Audit Guide

Audit Guide

Second Edition

STOY HAYWARD
A member of Horwath International

Butterworths
London Dublin & Edinburgh
1991

United Kingdom	Butterworth & Co (Publishers) Ltd, 88 Kingsway, LONDON WC2B 6AB and 4 Hill Street, EDINBURGH EH2 3JZ
Australia	Butterworths Pty Ltd, SYDNEY, MELBOURNE, BRISBANE, ADELAIDE, PERTH, CANBERRA and HOBART
Canada	Butterworths Canada Ltd, TORONTO and VANCOUVER
Ireland	Butterworth (Ireland) Ltd, DUBLIN
Malaysia	Malayan Law Journal Sdn Bhd, KUALA LUMPUR
New Zealand	Butterworths of New Zealand Ltd, WELLINGTON and AUCKLAND
Puerto Rico	Equity de Puerto Rico, Inc, HATO REY
Singapore	Malayan Law Journal Pte Ltd, SINGAPORE
USA	Butterworth Legal Publishers, AUSTIN, Texas; BOSTON, Massachusetts; CLEARWATER, Florida (D & S Publishers); ORFORD, New Hampshire (Equity Publishing); ST PAUL, Minnesota; and SEATTLE, Washington

A CIP Catalogue record for this book is available from the British Library.

First edition 1983

ISBN 0 406 67823 5

Typeset, printed and bound in Great Britain by
Butler & Tanner Ltd, Frome and London

Foreword

The first edition of the *Audit Guide* was published in 1983. This edition builds on the firm foundations of that *Guide*. The main revisions are to:

— describe some refinements to the audit approach including a specific risk assessment process;

— introduce new chapters describing how we adapt our audit approach for Computer Audits and the Audits of Small Companies;

— bring up to date the references to standards and guidelines issued since 1983.

Throughout the guide we continue to place great emphasis on an in-depth knowledge and understanding of each client's business and on the need to choose audit procedures or techniques which are appropriate to the circumstances.

We continue to be concerned with flexibility of approach rather than standard procedures and standard audit programmes. We have not changed our underlying philosophy. The choice of procedures and techniques continues to be influenced by the concepts of risk, analytical review and materiality. We adapt our auditing procedures to concentrate on those areas where there is the greatest risk of error and do less work where there is less risk. We do more work where the accounts do not make sense and less where we are satisfied that they do. We do more audit work on the bigger numbers in the accounts (or those which ought to be big) and less on those which we expect to be small. We concentrate our efforts on looking for errors which are large enough to influence the users of the accounts— we do not, unnecessarily, spend time looking for errors which are so small that they do not influence anybody.

We have continued to refine our approach to make it more effective. To this end we have introduced a risk assessment process which explicitly relates our knowledge of the business, analytical review procedures and review of the systems to our judgements concerning risk.

These concepts and our whole audit approach apply to all audits. They apply to the audit of a small business in the same way as for a large business and to the audit of a computer based system as a manual system. Of course, some of the procedures and techniques change but our approach does not. In this edition we have included two additional chapters which cover these special procedures and techniques and the ways that we may adapt our audit approach when faced with the audit of a small business or with the audit of a computer based system.

A feature of the guide continues to be that it contains very little by way of standard forms, schedules and checklists. The documentation, which supplements this guide and which must be used flexibly, is limited to:

— standard schedules and working papers which save time in both preparation and review (for example, standard lead schedules, internal control evaluation forms, fixed asset schedules, tax packages, risk assessment packages, disclosure checklists and so on);

— standard checklists which form part of the firm's quality control procedures (for example, the final checklist for the senior-in-charge which is used to evidence the fact that he has done everything expected of him); and

— lists of ideas of auditing procedures for each cycle and for various steps within the audit ('ideas lists').

Examples of this documentation are included in the Appendices.

We do more than just an audit in accordance with legal and professional standards. We carry out the additional work that clients have asked for. We also use our in-depth knowledge and understanding of each client's business to identify other ways in which we can provide help. The *Guide* does not tell us how to do this. Instead, it reminds us that, as auditors, we have a golden opportunity to provide such constructive services.

In conclusion, appreciation and thanks are due to all the people in Stoy Hayward who have helped in the production of the revised edition of this *Guide*, the members of the firm's Technical Department (on whom much of the burden has fallen), partners, managers and other staff in London and elsewhere in the United Kingdom (who have carried out field tests, commented on earlier drafts and discussed various problems as they have arisen).

August 1991
Stoy Hayward

Contents

PART B   TECHNIQUES

1 Introduction

This chapter summarises the legal and professional background to auditing in the United Kingdom.

1.01 An audit is defined in the explanatory foreword to the Auditing Standards and Guidelines issued by the governing bodies of the Auditing Practices Committee as:

'the independent examination of, and expression of opinion on, the financial statements of an enterprise'.

Audit Opinions

1.02 Most audits are carried out under the Companies Act 1985 with a view to expressing an opinion on the financial statements of companies whose shareholders have limited liability. The audit report in such cases is an expression of opinion, and not a certificate, on seven matters. Two of the seven matters are dealt with explicitly in the report; they are the opinions on whether the financial statements:
(a) show a true and fair view of the financial position, results and source and application of funds; and
(b) have been properly prepared in accordance with the Companies Act 1985.
Five other matters need only be reported on if the opinion is negative. These are whether:
(a) proper accounting records have been kept and proper returns received from branches not visited by the auditor;
(b) the financial statements agree with the accounting records;
(c) the auditor has received all the information and explanations required for the purposes of his audit;
(d) information in the directors' report is consistent with the financial statements;
(e) Statements of Standard Accounting Practice (SSAPs) have been complied with in all material respects (unless the auditor concurs with any departure).

Audit Evidence

1.03   The auditor needs to obtain and assess sufficient relevant and reliable audit evidence to reach these opinions and decide whether any uncorrected errors are sufficiently material to justify qualifying his report. In this context, the term 'errors' includes not only mistakes, but also departures from accounting principles specified in company law and Statements of Standard Accounting Practice. A material difference arising from a failure to comply with these principles results in a qualified audit report unless the auditor agrees that the departure is necessary to show a true and fair view.

Fraud

1.04   The auditor does not have a responsibility to detect all fraud, other irregularities or errors. The Auditing Practices Committee Guideline, *The auditor's responsibility in relation to fraud, other irregularities and errors,* states that:

> 'The auditor's responsibility is properly to plan, perform and evaluate his audit work so as to have a reasonable expectation of detecting material misstatements in the financial statements, whether they are caused by fraud, other irregularities or errors.'

However, some clients may expect him to scrutinise in more detail than he otherwise would certain areas where fraud is possible, such as the misappropriation of cash or goods. Such expectations must be clarified at the beginning of the audit.

1.05   Where the auditor discovers fraud, other irregularities or material errors he should normally report to senior management. Where he suspects that management are involved in or condoning fraud or other irregularities he must report to senior management unless he suspects them of being involved. In this case he may need to take legal advice about his reporting responsibilities.

1.06   For entities covered by specific legislation e.g. the Financial Services Act 1986, the auditor has a right to communicate directly with the appropriate regulatory body. The Audit Guideline: *Communications under the Financial Services Act* recommends that the auditor should report directly to the Regulator where there has been an occurrence which causes the auditor no longer to have confidence in the integrity of the directors or senior management.

Duty of Care

1.07 An auditor has a duty of care to those to whom he reports; in the case of a company, they are its members. Concern for the interests of members should be paramount throughout the audit. Audit procedures should be chosen to detect errors which would significantly affect the view members would take when they rely on the audited accounts.

1.08 Case law also requires the auditor to consider other possible users of the accounts. Although the law is uncertain, it appears that a duty of care could exist where it can be shown that the auditor knew the financial information upon which he was to give an opinion would be communicated to a third party and it was likely that party would rely upon it.

Independence

1.09 In reaching his audit opinion, the auditor must not be influenced by his relationship with management. Furthermore, he should be alert to factors which could be seen by a third party as diminishing his independence. With this in mind, we have adopted the following rules based on the Ethical Guide issued by the Institute of Chartered Accountants in England and Wales:

(a) No partner or member of staff may have any beneficial financial interest (shareholding, loan, debenture, etc) in any audit client.

(b) Any partner or member of staff having a common business interest with an audit client or an officer or employee of a client should not take part in the audit.

(c) Any member of staff having a close personal relationship with a client or officer or employee of a client should inform the partner responsible for the engagement who will decide whether the person should be involved in the audit. A partner with such a relationship should consider his own position and may ask another partner to take charge of the audit if there is a danger that his independence may be or appear to be impaired.

(d) Partners and members of staff should be wary of accepting goods, services or undue hospitality from audit clients. As a general rule, goods and services may be accepted on the same terms as those available to the client's staff, provided the amounts involved are small. More specific rules may be set for individual audits.

(e) We should not prepare accounting records for a public company client other than in exceptional circumstances. For a private company client, we need to ensure that we retain our objectivity in carrying out the audit if we have been involved in accountancy work. Accordingly, all such accountancy work should be reviewed by a person more senior to the preparer to ensure it is of the necessary standard.

Auditing Standards

1.10   Members of the United Kingdom accountancy bodies must carry out audits in accordance with Auditing Standards. These prescribe the basic principles and practices which members of those bodies are expected to follow in the conduct of an audit. The Auditing Standards are not, however, a set of rules sufficiently elaborate to cover all situations and circumstances which an auditor might encounter — indeed it would be impracticable to establish such a code. Instead, they are a framework within which the auditor must exercise his judgement in determining both the auditing procedures necessary in the circumstances to afford a reasonable basis for his opinion and the wording of his report. This audit guide is designed to help exercise that judgement and carry out audits in accordance with the auditing standards.

Part A The firm's audit approach

2   Our audit approach

This chapter summarises the approach used by the firm to obtain relevant and reliable audit evidence sufficient to reach the opinions referred to in Chapter 1. Some of the procedures and techniques are dealt with in more detail in later chapters.

2.01   There are many kinds of audit evidence which may be used and many ways of obtaining it. The aim should always be to obtain sufficient evidence of the right kind at the lowest cost. The approach set out in this chapter achieves this by choosing audit procedures to reflect:
(a) our knowledge of the client's business and accounting systems;
(b) the results of an analytical review of the management accounts and the draft accounts;
(c) an evaluation of audit risk based upon our business review and accounting systems review;
(d) an estimate of what is likely to be material in the accounts; and
(e) the interrelationship of different audit tests.

2.02   The audit is also the opportunity to provide a constructive service to clients. The audit team should look beyond the figures to the underlying facts. They should grasp the opportunity to use their professional and commercial expertise by standing back from the detail and recommending ways of improving the efficiency and profitability of the business. They should write management letters which are not only professionally sound but commercially realistic and in sympathy with the aims of the people running the business. They should draw attention to improvements in internal controls, reporting procedures and accounting systems which can lead to reductions in operating costs and audit time.

Planning the Audit

2.03   The planning of the audit as a whole is the first stage of our approach. The steps are summarised in *Table 1* (overleaf). For most audits, the planning process follows the sequence of these steps, although some are started before others are finished. Furthermore, the planning process itself does not stop until the audit finishes. We keep our assessments of audit risk and materiality under review throughout the audit and we use analytical review to give us audit assurance at various stages during the audit. We never stop using our understanding of the business and its accounting systems.

Table 1

Our audit approach — planning the audit

For the audit as a whole

> Understand the terms of the engagement including reports required and client expectations.

> Understand the business and its accounting systems by reviewing and assessing information on:
> (a) what the business does, how it is run and how it fits into its industry and markets;
> (b) the control environment including owner/manager controls;
> (c) its accounting systems and procedures and the effect of computers on them.

> Carry out analytical review procedures.

> Evaluate overall audit risk.

> Determine the preliminary estimate of materiality for the audit as a whole.

> Identify the cycles which are relevant and decide the types of testing and samples.

Understand the Terms of the Engagement

2.04   Most audits are carried out under the provisions of the Companies Act 1985 with the aim of expressing the opinions set out in Chapter 1. There are, however, other engagements described as audits which are dictated by other rules which specify the scope of our work, for example, where the client is a member of a Self Regulatory Organisation under the Financial Services Act 1986. Whatever the case, we should ensure that the terms have been agreed with the client and that they are covered by our letter of engagement.

2.05   One special area in which we carry out audits under different rules is for the UK subsidiary of a foreign corporation. Our duties may be extended (but never reduced) by the requirements of the country of the holding company and of its auditors. It is vital that we understand what is required of us and that we meet the expectations of the client and the primary auditors.

Client Expectations

2.06   As well as statutory requirements, there are also many clients who require or expect additional services as part of the audit. For example, some clients expect us to check if laid-down procedures are not being carried out, even though there may not be audit benefit, and report to them either orally or in a management letter. We should ensure that we are aware of these expectations. An extreme example of this is petty cash expenditure. Although the fact that petty cash vouchers have not been properly authorised is unlikely to affect the truth and fairness of the accounts, a client might expect a comment in the management letter if procedures are not being followed.

2.07   Similarly, the failure to reclaim full amounts of Statutory Sick Pay or cash discounts might not result in a material error in the accounts but the client may expect to have it pointed out. In other cases, clients may expect us to go beyond our statutory responsibilities in such areas as:

(a) the preparation of schedules during the audit for submission to taxation authorities;
(b) the examination of items of expenditure for evidence of waste or lack of control;
(c) the examination of areas (perhaps on the basis of one area a year) outside the normal scope of the audit but with the aim of finding improvements in efficiency, productivity etc;
(d) warning of problems in the application of the rules relating to VAT, PAYE and Social Security;
(e) reviewing their computer systems to give them an independent view of their effectiveness.

2.08   These tasks should always be carried out when requested or expected. Nevertheless we should always bear in mind that there are those clients who do not expect and would not wish to pay for such services. For this reason, the extent of such additional work must be identified when the job is planned.

Understanding the Business and its Accounting Systems

2.09   The audit approach depends upon a thorough understanding of the client's business. This not only helps provide timely relevant advice on all financial and commercial matters, but it also ensures that audit procedures are designed and implemented in a cost-effective manner. It assists us to review critically any management accounts or the draft statutory accounts and assess the risk of errors. It helps us to understand better the results of our audit work and to distinguish between errors that matter and those that do not. It ensures that the implications of the work in one audit area for another are followed through. It helps us choose whether or not to rely on controls in the accounting systems.

2.10   In order to plan the audit we need to gather information about the business on:
(a) what it does and how it is run;
(b) the industry and markets in which it operates and where it fits into them;
(c) the control environment, including the effect of the proprietor's personal involvement;
(d) its accounting systems and procedures, including the effect of computers on them.

2.11   Not only should the partner and manager responsible for the audit have a thorough knowledge and understanding of the client's business but so should every member of the audit team from the senior to the most junior assistant. All should try to understand the long-term objectives of the owners and management and the way in which they run the business on a day-to-day basis. They should have a good idea of the commercial and financial history of the business and how well it is doing currently and its prospects. They must know what it does, what it sells, what it buys, who are its customers and suppliers, as well as how the transactions are recorded in the books and records.

2.12   As part of our risk assessment we carry out a business review and a review of the accounting systems. This helps us to ensure our knowledge of the business is up to date and accurate, assists in the assessment of risk and helps us plan our audit procedures. The business review focuses on both external factors, for example, the conditions in the markets in which the client is operating, and internal factors such as the control environment and results in a business review report which brings together all the relevant information in one summary. The accounting systems review ensures that the client has a level of basic controls adequate to ensure correct processing of accounting information.

2.13 As our understanding of a business is built up over the years much information of continuing relevance is contained both in permanent audit files, past years' working paper files including previous risk assessments and in such documents as annual reports, investigation reports, industry information files and so on. The partner and managers who have dealt with and are dealing with particular clients and industries also have a vast wealth of knowledge and experience. Our understanding is, however, more than all this information — it is an attitude of mind which distinguishes the good auditor from the indifferent auditor.

2.14 As the understanding of the client's business and accounting systems increases with the experience of a number of years' audits, so the efficiency of our audits improves further. The records and knowledge carried forward from one year to the next give the next audit team a head start. Each person involved in work for a client should regard it as one of his prime duties to update the permanent file and make sure that the records he leaves are an investment in time which will pay dividends at the next audit. Apart from saving time, they will reduce the need for the client to answer the same questions year after year.

Carry out Analytical Review Procedures

2.15 Our understanding of the client's business helps us to review critically the accounting information which is available at the start of the audit. This may vary from a rather incomplete and poorly written up set of basic records to full draft accounts supported by up-to-date management accounts. A review of whatever information is available helps to:
(a) identify areas of the accounts which are important because of their size;
(b) highlight unusual or unexpected figures or relationships in the accounts;
(c) design audit tests which concentrate on the important and unusual items;
(d) obtain sufficient audit assurance to allow the reduction or even elimination of detailed testing in some areas.

2.16 The earlier such a review is carried out, the greater its impact on audit efficiency. If the review indicates that the figures make sense, we may reduce the level or alter the nature of subsequent audit tests. If a problem is identified early in the audit, the testing can easily be adapted to investigate it. A problem which is not detected until the end of the audit may prove considerably more time consuming and expensive to deal with.

Evaluate Overall Audit Risk

2.17   The nature and extent of our work is also affected by our assessment of the risk of different types of errors in the accounts. We distinguish between audits (or audit areas) where the risk is 'normal' and those where it is 'higher than normal'. Where the level of risk is normal, we must do sufficient work to provide a reasonable basis for our audit opinion. A higher than normal risk may lead to more extensive tests and a more sceptical attitude towards any errors or inconsistencies found during testing.

2.18   The assessment of risk is based upon our understanding of the business and our analytical review procedures. It is kept under review throughout the audit. Some factors affect the audit as a whole, some are restricted to one cycle. For example, financial pressures on a company and its desire to impress its bankers may increase the overall risk. A change in accounting policy for the valuation of stock or changes in the staffing of the departments responsible for the pricing of stock may increase the risk of errors in the valuation of stock (but not in the quantities of stock).

2.19   The work for each audit area should take account of any identified risk of error in that particular area. Thus, if there is a higher than normal risk of debtors being overstated, audit tests relating to the overstatement of sales and debtors would not normally be reduced for reliance on other areas such as analytical review. In addition, we would adapt the nature of our procedures to cover the specific risks of error identified. Tests on the understatement of sales, however, may be reduced by reliance on these factors if there is only a normal risk of errors.

Materiality

2.20   The review of the accounts is one of the factors that helps establish a preliminary estimate of the level of materiality for the audit. In some cases, however, our estimate may have to be based on last year's accounts adjusted for any major changes that have taken place. This estimate enables us to define the extent of our audit work. We concentrate on material items and do not look for errors which would be so small that they do not affect the impressions gained by users of the accounts. Thus, we ensure that the audit is carried out as efficiently as possible. It also helps avoid aiming for an unnecessary level of accuracy when assessing subjective judgements of value, for example, estimates of accruals.

2.21 Normally there is an estimate of materiality for the audit as a whole. Sometimes the same figure can be used for all audit areas. At other times, it may be necessary to audit some areas more closely.

2.22 The materiality level is kept under review throughout the audit but the preliminary estimate may form the starting point from which we decide whether to seek adjustments for errors which we have discovered. Errors which are singly or in aggregate immaterial need not be adjusted (but they often will be because the client so wishes). Errors which are singly or in aggregate material must be adjusted; otherwise a qualified audit opinion is required.

Cycles

2.23 We analyse accounting transactions into 'cycles', each corresponding to a major balance sheet heading and related profit and loss items. For example, the revenue cycle deals with debtors, sales and cash receipts; the expenditure cycle includes creditors, payments, purchases and all overheads. We need to identify the cycles which are relevant to the audit. For example in a manufacturing company with an integrated costing system, it may be more helpful to distinguish between:
(a) the conversion cycle, which deals with the purchase and conversion of raw materials and bought-in parts, production wages and production overheads; and
(b) the expenditure cycle, which deals with other purchases and overheads.
For an advertising agency on the other hand, one would not need to consider the conversion cycle but would concentrate on the expenditure cycle.

2.24 We must also decide whether it is more efficient to combine cycles and whether any cycles do not give rise to a risk of material error and may therefore be ignored. For example, we may combine payroll and expenditure cycles where there are few employees. Alternatively we may ignore payroll altogether if the amounts involved are not large and there is no risk of material error.

2.25 Although audit procedures are designed and carried out cycle by cycle, it is important not to overlook the inter-relationships of the cycles and especially not to omit to check that the results of one cycle make sense when compared with those of all the others.

2.26   The planning steps for each cycle are summarised in *Table 2* (opposite) — they are the next stage after planning the audit as a whole. We must begin by understanding those aspects of the business relating to the cycle. For example, when considering the revenue cycle, we need to know:

(a) what does the company sell?

(b) who are its customers and what terms are available to them?

(c) who are its competitors?

(d) how does it market, sell and distribute its products?

2.27   We must also understand the accounting policies relating to the cycle so that we can ascertain whether transactions have been dealt with correctly. We should know whether the policies comply with company law and other requirements and whether they involve estimates or judgements. We should pay special attention to policies which are unusual, those which do not comply with the law or accounting standards and those which are influenced by foreign requirements.

2.28   Finally we need to understand what transactions take place and how they are recorded. For example, as many tests are concerned with omissions or understatements, it is only if we know how all transactions are captured within the accounting system that these tests can be successful. The permanent audit file should contain flowcharts or narrative notes describing the system currently in use. These should be reviewed each year and updated as necessary.

Audit Objectives

2.29   The financial statements comprise a series of 'representations' or 'assertions' by management concerning the ownership, existence, valuation and completeness of assets and liabilities and the presentation and disclosure of all items. From the representations we can derive audit objectives, five of which summarise the areas in which sufficient relevant and reliable audit evidence must be obtained. They are:

(a) income is not understated;

(b) expenditure is not overstated;

(c) assets are not overstated;

(d) liabilities are not understated; and

(e) assets, liabilities, income and expenditure and other items required by law are
     properly presented and disclosed in the financial statements.

2.30   The first four objectives are designed to take advantage of the double-entry system and so minimise audit work. If an asset, say a debtor, has been overstated in the accounts, double entry means that a corresponding credit

[*text continues on p 16*]

Table 2

Our audit approach — planning the audit

For each cycle

Understand those aspects of the business which relate to the cycle, considering any matters identified during our risk assessment.

Understand the relevant accounting policies.

Understand how the transactions take place and how they are recorded.

Consider the financial statement representations and identify audit objectives taking into account the type of errors which could occur together with the risk of those errors occurring.

Based on our assessment of risk determine the audit evidence which will be obtained by analytical review procedures, tests in total and substantive tests of detail.

Determine the extent to which it is possible to reduce substantive testing based upon our assessment of risk, analytical review procedures or internal controls. If so identify procedures and key controls and design compliance tests.

Determine the audit evidence which will be obtained to verify unusual and related party items.

Determine sampling approach.

(for example, sales) will also be overstated. It may alternatively mean that a corresponding debit, for example, fixed assets or an expense account has been understated. By testing that the asset is not overstated we thus also gain assurance that related credits are not overstated or debits understated. This is called directional testing and it eliminates the need to test for the overstatement of income, the understatement of expenditure and assets, and the overstatement of liabilities — as all these possibilities are covered by one or more of the first four objectives.

2.31   We sub-divide the objectives to make easier the choice and design of audit procedures. For example, the objective that income is not understated is sub-divided to deal separately with despatches being recorded, invoices being prepared accurately and all invoices being recorded. These 'sub-objectives' may be different from one audit to another, because of the differences between clients' businesses and transactions.

2.32   Appropriate 'sub-objectives' should be identified for all areas of the accounts for which some audit work is necessary. Our choice is influenced by the sort of errors that may be in the accounts and the risk of those errors occurring. 'Sub-objectives' need not be identified for items which are so small that material errors cannot arise. However, where we are testing for understatement some audit evidence is normally required regardless of the size, as an item may be small because it is understated. We must not ignore the area on the grounds that the amount in the trial balance is small, where the objective is to test for understatement.

2.33   It should be borne in mind that the overall objectives of an audit are the same for all clients. The specific procedures followed to satisfy these objectives will however need to be tailored to suit the particular circumstances of each client, for example, where the accounting systems are computerised or where we carry out significant amounts of accountancy work.

Audit Evidence

2.34   Having identified the appropriate objectives and assessed the risks for each cycle, we decide how the audit evidence can be obtained for each objective. Audit evidence for the cycle may be obtained from:
(a) substantive tests of detail (direct tests of individual transactions or balances);
(b) tests in total;
(c) analytical review procedures; and
(d) reliance on internal control.

2.35   Substantive tests of detail are the most reliable source of evidence as they give direct audit assurance that specific transactions and balances are correct. Areas of the accounts which are important because of size or which have been identified as potential problem areas because of a higher than normal risk of error always require some substantive tests of detail.

2.36   In some audit areas, all or part of the evidence may be obtained by tests in total. For example, the depreciation charge can often be tested by multiplying the total cost of the category of assets by the depreciation rate (although a small number of individual items may need to be tested to ensure that the company has not, for example, depreciated fully written-down assets). Tests in total often take very little time to perform and can prove to be both efficient and reliable forms of evidence.

2.37   Where an item is small and there is only a normal risk of error, it may be possible to rely entirely on analytical review procedures. This is also the case when dealing with branches or divisions for which no separate audit opinion is required. Where it is not possible to rely entirely on analytical review procedures some audit assurance may be derived from them in order to reduce the level of substantive tests of detail.

2.38   The level of substantive tests of detail may also be reduced where there are internal controls within the client's accounting systems which prevent material error in the objective under review. These controls (called 'key controls') must be tested to ensure they were operating properly throughout the period under review. Only those key controls that leave some evidence of their performance (such as initials on an invoice) or which can be observed directly (such as controls over the opening of post) can be tested and relied upon in this way. Tests of such controls are called 'compliance tests' and are only carried out where the time costs saved on the substantive test are greater than the time costs of the compliance test.

2.39   Where a client has an internal audit function we should determine whether we can place reliance on its work when deciding the nature and extent of our own tests. For example, the internal auditor's systems notes and compliance tests can be used as part of our documentation and evaluation of accounting systems and as evidence that internal controls are functioning. However, we should be involved in the audit of all matters in the financial statements where there is a risk of material error.

Sampling

2.40   Whatever the form of testing, sampling procedures are used because it is inefficient and unnecessary to examine every transaction or balance in a population. Sampling procedures may be either statistical or non-statistical, both methods involving judgement. Whatever method is used, we must examine unusual and related party items, those balances or transactions which are most likely to be in error and those which are the most significant.

2.41   Statistical sampling methods provide a framework for linking the risk of error and the materiality of transactions and balances with the sample size. They also allow us to demonstrate the link between different types of tests and show, for example, how the size of substantive tests has been reduced by successful compliance tests. For these reasons, statistical sampling techniques should be used where practicable. However, there may be occasions when such procedures would not be cost effective, particularly with small populations, and non-statistical sampling methods should be used in their place.

2.42   Whatever form of sampling is used, it is important to remember that its purpose is to reach a conclusion about the population of balances or transactions. Having carried out appropriate audit procedures on each sample item we must:
(a) analyse any errors detected in the sample;
(b) project the errors found in the sample to the population; and
(c) assess the sampling risk i.e. the risk that the sample is directing us to the wrong conclusions.
The total projected error must be assessed to see whether there is an unacceptably high risk of material errors in the population.

Audit Plan and Programme

2.43   One result of the planning process is a written audit plan which must be approved by the partner and manager before any audit tests are performed (in larger or more complex engagements they will have already been heavily involved). The plan should contain the results of our initial analytical review procedures and the assessments of materiality and overall risk. It should be supported by a risk assessment which contains a business review report and an accounting systems review. It should set out, for each cycle, the objectives which are important, the way in which audit evidence will be obtained and the sampling approach to be adopted. The audit plan should include a detailed budget and, in many cases, a timetable.

2.44 A detailed audit programme should also be prepared setting out the tests and procedures to be carried out on each cycle. It must be based on the audit plan and tailored to meet the needs of the particular business. It should be specific in its instructions. The programme should be approved by the manager before any tests are carried out.

2.45 During the audit both the audit plan and the audit programme should be kept under review. Even though they have been committed to paper they should not be regarded as fixed. They must be adapted to reflect the results of audit work and any unexpected changes in the business or the draft accounts.

Joint Audits

2.46 We should always remember that we are responsible for our opinion on a joint audit irrespective of the allocation of work. When planning a joint audit we must ensure that all the above planning steps are carried out. How we allocate responsibilities is a matter for agreement between the two firms and not a matter which requires the client's agreement. We need to ensure that all aspects of the audit are fully considered, that there are no areas either of omission or unnecessary duplication of effort and that there are satisfactory arrangements to review the work of the joint auditor. We should record what we have agreed with the other auditors in respect of the work to be carried out and the various responsibilities.

The Audit of Each Cycle

2.47 The usual sequence of the work on each cycle is summarised in *Table 3* (overleaf); this links in to the approach set out in the audit plan and audit programme.

Audit Working Papers

2.48 All audit work should be recorded in the working papers. Each member of the audit team should ensure that his work is adequately documented so that a reviewer can understand exactly what work has been done, its results and conclusions and the reasons for the conclusions.

Table 3

Our audit approach — the audit of each cycle

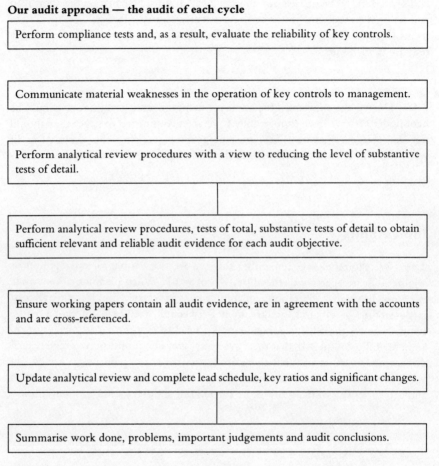

Perform compliance tests and, as a result, evaluate the reliability of key controls.

Communicate material weaknesses in the operation of key controls to management.

Perform analytical review procedures with a view to reducing the level of substantive tests of detail.

Perform analytical review procedures, tests of total, substantive tests of detail to obtain sufficient relevant and reliable audit evidence for each audit objective.

Ensure working papers contain all audit evidence, are in agreement with the accounts and are cross-referenced.

Update analytical review and complete lead schedule, key ratios and significant changes.

Summarise work done, problems, important judgements and audit conclusions.

2.49   At the end of any interim audit, notes should be prepared summarising the results of that work, any changes from the audit plan and any work outstanding; these notes should be reviewed by the partner and manager. At the end of each cycle we should summarise the work carried out, any changes from the audit plan, any problems experienced, the extent of unadjusted errors, and the conclusions reached.

Completing the Audit

2.50   The steps that the senior in charge should follow to complete the audit are summarised in *Table 4* (opposite). He should begin by reviewing the work of all assistants and ensure that the working paper file is complete in all respects before it is passed to a manager for review. In particular, he should:

[*text continues on p 22*]

Table 4

Our audit approach — completing the audit

Senior in charge

Review work of all assistants and check that audit plan and programme have been followed.

Ensure the permanent file has been updated throughout the audit.

Update overall analytical review.

Review unadjusted errors to determine whether individual and aggregate effect is material.

Review tax computation and supporting schedules; check accounts for current, future and deferred taxes.

Draft letter of representation and relevant board minutes (where appropriate).

Check compliance with Companies Act and other requirements.

Review post-balance sheet events.

Complete audit review check list and prepare points for partner.

Taking into account the results of work performed on each cycle and during the final review, draft audit opinion.

Prepare final management letter.

Compare budgeted time to actual and explain major variations.

Set up debriefing meeting with staff or client.

Complete staff evaluation forms.

Start planning next year's audit by writing debriefing memorandum and including it in the permanent audit file.

(a) update the overall analytical review to check that the accounts make sense (or where they appear not to, they are consistent with the audit evidence);
(b) prepare a summary of unadjusted errors and check whether they are material either singly or in aggregate;
(c) review the tax computation and supporting schedules and check the accruals for current, future and deferred taxes;
(d) draft letter of representation and relevant board minutes;
(e) complete a disclosure checklist to satisfy himself that the accounts comply with all statutory and other relevant requirements; and
(f) where appropriate, draft a management letter with a view to issuing it as quickly as possible.

2.51   Where we are carrying out a joint audit we need to ensure we have reviewed the other firm's working papers to assess the adequacy of their procedures and to consider fully any matters which have arisen which may affect our ability to give an unqualified opinion. We should take copies of their papers in all material areas.

2.52   The senior in charge should draw the partner's attention to:
(a) the results and financial position together with any significant changes from prior years, budget and expectations;
(b) any audit problems;
(c) any outstanding work;
(d) the costs of the audit together with explanations of variances from budget.

2.53   The manager should review the work of the senior and edit the points for the partner. The partner should review the work of the manager and indicate his approval of the working papers and the audit opinion. The manager and partner should both ensure that there are no uncleared points and that any decisions they have taken are adequately documented and are supported by the working papers.

2.54   Before the audit report is signed, the review of post-balance sheet events should be updated. The purpose of the review is to obtain assurance that all material events which require adjustments to or disclosure in the accounts have been identified and dealt with. It must be updated to a date as close as practicable to that of the audit report.

2.55   The final stage of any audit is to prepare the ground for next year. During the course of the audit, the team has learnt much which will help the next audit go more smoothly. The senior in charge should, therefore, prepare a list of points drawing next year's team's attention to likely audit problems, possible cost savings and known changes and must make sure that the permanent file is up to date.

Putting the Approach into Practice

2.56 In the remaining chapters we give guidance on how to put the audit approach into practice. The guidance takes two forms:

(a) Chapters 3–18 expand on some of the concepts and explain some of the techniques dealt with in this chapter. So, for example, Chapter 6 suggests how to determine and how to use materiality levels. Chapter 9 develops the concept of sampling and Chapters 17 and 18 explain in some detail the techniques of monetary unit and error rate sampling.

(b) The appendices contain examples of the 'ideas lists' for individual cycles. The 'ideas lists' give ideas on what objectives to test, what tests to perform, what controls to look for, what analytical review procedures to use. They are not checklists — but may be used as the basis for audit programmes or, in some cases, may be 'answered' and included as part of the audit working papers. There are also ideas lists dealing with particular tasks and topics such as stocktake attendance and audit planning. The appendices also contain examples of audit documentation, such as audit programmes, internal control evaluation forms (see Chapter 8), audit plans and risk assessments.

3   Understanding the business

This chapter sets out the sort of information we need to know so that we understand the business and the accounting systems sufficiently well to ensure that we:
(a) design and implement audit procedures in a cost-effective manner;
(b) review critically any management accounts or the draft statutory accounts;
(c) assess the risk of errors; and
(d) link together the results of the audit work.
We formalise our approach to gathering and retaining information by carrying out a business review and an accounting systems review. These reviews ensure we collect and evaluate information relevant to deciding the nature and extent of audit procedures. They are an integral part of our risk assessment (see Chapter 5).

3.01   Understanding a client's business includes obtaining, reviewing and assessing information on:
(a) what the business does and how it is run;
(b) the industry and markets in which it operates and where it fits into them;
(c) the control environment, including the effect of the proprietor's personal involvement;
(d) the accounting systems and procedures including the effect of computers on them.
Much of this information is readily available from permanent audit files particularly when partners and managers have maintained a close relationship with the client or have a specialised interest in its industry. Partners and managers in specialist departments who have done work for the client during the period under review may also be a useful source of information.

3.02   We expect every member of an audit team to take an active interest in the business of each client and understand how it works. Each member should try to understand the long term objectives of the owners and management and the way in which the business is run on a day-to-day basis. They should have a good idea of the commercial and financial history of the business, how well it is doing currently and what its prospects are. They must know what it does, what it sells, what it buys, who are its customers and suppliers, as well as how the transactions are recorded in the books and records.

3.03   It must be emphasised that understanding the client's business is not a separate stage of the audit; it continues all year round. Gaining such an understanding requires constant alertness. As soon as a senior knows he is booked out on a job, he should start obtaining a knowledge of the business by reading press articles on the client, competitors and the client's industry and by talking to others in the firm with previous experience of the client or specialist knowledge of the client's industry.

3.04   The knowledge we gain helps us in many ways. For a start, it makes possible a meaningful analytical review of management accounts or draft statutory accounts. It enables us to:
(a) decide whether the accounts make sense;
(b) expect certain results which we can compare with the management accounts or the draft statutory accounts;
(c) assess the reasonableness of any explanations given by management for any unexpected results; and
(d) assess the reasonableness of any other audit evidence which confirms or contradicts the accounts.

3.05   Our understanding of the business also helps us decide on the nature of audit tests. For example, in certain cash-based businesses, it may only be possible to verify income by observing and checking cash counts. Alternatively if a business only buys goods on receipt of a specific sales order, the audit of sales and purchases can be carried out together. Or if we know that demand for the products is declining — perhaps because of technological change or the introduction of cheaper competition from abroad — we may have to increase the amount of audit effort we direct at the obsolescence of stocks.

3.06   An understanding of the business influences the extent of audit tests; the knowledge helps identify the risk of error for each audit objective and this, in turn, affects the size of our samples. For example, if we know that as many sales as possible are put through in the last month of the year, we would extend tests on after-date cash receipts and after-date sales credit notes to ensure sales relate to the period under review. Having carried out the tests, the understanding and knowledge we have gained helps us assess the significance of any errors we have found.

3.07   The 'ideas list' for each cycle suggests points which we may like to consider when trying to understand how the business works. The suggestions are only a guide; it is not the intention that they be used as a checklist on which every question must be answered (although they can be if so desired). In some cases, the person dealing with the cycle may only need to run through the list quickly to check his knowledge — remembering of course to add points relevant to the particular client. In other cases, particularly new audits, they may form the framework of permanent file notes.

3.08   The remaining part of this chapter deals at some length with the four areas listed in paragraph **3.01**. The purpose is to highlight some of the general areas, rather than those specific to individual cycles, which the audit team may wish to consider. These areas are also covered at length in the business review and accounting systems review which form part of the risk assessment. This part of the chapter also gives background considerations to the issues raised by these documents. The chapter concludes by suggesting some sources of information, particularly where there are gaps in our knowledge, and refers to the method of documenting our understanding of the business.

What the Business Does and How it is Run

3.09   Before anything else, we need to know what the business does and how it is run. Is it a manufacturer, or distributor, a wholesaler or retailer? Does it sell goods or services? Does it buy to meet specific orders or does it hold stocks in expectation of orders? If it is a manufacturer, is it producing in bulk, in batches, by means of a continuous process or does it deal with individual jobs? Does it manufacture from basic raw materials or does it buy in components and assemble finished goods? If the business is that of a distributor or wholesaler, how wide is the range of suppliers, goods and customers? What product groups does a retailer deal in, and is it for cash only? If it is a service company, how does it provide the service, is it based on people or assets? Is the business trading entirely on its own account or are franchises or licences involved in some way?

3.10   We should ask ourselves:
(a) *What are the major products of the business and for which market are they intended?* This will enable us to consider how conditions in these markets are likely to affect the business, which may help identify audit problems. For example, if the market is in decline, special attention may need to be directed at the adequacy of provisions against the valuation of stocks (it may also give us the opportunity to advise on possible alternative business strategies).
(b) *Who are the major customers and suppliers of the business and are there any special terms available?* For example, reservation of title on sales may affect the recoverability of debtors. Major suppliers may give quantity rebates after the year end which must be accounted for.
(c) *Is the trade seasonal or spread evenly over the year?* From an audit point of view it may be more efficient to have the year end at a time of low stock levels.

3.11 Businesses may be structured in many ways and this may affect the way we tackle our audit. We need to know whether the business is centralised or whether it has branches, depots or outside warehouses. How is it managed, is there close involvement of senior management (possibly the proprietor) in the day-to-day transactions? Are there any special arrangements or terms with other group companies (for example, sales from one group company to another need only be tested in the books of one of the two companies provided the two are in agreement)?

3.12 In finding out what the business does and how it is run, it is helpful to be clear on the objectives of the proprietor and his plans for the business. Does he intend to stay in the business long term or is he taking advantage of a (possibly temporary) upturn in the market? Is he developing and expanding the business with a view to floating it on the Stock Exchange or Unlisted Securities Market? An understanding of these aims and objectives gives us an idea of what to expect; it forewarns us of major changes, it helps in assessing the risk of errors. It may, for example, lead us to think that the proprietor may want to present his business in the best possible light, which might lead to backdated sales and imprudent judgements.

3.13 We use the knowledge of the business to adapt our audit procedures. We would, for example, verify the work in progress of a construction company carrying out large single projects differently from work in progress at a manufacturing company producing goods to specific orders or at a professional partnership. The audit of a textile manufacturer producing garments for sale by and under the close supervision of a major departmental store gives rise to different audit problems on the valuation of stocks and debtors than those found at a more speculative fashion house. The audit of a company selling beauty treatment and hairdressing services involves different procedures for the verification of completeness of income from those used at a company selling consumer durables and operating a tight system of stock control and a strict pricing structure. We adopt different procedures to complete the audit of a professionally managed, tightly controlled subsidiary of a major corporation which has regular in-depth reviews of management accounts than we would for the company lacking management skills, with poor detailed records and little in the way of formal management information.

The Industry and the Markets in which the Business Operates

3.14 We can begin by finding out about the development and present state of the industry. This helps us understand whether it is growing, has reached its peak or is in decline; whether the industry is international or regional, or dominated by particular companies (either as members of the industry or as suppliers or customers). Are there new businesses entering the industry or are there barriers to entry protecting the present members?

3.15   We might find out about other businesses in the same industry who may be competitors, either on a local, national or international scale. This may tell us whether the business has scope to continue expanding, or whether it must hold down prices to maintain market share. Alternatively it could show that the business is the market leader and plays a dominant role in fixing selling prices, controlling supply or even expanding the market.

3.16   We are interested in the current financial trends in the industry. These may suggest the problems and opportunities facing the client and may lead us to expect certain results in reviewing the accounts. They may confirm or suggest that there are too many companies fighting for the same market so that margins are squeezed — this leads us to expect lower profitability for our client and possible problems on the valuation of stocks.

3.17   We need to look beyond the industry itself and find out the effects of other industries and the economy generally upon the business. For example, a hotel in London that relies heavily on overseas tourists would be adversely affected by a strong pound and we would expect to see sales decline unless special promotional measures were undertaken. Alternatively the same hotel may benefit from an economic upsurge in the countries supplying its guests which may lead to an increase in overseas tourism.

3.18   We need to find out about special legislative and other requirements relevant to the industry. For example, we may need to know about the special accounting rules for estate agents or about the statutory ban on credit in casinos. Alternatively, the introduction of new safety regulations or pollution control could affect capital expenditure and hence cash flow (they may even affect the valuation and depreciation of the premises and equipment).

3.19   Often there are special auditing problems common to an industry. For example, the presence of substantial numbers of casual workers in the construction industry and little in the way of formal records of engagements and dismissals may lead to problems in the verification of payroll (and even the cost of work in progress). A similar problem arises in the hotel industry. There are also problems in valuing stocks at a jewellers and fixed assets at a property company.

3.20 Some of these audit problems relate to special accounting problems common to the industry. For example, the practice of distinguishing capital profits from revenue profits in a property investment company requires special consideration in the context of the formats for the profit and loss account in the Companies Act 1985 Sch 4. The treatment of exploration costs at an oil company and royalties paid in advance by a record company are other examples.

3.21 Finally, we need to understand how the industry is treated for Value Added Tax purposes, and, where appropriate, other sales and production duties. If the industry supplies goods or services which are exempt from VAT this can cause considerable accounting and auditing problems. If there is some doubt about whether the sales are zero or standard rated, we must be sure that the correct treatment is adopted and that the company does not have a substantial creditor which is not included in the accounts.

Control Environment

3.22 The term 'control environment' refers to the attitude towards discipline and control in the recording of transactions and balances. It represents the total of all the methods and procedures used to enforce controls. Its strength or weakness is an important factor in evaluating audit risk and may indicate whether specific controls may be relied upon or not. For example, at a company where the attitude to laid down procedures is poor and uncorrected errors frequently arise, our past experience tells us not to rely on internal controls which are apparent from the record of the system. Conversely, where management exercises a tight control over its procedures and employees and the attitude is generally one of 'getting things right quickly', we may be able to place reliance on internal control and to reduce our audit procedures to reflect the lower risk of errors.

3.23 The control environment is greatly influenced by the attitude and capabilities of management and employees. Indications of the control environment might be found in management's commitment to control, the organisational structure of the client, the way control standards are communicated to employees and monitored and the presence of an adequate number of competent employees. These aspects are considered as part of our business review.

3.24 For many smaller companies an important consideration in the control environment is the active participation of the proprietor. The proprietor whose own money is at stake in the business and who takes an active day-to-day role in the business has the potential to provide a high level of control. His knowledge of what the accounts should show, what the stock levels are, who the major customers and suppliers are, and what are reasonable transactions often helps to prevent and detect major errors in day-to-day transactions (on the other hand he may have the authority to override controls and enter incorrect or false data — this is a separate problem which is discussed in Chapter 5).

3.25   The accounting systems review (see Appendix 6) is designed to help us perform an overall review of the client's accounting systems when planning the audit and to help identify areas of weakness that may lead to errors in the financial statements. Before we complete the review we should have an up-to-date record of the systems. The checklists which form part of the review set out a number of procedures and controls which, if present, ensure protection of a company's assets and correct recording of its transactions. If absent they may increase the risk of error. We use it to gain evidence that the client's accounting system is capable of producing reliable accounting information.

Accounting Systems and Procedures

3.26   Before any audit tests can be designed, it is necessary to understand the accounting records kept and their format and the way in which items are processed through the accounting system. This is necessary whether or not internal controls are likely to be relied upon in our audit tests. Without this knowledge, we are unable to decide upon the most efficient way of carrying out the audit and to tell whether all transactions and balances have been captured in the accounting records. Hence in all cases, including even the smallest of businesses, we need to know what transactions take place and how they are recorded. This is recognised in *The Auditor's Operational Standard,* which says:

> 'The auditor should ascertain the system of recording and processing trans-actions and assess its adequacy as a basis for the preparation of financial statements'.

The most effective way of obtaining this understanding, and one which is an essential part of the audit process, is to document fully details of the accounting system on the permanent file. Chapter 15 explains some of the techniques of recording accounting systems, for example, narrative notes and flowcharts.

3.27   Walk-through tests on one item for each cycle should be done every year before starting audit tests. They involve tracing a transaction through the system to ensure that our record of the system is correct. If an 'error' is found, it could mean that our record is wrong and it should be changed before we do any tests.

3.28 For new clients (or clients whose systems have changed substantially) we need to record the systems from scratch. If the client has his own record of the systems then we should use this as far as possible; alternatively we may ask the client to prepare such a record. If neither of these options is available to us, we must prepare our own record based on discussions with those responsible for the implementation of the system and those who actually operate it from day to day. Once we have the record of the system, we must check it by means of a walk-through test.

3.29 Where part or all of the client's accounting systems are computerised, we need to know how computer processing may influence our audit procedures. Some of the information which might be useful in helping us to make that decision includes:
(a) the organisation of the computer department (if any);
(b) the basic hardware;
(c) the accounting applications processed by the computer;
(d) the significant documents associated with each application;
(e) any changes to accounting applications, either during the period under audit or planned for the next year;
(f) any factors which affect our use of computer-assisted audit techniques.

3.30 We need to know this information to adapt our audit procedures to suit the characteristics of the computerised system. Although the accounting and auditing objectives do not change, the control techniques used by the business may. For example, the controls which monitor the flow of data in a computerised system are frequently different from the controls used in a manual system. Accordingly, the review, evaluation and testing of the internal controls might be affected. We may also modify our substantive tests, perhaps by using the computer to assist in certain audit tests.

Sources of Information

3.31 Much of the information referred to in this chapter should be available from one source — namely the permanent audit file. Its most important advantage is that it forms a record of our accumulated knowledge of the client's business. Other advantages are that it keeps all permanent information in one place, makes it easier and quicker to refer to and helps ensure that certain details or changes are not overlooked. It also gives more flexibility in the way information is recorded and avoids duplication, which can occur if information is kept in various parts of the current file. It also enables us:
(a) to avoid re-collecting audit evidence in future years;
(b) to pass on information easily to members of the audit team;

(c) to save time when planning the audit, since all the necessary information is easily available;

(d) to avoid duplication of questions to the client's staff by using the permanent file as a point of reference during the course of the audit.

3.32   Permanent files must be used on all audits. To gain maximum benefit they should be updated both throughout the year and throughout the audit. They should be used flexibly and their nature should vary depending on the client so that the information is recorded in the most efficient way.

3.33   Other useful sources of information are the partner and manager on the job. Between them they may have many years' experience of the client. There are also others within the firm with specialist knowledge of particular industries who may be consulted, particularly with a new client about whose business we have not yet built up a great deal of knowledge.

3.34   Other sources within the firm are:

(a) previous year's planning notes and risk assessment documentation, which give background information and summaries of accounting systems and audit problems;

(b) the library, which has access to industry background papers and guides, journals and other publications issued by the industry's representative body and general press comment;

(c) other specialist departments which may have done assignments for the client or in the industry.

3.35   Once at the client's premises the senior should arrange for the audit team to be shown around the client's premises to see how the business operates. Such a tour:

(a) introduces the audit team to the client's staff;

(b) gives the audit team a greater interest in the business by taking them behind the accounting records;

(c) may point to problems which may not become apparent in any other way, such as obsolescence of plant, dilapidated buildings and slow moving stocks.

Where the business is conducted at different locations, we should ensure that we visit every site. Depending on the significance of the different locations, this may not be every year.

3.36   Other sources of information at the client's premises may include:

(a) organisation charts, procedure manuals or publications by the client;

(b) trade journals;

(c) our own observation and walk-through tests;

(d) discussions with non-accounting staff.

Documenting our Understanding of the Business

3.37   Knowledge of the business is fundamental to our audit approach. To gain the greatest practical benefit from this knowledge it must be thoroughly documented and kept up to date. We therefore formally record our understanding of the important aspects of the client's business in our business review report and accounting systems review (see Chapter 5). These reviews are an integral part of our risk assessment process and form the basis for planning the audit work we will carry out.

3.38   The business review report and accounting systems review are part of the risk assessment which are the responsibility of the partner and manager. It will normally be the senior's responsibility to collect together the information to be included in the business review report and accounting systems review. This will usually involve meeting with the client before the audit fieldwork begins.

4 Analytical review

This chapter explains what is meant by analytical review, gives guidance on how such a review is carried out and documented, and explains how the results of the review affect subsequent audit tests. Chapter 16 explains some of the procedures which may be used to review the profit and loss account and balance sheet and points to some client-specific procedures.

4.01 Analytical review is the process of examining and comparing the financial and non-financial figures of a business with internal and external information in order to help us form a judgement on the truth and fairness of the accounts. It may be described as the process of looking at the figures to see if they make sense and, if they do, using that fact to reduce our later audit work. If it is to be effective, it must make full use of our knowledge of the business.

4.02 Analytical review is one of the ways of providing audit evidence about the completeness, accuracy and validity of the transactions and balances. It can be used at several stages in the audit, for example:
(a) as a planning tool to identify areas of the accounts which are important because of their size and to highlight unusual or unexpected figures or relationships which may influence our assessment of risk and should be investigated;
(b) as a substantive test to obtain limited assurance about transactions and balances and so reduce the level of (or in some cases eliminate) tests of detail; and
(c) as part of the review procedures at the end of each stage of the audit.

4.03 Analytical review assumes that there are relationships between items in the accounts (and between items in the accounts and non-financial data) which may be expected to continue in the absence of evidence to the contrary. For example, in many businesses there is a relationship between gross profit and sales which can be expected to remain constant unless there are changes in prices, sales mix and cost structures. Where the relationship changes, we normally expect to identify the reason from our knowledge of the business and industry, or we might already have anticipated it. Where we cannot identify the reason, it suggests an error in the accounts; so we can choose appropriate audit procedures.

Procedures

4.04   Analytical review procedures can include:

(a) comparisons of an item or ratio with comparable prior periods;
(b) comparisons of an item or ratio with anticipated results (budgets, forecasts etc);
(c) studies of the relationships between items in the accounts that are expected to conform to predictable patterns;
(d) comparison of the financial information with similar information for other companies and the industry as a whole; and
(e) studies of the relationship of financial information with non-financial information.

Comparisons should also be made with other branches or divisions in the same line of business which are part of the same company or group or with other companies. It is often helpful to make comparisons on a monthly or quarterly basis where such figures are available. This can eliminate any distorting effects of seasonal trade and may enable us to distinguish genuine seasonal fluctuations from window dressing around the year end.

Example 1

A company had 60 employees last year with total wages of £210,000 and 60 employees this year with a wage bill of £262,500, an increase of 25%. We know that the annual pay rise was 12% and the level of business has remained approximately constant.

At first sight, the figures do not appear to make sense because the increase is substantially greater than expected. There may, however, be satisfactory explanations. For example, there may have been a change in sales mix with previously bought-in goods being replaced by goods manufactured in house, resulting in substantial authorised overtime. This could be verified by looking at the sales figures for different products as well as the payroll. Alternatively there could have been a switch to more skilled, and hence more expensive, labour; this could be verified from payroll and production records.

If no such explanation is available, it is possible that the payroll has been inflated by, for example:

(a) misposting in the general ledger;
(b) 'dummy' employees on the payroll;
(c) unauthorised overtime being paid;
(d) employees being paid at higher rates of pay than authorised.

We direct our substantive testing towards finding any errors of this nature.

4.05   In our analytical review procedures we make full use of our knowledge of the business, the industry in which it operates and the economy as a whole. Hence, if we know that interest rates have been falling, we expect to see the charge for overdraft interest falling (if the overdraft has remained constant). If we know that the technology in the industry is changing in such a way as to reduce costs and selling prices, we do not expect to find increases in sales attributable to higher prices. If we know that a particular hotel relies heavily on overseas tourists, we do not expect to see it do well in a period when sterling is high.

4.06   Throughout our analytical review procedures, we are conscious that figures, ratios and percentages which do not appear to make sense may indicate errors. We may, however, find there are valid explanations for apparently wrong figures — the review merely alerts us to the possibility of errors and allows us the opportunity to seek explanations immediately or to plan substantive tests which will provide them.

Timing of Analytical Review Procedures

4.07   The review of clients' figures should begin as early as possible so that the maximum benefit is obtained in planning the audit and in reducing detailed testing. If analytical review procedures are not applied until the end of the audit, many of the benefits of such procedures are lost. For example, where substantive tests of detail are performed on the year's transactions prior to the analytical review, the analytical review may identify fluctuations which require some retesting of the transactions. Obviously, it is more efficient to examine each sample only once, which would be the case if analytical review procedures are performed and followed up prior to the detailed testing.

4.08   Analytical review procedures applied early in the audit tend to indicate errors and omissions, changes in accounting practices or unusual trends that tests of detail might not reveal. We need to investigate items of this nature and discuss them with the client at the earliest possible opportunity to avoid last-minute adjustments or discussions about qualifications to our audit opinion.

Information Available for Review

4.09   Individual figures should be reviewed as soon as they are available (as long as major adjustments are not expected). For example, if the client prepares interim management accounts, a review of the latest accounts should be carried out while planning the audit. This enables us to take account of any possible problems and gives us some audit assurance. In these cases, we should make use of the figures management uses to control and review its business — including any data which is not part of the formal management accounting package. Often we will find the information we want to use is already included in management and board reports. Where we produce interim accounts for a client, we should use them and the knowledge we have gained in preparing them to identify audit problems and thus to direct our efforts to significant areas and reduce the level of detailed testing.

4.10 Where the company produces a trial balance, it can be used for an initial analytical review. Care is needed, however, where the trial balance does not include all the accruals and prepayments and final adjustments. Ratios calculated from these figures may require adjustment if they are to be compared with a previous period's final accounts. Nevertheless, much useful information may be obtained from such a review. Furthermore, as soon as final figures for any item are available, they can be subject to review to check that they make sense in the context of the business and the rest of the accounts.

4.11 Even where the client does not produce a trial balance, certain figures are available before the draft accounts are prepared. For example, the sales ledger control account in the general ledger is likely to be agreed at a fairly early stage. Then we can review sales from the sales day book and debtors (the total of sales ledger balances) and possibly draw some conclusions about whether sales and debtors make sense.

Comparisons with Other Companies

4.12 Our review should not be limited to information produced internally by the client. Unless it is highly specialised or has no equivalent competitors, it is always helpful to compare the figures and ratios revealed by one business with other similar companies. This may involve consulting colleagues, managers or partners who have dealt with similar companies and are able to help interpret the results of the review. In addition, inter-firm comparisons may be a useful tool in judging how the client is performing, although care is required because they may be out of date, calculated on a different basis or distorted because some firms decline to take part in them.

Comparisons Generally

4.13   Whenever comparisons are made of absolute figures, ratios or percentages, care is required to ensure that:

(a) they are computed on a consistent basis for each period or location under review. Where there is a change in the basis of the calculation of a ratio or in the relationships which make up the ratio, comparability may be lost. The ratio for the prior year may be restated to obtain a meaningful comparison. For example, if stock turnover was calculated using average stocks last year, it is no good trying to make a comparison with a ratio for this year using year-end stocks. Major changes in pricing policy and product lines may also render past relationships inconsistent with current results;

(b) we are comparing items where there ought to be a meaningful relationship. For example, there is little point in comparing head office overheads with sales since there is unlikely to be any connection between them. Similarly there is little point in examining the relationship between sales and gross profit if stocks are valued by reference to a fixed gross profit ratio;

(c) results and balance sheet values are not distorted by the effects of changing price levels. For example, under historical cost accounting, assets acquired at different times are stated at different price levels. This means that any ratio involving fixed assets is affected by when the assets were purchased. Hence ratios such as return on capital employed and fixed asset turnover can be distorted and comparisons between different companies made meaningless unless they are done on a current cost basis;

(d) they are not distorted by exceptional or extraordinary items. Such items are often first detected by means of analytical review procedures and once detected, they should be investigated separately and their effects removed from any ratios and trends;

(e) they are not distorted by changes in accounting policy or accounting estimates. It is necessary to adjust the figures for the prior year in order that comparisons can be made. It may also be useful to calculate the figures or ratios using the old accounting policy or estimate; this is not always possible but, if it is, it may give some indication of the effects of the change.

Results of Analytical Review Procedures

4.14   Having calculated appropriate ratios and made appropriate comparisons, we should compare the results with our expectations based on our knowledge of the business, budgets, forecasts, etc. Expected results need no further investigation and allow us to reduce the size of our substantive tests of detail.

4.15 Unexpected results must be investigated and verified before they can be accepted. This is true whether the change in the figures is small or large. For example, if we know that the market for men's clothing is being hit by cheap imports, we may expect a UK manufacturer of menswear to show declining sales and reduced margins. A 5% increase in sales without a reduction in margins is, therefore, unexpected unless we know of any special circumstances affecting our client's sector of the market.

4.16 Unexpected results may occur because of:
(a) actions of the company of which we are unaware when we do our review;
(b) external factors not controllable by the client, such as increased costs of raw materials, of which we are unaware when we do our review;
(c) errors or omissions.

4.17 Actions of the company should not normally lead to 'unexpected' results since we should know about them from our knowledge of the business and our contact with the client throughout the year. We may, however, be unaware of some actions, particularly where the business has a decentralised management structure.

4.18 All material variations, whether expected or not, should be discussed with management and explained in the working papers. Explanations should be specific and quantified and in such terms as:
(a) an 8% wage increase for all sales staff from 1 January, costing £40,000 in the year;
(b) a loss of 10 days' production due to a strike resulting in lost sales of £460,000 and a reduction in gross and net profits of £84,000;
(c) a 5% across-the-board increase in sales prices which increased sales by £62,000 in the year;
(d) a 10% increase in quantity sold amounting to increased sales of £608,000 and gross and net profit of £41,000;
(e) a change in accounting policy for dealing with the treatment of finance leases; this has increased indebtedness by £168,000 and fixed assets by £154,000.

4.19 Explanations should avoid using:
(a) vague phrases, such as 'inflation', 'economics' or 'growth'. The cost of electricity goes up because the electricity company has increased its prices not because of 'inflation'. If stocks have been increased because of a growth in the business be more specific — relate the change to increased purchases and sales, selling area and so on;
(b) self-fulfilling or incomplete relationships. Stock may have increased because there is more storage space — but why is there more storage space? Fixed

assets may have increased because of additions in the year — but why has the company bought more of them?;

(c) circular logic resulting from having only variables (and no 'constants' or reliable amounts) in the figures. Hence, if we are unhappy about the accuracy of the level of the bank overdraft, we cannot use it to verify interest paid. We cannot gain comfort on cost of sales and gross profit from their relationship with sales if sales are only verified by reference to gross profit.

4.20   Explanations must be adequately verified to ensure that they are genuine and correctly account for the results seen. Where, for example, an increase in wages is explained as a 10% uplift in wage rates, we should check this to wages records and any union agreements and satisfy ourselves that it accounts adequately for the variation.

4.21   Not all explanations are capable of verification; nevertheless we may be able to decide on their reasonableness. For example, if a decrease in sales is attributed to a fall in demand, we may not be able to verify this explanation directly nor quantify its effect (unless there are total market figures published and available in time for our audit). If the decrease is in line with our knowledge of the industry and market conditions, we may accept it as being reasonable. If the explanation cannot be verified, we cannot reduce our detailed substantive tests on sales.

4.22   As we will often use the results of our analytical review to justify reduction in the level of detailed substantive testing it is important that we clearly document the results of our review, the explanations we have received and the work we have been able to do to corroborate these explanations.

Effect on Substantive Tests of Detail

4.23   Once explanations have been obtained and verified, we can decide how to reduce the level of subsequent substantive tests or, in appropriate cases, rely entirely on the results of the review. If the figures make sense, or unexpected results have been satisfactorily resolved, detailed substantive tests covering appropriate audit objectives may be reduced. The working papers should state which audit objectives are affected and the audit programme will show by how much the detailed tests will be reduced. The appropriate sample size reductions are explained in **9.18**.

Example 2

At a manufacturing company, in our analytical review procedures we might:

(a) compare sales for each major product with budget and previous years' actual, and assess the reasonableness of explanations for variances shown in the monthly sales report;

(b) compare monthly figures for each major product to establish trends and seasonal fluctuations. This may help to verify explanations about the performance of individual products;

(c) compare sales quantities for each major product, in relation to budgets and previous years;

(d) reconcile sales quantities to production schedules and opening and closing stocks for each major product;

(e) compare ratios such as gross profit, stock turnover, debtors collection period, with budget and previous years. Gross profit and stock turnover may be calculated on an individual product basis;

(f) examine price lists to establish the effect of changes in prices.

If the results of these procedures are satisfactory, we may decide to reduce our sample sizes for sales and debtors (see Chapter 9).

4.24 Where management itself uses and reviews management accounts and budgets and takes appropriate action to investigate unusual or unexpected results, we may be able to place extensive reliance on our analytical review procedures in determining the level of substantive tests. If such a review by management is limited to certain figures, such as sales and debtors but not, say, all the overhead expenses, we can place greater reliance on the results of our analytical review procedures on the revenue cycle than elsewhere.

4.25 Even where our analytical review procedures are limited by the lack of management accounts and budgets or by a lack of experience and knowledge of the client in the first year audit, we should still look at all relevant figures that are available and consider any figures used by the management to control the business. We may still be able to place limited reliance on them and reduce the level of our substantive tests.

4.26 If unresolved problems remain, the working papers should specify which audit objectives are affected and how this will affect the tests on those objectives. For example, if there appears to be a possibility that sales are understated and, from the monthly sales figures, we suspect the understatement may have occurred in June and July, we increase our sample of sales for those two months.

Working Papers

4.27   The form of the working papers for an analytical review depends upon the type of business involved and what is already available from the company. Whatever is chosen, we must:

(a) set out clearly the figures and ratios that we have considered;
(b) set out our expectations relating to the figures and ratios reviewed;
(c) state any unexpected results and the effect on our audit objectives;
(d) note the explanations of the client for unexpected results;
(e) refer to the relevant working papers schedules on which we have set out the way in which these explanations have been verified;
(f) state how our tests are to be adapted to take account of the results of the review;
(g) state on which audit objectives sufficient assurance has been obtained from the analytical review to reduce sample sizes and by how much;
(h) leave space for year end figures to be inserted as and when they become available.

5 Risk

This chapter explains how we assess the overall audit risk and the specific risks affecting different cycles of the audit. It also describes how this assessment of risks affects the design of audit tests.

Evaluate Overall Audit Risk

5.01 The nature and extent of our work is affected by our assessment of the risk of different types of errors in the financial statements. Where we have assessed risk and there is no indication that material errors may be present, we are justified in carrying out the minimum amount of audit work consistent with reasonable caution. Where on the other hand it appears, either from our analytical review or our past experience of the company or from our knowledge of its business and industry, there could be material errors, we need to investigate further until we have determined the extent of error or satisfied ourselves that the accounts give a true and fair view.

5.02 Hence we identify audits where there is a 'normal risk' of material errors and those where there is a 'higher than normal risk' of material errors. We do not recognise any situations where there is less than normal risk.

5.03 Audit risk consists of:
(a) inherent risk: the susceptibility of a balance or class of transactions to material error;
(b) control risk: the risk that the controls will not detect material error on a timely basis;
(c) detection risk: the risk that our audit procedures do not discover material error that is present. Our audit procedures are designed to minimise detection risk.

5.04   Detection risk is itself a combination of:
(a) sampling risk, which is the possibility that a test based on a sample (whether statistical or not) might lead to conclusions different from those we would have reached had we applied the test to the total population; and
(b) the risk that we apply the wrong procedures or fail to recognise errors or draw conclusions which are inconsistent with the evidence.

5.05   Sampling risk can be quantified and is dealt with in Chapter 9. The other risks can be minimised by adequate planning and supervision and review of the audit work. Proper quality controls within the firm also minimise these risks. They are not dealt with in this guide.

Assessment of Risk

5.06   At the planning stage of the audit we should assess the risk of material errors for:
(a) the accounts as a whole; and
(b) each individual cycle.
We should keep this assessment under review throughout the audit and where it changes, perhaps because of developments in the company or because of the results of our audit work, we should adapt our procedures as necessary.

We carry out our risk assessment by means of:
(a) business review; and
(b) accounting systems' review.

5.07   The business review involves an in-depth enquiry covering the following areas:
(a) the business, its structure and ownership;
(b) industry, markets and products;
(c) financial position;
(d) initial results review;
(e) control environment;
(f) review of departments.
The review consists of a structured analysis of the above areas. It is recorded in the business review report. During the review and at its conclusion, we identify any negative factors — those leading to the conclusion that risk is higher than normal, and any positive factors — those leading to the conclusion that risk is normal. We weigh these factors together before reaching an overall conclusion.

5.08 The accounting systems' review is designed to identify any areas of weakness in the client's accounting system. The presence of these weaknesses, in the absence of mitigating strengths, leads us to the view that there is a higher than normal risk of error.

5.09 The accounting systems' review consists of two checklists: an accounting systems checklist — which covers the client's systems cycle by cycle, and a computer controls checklist — which covers general computer controls, i.e. controls covering access to the computer, disaster planning, etc. It is essential before completing these checklists to have an up-to-date record of the system.

5.10 In our assessment of risk we consider such matters as:
(a) the financial position of the company;
(b) whether the company is likely to be encountering liquidity problems in the current and future years;
(c) the integrity of management;
(d) our audit experience in recent years;
(e) our recent experience of the industry and markets in which the client is operating;
(f) the existence of an appropriate control environment;
(g) management's (or the owner's) plans for the company;
(h) the significant audit areas and anticipated problems.

5.11 We also need to consider the uses to which the accounts are to be put. We need to ask who are the users and what are their needs so that we can be responsive to them. If we know that the accounts are to be used to help justify increased borrowings from the bank, we should be conscious of what the bank manager will be looking for and the risk of errors which may lead him to make wrong decisions from the bank's point of view.

Negative Factors

5.12 During our assessment we should recognise both the negative factors which tend to lead to higher than normal audit risk and the positive or mitigating factors which tend to lead to normal audit risk. The negative factors which might lead to a higher than normal risk decision could include:
(a) excessive debt;
(b) a possible purchase or sale of a business (including a flotation on the Stock Market);
(c) a poor control environment;
(d) poor management; and

(e) a poor history with regulatory bodies.

The list is not exhaustive nor are all the above factors expected to be present to enable us to decide that the audit risk is higher than normal. Any one factor by itself might lead to such a conclusion.

Positive Factors

5.13   Some positive factors which might lead to a 'normal risk' decision include:

(a) we have audited the client for a number of years and found good records and no significant internal control or audit problems;

(b) the company's accounting personnel are competent;

(c) the control environment is strong;

(d) the company is privately held and financially stable without an excessive amount of debt and it is highly likely that it will remain so for the next two or three years;

(e) the proprietor takes an active role in the business;

(f) the business is successful;

(g) the company's history with the Inland Revenue and Customs and Excise has been good;

(h) management is generally conservative and interested in long term growth, with no intentions of selling the business;

(i) there is an active board of directors including non-executive directors or even an audit committee.

Again this list is not exhaustive.

Other Considerations

5.14   Note that many of these factors relate to a company's current position and past history; audit risk is assessed partially by what has happened in prior years and what is happening now and partially by our judgement about the future of the business. For example, the fact that a client is a private company is a statement about the past and the present. On its own it is not a positive factor; if, however, we anticipate that the status will continue in the foreseeable future then it may be. If, on the other hand, we do not expect the company to remain private, we might start to think in terms of 'higher than normal' risk.

5.15   Changes in accounting policy (or even changes in the way certain policies are implemented) may be a factor indicating a higher than normal risk. For example, a change in policy so that income is recognised earlier than in the past may, coupled with other factors, suggest a higher than normal risk in overall terms (the change itself may even be an 'error'). A change in the method of computing overheads for inclusion in the valuation of stock may indicate a higher than normal overall risk (the company is trying to influence its profits by changing the way it values stock) or a higher than normal risk on stocks (the change may give rise to errors because it is a new method and the company's staff are unfamiliar with it and have not coped well with changes in the past).

5.16   The involvement of the proprietor in the running of the business or the existence of an internal audit department has a bearing on the control environment and hence the risk of errors. Where the proprietor monitors the business closely, reviewing transactions for reasonableness and supervising staff, there is likely to be a normal risk of errors. However, where the proprietor of a closely held business is in a position to override normal control procedures particularly for unusual transactions, such as special orders that have to be processed quickly, there may be a high risk of errors for those objectives concerned with these transactions.

5.17   When auditing small businesses special attention must be paid to particular audit risks such as:
(a) the failure of an owner/manager to distinguish between personal and family affairs and those of the business. This may increase the risk of certain types of errors in the financial statements, such as misclassifications or overstatement of expenses;
(b) errors in the accounting records which arise because of undermanning or inexperienced staff;
(c) the lack of segregation of duties (all or many of the accounting entries may be made by one person, and not all of the entries may be checked) increases the risk of certain types of errors (and sometimes fraud).

How Risk Affects Audit Work

5.18   In the absence of any indication of a 'higher than normal' risk of errors, we are justified in reducing the level of our audit work to the minimum consistent with reasonable caution and care. However, we should never do less work than is required by auditing standards; to do otherwise would both violate professional standards, with the risk of damaging the reputation and standing of the firm and the profession, and fail to meet the expectations of users of the accounts.

5.19   Where we have completed and fully documented risk assessment and have concluded that overall risk is normal and that the risk is normal for a particular cycle we may take reliance from this to reduce the level of tests in that cycle. We should also be able to reduce the level of our substantive tests of detail by placing reliance on:

(a) analytical review procedures;
(b) compliance tests of key controls;
(c) substantive tests in total;
(d) other substantive tests covering the same audit area.

5.20   For example, where there is a normal risk of the understatement of creditors, it may not be necessary to circularise suppliers to seek confirmation of amounts owed to them by the company. Instead, reliance can be placed on analytical review (checking to see that creditors make sense in the context of the other figures in the accounts and our knowledge of what has gone on in the business) and internal controls over the recording of liabilities supported by limited checks of suppliers' statements available at the company.

5.21   Detailed testing on small items may be eliminated entirely and replaced by analytical review procedures and possibly tests in total. On larger items, it is normally necessary to carry out some detailed testing, although reliance on analytical review and tests in total may reduce them to a minimum.

5.22   When planning the audit, or when our assessment of risk changes, we should specifically consider what procedures can be reduced or eliminated in the normal audit risk situation. For example, where there is normal audit risk based on a strong control environment, we can probably restrict our work considerably. It may, for example, be possible to exclude:
(a) circularisation of creditors (and rely entirely on evidence available at the company);
(b) tests of additions to fixed assets (except if they are very large or unusual);
(c) detailed testing of prepaid expenses and deferred charges;
(d) tests of accruals for normal, recurring transactions;
(e) detailed testing of some profit and loss expenditure; and
(f) detailed testing of credit notes.

5.23   Where we have identified a higher than normal risk of errors, the effect on the audit work depends on the precise nature of the risk, that is the type of errors that appear likely. Certain higher than normal risks might lead to specific audit steps. Others make us more sceptical about errors. For example: the possibility that management is keen to maintain the trend of increasing earnings per share might mean we have to increase tests of sales and purchase cut off, obsolescence and provisions for doubtful debtors. Where there is a higher than normal risk of understated creditors (perhaps because errors have often occurred in the past, the control environment is poor and the company is eager to show large profits), a circularisation of a large sample of suppliers may become a vital procedure.

5.24 Usually where there is a higher than normal risk of errors, we recognise that certain types of error are most likely to occur (but other types of error may be no more likely than normal). More often this occurs in the judgemental areas, such as the valuation of stock and the recoverability of debtors. For example, our review of the accounts may indicate that stock may be overstated and we know that errors have occurred in the past and the company wants to show good results, but all other figures may appear reasonable. In this case we would bias our tests towards the risk of errors in stock and reduce to a minimum our work in other areas.

5.25 Where there is a higher than normal risk for the audit as a whole, but we have not been able to assess what specific types of error are likely (for example, because we are concerned about the general competence of management or the accounting staff or the effects of major litigation), we treat any errors or unusual items found with a greater degree of scepticism than in a normal risk audit. We investigate the errors and unusual items thoroughly.

Documenting the Risk Assessment

5.26 The risk assessment brings together the risk factors identified from:
(a) the business review; and
(b) the accounting systems' review.
Negative factors leading to higher than normal risk should initially be documented in our risk assessment along with mitigating positive factors. Where negative risk factors cannot be offset by positive factors the cycle affected and appropriate programme steps should be identified. A summary of our assessment of these risks and their effect on the nature and extent of our audit tests should be included in the overall audit plan.

5.27 The information documented on the business review report and the accounting system review provide the basis for the assessment of overall risk. It is the manager's and partner's responsibility to assess and sign off the overall risk assessment for the audit using all available information.

Conclusion

5.28 The overall conclusion on the risk assessment which must be approved by the partner will either be that:
(a) There is a higher than normal risk of error which affects every cycle.
(b) There is a higher than normal risk of error in certain cycles but a normal risk elsewhere.
(c) There is a normal risk of error throughout the audit.

6 Materiality

This chapter describes what is meant by 'materiality', gives guidance on how a materiality level for the audit is determined and explains how the preliminary estimate of materiality affects the extent of our audit tests. It concludes by showing how the materiality level is used in deciding whether to seek adjustment for errors or qualify an audit opinion.

6.01 The main purpose of an audit is to express an opinion on the truth and fairness of the results and financial position shown by the accounts. For the most part, we tackle this job by looking for errors in the figures presented to us by management. It would, however, be both foolish and wasteful to look for and adjust every single error. It would take too long and it is, in any case, usually impossible because some items in the accounts are estimates which are inherently imprecise. All that is expected of us is that we look for and request the adjustment of material errors (management can, if it wishes, adjust for any immaterial errors that are discovered).

6.02 The concept of materiality is included in both company law and accounting standards, neither of which is concerned with the treatment of immaterial items. So, for example, it does not matter whether a provision is made for bad and doubtful debts if the amount involved is small by comparison to the rest of the accounts. Similarly, it is unnecessary to disclose the accounting policies for items which have little bearing on the results or the financial position. The only occasion where the materiality concept does not apply is for some specific disclosure requirements, such as directors' remuneration and loans.

6.03 A matter is regarded as being material if its non-disclosure, misstatement or omission is likely to distort the view given by the accounts to their users. So, for example, the overstatement of debtors and profits by £50,000 would be material for a small company where it would give a totally different impression to users than the correct figures. In a much larger company, the £50,000 error might not be material because it would not affect the view of users.

The Effect of Materiality on Audit Work

6.04   The first way in which the concept of materiality affects our audits is that it is one of the factors which influence the nature and size of our audit tests; we need to design audit procedures to verify only those items which could be materially wrong and we need do only sufficient work to satisfy ourselves that balances and transactions do not contain material errors. Hence, where we have decided on a materiality level of £50,000, we do not direct much (if any) audit effort towards verifying prepayments totalling £10,000. For those procedures we decide to carry out, the sample size reduces as the materiality level increases (and vice versa). So, if debtors total £250,000 we test more items (all other things being equal) if the materiality level is £10,000 than if it is £50,000.

6.05   The second way in which the concept of materiality affects our audit work is when we are deciding whether to seek adjustment for errors we have found. We are not concerned whether or not management adjusts for immaterial errors. We are concerned that adjustments are made for material errors.

6.06   There are cases where management wants to adjust for all errors — or at least some of those which are immaterial to the audit opinion. If this is so, we should agree this with the client before we start our audit work (often, from past experience, we know that certain clients prefer to adjust for all errors, or at least have the opportunity to consider them). There may also be cases where the client expects us to discover immaterial errors — again, this should be agreed in advance, particularly as it may substantially increase the costs of the audit and the risks to ourselves.

Setting the Level of Materiality

6.07   To set the materiality level, we need to decide the level of errors which would distort the view given by the accounts. Because most users of accounts are primarily interested in the success of the business, the level is often expressed as a proportion of its profits. It is better, however, to think of materiality in terms of the size of the business and recognise that, if the business remains a fairly constant size, the materiality level should not change. Similarly, if the business is growing, the level of materiality increases from year to year and if it shrinks, the level of materiality decreases.

6.08   The size of a business can be measured in terms of turnover and total assets (before deducting any liabilities) both of which tend not to be subject to the same fluctuations which may affect profit. As a guide, between $\frac{1}{2}$% and 1% of turnover and between 1% and 2% of total assets gives an indication of what is material. These figures, based on the latest available information (last year's accounts if nothing else is available), should be the starting point in the estimate of the level of materiality.

Example 3

A company's accounts show the following:

	£
Total assets	15,000,000
Turnover	20,000,000

The estimate of materiality is likely to be in the following ranges:

	$\frac{1}{2}$%	1%	2%
Total assets		£150,000	£300,000
Turnover	£100,000	£200,000	

These give a starting point in deciding the level of materiality. We must also take into account what we know the users of the accounts are interested in and consider any other relevant figures in the accounts. This will allow us to refine our judgement within the range or, in some cases, take us outside the range.

6.09   The use of turnover and total assets has particular advantages over the use of profits as the base figure for the estimate of the level of materiality. It helps to remind us that the level should remain constant from year to year unless the size of the business changes. In addition, problems do not arise when the business makes a loss, or breaks even or earns only a small profit. Nor do turnover and total assets need adjustments for items such as directors' bonuses, additional pension contributions and so on, which may distort the profit before taxes.

6.10   Profits can, however, enter into the calculations. Again as a guide, between 5% and 10% of profit before taxation is the usual range. Profits are, however, also likely to vary from year to year and there is the risk of increased audit work in years of low profits, even though the company is roughly the same size.

6.11   When using profits in the calculation of materiality levels, adjustment should be made for the effect of such items as management charges or directors' remuneration which may vary with profits. They may need to be added back to the profit figure before using it as a basis for any calculation.

Example 4

Extending *Example 3*, suppose that the company's profits before tax were likely to be of the order of £2m. A materiality level based on pre-tax profits would be between £100,000 (5%) to £200,000 (10%).

Example 5

Continuing *Examples 3 and 4*, if the company expects profits before tax of only £10,000, a materiality level based on such profits would be in the range £500–£1,000. It would involve a considerable amount of work looking for £1,000 errors in total assets of £15m. Indeed, within that £15m, there are, undoubtedly, subjective judgements of value which are not right to within £1,000; hence we would be wasting our time looking for such small errors.

Example 6

Suppose a company has the following results:

		1987 £	1988 £	1989 £	1990 £
Profits before tax		100,000	60,000	106,000	20,000
Materiality level, based	5%	5,000	3,000	5,300	1,000
on profits	10%	10,000	6,000	10,600	2,000

Another effect of using each year's profit figure as the basis for the materiality level is that the size of the audit test varies. Hence in 1990, far more audit work would be done than in 1989, a situation which is unlikely to be correct. One way of overcoming the problem is to ignore isolated fluctuations and average the profits in some way. If materiality levels are based on a 3-yearly moving average of profits before tax, then

		1987 £	1988 £	1989 £	1990 £
3-year moving average		86,000	74,000	89,000	62,000
Materiality level, based on:	5%	4,300	3,700	4,500	3,100
	10%	8,600	7,400	8,900	6,200

Even this leaves some fluctuation in the materiality level, although the range (and hence the risk of over and under auditing) is reduced substantially.

Narrowing Down the Range of Materiality Levels

6.12   We can settle on a figure to use in our test design by starting at the upper limit of the range of possible values and then look for factors that require us to reduce the materiality level. Such factors might include:

(a) a wide level of exposure for the accounts, particularly where their publication attracts a lot of publicity;

(b) cases where the trend in profits is of particular importance to users; for example, where the company is seeking a listing or additional finance; or

(c) the fact that the company is close to breaching certain requirements such as a debenture trust deed.

6.13   One might use a lower point within the range where an error could move a company from low profits to a small loss. Such a change may have a strong psychological effect on management or users. However, such an error does not change the fact that the company is essentially of a particular size and we should be careful not to do excessive audit work just to find the small errors that will push the results one way or the other.

6.14   Whatever figure we settle on, we should try to ensure it remains constant from year to year unless the size of the business changes. We should also remember that, although we settle on a single figure expressed in money terms, it is an imprecise estimate. It is based on a judgement about what matters to users — this must inevitably be approximate. It involves an assessment of the size of the business based on figures from the accounts under audit or previous accounts; these can only give an approximate guide. For these reasons, materiality should be seen as a band around the selected figure rather than the particular figure.

Materiality and Sample Sizes

6.15   Although we have set a single figure on the level of materiality, it is often advisable to use a slightly smaller figure (say 10% smaller) for testing. This reduces the sampling risk. As explained in Chapter 9, the discovery of any error in a sample indicates that the population may be materially wrong. There is, however, the risk that the sample includes proportionately more errors than the total error in the population. In order to reduce the risk of wrong conclusions and of additional work at a late stage in the audit, sample selection can be based on a materiality level slightly reduced from the pre-set level. We then use the higher figure for deciding whether or not to require adjustments and the lower figure for determining sample sizes.

6.16 The other instances where we use a different level of materiality are where:

(a) the test only deals with balance sheet classification and we can use a higher figure (on rare occasions, a lower figure where balance sheet classification is especially sensitive); or

(b) we are checking those figures which company law requires to be accurate (for example, directors' remuneration).

Accountancy Work

6.17 Where accountancy work is involved, it is usually carried out with the intention of complete accuracy. Therefore, a materiality level is not used in the same way as for auditing. For example, when posting sales invoices to the debtors' ledger, we expect to be accurate to the penny. However, we do not waste time searching for errors of a few pounds in, say, the sales ledger control account (as long as we are happy it does not indicate large compensating errors); instead, we use a concept of materiality albeit with much lower figures in mind than when auditing.

6.18 Certain aspects of accountancy work require estimates which cannot be totally accurate. For example, prepayments and accruals are calculated to the nearest pound or preferably the nearest £10, £100 or even £1,000. Similarly, provisions for bad debts or against obsolete stock items are imprecise but within reasonable limits. The materiality level used in making these accounting estimates is likely to be smaller than for the related audit work.

Smaller Audits

6.19 Where audits involve accountancy work, a materiality level must be decided upon for the audit procedures, such as debtors' circularisations or observations of stocktakes. This is particularly important on small jobs which involve a significant amount of accountancy work. There is a danger on these engagements that, without a materiality level as a guide, we waste our time by testing everything possible.

Adjustments for Errors

6.20   Only errors that are material require adjustment for the accounts to show a true and fair view. However, as explained earlier, management may request that all errors found are adjusted (or considered). All errors (other than very small ones) found during the audit must be listed and their combined effect assessed. An error should not be ignored because it is less than the materiality level. A number of such errors, which are individually immaterial, may be material in aggregate.

Example 7

During the course of an audit, the following errors are discovered, all of which affect profits:

Debtors	— overstated by	£20,000
Stocks	— overstated by	£29,000
Creditors	— understated by	£40,000.

Assume errors of £50,000 are regarded as material because they distort the accounts. If the errors are assessed individually, no adjustment is required — each error is immaterial. If, however, they are aggregated, profit is overstated by £89,000, a sum well in excess of the materiality level. So if an adjustment is not made for at least £39,000, the accounts are likely to be materially wrong.

6.21   In assessing whether errors are material, the same factors apply as in setting materiality for testing. We must assess it in relation to the size of the company, the nature of the item and the nature of the error. Where errors are in different directions, it is possible that, taken together, they are not material in terms of the size of the company, but that they are material in relation to particular balance sheet items. For example, errors in recording items in creditors and stock may not be material overall to profit but may be material because of their effect on the creditors' or stock figures.

7 The audit programme — substantive procedures

This chapter explains how the audit objectives, which are appropriate to the client's business, are identified and gives guidance on the kinds of audit evidence required for each objective.

7.01 The audit can be divided into a number of 'cycles' corresponding to each major balance sheet heading and related profit and loss items. So, for example, the revenue cycle deals with debtors, sales and cash receipts; the purchases cycle includes creditors, payments, purchases and all overheads. At the beginning of the audit we choose cycles which match the client's business and accounting system. So, for example, the revenue cycle of a property company refers to rents and service charges received rather than sales; at a manufacturing company with an integrated costing system, separate cycles would deal with 'conversion' (the purchase of raw materials, production wages and the overheads included in the stock valuation — together with related creditors and payments) and 'overhead expenditure'.

Audit Objectives

7.02 Having identified the cycles, we must identify appropriate audit objectives for each of them. The objectives are derived from the representations made in the accounts. For example, management represents that the amounts shown in the balance sheet as fixed assets are not misclassified revenue expenditure and that the assets owned by the company are properly valued and have not been sold or otherwise disposed of. Management also represents that the sales figure in the accounts fairly reflects all the despatches made by the company during the period, that the despatches have been properly evaluated and recorded and that unrecorded credits are not due in respect of any of them.

7.03 From the representations we derive audit objectives which identify the areas in which we need to obtain sufficient relevant and reliable audit evidence. The objectives can be expressed in summary form as:
(a) income is neither understated nor overstated;
(b) expenditure is neither understated nor overstated;

(c) assets are neither understated nor overstated;

(d) liabilities are neither understated nor overstated; and

(e) assets, liabilities, income and expenditure and other items required by law are properly presented and disclosed in the financial statements.

7.04 It is, however, inefficient to carry out both understatement and over-statement tests on each of income, expenditure, assets and liabilities. The double entry bookkeeping system means, for example, that if an asset is understated, then either another asset or expenditure is overstated or income or liabilities are understated.

Example 8

If a test shows that debtors are understated by £10,000, then either:

(a) another asset must be overstated by £10,000 (for example, cash at bank or other debtors); or

(b) income is understated by £10,000 (for example, sales); or

(c) liabilities are understated by £10,000 (for example, bank overdraft); or

(d) expenditure is overstated by £10,000; or

(e) any combination of the above totalling £10,000; or

(f) the accounts do not balance (when debtors are adjusted by £10,000).

7.05 We take advantage of the double entry system to minimise our testing. The way we have chosen to do this is by testing to ensure that:

(a) income is not understated;

(b) expenditure is not overstated;

(c) assets are not overstated; and

(d) liabilities are not understated.

In practice, this means we are testing the debits in the trial balance for over-statement and the credits for understatement. So, for example, we test debtors for overstatement but sales for understatement and we test creditors for under-statement and purchases for overstatement.

7.06 In addition to these four objectives, we must also ensure that the presentation and disclosure in the accounts complies with all relevant requirements. Each cycle should contain an objective to deal with this.

7.07 We sub-divide the objectives to make the choice and design of audit procedures easier. For example, if tests are designed to check that income is not understated, there is the risk of missing certain areas because the objective is so broad. Therefore we may sub-divide the objective and check that:

(a) despatches are recorded and give rise to an invoice;

(b) invoices are correctly computed;

(c) invoices are recorded in the sales ledger and sales day book;

(d) cash receipts are accounted for.

7.08   The objectives must be adapted to meet the requirements of the client's business and accounting system. For example, at a retailers we check that:

(a) all goods leaving the shop are correctly recorded on the cash register and the correct amount of cash is put in the till; and

(b) all cash put in the till is accounted for.

Where a manufacturing company has an integrated costing system which is used to value stocks, the objectives are directed towards the correct classification of costs and the accurate recording of movement of stocks. Where there is a less sophisticated system and stocks are only valued at the year end, the sub-objectives are concerned less with movements and more with the correct identification of items at the stocktake and pricing of the stock sheets.

7.09   The objectives always use words appropriate to the client's business. Where, for example, 'sales' are commissions or rents, use the right word! — it helps design the right tests and understand the consequences of errors. It also demonstrates to the client that we know what we are talking about and we don't churn out a 'standard' audit whether we are dealing with a motor manufacturer, an estate agent, a property company, a beauty salon or a trade union.

The Audit Programme

7.10   Tests of balances and transactions should be designed for all objectives at the beginning of the audit. The manager should review the tests and approve them before they are carried out. Some or all of the tests may have been identified while preparing the planning notes; alternatively, it may be more appropriate to design the tests as a separate exercise. Where we perform accountancy work, the audit tests should be designed to take into account the assurance gained from the accountancy work. The nature and extent of our tests will also take account of our risk assessment for the cycle.

7.11   Tests are designed at the start of the audit so that an integrated approach may be adopted for all cycles, preventing any duplication of effort. However, the design of tests is based on an assessment of factors which may change during the course of the audit. Therefore we must be prepared to change or extend the tests. For example, a control may not prove as reliable as expected, or a review of the year-end accounts may reveal a problem which was not apparent from the management accounts at the interim visit, hence we may not be able to reduce the level of our substantive tests (as we had planned).

7.12   The tests that we include in the audit programme must provide sufficient relevant and reliable audit evidence to meet the objective concerned. Audit evidence may be obtained from the accounting system and underlying documentation, the company's tangible assets, management and employees, and its customers, suppliers and other third parties who have dealings with or knowledge of the business.

7.13   The evidence must be sufficient in terms of our knowledge of the business, the risk of errors, the materiality of the balances or transactions under review and the persuasiveness of the evidence itself. It must be relevant to the overall audit objective of expressing an opinion and to the specific objectives which have been identified. The evidence must also be reliable i.e. from a credible source.

7.14   The evidence may be obtained by the following substantive procedures:
(a) tests of detail (direct tests of individual transactions or balances);
(b) tests in total; and
(c) analytical review procedures.
In addition, it may be obtained by compliance tests which demonstrate that we can place reliance on internal controls and so reduce the level of substantive procedures (this is dealt with in Chapter 8).

7.15   The ideas lists for each cycle suggest possible tests that may be used in different circumstances. We should design tests that achieve the audit objective as cost effectively as possible. We are likely to use fewer tests than are on an ideas list because the ideas lists are designed to cover a number of different possibilities. We frequently use tests which are not on an ideas list but are appropriate to the particular circumstances of the business.

7.16   Where there is a higher than normal risk of error for an objective, the extent of work required is greater than the minimum allowed by auditing standards. It is unlikely that reliance on internal controls and review procedures is possible and little assurance is likely to be obtained from tests in total. A higher than normal risk for an objective often alters the nature of the detailed tests. For example, where there is a high risk that purchase invoices may be lost before posting and where goods inward records are poor, we may only be able to obtain sufficient assurance on trade creditors by circulating every major supplier. Where there is a higher than normal risk of the overstatement of debtors (perhaps because we suspect dummy sales invoices may be processed to inflate sales and profits), a debtors' circularisation alone may be inadequate; it may be necessary to trace individual debit items in the sales ledger to shipping documents.

7.17 The various tests involve one or more of the following techniques:

(a) *Inspection* — reviewing or examining records, documents or tangible assets. Inspection of records and documents provides evidence of varying degrees of reliability depending upon their nature and source. Inspection of tangible assets provides us with reliable evidence as to their existence and, sometimes, their value but not necessarily as to their ownership or cost.

(b) *Observation* — looking at an operation or procedure being performed by others with a view to determining the manner of its performance. Observation only provides reliable evidence about the manner of performance at the time of observation.

(c) *Enquiry* — seeking relevant information from knowledgeable persons inside or outside the company, whether formally or informally, orally or in writing. The degree of reliability that we attach to evidence obtained in this manner is dependent on our opinion of the competence, experience, independence and integrity of the respondent.

(d) *Computation* — checking the arithmetical accuracy of accounting records or performing independent calculations.

Substantive Tests of Detail

7.18 Tests of detail cover balances and transactions. If properly designed and carried out, they provide the most persuasive audit evidence because they indicate the accuracy of individual items. They are aimed at giving direct assurance on the transaction or balance concerned. Examples include:

(a) inspection and comparison of documents, for example, testing from purchase day book to purchase invoices to ensure invoice amounts are correctly recorded and analysed and comparing details to supporting goods inward notes;

(b) computation, for example, checking casts and extensions of stock sheets, checking reconciliations;

(c) third party confirmation, for example, debtors' circularisation and obtaining bank or solicitor's letters;

(d) physical verification, for example, test counts of stock items, inspecting a sample of fixed assets drawn from the plant register.

7.19 The level of assurance provided by a test of detail depends on the reliability of the information on which it is based. Third party information or physical verification is usually more reliable as audit evidence than information generated by the client's systems. We should always ensure that we see a reasonable proportion of the major asset items (fixed assets and stock) because this is good evidence of their existence and ownership by the company. It can also provide information about maintenance and replacement policies and hence their valuation.

7.20   Although third party evidence may be essential to the audit, we should not place reliance on such evidence unless we are satisfied that it is reasonable. Third parties are just as capable of making mistakes as the company and there is always a risk that major customers and suppliers may be motivated to confirm erroneous balances because of the importance of their trading relationship with the company. If third party evidence conflicts with the evidence obtained from the company, we need to investigate the discrepancy to decide whether the error is the company's or the third party's. Where there is no conflict, and the third party evidence is consistent with our expectations, we may place reliance on that evidence. Third party evidence is often used to verify such things as debtors, stocks held as custodian and investments where the certificates are held in safe custody.

Example 9

Objective	*Direction*	*Possible test*
All goods despatched have been invoiced.	Understatement of sales.	Test from despatches to invoices, checking quantities and descriptions of goods.
All purchases are valid expenses of the company.	Overstatement of purchases.	Test from purchases account in nominal ledger to invoices and goods inward documents, agreeing analysis, description of goods and invoice value.
Stock quantities are correctly recorded on final stock sheets.	Understatement and overstatement of stocks.	Attendance at stock count, with test counts in both directions (from floor to stock sheets and from stock sheets to floor). Control over sequence of stock sheets to ensure none is lost and none created between the end of the stocktake and the final audit visit.

7.21   Whatever tests are designed for each objective, it is essential that they help to achieve the objective for which they are designed. Objectives may deal with either understatements or overstatements or both. Tests for each objective should be designed to give assurance in the right direction.

7.22 Some tests provide assurance on more than one objective. For example, one possible test on the objective 'all sales invoiced are correctly recorded in the accounts' is a test of sales invoices, checking prices to price lists and checking calculations and casts. This test also helps achieve the objective 'all debtors are valid receivables' because it ensures the invoices making up debtors are correctly priced and arithmetically correct. Where a test helps to achieve more than one objective, the audit programmes for all relevant objectives should be cross-referenced to the test schedule.

7.23 Tests must be designed to cover all material aspects of each objective. For example, if the objective is 'purchases and expenses represents goods and services received during the accounting period', the sample should include items selected from all material purchase and expense headings.

Example 10

When designing tests on the sales cycle for the objective 'all despatches are invoiced in the accounting period', we should cover:
(a) despatch notes are accurately raised for all despatches;
(b) invoices are accurately raised for all despatches;
(c) all invoices relating to despatches before the year end are included in the year's sales.

It is not sufficient just to test despatch notes to invoices checking quantities and descriptions. We also need to ensure that despatch notes are raised for all despatches, possibly by examining and testing gate controls over the despatch of goods and by reviewing sales and cost of sales. We must also ensure that all despatches during the year are included in the year's sales and not held over to next year. This might involve looking at despatch notes raised in the two weeks before the year end and ensuring that they have been invoiced before the year end and are included in the sales ledger.

7.24 Although tests should always be adapted to suit the requirements of each client's business and systems, those that are always needed include:
(a) casting, cross-casting and checking calculations of any schedules supplied by the client for audit purposes;
(b) checking (or preparing) reconciliations of control accounts; and
(c) checking the trial balance and summary schedules to the accounts.

7.25 Tests common to the majority of audits include:
(a) physical verification of stocks and tangible fixed assets;
(b) third party confirmation of debtors, bank balances and creditors (creditors are often verified by reference to suppliers' statements rather than circularisation);
(c) transaction tests on sales, purchases and major expense items.

The precise nature and extent of these tests varies from one audit to another depending on the nature of the business, the accounting system and the risk of errors. For example, the debtors' circularisation may be on an individual invoice basis or it may be in terms of balances. Circularising individual outstanding invoices may produce a better response where customers' systems are not capable of producing a balance at any time.

7.26   The nature of our stocktake attendance also depends on the client's business and our assessment of risk. Where stock is held at a number of branches, we may decide only to visit a sample of locations every year. If controls are good, and the figures look reasonable, we may not need to make our visits last the entire length of the stock count. Where control is poor, however, we may need to be present throughout the stock count and make extensive test counts.

7.27   As detailed substantive tests are usually time consuming and expensive they should whenever possible be kept to a minimum if there is sufficient reliable evidence available from other more cost-effective sources. It may be possible to reduce the nature or extent of detailed substantive tests by placing reliance on tests in total, review procedures and tests of internal controls. (We may already have taken into account our risk assessment to reduce the level of testing.) These alternative procedures should be used wherever they are cost effective, that is if the costs saved by reducing the extent of the detailed tests is greater than the cost of performing the alternative procedures. They are unlikely to be of use where there is a higher than normal risk of material error.

Substantive Tests in Total

7.28   Substantive tests in total are tests aimed at verifying the total of a balance or the total value of transactions without looking at the underlying detail. For example, a test of sales in certain types of industry may be carried out by multiplying quantities of each product sold by the average sales price. Other examples include verifying:
(a) the provision for depreciation for each category of assets, by multiplying the total cost by the depreciation rate and making allowance for additions, disposals and fully written-down assets;
(b) wages and salaries, by multiplying the number of employees for each category by the average wage rate;
(c) a holiday pay accrual, by multiplying the average rate of holiday pay by the number of employees and the average holiday outstanding;
(d) sales commission, by multiplying sales by the average commission rate;
(e) investment income or interest payable/receivable, by multiplying the average amount invested or on loan by the yield or interest rate;

(f) advertising revenue, by multiplying the number of column centimetres by
   average rates.
Other forms of test in total may be equally effective in particular circumstances.

7.29 When carrying out tests in total, it is important to ensure the figures used
in the calculations are audited. For example, if calculating sales value from
quantities and prices, quantities must be verified, for example by reconciling to
known purchases and opening and closing stock and prices must be checked to
price lists.

7.30 The amount of assurance that is derived from a test in total depends on
the accuracy with which the result can be obtained. It may sometimes be possible
to obtain almost all the necessary assurance on an objective by a test in total,
although in different circumstances a total test may provide no more assurance
than review procedures. The way in which this assurance is taken into account
in determining the sample size for a detailed test is considered in **9.19**.

Analytical Review Procedures

7.31 The use of analytical review procedures is explained in Chapter 4. We take
assurance from these as described in Chapter 9. In certain circumstances analytical
review may provide sufficient assurance on its own. This is not the case for the
largest items in the accounts, such as sales and purchases, and where there is a
higher than normal risk of error, but is possible for smaller items.

Other Sources of Audit Evidence

7.32 Audit evidence comes from a number of sources apart from those mentioned above. These include reviews of correspondence and minutes as well as
discussions with the client's staff. The quality of such evidence varies considerably
and it is likely that such sources may point us to a problem which needs to be
verified by other means rather than providing direct audit evidence.

7.33 Correspondence often provides evidence that cannot be obtained from the
accounting records or client's staff. For example, correspondence with debtors
can give an indication of whether balances are recoverable or whether amounts
are disputed for any reason. Correspondence with the company's solicitors (and
fee notes) may indicate whether any legal actions are outstanding which give rise
to a contingent or actual liability. A review of legal fee notes and correspondence

may also indicate possible bad debtors against whom legal proceedings are pending. It is also usual practice to write to the company's lawyer seeking confirmation about any outstanding matters.

7.34   Board and shareholder minutes point to the most important events during the period including details of successful and unsuccessful deals, tenders etc. They may also give information about contingencies and financial commitments which need to be disclosed in the accounts.

Management Representations

7.35   While management representations constitute valid audit evidence we should not, in respect of any significant aspect of the audit, rely solely on unsupported oral representations of management as being sufficient reliable evidence. Most representations can be corroborated by checking with sources independent of the company or by checking with other evidence generated by ourselves. However, in certain cases, such as where knowledge of the facts is confined to management or where the matter is principally one of judgement and opinion, we may not be able to obtain independent corroborative evidence and could not reasonably expect it to be available. In such cases we should ensure that no other evidence conflicts with the representations of management and we should obtain written confirmation of the representations.

7.36   Representations are often useful, in conjunction with other audit work, in determining whether any transactions are omitted. For example, it may be difficult to establish whether all sales have been recorded in the accounting records. The only available evidence may be the results of an analytical review of sales, our observation of procedures and a representation by management that all sales have been included. This may be sufficient if there is no reason to doubt the results of the analytical review or the truth of the representation.

7.37   Another example where representations are useful is in meeting the disclosure requirements relating to directors' loans and other transactions. We should be alert to the possibility of such transactions throughout the audit and should carry out certain specific procedures, such as a scrutiny of the accounting records for unusual transactions and an examination of debtors' listings. However, some transactions can be difficult to detect, so it is important to obtain written confirmation from the directors that no such transactions existed apart from those disclosed in the accounts.

Accountancy Work

7.38   Although accountancy work performed by us is not primarily directed at achieving audit objectives, it may provide some of the audit assurance needed. The accountancy and audit work should, as far as possible, be planned together so that accountancy work is completed before the audit work on the same area and so that the audit work takes account of the assurance gained from it.

7.39   Some accountancy work provides much of the assurance which would otherwise come from substantive tests of detail. It may be regarded as a substantive test of detail in which we look at every transaction or balance. It can, for example, provide assurance on casts and calculations and on the completeness and accuracy of postings. If we write up the sales day book and sales ledger, we obtain complete assurance on the accuracy and completeness of posting of sales and debtors from the sales invoices, providing the work done is adequately evidenced and reviewed.

7.40   There are certain audit objectives which cannot be met by our accountancy work. Writing up the sales day book and ledger accounts will not ensure that all sales were correctly invoiced — nor will it provide any assurance on the recoverability of the sales ledger balances. Objectives concerned with the completeness of recording transactions at source, the existence of assets and with the adequacy of provisions require separate audit tests.

Computer Audit Enquiry Packages

7.41   Where a company uses a computer to process some or all of its accounting records, it may be cost effective to use an audit enquiry package to produce special reports for audit purposes. Such a package may be used to perform repetitive, time-consuming procedures with great speed and can enable the senior to test every item in the population (where necessary) at reasonable cost. In some cases the enquiry package may be supplied to the client by the software house as part of his software.

7.42   The use of an enquiry package may involve set-up costs in the first year of use, covering such matters as defining the data file layout, designing the tests and setting parameters. However, once set up, the package produces reports very quickly and may be used in future years with little modification provided the client's system does not change substantially. Specific uses for such packages are more fully discussed in para **14.20** below.

7.43   Because of the great speed of the computer, there is a temptation when using an enquiry package to carry out more procedures and print more comprehensive reports than are strictly required. This temptation should be resisted because it wastes time when reviewing the reports and following up items selected. Care needs to be taken in setting parameters for exception reports to ensure that only truly exceptional items are reported and that the particular exceptions tested for are of genuine audit importance.

Timing of Tests

7.44   The timing of tests depends largely on management's deadlines for the final accounts. If there is no time pressure, it is better to carry out most procedures after the year end so that the whole year's transactions may be covered at one time. However, they should not be delayed too long because:
(a) company staff may forget details of transactions;
(b) records may be disposed of;
(c) there may be undue delay in telling management about serious control weakness;
(d) the accounts cease to be valuable in, say, discussions with bankers if they are late;
(e) the accounts must be ready in time for submission to the members, the Inland Revenue and the Registrar of Companies.

7.45   Where there is pressure to finish the audit as soon as possible after the year end, as much of the audit work as possible should be performed before the year end. Although year end balances will not be available at the interim visit, certain audit work on them may be done at this time. At the year end it will only be necessary to reconcile movements in the intervening period and test a small number of transactions. This approach is often adopted for stock, debtors and additions to fixed assets, but it may be used for all balance sheet items where there are sufficiently good controls to ensure transactions in the intervening period are correctly posted. If errors are likely between the interim date and the year end, there may be no time saving in testing balances at the interim because extensive tests will be needed on movements up to the year end.

Group Audits

7.46   If we are the primary auditors of a group, we have responsibility for the opinion on the group financial statements, even when we have not audited all the subsidiaries. We should therefore ensure that we obtain all the information and explanations we consider necessary. Our procedures include:

(a) Sending out a questionnaire to the subsidiary auditors. We have two types of questionnaire, a long-form questionnaire where we ask for detailed information on the audit procedures followed and detailed accounting information and a short-form questionnaire where our questions are directed towards gaining an understanding of the overall audit approach.

The long-form questionnaire will be used where we are unfamiliar with the work carried out by the auditor or where they may not be used to carrying out their work in accordance with United Kingdom Auditing Standards. It would also be used where the client's consolidation package does not give us all the information we consider necessary. In all other cases it will normally be appropriate to use the short form.

(b) Reviewing subsidiary auditors' working papers. We should review these files for material subsidiaries and those which taken together could have a material effect on the group accounts. We may also review those subsidiaries where the questionnaires or the accounts highlight particular problems.

8 The audit programme — compliance procedures

This chapter explains how we decide whether to rely on internal controls for specific substantive tests, how we identify the key controls on which we can rely and how we design compliance tests to test the operation of the key controls.

8.01 In earlier chapters we considered how as part of obtaining knowledge of the business and of our assessment of risk we perform an overall review of the accounting system. As a result of this review we may seek to rely on the systems of internal control which management has set up to ensure that the possibility of errors is minimised. Before we can rely on the controls to reduce our substantive tests of details, we must test that they have operated properly throughout the year. These tests are called 'compliance tests'.

8.02 We only seek to rely on internal controls where it is cost effective, that is where:
(a) the reliance on internal controls enables us to reduce specific substantive tests;
     and
(b) the time costs of identifying key controls and carrying out the compliance test is less than the time costs saved by reducing the substantive test.

So, for example, if a company regularly reconciles suppliers' statements, investigates resulting differences and retains the evidence of the reconciliation and investigation, we may incur less time costs by:
(a) checking that the reconciliations and investigations are being done regularly and properly and, if they are,
(b) reducing the number of checks we have to do to confirm that creditors are not understated,

rather than checking a full sample of creditors for understatement. Where we use statistical sampling methods, we can compare the sample sizes for both alternatives and estimate the time cost saving.

8.03 The decision about whether to rely on internal controls may be influenced by our experience at past audits of the same company. If, for example, we discovered in the past that creditors' statement reconciliations that should be done are rarely done properly and the client tells us that nothing has changed, we may decide that it is not worthwhile even trying to rely on the controls because our compliance tests are likely to show that the control is not working. In such a case we carry out full substantive tests and we tell management of the fact and explain the additional audit costs of the controls not being followed.

8.04 Therefore, before evaluating the controls for a particular audit objective, we should check whether our reliance on them is likely to be cost effective. We must ask ourselves:
(a) are the controls likely to prove reliable?
(b) by how much can the substantive testing be reduced by reliance on controls?
(c) how much compliance work will be needed to permit reliance?

8.05 The audit plan should indicate whether or not we intend to rely on internal controls. If we decide not to rely on internal controls for an objective when the audit plan has indicated that controls should be relied upon, the decision and the reasons for it should be recorded in the working papers.

8.06 A client's accounting system will almost always have areas where controls are strong and areas where they are weak. The decision whether to carry out compliance testing should therefore be taken on a cycle-by-cycle basis and not necessarily for the accounting system as a whole. For example, we may decide to carry out compliance tests for the revenue cycle but not for the expenditure cycle.

Key Controls

8.07 If we want to rely on internal controls, the first step is to decide whether or not there are key controls, which have been evidenced and which are sufficient to prevent material error if they operate as recorded. The ideas lists suggest some key control questions which can be used to help identify such controls in each cycle.

8.08 A key control is one whose failure:
(a) could lead to a material misstatement in the financial statements; and
(b) is not compensated for by another control; if it is compensated for, then the control we have identified is not 'key'.

8.09   In addition, a control is only key if there are no weaknesses in the system or the control environment that prevent the control working properly. For example, apparently good controls may be rendered worthless by inadequate segregation of duties which allow staff to manipulate the accounting records. So, where the same person is responsible for recording and banking receipts and for maintaining the sales ledger, he can divert cheques to his own account and amend the sales ledger to cover up the theft. This renders useless any apparent controls over, say, the reconciliation of the sales ledger control account.

8.10   Another instance of where apparently good controls may have to be ignored is where they can be overridden by senior staff. For example, the proprietor may override the normal checks on credit worthiness for certain orders. This may or may not be a problem. It may represent an additional control where it is done for a good reason and it is documented. For example, the proprietor may override the credit checks for those customers he knows to be good risks. Provided he marks the orders to show he has done this we may still be able to rely on the control. Another example arises in computer systems where an 'intervention log' contains an automatic record of every operator intervention. The fact of the intervention may weaken controls but the record may reinforce them.

8.11   In the audit plan, our assessment of the control environment should refer to the proprietor's involvement and its effect on the reliability of controls. There may be areas where the proprietor has an interest in preventing errors and supervises his staff closely. This may, for example, include wages and purchases, where the proprietor is concerned to ensure 'his' money is not misspent. There may be other areas where the proprietor may be known or expected to override controls, perhaps for special last-minute deals which do not go through the normal processes. We need to decide whether the proprietor's supervision is a key control, on which we may rely if it is evidenced, or whether it constitutes a weakness which could outweigh some of the controls in the system.

Non-key Controls

8.12   Controls which are not key should not be tested nor should they be relied upon. They cannot give any audit assurance and any time spent testing them is wasted. The only exception to this rule is where we might test the operation of a control because the client wants us to, notwithstanding its lack of audit significance. We should point out the additional costs of such an exercise.

Types of Controls

8.13   The sorts of controls we should look for are classified in the appendix to the Auditing Guideline *Internal Controls* as:

(a) organisation controls; dealing with the allocation and formal recording of responsibilities;

(b) segregation of duties; the separation of responsibilities which, if combined, enable an individual to control all aspects of a transaction;

(c) physical controls; controls over access to assets and records and other security measures;

(d) authorisation and approval procedures for approving all transactions and the limits set on the amounts each official can authorise;

(e) personnel controls; ensuring that all personnel are suitably qualified and have the ability to perform their duties adequately;

(f) supervision; ensuring that staff are adequately supervised in their day-to-day activities;

(g) management; the overall supervision of management by periodical review, use of budgets, internal audit etc; and

(h) arithmetical and accounting; ensuring all items are correctly recorded and accurately processed, totals are checked, reconciliations performed etc.

8.14   It may also be helpful to look at controls in a slightly different way. As we want to find controls which ensure the accuracy of the accounting records, we want to find:

(a) boundary controls over the capture of information when assets move in and out of the business;

(b) processing controls over the processing of transactions from the boundary to the accounting records and accounts; and

(c) asset controls to ensure assets are protected from theft, deterioration etc. and to ensure that any loss is detected.

8.15   Boundary controls include those designed to ensure that all transactions are recorded, all transactions are genuine and that the initial recording of transactions is accurate. Examples include:

(a) use of pre-numbered documents or numerical document logs;

(b) gate controls to ensure all goods in and out are recorded;

(c) reconciliations in total to ensure, for example, that all chargeable time is billed;

(d) approval of transactions by an authorised person;

(e) checking computations; and

(f) comparing independently generated source documents, for example, telephone order forms with written order confirmations.

8.16   Good boundary controls require adequate segregation of duties. The following duties should be performed by different individuals, preferably in separate departments:

(a) authorising the transaction;

(b) committing the company to the transaction (for example, accepting or placing an order);

(c) handling the goods and cash receipts; and

(d) recording the transaction.

If any two of these duties are performed by a single individual, he may be able to conceal any errors or fraud for which he is responsible. If the last three duties are performed by a single employee, that employee is in a position to sell the company's product, divert the proceeds and prevent the transaction being recorded.

8.17   Processing controls ensure that the number of items being processed does not change during processing and that the information does not change during transfer from one document to another or from one medium to another (for example, entering on to a computer). They also include controls over the accuracy of calculations performed on data or the preparation of analyses and summaries. Examples of processing controls include:

(a) accounting for pre-numbered documents;

(b) batch controls;

(c) reconciliations;

(d) use of hash totals;

(e) review of one person's work by another;

(f) casting and cross casting of totals; and

(g) review of figures for reasonableness.

8.18   Asset controls designed to prevent loss or deterioration of assets include:

(a) restrictions on access (stocks only accessible to storeman, post opened in a separate room etc);

(b) authorisation of all movements (stock requisitions, cheque requisitions backed by invoice etc);

(c) inspection of goods in and out; and

(d) assignment of assets to the responsibility of a particular person, possibly with a rotation of that responsibility.

8.19   Asset controls should also be sufficient to ensure that any loss or deterioration is detected. Hence they include checks of physical quantities against accounting records to discover any discrepancies which may indicate an error in the accounting records. Such controls should be the responsibility of someone not involved in handling the assets on a day-to-day basis so that the control is independent. Examples include monthly stocktakes and surprise independent cash counts.

8.20   The types of controls we might rely on depend on the audit objective. For example, if the audit objective is 'To ensure that goods cannot be despatched without a sale being recorded', the controls we should look for are boundary and, possibly, asset controls. Thus we may look for such controls as:

(a) the gateman checking all despatches against a copy despatch note;

(b) pre-numbered despatch notes subject to a regular check that all have been converted into invoices; and

(c) monthly stock counts with follow-up of differences.

Computer Controls

8.21   The same auditing principles apply to computer systems as to any other system; key controls should be identified and tested if we wish to rely on the controls. A separate ideas list for computer controls is available to help identify the types of controls which may be present. These may be divided between 'general controls', that is controls over the development of programs and operation of the computer installation, and 'application controls', which cover the transactions and data used by each application and are therefore specific to applications.

8.22   If there are weaknesses in general controls we must consider the likelihood of specific application controls being rendered ineffective. We may decide that computer controls cannot be relied upon for all or some applications. Alternatively, we may decide that the weaknesses in general controls are counter-balanced by adequate application controls.

8.23   More and more computer installations and companies using computers have no, or very few, specialist data processing staff. Hence there may be a lack of segregation of duties and little restriction of access to data and programs. There may also be a lack of physical security over files and the computer itself. In such cases, the weak general controls may prevent us placing any reliance on some application controls. With larger systems, adequate segregation of duties is more likely, both between the computer department and user departments and between the different functions within the computer department such as operation, programming and application development. Access to the computer and to specific data and programs is also likely to be restricted, although an in-house programmer may be able to make unauthorised and unrecorded amendments to programs.

8.24   The increased use of on-line terminals situated in user departments makes data entry and retrieval quicker and more efficient and leads to a more effective use of the computer and a better flow of information. It tends to be achieved by a reduction in controls, unless the user is restricted to accessing information such as an account balance or stock quantity ('on-line enquiry'). Where data is entered or programs developed on-line, there are risks such as the corruption of data files and unauthorised program amendments. They may be such that we cannot place any reliance on certain controls.

8.25   Application controls are examined in the context of the key control questions and the audit objectives. The application controls should cover:
(a) input to the computer, including authorisation, cancellation of items to avoid double processing, treatment of rejected items and error reports;
(b) output from the computer, including completeness and accuracy of output, distribution and use;
(c) processing of data, such as the accuracy of calculations, by ensuring calculated data is within pre-determined limits and in appropriate format;
(d) master files, including preparation of files, authorisation of changes, use of correct files.

Compliance Tests

8.26   Compliance tests are designed to check the operation of each key control on which reliance is to be placed. We usually test only for evidence of the control being performed, for example completion of an invoice grid stamp. This means that a control can only be tested (and therefore relied upon) if there is some evidence of its performance. This evidence typically consists of a signature (or initials) on a document or the handwriting of the person carrying out a reconciliation.

8.27   Where the control does not leave permanent evidence of its performance, it may be possible to test it by observing its performance or attempting to defeat it. For example, controls over the opening of post may be observed on a surprise basis. Password controls on on-line computer terminals may be tested by attempting to defeat the control and by examining the record of passwords issued and password changes. Such tests should be described in the working papers, including the dates and times of the procedures.

8.28 Compliance tests should ensure that the key controls have functioned properly throughout the period under review so the sample needs to cover the whole period. When tests are carried out at an interim visit more than 2 or 3 months prior to the year end, it is necessary to cover the rest of the year. If tests are carried out within two or three months of the year end a limited review to ensure key controls are still functioning will suffice.

8.29 Where a compliance test involves observation of the control, it is not possible to cover the entire year. We need to assess the results in the context of changes in staff during the year or the likelihood of the control being performed more rigorously during our presence.

8.30 Where a compliance test is carried out on a sample basis, we should consider whether the same sample can be used for (or as the basis for) any substantive test on the same documents. Tests should be planned so that either the compliance and substantive tests are carried out simultaneously or the documents extracted for the compliance test are retained until the substantive test can be done.

8.31 It may be both quicker and sufficient to carry out a compliance test by flicking through the documents being tested. For example, if purchase invoices are being tested for a properly completed and initialled grid stamp, the best way may be to flick through invoice files to ensure that all invoices appear to bear the completed stamp.

Table 5

Examples of compliance tests may include:

Key control	*Possible compliance test*
1. Matching of purchase invoices to goods received notes and purchase orders before processing, evidenced by initials on approval grid.	Extract sample of purchase invoices and ensure grid stamp properly completed and signed (same sample may be used for substantive tests on the validity and accuracy of purchase invoices).
2. Bought ledger control account reconciled with list of balances monthly.	Check that a reconciliation has been prepared for each month and that any differences have been followed up and resolved.
3. Monthly counts of stock lines on a rotational basis. Any major differences investigated by management.	Review reports of four stocktakes, noting whether procedures appear to have been followed. Check that any large differences have been investigated and satisfactory explanations obtained.

8.32   The design of compliance tests in computer systems follows the same principles as manual systems. However, it may be more difficult to obtain evidence of the performance of controls in a computer system. It may be necessary to employ techniques such as observing the operation of the system to see that all system checks operate properly or attempting to defeat controls by such methods as attempting to enter invalid data, or bypass a password control. Alternatively we may decide to 're-perform' the control or the operation being controlled.

Documenting the Audit Plan

8.33   The evaluation of internal controls and the nature of the compliance tests are recorded on *Internal Control Evaluation* forms (ICE). These must be linked to one or more of the audit objectives identified in the previous chapter. An example of an ICE is included in Appendix 4.

8.34   In many cases it is necessary to record details of the compliance test on separate schedules cross referenced to the ICE. These separate schedules should not, however, repeat information already on the ICE. They should only contain extra details, such as the sample selected and the detailed results and follow-up procedures. The details recorded depend on the exact nature of the test. Some tests, such as checking that monthly reconciliations have been prepared or a 'flick through' test of invoices and tests involving the observation of procedures or attempting to defeat a computer input control may require a narrative explanation of what was done and the conclusions reached. On the other hand, a check of signatures on purchase invoices requires the listing of the items selected.

Results of Compliance Tests

8.35   The result of each compliance test should be recorded in the column headed 'errors?' on the ICEs. If no errors have been found for a particular compliance test, our conclusion is that the control may be relied upon. This should be recorded on the ICE, which is cross referenced to the working paper describing the details of the test.

8.36   If one or more errors have been found for a compliance test, more work is necessary before a conclusion on the test can be drawn. If the compliance test was based on a sample, the errors may indicate that the frequency of errors in the population may be unacceptably high. If only 1 or 2 errors have been found, we need to find out whether or not they are a 'false alarm' or whether there really is an unacceptable level of error throughout the population. If there are several errors or the 1 or 2 errors are not a 'false alarm', then no reliance can be placed on the key control. We should, however, investigate the errors thoroughly as they may give us an idea whether there is material error in the accounts.

8.37   Errors may occur because of a specific cause, such as staff absence or unusual circumstances surrounding a particular item, or they may just be random human errors. Where there is a specific cause, this should be confirmed where possible (for example, by testing more items in the period before and after the staff absence which has given rise to the error). If there is no specific reason for isolated errors, we need to decide whether the internal control is satisfactory. An additional sample of items should be tested to confirm that there is not an unacceptable error rate in the population. This sample should usually be chosen on a non-statistical basis. (It may, however, be more cost effective at this stage to treat the control as unreliable and revert to full substantive tests.)

8.38   When investigating 'errors' in compliance tests, it is important to ensure that they genuinely are errors. We may think they are errors but we may have identified the control incorrectly. For example, a control may only be applied to items greater than £50 because management does not find it effective to look at all trivial items. If we had assumed that the control applies to all items, irrespective of value, then we may discover a number of 'errors'. Provided we are satisfied that the restriction of the control to non-trivial items is acceptable, then we must not treat the application of the restriction as an error.

8.39   Once errors have been investigated then we may conclude either that the key control is effective or that it is not. When all relevant and material key control questions have been completed for an objective, it is possible to draw a final conclusion about the effect of internal controls on the relevant substantive tests. If a substantive test consists of a number of parts, such as a test from despatch notes to invoices and from invoices to sales day book, then the parts may be treated separately. So for example, the test from invoices to sales day book may be reduced (because the controls are proved to work), but the test from despatch notes to invoices may have to be done fully because the controls have been shown not to work.

9 Sampling

This chapter introduces the approach to sampling and explains how to identify the most suitable method for each audit procedure. It also identifies the procedures where sampling is not appropriate. The statistical sampling techniques we use — error rate and monetary unit — are described in Chapters 17 and 18.

9.01 Audit sampling is the application of an audit procedure to less than 100% of the items within an account balance or class for the purpose of evaluating some characteristics of the balance or class. Sampling procedures are used because it is inefficient to examine every transaction or balance in a population. The procedures may be statistical or non-statistical.

Non-sampling Procedures

9.02 Sometimes it is necessary to examine every item of a particular kind. For example, where we suspect there are many errors we may examine every item in order to find the total value of errors. Alternatively, we may decide to examine every item over a certain value and a sample of the remainder in order to identify all material errors. A test of every item of a particular kind is a non-sampling test.

9.03 The results of a non-sampling procedure cannot be extended to items of a different kind. For example, if we test every purchase invoice over £1,000, we can draw no conclusion about smaller invoices. Similarly, a test of every sale in March does not tell us anything about sales in the remainder of the year. A sequence test of 100 invoices in July does not tell us anything about the completeness of the population of invoices in the year. The use of analytical review procedures, inquiry and observation are all further examples of non-sampling procedures the results of which cannot be extended to items of a different kind.

Sampling Risk

9.04 The rest of this chapter is devoted to sampling procedures, that is those where we look at some items in order to form a conclusion about the population. Sampling means that we must accept a risk that the sample is not representative of the population from which it is drawn and we may draw the wrong conclusion on the test. Correct sample design, including an appropriate choice of sample size and selection method, ensures that this sampling risk is kept to a minimum.

9.05 Sampling risk may result in:
(a) a population, which is acceptable, being rejected because the sample happens to pick a large proportion of the items in error. This leads to additional, unnecessary, audit work but should not affect the validity of the final audit conclusion;
(b) a population, which contains a material error, being accepted as satisfactory because the sample happens not to select any of the items that contain errors. This risk is more serious because there is the possibility that an unqualified audit report is issued when a material error exists in the accounts (although we should organise our other audit procedures so that it is, in fact, unlikely that such an error escapes detection).
As we shall see later, we are able to quantify the latter risk when we use statistical sampling methods.

Statistical and Non-statistical Sampling

9.06 We use both statistical and non-statistical sampling and there are several similarities between them. Both are sampling techniques which involve examining less than the total population to reach a conclusion about the population and both involve sampling risk. Both give us approximate, but not exact, knowledge about the population; however, the amount of approximation can be measured using a statistical sample. Even though non-statistical sampling cannot result in a mathematical conclusion about the population, it does require the expression of a conclusion about the possible range of error in the population. Both statistical and non-statistical sampling involve the same audit steps. Both methods involve audit judgement. One major difference between statistical and non-statistical methods is that a statistical sample must be selected at random from the population; this is desirable, but not essential, for non-statistical methods.

9.07 We should always exercise judgement in determining the size of audit samples, whether statistical or non-statistical. However, judgement is generally more consistent if we quantify the sample size needed by reference to the various risks, expected error rate and materiality factors. Thus, we should generally use statistical sampling techniques (such as error rate and monetary unit sampling) as a starting point in determining the size of samples.

9.08   Whether using statistical or non-statistical methods, we must use our knowledge of the business and the results of our analytical review procedures. If the population includes unusual or related party items we must, if they are material, extract them and verify them separately. We cannot hide behind statistical theory or any other procedures to justify our failure to verify items which arouse suspicion or where there is a higher than normal audit risk.

9.09   Although it is our policy to use statistical methods wherever possible, it is important to emphasise that this does not reduce the need for judgement. We use our judgement in designing audit procedures, in identifying unusual and related party items, in carrying out and attributing assurance to analytical review procedures and other tests and in interpreting the consequences of errors. Statistical methods are not a substitute for judgement. They are a framework to link judgements as effectively as possible.

9.10   Not every audit sample is worth performing on a rigorous statistical basis. Non-statistical sampling may be used whenever we conclude that the additional costs of statistical sampling (for example, set-up time) are in excess of the benefits to be obtained (for example, objectivity of sample selection and evaluation). Non-statistical sampling may be preferable in situations where the statistical selection is difficult to make because the records are not readily accessible or are in a form which makes it difficult to make a valid statistical selection (for example, when we are selecting items for test counting at the physical stocktaking). In these cases, we should still use the statistical sample size tables to get an idea of an appropriate sample size.

9.11   When using non-statistical methods, we also need to be satisfied that the selection is appropriate to obtain a reasonable conclusion and that we have not used them to exclude difficult items. Neither non-statistical sampling nor non-sampling should be used as a smokescreen for inadequate auditing. Non-statistical sampling does not automatically solve problems or make documents with errors into correct documents. Every item selected should be audited (and not replaced if not found). A conclusion about the population should be made from the sample evidence.

9.12 Statistical sampling should be used whenever the auditor concludes that the benefits are greater than the costs. Examples of when this is likely to be true include situations where:

(a) the set-up time and selection time are reasonable in relation to the time required to test the selected items and follow up on discrepancies (more likely to be true for larger tests than for smaller ones);

(b) the most extensive part of the test is a representative selection, not the selection of material or unusual items;

(c) records of the entire population are reasonably accessible for purposes of making the selection (although even if they are not readily accessible, statistical sampling could be desirable if it is likely that a non-statistical selection would yield an inappropriate conclusion because of a failure to include inconvenient records in the selection); and

(d) the selection of the statistical sample can easily be effected, perhaps with the aid of computer-assisted techniques.

Statistical Sampling and Sampling Risk

9.13 When an audit sample is designed using a statistical sampling method, it is possible to measure sampling risk. In practice, only the risk of accepting a population which does contain material errors is measured. The risk is expressed as a percentage; for example a risk of 5% means that there is a 1 in 20 chance of a material error going undetected. It is the firm's policy to accept a 5% risk of failure to detect a material error in any given test. This figure is a judgement based on experience. It does not mean that 5% of our audit tests incorrectly accept material error because, if such an error does exist, it will probably be detected by other audit procedures.

9.14 This risk can be represented in two other ways: confidence levels and R-factors. The confidence level is the degree of assurance we have that a material error does not exist in the population; it is the reciprocal of risk. If there is a 10% risk of a material error going undetected, then we are 90% confident that there is no material error.

9.15 R-factors are another way of expressing risk; they have been devised to simplify the use of statistical sampling and are derived from the same statistical theory as the confidence levels. They make the selection of samples much easier and avoid the necessity to carry tables. The relationship between R-factors, risk and confidence levels is as follows:

R-factor	Risk	Confidence level
	%	%
3	5	95
2.5	8	92
2.3	10	90
2	14	86
1.5	22	78
1	37	63

9.16   The R-factors are used to calculate sample sizes by means of the formula:

$$\text{Sample size} = \frac{\text{R-factor}}{\text{Precision}}$$

where the precision is the acceptable error rate in the population expressed as a decimal (this is explained in more detail in Chapter 17).

Example 11

If we are prepared to accept an error rate of 2% in a particular population, the sample size for given R-factors is:

R-factor	Precision	Sample size
3	0.02	150
2	0.02	100
1	0.02	50

Reverting to confidence levels and risk, where no errors are found the above means that:

(a) with a sample of 150 we are 95% confident that the error rate does not exceed 2% (or there is a 5% risk that it does exceed 2%);

(b) with a sample of 100 we are 86% confident that the error rate does not exceed 2% (or there is a 14% risk that it does exceed 2%);

(c) with a sample of 50 we are 63% confident that the error rate does not exceed 2% (or there is a 37% risk that it does exceed 2%).

9.17   As explained later in Chapter 18, the R-factors are used slightly differently when we are interested in error values rather than error rates. Instead of calculating a sample size, we work out a sampling interval:

$$\text{Sampling interval} = \frac{\text{Materiality level}}{\text{R-factor}}$$

(the sampling interval is the value of the population divided by the sample size).

Example 12

If we are prepared to accept errors of up to £50,000 in a population of debtors totalling £800,000, the sampling interval for given R-factors is:

R-factor	Precision	Sampling interval
3	50,000	16,667
2	50,000	25,000
1	50,000	50,000

This means that we select and verify every 16,667th, 25,000th or 50,000th £ unit in the population of £800,000. This in turn means that for an R-factor of 3 we would test a sample of 48 £1 units, 32 £1 units at an R-factor of 2 and 16 £1 units at an R-factor of 1 (and the balances they form part of).

Again we can revert to confidence levels and risk. For example, using a sampling interval of £16,667 and finding no errors, we conclude that we are 95% confident that debtors are not in error by more than £50,000 (or there is a 5% risk that they are in error by more than £50,000).

9.18 Our policy is normally to accept a 5% risk and so aim for an R-factor of 3. However, not all tests need to be carried out at this level because audit assurance comes from a number of sources the results of which can be combined. As well as substantive tests of detail, the other sources of direct audit assurance are risk assessment, analytical review procedures, tests in total and compliance tests on key controls. In order to combine any assurance derived from these sources, R-factors have been attributed to them as follows:

	R-factor
Risk assessment results in normal level of risk	1
extensive analytical review	1
limited analytical review	0.5
reliance on internal control	1

The appropriate factors are deducted from the required R-factor of 3 in order to obtain the R-factor for the substantive tests. There is an overriding constraint however, that the R-factor required from substantive tests may never be reduced below 1. This ensures all material items are tested.

Example 13

A test is planned to confirm debtors. If risk is assessed as higher than normal no reliance can be placed on internal controls or analytical review, all the audit assurance must be obtained from the confirmation procedures. Hence, the test is carried out at an R-factor of 3. If risk is assessed as normal, this contributes 1.0 of our target of 3.0 and we select a sample of debtors based on an R-factor of 2.0.

9.19   No specific R–factor has been attributed to tests in total because such tests vary considerably in the degree of audit assurance they provide. In addition, tests in total usually replace (rather than contribute assurance towards) substantive tests of detail. Where, however, a test in total is carried out the R–factor for the subsequent substantive tests of detail should reflect the assurance gained from the test in total.

Example 14

Wages are tested by a test in total, based on numbers of employees verified from clock cards and changes in wages rates verified by reference to union agreements. Some detailed testing of wages calculations is also necessary. An extensive analytical review has indicated that the wages figures are in line with expectations and risk has been assessed as normal.

Overall R–factor required		3
Less R–factor contributed by: risk assessment results		
in normal level of risk		1
analytical review		<u>1</u>
R–factor required from substantive tests		<u>1</u>

After the test in total has been carried out, some confidence can be attributed to it, say equivalent to an R–factor of 0.5 then:

Overall R–factor required		3
Less R–factor contributed by: risk assessment results		
in normal level of risk	1.0	
analytical review	1.0	
test in total	<u>0.5</u>	<u>2.5</u>
R–factor required from other substantive tests		<u>0.5</u>

9.20   In rare instances two substantive tests of detail cover an aspect of the same audit objective. If this occurs, an R–factor should be attributed to the first test to be carried out so as to reduce the sample size for the second.

Random Samples

9.21   When carrying out a test on a sample of items, the sample should be chosen so as to be representative of the population from which it is taken. This can only be achieved by selecting every item of the sample at random from the whole population. For example, if a sample of 45 items is to be selected from a population of invoices numbered 369 to 1895, we would take 45 random numbers (from tables or generated by computer) in the range 369 to 1895 inclusive. Other methods of selecting a 'random' sample are described in Chapters 17 and 18.

9.22   Any form of bias in selecting the sample tends to make the sample less representative of the population and invalidates any conclusions drawn from it. For example, suppose in the previous example instead of choosing all 45 invoices at random, a starting point was chosen randomly and then the next 45 invoices were taken as the sample, say invoice numbers 1373 to 1417. This is a highly biased sample because a large proportion of the population is unrepresented. The invoices selected probably only cover a week or two of the year, so it is impossible to draw any conclusions about the other 50 or 51 weeks.

Monetary Unit Sampling (MUS)

9.23   For substantive tests, we concentrate on those items where the scope for material error is greatest. If the test is designed to look for overstatements, we tend to look at the largest items. If, however, the test is designed to look for understatements, we seek items which we expect to have high values, even if their recorded values are low. Hence, we do not necessarily pick the largest items in the recorded population. So, for example, when testing creditors for understatement, we test the balance due to a major supplier even if the recorded liability at the year end is small. For substantive tests we use monetary unit sampling wherever possible (although some tests of transactions may have to be done using error rate sampling).

9.24   MUS automatically concentrates on high value items and is, therefore, suitable for many substantive tests. It also enables conclusions to be drawn in money terms when used for testing balances. MUS is particularly useful when testing for overstatement, such as testing the validity of purchases, or a debtors' circularisation.

9.25   MUS cannot be used directly for tests of understatement where omissions are possible but it may be cost effective to apply MUS indirectly. For example, when testing for understatement of creditors, we could use an MUS test selected from after-date payments or from the total purchases from each supplier so that we bias the test towards the largest suppliers rather than the largest purchase ledger balances.

9.26   Any unusual items which are identified as having a high risk of error may need to be tested in addition to the sample — particularly if they are zero or negative items (for example, credit balances on the sales ledger or purchase credit notes). It may be necessary to select an additional sample of these items.

9.27 MUS should not be used when a large number of errors is expected because the method becomes less accurate the more errors are found. If, however, an MUS test is carried out and detects a large number of errors, it may be cost effective to extend the sample and evaluate the results using other statistical techniques more suited to high error situations. Before using these, it is important to discuss the errors with the client — he may prefer to carry out a full check and may resist adjustments (even when supported by a large sample) based on statistics.

Error Rate Sampling (ERS)

9.28 Error rate sampling involves the selection of items at random, without bias; in other words, every item has an equal chance of selection irrespective of its value. It is, therefore, a suitable technique for compliance tests because monetary values are not important and any substantive tests of transactions where monetary values are not available (for example, testing despatch notes to sales invoices). The population does not need to be expressed in money terms for selecting the sample and ERS can be used to select samples from despatch notes, clock cards, and other similar documents. It can be used directly for tests of understatement because it detects omissions and is, therefore, effective at testing completeness.

9.29 When using ERS for substantive tests it may be necessary to bias the sample towards the larger items and unusual items with a high risk of error. If the test is one of overstatement, we may decide to look at all material items and an ERS sample of the others. Or we could split the smaller items into two or more 'strata' by value and take a proportionately larger sample from the higher value strata.

9.30 If the test is for understatement (or if the test is in both directions) it is necessary to look at those items which might be expected to be large, for example balances with major suppliers, transactions with major customers and so on. Such items may need to be treated separately.

Group Audits

9.31 Many of our clients will be groups comprising a holding company and numerous subsidiaries. Where these subsidiaries are incorporated in Great Britain they will each be required to file audited accounts with the Registrar of Companies. As we have to carry out sufficient tests to be able to form an opinion on the individual accounts of each company within the group the sample sizes we use for each company should be chosen following the principles set out above.

9.32 Where a client operates a common accounting system for all (or several) companies in the group we may find it cost effective to carry out compliance tests on the controls that are in operation. If we decide that the controls over the system are adequate and are operating properly it is acceptable to place reliance on these results and reduce substantive tests for all the companies using the system.

Small Populations

9.33 Where the population being tested is very small, say less than 100 items, error rate sampling may not be appropriate because it produces excessively large samples or the set-up cost outweighs the benefits. Therefore it may be necessary to apply additional judgement to decide on a suitable sample to reflect the size of the population and the nature of the test. With monetary unit sampling the same problems do not usually arise as the sample size is closely related to the population size.

9.34 For compliance tests, it is normally sufficient to cover a reasonable proportion of the population, such as no more than 20% to 30% of the items. For example, a compliance test on monthly reconciliations may be based on 3 or 4 reconciliations out of the 12 for the year. A compliance test of weekly cash takings summaries may be limited to, say, 10 to 15 summaries out of 52.

9.35 When a substantive test is based on a small population, it may be necessary to test the whole population. For example, if a record company's turnover consists of 12 monthly invoices under a single pressing and distribution agreement, it may be essential to look at every one of the 12 invoices since each one represents a large proportion of turnover. Sampling is, however, used when testing the make up of each invoice.

9.36 Even with small samples the respective values of each item in the population need to be considered. For example, where a company holds stock at 60 locations, it is possible to visit only a sample of these to observe stocktakes. The sample should include the locations with the highest stock values, any locations where problems exist and a random sample of the remainder.

10 Documenting the audit plan

This chapter explains how the information and decisions arising from planning the audit can be documented.

10.01 The audit plan must be documented. It should contain information on:
(a) the terms of the engagement;
(b) the company and its business;
(c) the results of analytical review procedures;
(d) the assessment of overall audit risk and the risk attributable to each cycle;
(e) the preliminary estimate of materiality;
(f) the audit aproach to be adopted; and
(g) the allocation of responsibilities in the case of a joint audit.
For each cycle it should set out the objectives which are important, the way in which audit evidence will be obtained and the sampling approach to be adopted.

The audit plan should include a detailed budget and, in many cases, a timetable. It should also include lists of key personnel, contacts, telephone numbers and so on.

10.02 The audit plan must be documented no matter what the size of the business and no matter what the extent of any accountancy work. There is a risk that everything in sight will be audited on small jobs unless they are planned properly. The plan must also be documented if deadlines are tight and time is short — it is more likely that the planning process itself will save more time than could be saved by not planning at all. A written plan cannot be replaced by an oral briefing — auditing standards require us to document what we have done — and the briefing should support (not replace) the plan.

10.03 As can be seen from the examples in the appendix, the size of an audit plan can vary substantially. For a very small job it may only be brief notes under each of the headings in paragraph **10.01** above. For a group of companies there will usually be separate detailed plans for each subsidiary as well as the group itself. There is no such thing as a 'standard plan'; our only requirements are that the audit is planned, that the plan be documented and that it addresses the points in **10.01** above.

10.04 Some of the information which should be included in the plan will also be contained in the permanent audit file and previous year's current working paper files. This is not wasteful (unless there is an excessive amount of detail in the plan) because every member of the audit team is given a copy of the plan and must be familiar with its contents. It is impossible to circulate the permanent audit file in time for everybody to read it and, even if it were possible, it would contain too much information specific to locations and cycles for each member of the team.

The Terms of the Engagement

10.05 The plan should specify:
(a) the legislation under which the audit is carried out, for example, the Companies Act 1985;
(b) other statutory or regulatory requirements; for example, a report is required in accordance with US generally accepted auditing standards or the accounts must comply with US generally accepted accounting principles; alternatively, a report must be made to a Self Regulatory Organisation (SRO) under the Financial Services Act 1986;
(c) client expectations including any review of systems or procedures, reporting of errors or other deficiencies, preparation of schedules for tax purposes, accountancy work and so on.

The Company and its Business

10.06 The plan should contain a summary of our knowledge of the company and its business, especially with respect to changes since last year. Much of this information will be documented in detail in the business review report part of our risk assessment, so it will be appropriate simply to summarise on the audit plan itself those major developments which have occurred. For example:
(a) new and discontinued products;
(b) important contracts gained and lost;
(c) new agreements and their consequences;
(d) new business activities started or the cessation of an activity;
(e) opening or closing of branches and depots;
(f) acquisition and disposal of subsidiaries; and
(g) current financial position.

10.07 The plan should also refer to the accounting systems and procedures and note the effect of any recent changes therein, including:
(a) implementation of management letter points;
(b) computerisation; and
(c) centralisation or decentralisation of accounting.

This will draw on information in the accounting systems' review which is contained in the risk assessment.

10.08   The business review report itself, which is an integral part of the planning documentation, documents our understanding of the business in general and those aspects which in particular can affect audit risk. It should cover:
(a) the business, its structure and ownership;
(b) industry, markets and products;
(c) financial position;
(d) initial results review;
(e) control environment;
(f) review of departments.

Analytical Review Procedures

10.09   The audit plan should summarise the results of any analytical review procedures carried out as part of the planning process. It is unlikely and unnecessary to include all the details, as these should be on the current working papers file, but it should be sufficient to enable each member of the audit team to understand the trends in the business, where any problems are likely to arise and whether any audit assurance can be attributed to the procedures.

Risk

10.10   The audit plan should refer to the overall audit risk and the significant risks specific to each cycle. We identify risk as a result of our risk assessment and our plan should contain a summary of our detailed asessment of these risks and their effect on the nature and extent of our audit tests.

Preliminary Estimate of Materiality

10.11   The preliminary estimate of the level of materiality should be included in the written plan. It should refer to the factors taken into account in arriving at the level and also any special considerations which apply. For example, the plan may refer to the fact that some tests should be carried out using lower (tighter) materiality levels. It may suggest using different materiality levels for each cycle. Alternatively, the plan may refer to the fact that certain balance sheet ratios are both critical and sensitive and that tests involving items which affect them must be carried out using very much lower materiality levels.

Audit Approach

10.12 The audit plan should show for each cycle (alternatively some of the detail may be cross-referenced to an audit programme which has already been prepared):

(a) audit objectives;

(b) an outline of the approach to each objective, for example, are we seeking to rely on internal controls or should all our audit assurance come from substantive tests;

(c) the use of statistical and non-statistical sampling methods and the use of non-sampling procedures;

(d) the arrangements for stocktake attendances and review of the client's stocktake instructions and debtors' and creditors' circularisations;

(e) certificates required, for example bank certificates which need to be requested before the year end, and letters from solicitors; and

(f) schedules to be prepared by the client. In many cases much of the work of preparing schedules and extracting figures can be carried out by the client, thus enabling the audit time and costs to be reduced.

Consideration should also be given to providing the client with skeleton schedules designed to give the information required in the most useful format. The blank schedules should be prepared and sent to the client on a mutually agreed date. Once designed, copies of these schedules can be used in subsequent years, suitably updated for any necessary changes.

Audit Problems

10.13 The plan should refer to known or expected audit problems. These may have been identified in previous years and highlighted as part of the risk assessment perhaps arising from the nature of the company's business. For example, the valuation of long-term contracts may be a recurring audit problem at a construction company. A change in the nature of a trade may give rise to stock obsolescence problems. A switch of suppliers may change the way creditors are confirmed. The response rate on debtors' circularisations may have been historically poor.

10.14 Other problems may emerge from our analytical review procedures. For example, debtors may have increased substantially as a proportion of turnover;

although the reasons for this may be explained to and verified by us, it may give rise to problems in our confirmation procedures and in ascertaining the recoverability of debtors. Gross profit percentages may look wrong, meaning that we could have problems on cut off or the valuation of stock.

10.15   Some problems arise because of changes in accounting standards or the law. For example, SSAP 24 on pension costs means that most companies which operate pension schemes must set up triennial actuarial valuations.

Budget and Timetable

10.16   The written audit plan should include a detailed budget for the audit, analysed by cycle and staff member. The budget should seek to ensure that all work is done by the least expensive person capable of doing it (subject to the constraints of deadlines).

10.17   In order to avoid any confusion and delay, we should agree a timetable with the client in as much detail as possible. It may include the dates:
(a) of the various audit visits, including visits for stocktake attendances, and visits by specialist departments (such as computer audit);
(b) interim and final management letters are to be sent;
(c) particular schedules, the trial balance, draft accounts and final accounts are to be available;
(d) the representation letter is to be signed or minuted;
(e) the consolidation packages are to be completed;
(f) the accounts are to be printed and the audit report dated;
(g) audit fees are to be submitted and settled.
As well as agreeing a timetable, the audit team may find it useful to agree the sequence in which the work will be done and the deadlines for individual cycles.

Other Matters

10.18   Other matters which may need to be dealt with in the audit plan include:
(a) Taxation — including any special work to be carried out or schedules to be prepared, arrangements for the review of tax computations (company and group) and the present status of prior year liabilities. The plan might also refer to specific tax problems which have arisen in the past or are likely to arise in the current period;

(b) The involvement of other offices — we should ensure that there is liaison at an early date to agree on the work to be done. For example, where the client operates from several locations it may be cost effective for an associate close to the client's premises to carry out certain work. The work to be done should be discussed with the other office well in advance and an outline programme of work agreed;

(c) The involvement of specialist departments — we should ensure they receive adequate warning and that the precise nature of work to be done is agreed. Where the audit work involves computer-assisted audit techniques, it may be necessary to seek help from specialists to discuss what work is required;

(d) Liaison with or reliance on internal auditors — the internal auditors may have done some tests on which we can rely to reduce the level of our own work. It may also be possible to identify areas where the internal audit department may carry out some of the tests which we have designed for our audit and again make it possible to place reliance on their work;

(e) Joint auditors — we should ensure the audit plan clearly documents the way in which the responsibilities of the two firms have been allocated and the agreed procedures for reviewing the other firm's working papers. We need to ensure that all aspects of the audit are fully considered

(f) The involvement of secondary auditors — where other firms act as auditors to subsidiaries we should ensure that there is liaison concerning dates by which reports are expected, the type of report they will give and any arrangements for the review of their working papers.

10.19   Care is needed if the written plan needs to contain anything that may be construed as casting doubt on the competence or integrity of client's management or staff. In the rare circumstances where such doubts exist and are relevant in determining the nature of audit work, the precise nature of the problem may need to be omitted from the written plan. The details should be communicated orally to members of the audit team; the written plan should be limited to the effects of any such doubts on the assessment of the risk of errors for each objective and the description of the audit approach to be adopted.

Timing of Planning

10.20   The main planning work should be completed before staff go down to the client for the first audit visit (certain arrangements, such as allocating staff and agreeing a timetable with the client, will have been dealt with considerably earlier). This ensures that the audit team arrives at the client's premises knowing what work is to be done and in what order. The manager and partner should have approved the written plan before it is distributed.

Briefing of the Audit Team

10.21   Copies of the audit plan are generally distributed to:
(a) the partner;
(b) the manager;
(c) all members of the audit team;
(d) any specialist staff involved; and
(e) any associated offices involved.
On a larger audit, not all sections of the plan are relevant to every assistant but the whole plan may still be given to everyone to encourage them to take an interest in other aspects of the audit and the client's business. Paragraphs relevant to the particular audit cycle on which the assistant will be engaged should be highlighted.

10.22   A formal briefing meeting may be held to discuss the salient points of the audit plan. It may be led by the manager or partner. The briefing gives members of the audit team the opportunity to discuss any queries arising from the audit plan. It is also a chance to deal with sensitive audit areas and with administrative details, such as the protocol for dealing with the client's staff. All staff involved in the audit should attend the briefing, including members of any specialist departments involved. The briefing normally concentrates on matters of general relevance; matters of specific concern to individual assistants being dealt with on a one-to-one basis by the senior.

11   Completing each cycle

This chapter explains the use of audit working papers in each cycle. It also sets out the procedures which should be followed at the end of the work on the cycle by the person responsible for it.

11.01   The sequence of steps in each cycle is set out on *Table 3* on page 20. Most of it is self-explanatory, although one point worth emphasising is the timing of compliance tests. As explained in Chapter 8, compliance tests are carried out only when they lead to a saving in audit costs. Hence they are designed *after* we have identified the relevant substantive tests. The compliance tests are then carried out *before* (or sometimes at the same time as, but never after) the relevant substantive tests.

11.02   There is a checklist for each cycle which summarises the main steps to be followed. Each is based on *Table 3* and one should be completed for every major cycle. An example of the checklist is included in Appendix 2.

Working Papers

11.03   The audit evidence, including oral representations, is recorded on audit working papers, the main objectives of which are:
(a) to record in a clear and convenient form the information concerning the scope of the audit and the results of audit tests applied, so that the accounts and audit work can be reviewed and evaluated;
(b) to provide, after review and evaluation, all the information necessary to enable the firm to express an opinion on the accounts or other financial statements under examination and the information required to support any special reports to clients, including the management letter;
(c) to provide for future reference a record of:
   (1) all material features of the accounts;
   (2) the audit tests applied;
   (3) the information and explanations received.
     This information is necessary:
      (i) not only in order to justify decisions taken, in the event of any

subsequent challenge or enquiry, but also in order to provide guidance and a saving of time for staff coming new to the job on a subsequent occasion, and;

(ii) to provide a guide to the planning of future audits and to indicate those areas where remedial action can be taken to overcome any serious difficulties and delays previously experienced.

11.04   Much inconvenience, loss of time and even embarrassment can be caused to the firm because of incompleteness, ambiguity, inadequate referencing or other deficiencies in audit working papers. Apart from the normal audit requirements, information may be required from the audit working papers by:

(a) the tax department, for the purpose of submitting tax computations to the Inland Revenue and answering queries thereon;

(b) the investigation department or an outside firm of accountants, who may be making enquiries in preparation for an acquisition or public flotation;

(c) clients who may want, often at very short notice, information concerning certain items in the accounts;

(d) other auditors who may wish to review the firm's audit working papers where, for example, the firm is not the auditor to the holding company.

Also, the importance of good handwriting and clear layout cannot be over emphasised. The written explanations and notes, however complete they may be, will be of little use unless they can be easily read.

11.05   The responsibility for the control and sequence of the working paper references rests with the senior in charge of the audit. Schedule references should be inserted as each section or sub-section is completed. All notes, schedules, audit programmes and internal control evaluation forms should be cross-referenced both to the source and destination of information.

11.06   Because of a wide variety of circumstances in which they have to be prepared and the many types of business transactions to which they relate, it is not practicable to lay down a standard form for the preparation of working papers suitable for each and every situation. How the relevant information can best be shown, what audit tests need to be applied and how the results of the audit work performed can best be summarised is a matter for the particular circumstances. They should, however, be set out in such a way that the salient facts are readily apparent. They should be sufficiently clear and complete in themselves for the reviewer to complete his examination without the presence of the staff member to explain them (although the reviewee is normally present at the time of the review).

11.07 Details of the audit tests should be recorded in the audit programme or the internal control evaluation form. These details should be sufficient for a reviewer to understand exactly what the test is, how it is to be carried out and how it helps to achieve the relevant objective. They should also be adequate for an audit assistant to understand what he has to do. In some cases, it is necessary to prepare a separate test schedule to explain the details more fully. For example, where a debtors' circularisation is carried out it may be better to enter the type of test on the audit programme and then include a more detailed schedule showing the precise procedure to be followed.

11.08 Where the audit includes one or more interim visits, the audit programme should indicate whether the test is to be carried out at the interim or the final. Where tests are to be started at the interim and completed at the final, this should be mentioned in the interim notes (see Chapter 12). The interim notes should also set out what steps are to be taken to cover the gap between interim and final.

Compliance Test Errors

11.09 Compliance test errors are dealt with in Chapter 8; such tests are carried out in order to decide whether or not we can rely on the system of internal control. If we cannot rely on it, we have to revert to full substantive tests — hence compliance errors should have been dealt with fully by the time we are completing a cycle.

Substantive Test Errors

11.10 If any errors are found in a substantive test, it is necessary to assess the effect of these on the accounts to determine whether a material misstatement is likely. If the substantive test is a non-sampling procedure (for example, a test in total or a 100% test of detail), then the error found may be the total error in that account item. If, however, the test is based on a sample of transactions or balances, the results must be projected to the whole population.

11.11 Before reaching any conclusions on errors, it is important to ensure that what constitutes an error is correctly specified in designing the rest. Otherwise, there is a danger of misinterpreting test results. For example, a disagreed balance in a debtors' circularisation is not an error if it is due to the timing of movements around the year end and we are satisfied that it has been properly treated. A non-reply to a circularisation request is not an error, provided that the balance is verified satisfactorily by other means e.g. the receipt of after date cash in respect of that balance.

11.12   We must investigate all substantive test errors to establish their cause. Isolated errors, which are not material in themselves, may be accepted if we show that they are not indicative of a material error (if they are material they may have to be adjusted).

11.13   When errors cannot be dismissed as isolated, it is often necessary to use additional procedures to establish the total error value. These procedures are designed to look for errors rather than prove no errors exist. They include:
(a) a test of every item making up the account balances or transaction stream;
(b) a mixture of non-sampling and non-statistical sampling, for example a test of every item greater than £1,000 and a random sample of 50 smaller items; and
(c) the use of a statistical technique which is capable of estimating error values (provided the client is happy to consider adjusting for a statistical estimate).
Error searches are usually time consuming and add considerably to the costs of the audit. Management should be asked if it would prefer to carry out the procedure with its own staff.

11.14   The effect on the cycle of the results of other cycles should also be taken into account. For example, an error which results in debtors being overstated and fixed assets understated may not be discovered during the work on the fixed assets cycle as they are primarily tested for overstatement. It should be discovered (if it is material) during the work on the revenue cycle as this deals with the overstatement of debtors.

Lead Schedules

11.15   The balances and transactions on each cycle are summarised on the lead schedule. This is supported by:
(a) the important ratios and other statistics for the cycle; and
(b) a note of the significant changes from last year (the lead schedule provides for four years' figures to be shown where this proves useful).
The lead schedule is cross referenced to the working papers and to the appropriate figures in the draft accounts.

Top Memos

11.16   The top memo summarises the audit work and conclusions on each cycle by showing:
(a) the work performed;
(b) how any audit problems (including higher than normal risk situations) were coped with;
(c) the nature and extent of important acounting and auditing judgements; and
(d) the audit conclusion on the cycle.
Example 15 (overleaf) shows a top memo for the fixed assets cycle.

11.17   The purpose of the memorandum is to collate, at the front of the working papers dealing with each cycle, the major points which require the attention of the reviewer. Hence it refers to occasions where we have not been able to carry out the work we planned or where the test showed worse results than we expected. It may summarise the adjustments the client has already made for errors discovered during the audit.

11.18   The audit conclusion states that either:
(a) the balances and transactions relating to the cycle are fairly stated; or
(b) the balances and transactions relating to the cycle are fairly stated subject to certain adjustments (which are summarised at the front of the working papers).

11.19   In some circumstances, the conclusion may state that it is subject to:
(a) obtaining further audit evidence; or
(b) the partner's or manager's approval of certain accounting judgements.
Ideally the circumstances in which such conclusions are used should be rare. However, in practice it may be necessary more frequently; the senior in charge should liaise with the manager who may prefer a 'qualified' conclusion rather than wait for audit evidence. Whenever such conclusions are used, the partner and manager should ensure that the missing evidence is obtained or their approval is given and both are recorded before the audit opinion is signed. The conclusion should then be updated.

11.20   Where we are carrying out an audit jointly with another firm we may not have carried out the detailed audit tests for a particular cycle. In such a case we should ensure that the relevant section of our audit file includes:
(a) a lead schedule;
(b) a summary of the procedures followed by the other firm and their conclusions (or copies of the relevant working papers);
(c) details of our review procedures and our conclusion of the cycle.

Example 15

Client:	TONNEX LTD	Prepared by:	AMH N3
		Date started:	16.2.91
Accounts to:	31.12.90	Date finished:	23.2.91
		Reviewed by:	
Subject:	FIXED ASSETS — TOP MEMO	Date:	

---

1. *Work done*

   The audit of fixed assets has been carried out using the procedures listed on N5* to N6*. A full check from the assets to the plant register and a reconciliation of it with the nominal ledger was carried out because of the problems detailed in paragraph 2 below. In all other respects the work was carried out in accordance with the audit plan and audit programme.

2. *Special problems*

   As referred to in the planning notes, the client has put fixed assets on to a computerised plant register for the first time this year. They had considerable difficulty in reconciling the nominal ledger with the plant register. Because of the materiality of this area, we did a 100% check from the plant register print-out to the assets and to the nominal ledger. We discovered that assets shown at net book value of £14,200 (42,600 cost, £28,400 depreciation) were on the register but did not exist. This amount has been scheduled for adjustment (N10*). This work involved 14 hours' additional time over and above that budgeted for the section.

3. *Judgement*

   For the purpose of calculating depreciation, the buildings element in land and buildings at Enfield has been assumed to be 85% of the value. This is reasonable and is similar to the proportion used for the Watford factory, which was confirmed by independent surveyors, and which is a similar site.

4. *Conclusion*

   Subject to the adjustment for errors totalling £25,171 (see N10*), fixed assets are fairly stated.

*not reproduced

11.21 We should conclude in a top memo on any section of the audit file other than a 'cycle' where we have carried out audit procedures. For example, there should always be a top memo covering analytical review procedures or work carried out on a consolidation.

12   Completing the audit

This chapter sets out the procedures at the end of the interim audit and at the end of the final audit. It explains the review responsibilities of the senior in charge, the manager and the partner. It also describes other procedures which need to be completed in the final stages of the audit. The responsibilities and procedures provide a check that the audit has been performed to an acceptable standard and the opportunity to review the service given to the client. They also form the foundation for the following year's audit.

12.01   The work performed by each staff member of the audit team must be reviewed by a more senior member of the firm. This is necessary to ensure that the work has been adequately performed and to confirm that the results support the audit conclusions which have been reached.

12.02   This review process does not replace the need for consultation with colleagues or more senior members of the firm where matters of principle or contentious matters arise. Indeed, such consultation is vital not only to maintain the quality of the firm's work but also to ensure an efficient and effective service to our clients.

12.03   The final review fulfils the following audit functions. It enables us to:
(a) ensure that the figures in the draft accounts make sense in the light of the audit evidence;
(b) assess the impact of any unadjusted errors and decide whether to press for adjustments;
(c) check that all appropriate disclosure and other requirements have been complied with in the accounts;
(d) check that there is sufficient relevant and reliable audit evidence to support the audit opinion;
(e) consider what recommendations we can make to the client in a management letter; and
(f) prepare the way for the following year's audit by summarising any points which have come to our attention which will be relevant to that audit and by leaving an up-to-date permanent audit file.
In addition, a review of the work carried out during a separate interim audit visit provides a link between that visit and the final audit.

12.04   Where we are acting as joint auditor, our responsibilities as set out in **12.03** are not diluted. We must ensure that each cycle has been adequately audited whichever auditor has carried out the initial work. We must also ensure that we have fully reviewed the working papers of the other auditor, and have recorded the results of this review. We should also take copies of papers which report problems and conclusions in the major cycles.

12.05   The responsibilities of the senior in charge and the manager are summarised in *Tables 6 and 7* (overleaf). These must only be seen as a guide as it is difficult to lay down hard and fast rules, given the wide range of clients and the differing experience and skills of individual members of staff. For many clients there are additional tasks which increase the responsibilities of the senior and the manager. At the simplest level, these may include obtaining information for P11Ds and company annual returns. Alternatively, they may include reports upon the efficiency of departments within the client's business or advice on the tax effectiveness of particular courses of action.

Partner Responsibilities

12.06   In order that the partner can be satisfied that the audit has been properly performed and that material matters requiring his consideration or approval are referred to him quickly, it is essential that he is involved at each phase of the audit. His role as a reviewer should include the following:
(a) examine and review the audit files in sufficient detail to be satisfied that the audit team, including the manager, has done its work satisfactorily;
(b) consider the points for partner and formulate decisions;
(c) approve the final management letter for submission to the client;
(d) approve the form and content of the accounts;
(e) ensure that all material outstanding points are cleared. This normally requires a meeting with the client and may require consultation with another partner;
(f) review and approve the representation letter;
(g) agree the wording of the audit opinion.
The partner should approve the final typed accounts and sign and date the audit report when he is satisfied that all the necessary pre-signing procedures have been carried out.

12.07   The review stage is not only a check on the quality and effectiveness of our audit work, it is also the opportunity to assess the service we have given to the client and to decide upon improvements that can be made in future years. We may identify changes in the way in which the audit is carried out. We may suggest improvements in the client's systems which will improve the efficiency of the audit (without an equivalent increase in the internal costs of the company).
[*text continues on p 108*]

Senior and Manager Responsibilities

Table 6
Completing the audit — responsibilities of the senior in charge

---

Review responsibilities

Review in detail the work of all assistants.

Check that all working papers on the current and permanent files are complete; working papers should identify:
(a) name of client;
(b) balance sheet date of the accounts covered by the audit;
(c) name or initials of member of staff who prepared the working paper and date of preparation;
(d) clear and accurate heading indicating purpose of working paper and a cross reference to the audit programme or internal control evaluation form;
(e) details of work performed;
(f) results of work, together with any further action required;
(g) schedule reference and cross references to other working papers;
(h) comparative figures (where appropriate).

Check that all necessary audit work has been done.

At the end of the interim visit

Prepare 'interim notes' linking interim and final visits.

Other responsibilities

Update the overall analytical review to check that the accounts make sense.

Prepare a summary of unadjusted errors and check whether they are material either singly or in aggregate.

Prepare or review the tax computation and supporting schedules and check the accruals for current and deferred taxes.

Draft letter of representation and any relevant board minutes.

Complete a disclosure checklist to ensure that all appropriate requirements have been complied with.

Review post-balance sheet events to ensure that all material adjusting and non-adjusting events have been taken into account.

Prepare a list of points for partner, dealing with:
(a) the results and financial position, together with any significant changes from prior years, budget and expectations;
(b) any audit problems;
(c) any outstanding work;
(d) the costs of the audit, together with explanations of variances from budget.

Draft the audit opinion.

Prepare the management letter from the draft paragraphs written on each cycle.

Complete staff evaluations.

Write points forward to the next audit and update permanent file.

Table 7

Completing the audit — manager responsibilities

Review the detailed working papers prepared by the senior and assistants in the context of the audit plan, the audit programme, facts and developments which have emerged during the audit and his own knowledge of the client. As a result ensure there is sufficient relevant and reliable audit evidence to support the audit opinion.

At the end of any interim visit, review the interim notes and take appropriate action.

Consider the results of the analytical review and ensure that the accounts make sense.

Review all unadjusted errors and, in the context of an updated estimate of materiality, make recommendations about adjustments/audit opinion.

Review tax computations and check the accruals for current and deferred taxes.

Review the letter of representation/draft board minutes and ensure that they are appropriate.

Review the draft accounts and ensure compliance with appropriate requirements.

Edit and review the points for partner and recommend action to be taken.

Where there is a second independent partner, ensure that all points raised by him on the audit work and accounts are cleared.

Review the audit opinion and if qualified agree with the appropriate independent partner.

Review the management letter and ensure that it is commercially realistic, professionally sound and in sympathy with the aims of the people running the business.

Review our performance on the job, including the time costs summary and variances from budget, staff evaluation and the service given to the client.

Review the points forward to the next audit and check that the permanent audit file has been updated.

Immediately prior to audit opinion being signed, ensure that:
- post-balance sheet review has been updated to current date;
- working papers contain all audit evidence — particularly where matters have involved exercise of judgement;
- all review points are cleared and reflected on the relevant working papers;
- financial statements reflect any changes in legislation and accounting standards which have taken place since the accounts were first drafted;
- the appropriate independent review of the file, of treatments that do not comply with the Companies Act or of qualified reports has been carried out;
- all firm's policies and procedures now complied with.

We may want to review the effectiveness of the service given by specialist departments to the client. While all of these and many other aspects of our service should be kept under constant review, the end of the audit provides a special opportunity for an annual assessment.

Interim Notes

12.08   When a separate interim audit visit is made, it is normal to complete all the initial internal control testing at this time. If, for any reason, part of this work is unfinished at the end of the interim, the senior in charge should make sure that the reasons for it are recorded in the working papers together with brief details of what needs to be done at the final and details of any work necessary to complete the testing in this area. It may mean that no definite conclusions at the interim stage can be drawn about the reliability of internal controls on certain objectives.

12.09   Whether or not all the interim work is finished, the senior should prepare some notes linking the interim and final visits. Their purpose is to assess whether any changes are necessary in the work planned for the final. The notes should refer to:
(a) whether all work which should have been undertaken at the interim has been completed and, if not, what is outstanding;
(b) proposals for further reductions of work at the final visit in areas where controls are stronger than was expected at the planning stage (or increases in work where controls have proved to be unreliable);
(c) confirmation that such things as dates of stocktake attendance or debtor circularisations have been arranged;
(d) an outline of possible problem areas which have become apparent for the final visit;
(e) any points arising from analytical review procedures which may suggest audit or commercial problems;
(f) any changes in the assessment of materiality or risk;
(g) any other matters which need to be considered before the final visit; and
(h) a summary of time costs to date versus budget with an explanation for any variances.
An example of interim notes is included in Appendix 7.

Points for Partner

12.10   One of the most important tasks of the senior in charge at the end of the final audit is to prepare a list of points for partner. It should be restricted to material points and include:

(a) a brief explanation of the results and financial position as shown by the draft accounts and of any changes from prior years, budget and expectations. It is important that the senior gives explanations; if he limits himself to stating facts (for example by saying that gross profit percentage has decreased from 26% to 19%), he has failed to carry out his responsibilities properly by leaving the partner and manager to form their opinion on the accounts on the basis of incomplete information;

(b) an explanation of any audit problems including areas where major judgements have been exercised. The points should include sufficient detail for the partner and manager to grasp the extent of the problem and understand what action has already been taken. Wherever possible, the senior should give his recommendation as to the appropriate course of action. The problems should be cross referenced to the relevant working papers and to the audit plan;

(c) a brief explanation of any outstanding work which it has proved impossible to complete. This should not include unexplained variations in the figures. Nor should it include areas where relevant and reliable audit evidence is missing, unless it has proved impossible to obtain even after full investigation;

(d) a summary of the costs of the audit to date (plus an estimate to complete) together with an explanation of any variances from budget.

12.11 The senior should include, as an appendix to the points for partner, a schedule of unadjusted errors. This should show, cycle by cycle, the effect of these errors on the profit and loss account and the balance sheet. The schedule should contain a conclusion about whether or not any adjustments should be made (or whether or not our audit report should be qualified) in the light of an updated estimate of materiality.

Letters of Representation

12.12 Oral representations by management should be summarised in the working papers. Where they are uncorroborated by other audit evidence and where they relate to matters which are material to the accounts, we should ensure that they are also formally minuted or included in a signed letter of representation. The minutes or letter should also confirm management's responsibility for the accounts, particularly in those cases where we have been heavily involved in their preparation.

12.13 The precise scope and wording of the minutes or letter of representation should be appropriate to the circumstances of each audit. Hence, standard letters or minutes may not be appropriate. Whatever the scope or nature of the representations, management should be encouraged to participate in their drafting (or to comment on our drafts) and make appropriate amendments, provided that the value of the audit evidence obtained is not diminished.

12.14   It is the audit senior's responsibility to draft the letter or the minutes. He should be aware of the areas for which we have received only oral representations which are uncorroborated by other audit evidence. He may use the appendix to the Auditing Guideline on *Representations by Management* as a guide for the format of the letter or minutes.

Review of Statutory Accounts

12.15   Throughout the audit we are building up a picture of the company's activities and position at the year end. At the final review state, we must confirm that the picture shown by the financial statements matches these expectations and the audit evidence we have obtained. For example, if an increase in debtors was justified by reference to an increase in turnover, the conclusions made on debtors should be re-examined if the draft accounts do not show such an increase in turnover. We should also be on the lookout for 'window dressing' or other artificial entries put through to mask the true results or state of affairs. For example, the repayment by a debtor of a loan before the year end and its subsequent re-advance immediately after the year end may give a false impression of a company's liquidity and should be disclosed as a post-balance sheet event.

12.16   During this review we should:
(a) update our earlier analytical reviews to take account of adjustments and to reflect the effect of unadjusted errors; and
(b) examine explanations given to points arising during the audit and ensure that they are compatible with the final accounts.

12.17   Adjustments made to figures during the course of the audit — and particularly at the final review state — may highlight new relationships between figures which may cause us to change our opinion about the reasonableness of certain figures. For example, an adjustment to the closing stock to correct errors found in valuing it may force the gross profit percentage out of line and so lead to a re-examination of purchases and sales.

12.18   The accounts must comply with the Companies Act and Statements of Standard Accounting Practice, as well as showing a true and fair view. These requirements ensure consistency between different sets of accounts and give a measure of certainty to users of the accounts that items will be treated in a standard way. They also require certain disclosures. Our checklists assist in checking (and evidencing the check of) compliance with the disclosure require-ments and have been designed to highlight any failures to comply with the requirements. They must be completed for all audits and filed on the current working papers file. It is the senior's responsibility to see that this is done.

12.19 Very rarely, a client may need to override the requirements of the Companies Act and Accounting Standards to enable the accounts to show a true and fair view. Where a client proposes to do this, it must be discussed with and agreed and evidenced by a designated independent partner.

Post–Balance Sheet Events

12.20 The review of post-balance sheet events is an important aspect of the examination of the draft accounts. It may highlight:

(a) adjusting events, which are those post-balance sheet events which provide additional evidence of conditions that existed at the balance sheet date; and

(b) non-adjusting events, which are those post-balance sheet events which concern conditions which did not exist at the balance sheet date but which may, in certain circumstances, require disclosure.

12.21 The review should consist of discussions with management relating to, and consideration of:

(a) procedures adopted by management to ensure that all events after the balance sheet date have been identified, considered and properly evaluated as to their effect on the accounts;

(b) any management accounts and relevant accounting records;

(c) profit forecasts and cash flow projections;

(d) known risk areas and contingencies, whether inherent in the nature of the business, revealed in our risk analysis or discovered on previous audits;

(e) minutes of shareholders, directors and management meetings and related correspondence and reports; and

(f) relevant information from outside the business, including that relating to the competitors, customers, suppliers and the economy generally.

12.22 Our checklist for post-balance sheet events reminds us of procedures we should carry out to identify post-balance sheet events. The audit senior should carry out such a review to a date as close as possible to the end of his fieldwork. The senior must clearly document this review. The partner and manager must ensure that the review is updated for events which have taken place since the fieldwork was completed up to the date on which the audit opinion is signed.

Going Concern

12.23   Where we are uncertain about the client's ability to continue to operate as a going concern this must be a major consideration throughout the audit and in our post-balance sheet review. Here, it is especially important to document the evidence considered (for example, cash flows and budgets), the procedures we have carried out, and our conclusions based upon this evidence on whether the company will continue to operate in the foreseeable future.

Audit Opinions

12.24   The audit senior should draft the audit opinion based on the results of the work carried out. Wherever possible, the opinion should be unqualified. Where the draft accounts contain material errors, we should try to convince the client to make the necessary adjustments. Where the client is unwilling to do this, we must qualify our opinion. We also need to qualify our opinion where there are material uncertainties about the accounts. The partner must discuss and agree the wording of any qualified audit report with a member of the Technical Committee.

12.25   Before giving an unqualified report we must be satisfied, based on the audit evidence we have obtained, that the accounts show a true and fair view and are properly prepared in accordance with the Companies Act. We must also be satisfied that:
(a) proper accounting records have been kept;
(b) the accounts agree with the accounting records;
(c) we have received all the information and explanations required for the purposes of our audit;
(d) information in the directors' report is consistent with the accounts; and
(e) all relevant Statements of Standard Accounting Practice have been complied with, apart from departures with which we concur.

12.26   The form of any qualification depends upon the reasons for the qualification — whether it is due to uncertainty or disagreement and whether it is material or fundamental.

12.27   Circumstances giving rise to uncertainty include:
(a) limitations on the scope of the audit (for example, our inability to carry out necessary audit procedures or the absence of proper accounting records);
(b) inherent uncertainties where it is not possible to reach an objective conclusion as to the outcome of a situation (examples include major litigation and doubts about the company's ability to remain a going concern).

12.28   A qualification arising from a disagreement may be caused by:

(a) departures from generally accepted accounting principles (including State-
    ments of Standard Accounting Practice) where we do not concur with the
    departure;

(b) unadjusted errors in the accounts;

(c) inadequate disclosure of events or amounts; or

(d) failure to comply with the legislation dictating the form and content of the
    accounts.

12.29   An audit opinion should only be qualified if the uncertainty or disagreement is material. In extreme cases, the uncertainty may be so material that
it renders the accounts meaningless or the disagreement so material that the
accounts are misleading. In such cases, the term 'fundamental' is used instead of
material.

12.30   The appropriate form of opinion can be established from the following
table taken from the Auditing Standard *The Audit Report*:

	MATERIAL BUT NOT FUNDAMENTAL	FUNDAMENTAL
Uncertainty	Subject to	Unable to form an opinion
Disagreement	Except for	Accounts do not show a true and fair view

12.31   Hence, where a matter is 'material but not fundamental', the audit opinion
should conclude that the accounts show a true and fair view, either 'subject to'
(uncertainty) or 'except for' (disagreement) the matters referred to. Where the
matter is fundamental, then we must state that we are 'unable to form an
opinion' (uncertainty) or that the accounts 'do not show a true and fair view'
(disagreement). In all cases the opinion should state clearly the details of the
matter giving rise to the qualification.

12.32   In rare circumstances, we may want to bring some matter to the attention
of the reader without qualifying the report by the use of 'emphasis of matter'.
We should not use this to amplify a matter which is inadequately disclosed
elsewhere in the accounts but merely to draw attention to important matters in
the financial statements to ensure they are not overlooked. Where we consider
this necessary we should include a reference to them in a separate paragraph at
the end of the audit report to avoid it being confused with a qualification.

12.33   Where we take management representations as part of our audit evidence we should evaluate them in the light of all other audit evidence obtained. If we conclude that we have insufficient supporting evidence to place reliance on the representations, we must qualify the audit report where the matter concerned is material. Where representations are accepted there should be no reference to them in our audit report.

12.34   Some clients will be governed by the rules of other bodies or legislation, for example, the Financial Services Act 1986. To comply with those rules we will have to report on an additional set of financial statements for submission to the relevant body. In such instances we must ensure that we are aware of the requirements of the body, that we have done sufficient work to allow us to issue the report required by the body and that we word our report as they require.

12.35   Before signing the audit report the manager should complete and both the manager and partner sign the pre-signing checklist. This records that the partner and manager are satisfied that the audit working papers support the opinion, that all the firm's policies and procedures have been complied with and that the work has been updated to the date of signing.

Management Letters

12.36   The audit is far more than a review of past events; it also enables us to give the client advice for the future. This is normally done by way of a management letter informing the client of shortcomings in the systems of internal control which have been found during the course of the audit, pointing out the effects of such shortcomings and making constructive recommendations in order to eliminate or reduce these in future. We should also include in the letter any other points arising from the audit which need to be drawn to the client's attention. The letter should deal with major points (although some clients may want all errors and weaknesses listed in an appendix).

12.37   The management letter is not a substitute for:
(a) informing management on a timely basis of problems which have emerged during the audit;
(b) adjusting for errors in the accounts; or
(c) qualifying an audit opinion because material errors have not been adjusted or proper accounting records have not been maintained.

12.38 Where there is a separate interim audit, it is usual to send an initial management letter at the end of it dealing with:
(a) weaknesses in existing systems of financial and accounting control, such as a failure to check credit worthiness before despatch of goods;
(b) errors in the operation of the systems which affect transactions and balances, such as a failure to record all purchase invoices, account for VAT or PAYE properly or take discounts available for prompt payment;
(c) inadequate bookkeeping or data processing, such as failure to carry out regular bank reconciliations. We may also point out areas where we have had to do extra work to compensate for these inadequacies;
(d) possible improvements in the production of accounting information for management, such as producing cash flow statements; and
(e) managerial and operational activity insofar as we can make realistic comments based on the work we have done.
The initial letter also points out any problems we foresee in carrying out the final audit. For example, the failure to record all purchase invoices may make it difficult to verify creditors at the year end or an accounting policy may be inappropriate for certain transactions which have arisen during the year.

12.39 After the final audit, a second letter normally includes:
(a) any additional matters under the same headings as the initial letter;
(b) inefficiencies or delays in the agreed timetable for preparation of the accounts or of working schedules which delayed the completion of the audit and may have resulted in increased costs;
(c) any significant differences between the accounts and any management accounts or budgets which not only caused audit problems but also reduced the value of management information; and
(d) any results of our analytical review procedures of which management may not be aware.

12.40 The letters should be addressed to the directors — although it is usual that they are discussed with the senior accounting executive first. They should invite a reply on the action taken by management. They should also make clear that the matters raised are only the major points that came to our attention and that our audit should not be relied upon to detect all errors and frauds.

12.41 In drafting the letters we should take into account the additional costs and benefits to the client if recommendations are carried out. We should not make recommendations that would increase costs without any benefit either in cash or information terms. The recommendations should be commercially realistic — there is no point putting forward proposals which we know the company could not implement (although we may still want to point out the weakness).

12.42   The individual paragraphs should be drafted during the audit as and when any points arise. They should specify:

(a) the weakness or error and its cause, together with examples of specific cases. The client should not be left in any doubt as to the matter we are referring to. We should also state whether we have found any evidence to suggest that the weakness has actually led to error in the period under review. If so, we should provide sufficient information to enable the client to trace the problem himself and, if necessary or possible, make corrections;

(b) the precise effect of the weakness; and

(c) recommendations to prevent such weaknesses and errors occurring in the future. These should always be specific suggestions about procedures that could be adopted to rectify the weakness.

In the draft letter, paragraphs should be cross referenced to the appropriate audit working papers.

Points Forward to the Next Audit

12.43   The senior should prepare a list of 'points forward' for the attention of the following year's audit team. Its purpose is to provide a link between the end of the final visit and the planning of the following year's audit work by ensuring that any ideas on improving the efficiency of the audit and any problems, of which we have received advance notice, are written down for the benefit of the staff handling the audit in future years. The document is the start of next year's planning; it should neither be a substitute for dealing with the current year's problems immediately nor an excuse for delaying the update of the permanent audit file.

12.44   The points normally included are:

(a) items raised at manager/partner review or in the management letter which may need attention next year;

(b) recommendations to restrict audit work in certain areas or to reduce the importance of certain audit objectives;

(c) recommendations of alternative audit tests to overcome difficulties or improve efficiency;

(d) different forms of third party confirmation;

(e) practical difficulties faced in carrying out tests and recommendations as to how to deal with these;

(f) proposed changes in the company's systems, including any plans for computerisation;

(g) advance warning of major changes in the business that could lead to the disappearance of or introduction of audit areas or changes in the relative importance of areas of the business;

(h) changes in legislation and accounting policies which may affect our work; and

(i) any suggestions for improvements in timetabling and staffing arrangements. Wherever possible, the effect of the changes proposed should be quantified in terms of man hours. An example is included in Appendix 8.

13 The audit of small businesses

The audit of a small business may present us with a number of special problems which may require us to modify our audit approach. This chapter highlights some of the problems and suggests ways of doing this.

The Characteristics of a Small Business Audit

13.01 A small business is not best viewed by reference to some measure such as size of turnover, assets or number of employees. We find it is more useful to identify those characteristics which small businesses share and which cause us to modify our procedures. The chief characteristics of a small business are:

(a) Lack of accounting expertise: a small business will not have experienced accountants as staff members. This may result in poor accounting records and preparation of accounts.

(b) Dominance over business operations by one or two individuals: whilst this can have positive effects especially if there is close involvement in the day-to-day running of the business, it can also have detrimental effects because of their ability to override controls and, for example, to exclude or wrongly record transactions.

(c) A tendency for the owner/manager to confuse company and personal property which if reflected in the accounting records would lead to errors in the accounts and problems with the taxation authorities.

(d) Lack of sufficient employees to maintain controls: because of low numbers of staff, segregation of duties is not possible and all of the accounting responsibilities for a particular type of transaction often fall upon one employee.

(e) Lack of understanding why an audit is necessary: because of the lack of accounting expertise small clients are often unaware of what an audit entails and why it is necessary. Even where they do understand, they may see it as something from which they obtain little benefit as the shareholders and directors are the same people. They tend to see the audit engagement as being primarily for the purpose of producing accounts and agreeing the tax liability. This can result in fee and time pressure on the audit part of the engagement which increases the necessity to employ efficient procedures.

13.02   Not every small business will have all these characteristics. Some will have all whereas others will have only one or two. Equally some larger businesses will share them. Each of the characteristics gives us different problems in achieving an effective and efficient audit and in reporting on it. Whilst our basic approach outlined in the rest of the guide applies equally to all sizes of businesses, for many small businesses we will need to refine our detailed procedures. The rest of this chapter examines ways in which this may be done.

13.03   The same concepts apply to the audit of small businesses as to the audit of larger businesses. The scope of the audit and accounting work is determined by our statutory and professional responsibilities — and by the expectations of our clients. Our audit work reflects the nature of the client's business, the risk of material errors and the results of any analytical review procedures. It includes sampling techniques to carry out substantive tests in the most cost-effective manner. In particular, we coordinate our accounting work and audit work. It is, however, extremely unlikely that the audit of a small business will involve compliance tests (where controls exist, it is rare that it will be cost effective to use the compliance test/reduced substantive test route).

Terms of Engagement

13.04   A characteristic of small businesses is a lack of skilled accounting staff. As a result we are often expected to assist with accountancy work, such as recording transactions in the books of prime entry, posting the books to the nominal ledger, extracting a trial balance and preparing draft accounts. We may also be required to provide the company with regular management accounts. Whatever accountancy or other work we are required to do, we must take it into account in planning the nature and timing of our audit work.

Understanding the Business and its Accounting Systems

13.05   It is as important to understand the business of a small company as a large one. We may understand the business of a smaller client more easily as:
(a) the business and its systems will usually be less sophisticated and will be more easily understood;
(b) we will often provide general business and accounting advice during the course of the year and will therefore have considerable knowledge of the client's affairs.
Usually the manager can brief the senior in charge quickly. They may find it helpful to do this while completing together the business review checklist. A permanent audit file should be maintained; it will, of course, be much briefer than one for a larger business and it may combine certain sections of information.

13.06   The permanent file must include a record of the accounting systems and procedures. Audit and accountancy work can only be carried out if we know the systems and procedures used by the client — even with a small business. We need to know how sales take place and how they are recorded so that we can check for the understatement of income. For example, if we are dealing with a service company such as a road transport company, large or small, we need to know what records exist which enable invoices to be raised. If we are dealing with a retailer, large or small, we need to know how it records both cash and credit sales and what system it has for recording purchase invoices.

Understanding the System

13.07   Many controls which would be relevant to the large business are not practical, necessary or appropriate in the smaller business. However, from an audit point of view, certain basic controls should be found in all the accounting records such as:
(a) the list of debtor balances are regularly reviewed and reconciled to the sales ledger control account;
(b) purchase invoices are checked against orders and goods received notes;
(c) all payments are checked to supporting documentation.
The accounting systems' checklist will help us to identify whether basic controls exist which are necessary for our client's accounting system to work effectively.

13.08   Absence of any of these controls will not necessarily constitute a serious weakness and lead us to carry out additional testing but should cause us to question what alternative method the company uses to protect those assets or ensure correct recording of transactions. In many small businesses these controls may be exercised by an owner/manager.

Analytical Review Procedures

13.09   Analytical review is an extremely valuable tool in the audit of small businesses. As well as being used on whatever reliable accounting information is available while planning the audit, it has the following uses:
(a) we should apply analytical review procedures to the results of any accountancy work which precedes related audit work. For example, where we have to extract debtors' ledger balances and reconcile the control account, we should review the reasonableness of debtors and the ageing (which we will have done while extracting the balances) before deciding on the nature and extent of audit procedures (for example, checks from debtor balances to despatch records, circularisation of balances, review of after-date cash, etc).

(b) analytical review may provide sufficient relevant and reliable audit evidence for certain items including profit and loss overhead expenditure (plus some direct costs), accruals and prepayments and, possibly, fixed assets. The use of analytical review procedures will point to any items which, because of their nature, incidence or size, require further investigation.

(c) analytical review procedures supported by reasonable oral explanations are essential in those cases where other audit evidence is not available.

Assessing Audit Risk

13.10   Our assessment of risk is an essential part of an audit for all types of client. Many of the characteristics of small businesses give rise to an increased risk of error in the financial statements and should mean that our work is directed into different areas than would be expected for larger businesses. Some areas we need to consider are:

(a) The close involvement in the business of the owner/manager. His close control over employees and detailed knowledge of transactions may reduce the risk of their making errors or such errors going uncorrected. However, errors or deliberate misrepresentations may go undetected because of his ability to override controls, include or exclude transactions and put through transactions of an unusual or unexpected nature.

(b) The failure of an owner/manager to distinguish between personal and family affairs and those of the business. This may increase the risk of certain types of errors in the financial statements, such as misclassifications or overstatement of expenses.

(c) Errors in the accounting records, which may arise because of undermanning or inexperienced staff.

(d) The lack of segregation of duties (all or many of the accounting entries may be made by one person, and not all of the entries may be checked) increases the risk of certain types of errors (and sometimes fraud). For example, one employee may send out invoices, record them in the sales day book and sales ledger, open the post, record and bank the receipts and update the cash book and sales ledger. In such a case, there is an increased possibility of error due to either accidental or deliberate failure to record some or all of the transactions.

13.11   In many small businesses there will be no formal system of internal control. This does not make such businesses 'unauditable' as it only raises the possibility of a risk of error. Such a risk may be offset by a number of factors and the absence of error may be established by reference to evidence obtained externally to the company. In fact, a strong control environment will more often than not offset the potential problems which could result from lack of formal internal controls.

Materiality

13.12   The need for, and the use of, an estimate of materiality are the same for the audit of small businesses as for large businesses. We use an estimate of materiality for determining sample sizes for audit work and deciding whether or not to adjust for errors. It must not be used for accountancy work; this must be carried out with a far greater degree of precision.

13.13   When auditing small businesses, it is often the case that we can:
(a) identify certain key audit tests; and
(b) rely on analytical review procedures for many audit objectives particularly those relating to the overstatement of expenditure and payroll and the over and understatement of small balance sheet items (we will, of course, investigate further those items which do not make sense or which are unusual).

13.14   In choosing the tests we need to do, it is vital that we concentrate on the important matters. There can be a temptation to audit everything in a small company because it is relatively easy to do and it does not appear to take long to do it. Unless the client wants us to check everything, we should identify those audit objectives with a higher than normal risk of material error and concentrate on them.

13.15   We should also make use of the sampling techniques which form part of our audit approach. Monetary unit sampling can be applied, without modification, to small businesses (it only becomes unreliable when the population is less than £5,000).

13.16   Care is required, however, with error rate sampling which may lead to unnecessarily large sample sizes when the population size is small. The advice given in paragraphs **9.33** to **9.36** deals with small populations and should be followed where such circumstances arise in small businesses. Alternatively, we may be able to obtain sufficient relevant and reliable evidence from a smaller, carefully selected sample or from adopting a different audit strategy.

Planning the Audit of Small Businesses

13.17   The best approach to planning the audit of a small company is to spend a few minutes discussing the first five points set out in **10.01**, and agreeing the answers to them with the manager. Then, for each cycle and for the financial statements as a whole, list the accountancy work that must be done and any additional work expected by the client. Only at this stage should we decide what audit work must be done. So, for example, before deciding the audit work on the expenditure cycle of a small company where the bookkeeper writes up the day book and creditors' ledger (but not the nominal ledger) we must first list the postings to the nominal ledger. (We may need to check entries in the day book to supporting vouchers and reconcile balances due to major suppliers to statements.)

13.18 The accountancy work programme provides guidance on how we should carry out an accountancy-based assignment. It covers the major sections of the working paper file and details the general procedures. However, there may be work on particular areas which will need to be added to the programme to make it appropriate for individual clients.

Obtaining Audit Evidence

13.19 Where accountancy work is carried out for a client it may be possible with a minimal amount of independent checking to obtain audit assurance. The way in which accountancy work can allow us to adapt our procedures depends on its extent and nature. It will never replace all other procedures, for example, where we have written up the cash book and carried out the bank reconciliation it will still be necessary to obtain a bank certificate. However, in this example we should be able to reduce significantly the work that would have been carried out in the areas where we performed the accountancy work.

13.20 Accountancy work seldom affects our work on understatement, e.g. we may have posted all the sales invoices given to us by the client but this does not give us any assurance that sales invoices have been raised for all despatches made by the client.

13.21 Our audit files should record:
(a) details of accountancy work which we have carried out;
(b) the type and extent of audit assurance this work has given us; and
(c) its effect on our detailed audit procedures.

Management Representations

13.22   A major issue in respect of the audit report on small businesses is that of acceptance of management representations. In many smaller businesses because the accounting system is controlled by one or two individuals, we may have difficulty in obtaining sufficient reliable evidence to assure ourselves, for example, that all income has been included. This is particularly the case in a cash business but may also be the case in the service industries or in businesses where stock is not purchased for specific customers. We may also have difficulty, for example, in establishing that all expenditure is a valid charge on the business given the confusion between the company and the owner in many small companies.

13.23   In these cases we may feel that we have to rely upon management representations as to the completeness and accuracy of the accounting records. On their own these representations cannot be sufficient. Where they are supported by the results of substantive tests of transactions and an analytical review of costs and margins (or possibly one of them) it may be possible to conclude that there is sufficient evidence on which to base an unqualified report.

Qualified Audit Reports

13.24   Where, however, it is not possible to obtain sufficient supporting evidence from these sources on the point upon which representations are sought, it is necessary to qualify the audit report on the grounds of uncertainty. In most cases there will be a specific area or specific areas of concern. The Auditing Standard — *The Audit Report* — says that the qualification should be on a 'subject to' basis and the report should specify the reasons for the qualification and the areas and amounts affected by the uncertainty.

13.25   The standard also deals with cases where the uncertainties are pervasive to the financial statements. Here we should consider disclaiming our opinion as pervasive uncertainty could well throw doubt on what other evidence we have collected. However, the standard allows for rare cases where the other evidence is considered to be reliable enough so that a disclaimer is not justified. Here a general qualification, for example 'in regard to the completeness and correctness of recording of transactions' is permissible.

13.26   In many small businesses the need for representations will not arise. We will be able to obtain sufficient evidence upon which to issue an unqualified audit report. There can be no doubt, for example, whether all income has been received for a small property investment company with two properties, where income is determined by the leases. Alternatively, where all purchases are obtained from a small number of suppliers, the verification of purchases together with a thorough analytical review of margins should give sufficient assurance about completeness of income.

14 Audit of computer-produced information

This chapter sets out how we adapt our audit approach to take into account the use by a client of computers to process information.

14.01 The use of computers by our clients does not alter the basic principles which underlie our audit approach. Our audit objectives are the same as for a manual system. However, as computers may have a far-reaching effect on the way in which a client collects and stores its accounting information they will often have a significant effect on the detailed procedures which we choose to collect the necessary audit evidence.

14.02 The principal characteristics of a computer system which cause us to modify our audit approach are that:
(a) The extent to which accounting systems are computerised and the complexity of the system may lead to a loss of audit trail. As a result audit risk may increase and there may be difficulty in identifying any problems in the computer programs.
(b) Despite the above, computer controls may often impose discipline upon a system and as a result may be relied upon to a significant extent to reduce errors in the accounting system. This may allow us to conclude that there is a normal risk of material errors and to reduce our audit testing accordingly. Further, it is more likely that we will be able to rely upon controls to reduce substantive testing where this proves cost effective.
(c) Because the computer routinely processes large volumes of transactions it may make clients over-dependent and vulnerable to its failure.
(d) A computer is capable of consistent operation so that if it processes one item correctly it may be relied upon to process all similar items correctly. By contrast, if one item is processed wrongly there is a risk that all items are processed wrongly.
(e) The computer lends itself to the use of computer-assisted audit techniques which allow us to carry out our audit procedures more cost effectively.
Because of the above characteristics, a computer system may affect the decisions we make about what to audit and how we are going to audit it.

14.03 Our audit work should reflect the expectations of our clients and those with computerised systems often expect us to carry out checks or tests which are not needed to support our audit opinion but which enable them to obtain an independent view of their systems and procedures.

Understanding the Business

14.04 A fundamental part of our planning process is to gain an understanding of the client's business and the way in which it operates. A key feature of the process is the documenting of the client's system. Where the system is computerised and the processing of transactions and the controls operated are complex it is important that we have a comprehensive record, usually in the form of a flowchart, as this will help us:

(a) identify any risks associated with the processing of transactions;

(b) devise audit tests which are most appropriate; and

(c) highlight opportunities for providing advice and assistance to our client.

14.05 Our record of the system must include details of those computer installations and applications which are used to process accounting information. Our record will normally comprise:

(a) details of installations;

(b) details of types, volumes and values of transactions; and

(c) a schematic overview flowchart.

Details of Installations

14.06 As a minimum we should record details of:

(a) organisation of the data-processing function;

(b) hardware used by our client;

(c) operating environment; and

(d) computerised accounting applications. We should distinguish between those applications developed in house and those supplied as a package by software houses.

There is an installation details form to assist our recording of these.

Types, Volumes and Values of Transactions

14.07 To give us an indication of the materiality and significance of the computer systems we should also record details of the various types of transactions processed, the normal values associated with those transactions and the number of transactions normally processed.

In practice this is a summary of the information either input or produced by an accounting system. We may combine it with the overview flowchart or set it out on a supporting schedule.

Example 16

Sales Ledger, XYZ Limited

Transaction type	Number of transactions per annum	Average value £
Sales invoice	1,000,000	500
Credit notes	11,000	200
Adjustments	500	50
Cash	100,000	5,000
Average sales ledger balance		400,000

Schematic Overview Flowchart

14.08 A schematic overview flowchart sets out the main details of each application on one sheet of paper (see **15.32**). Where we decide to attempt to place reliance on internal controls we may also need full document flowcharts (see **15.10**).

Simpler Systems

14.09 Our approach differs depending on the complexity of the system. Where the processing carried out is of a routine nature it is often possible on the basis of a review of the systems' documentation and after completing the computer controls' summary to make a judgement about the risk of material error and the need for additional audit procedures. This is the case particularly when smaller clients are using standard or bespoke packages obtained from software houses to perform basic processing. If the control environment is good we may be able to rely entirely on substantive tests and need not carry out a detailed audit of the computer's internal processing and control procedures.

14.10 To follow this approach, which is often known as 'auditing around the computer', we need to ensure that there is no loss of audit trail as the transactions are processed by the computer and that there is sufficient 'hard copy' record of the transactions. Under this approach we must also ensure that we test the same things as we would in a manual system, for example, we should test the ageing of debtors and the casts of stock lists and not assume they are satisfactory because a computer produces them.

Complex Systems

14.11 Where there is an extensive use of computers and the features of the system are such as to make a 'round the computer' approach inadequate to detect all errors because, for example, of loss of audit trail, we will need to perform a more comprehensive evaluation of controls before assessing risk. Here we have to evaluate:

(a) application controls i.e. controls over inputs to, outputs from, and standing data specific to each application. We do this by completing the summary of controls schedule (see Appendix 9); and

(b) general controls i.e. controls over development and maintenance of programs and the operation of the computer installation. We do this by completing the computer controls summary.

Application Controls

14.12 We aim to identify internal controls covering completeness, accuracy, validity and maintenance of accounting information which ensure that:

(a) all items which should be entered on to the computer are input and accepted once only;

(b) only valid transactions are processed;

(c) all items are entered accurately;

(d) exceptions are investigated where appropriate and rejections are corrected and resubmitted;

(e) all accepted items completely and accurately update the appropriate master-files;

(f) data held on masterfiles, both transaction and reference, remains up to date and is not subject to erroneous or unauthorised amendment; and

(g) any procedures initiated by the computer, for example, the automatic charging of interest or the production of an aged debtor list, are properly carried out.

General Controls

14.13   When seeking to rely on the computer system, we carry out a review of general controls. Good general controls contribute to the effectiveness and efficiency of the client's data-processing function. In the worst case, an absence or breakdown of general controls may, for example, result in a 'going concern' problem where there is the lack of an effective disaster recovery plan. Whilst their absence or breakdown will usually not have such an effect we will usually seek to advise our clients where improvements may be made. In addition, where we are evaluating application controls it is necessary to perform a thorough review of the general controls which underlie them.

Assessment of Risk

14.14   The information obtained above provides us with a basis to assess whether computer processing results in a higher than normal risk of error. The major areas of risk resulting from the use of computers may be summarised as follows:
(a) loss of audit trail because the computer is being relied upon to process transactions without any independent confirmation that it is doing so correctly;
(b) over reliance on computer controls, for example, on the completeness of exception reports;
(c) lack of appropriate controls over applications;
(d) lack of appropriate general controls, for example, controls to prevent the wrong data files being used or lack of adequate back-up facility in the event of computer failure or damage to the computerised records.

14.15   As with any assessment of risk we should not consider these factors in isolation. Compensating factors outside the computer system may offset an apparent risk, for example, manual control procedures may compensate for weaknesses in the computer system.

Reliance on Internal Controls

14.16   If our assessment leads us to conclude that there is normal risk, we may choose to rely on the key controls which we have identified to reduce detailed substantive testing. As with a manual system this decision depends on whether:
(a) key controls have been identified;
(b) there is evidence that the controls are applied;
(c) it is cost effective to rely on controls as opposed to performing full substantive testing.

Placing Reliance on General Controls

14.17 Where we are relying on application controls to reduce substantive tests we may have to place reliance on general controls which underlie them. In this case we must consider whether it will be cost effective to evaluate and test them. In practice such a review should be carried out by computer audit specialists who would also be responsible for the design and performance of the compliance tests. Because such a review requires special expertise it is unlikely to be cost effective to test general controls except for clients with highly computerised systems.

Design of Substantive and Compliance Tests

14.18 When designing substantive and compliance tests for computer systems there are several factors to bear in mind:
(a) the extent to which the use of Computer Assisted Audit Techniques (CAATs) is possible;
(b) the need to design tests to ensure that the computer has operated properly when carrying out computer-based control procedures;
(c) the way that the consistent operation of the computer system allows us to modify our tests and reduce our samples.

14.19 The main type of CAAT is an audit enquiry package (see **7.41**). We use these to carry out substantive tests, compliance tests and analytical review procedures including:
(a) reperforming calculations and casts, such as payroll calculations, calculations of royalties payable, casts of debtor balances etc;
(b) selecting samples. Random samples for use in error rate and monetary unit sampling may be selected; alternatively, the population may be divided into sections and random samples selected from each. It is also possible to check the population, while extracting the sample, for unusual conditions, such as duplicated items;
(c) testing items for certain conditions and printing out exceptions. For example, listings of debtors older than a specified period, employees with exceptionally high gross or net pay, customers exceeding credit limits, stock items with no or very small movements may be produced;
(d) comparing files at two points in time to detect records that have been added or deleted so that we can examine the reasons and authority for these. This could be used, for example, to ensure the correct treatment of starters and leavers on the payroll; and
(e) creating information not otherwise available from or reported by the client's system.
We may use these techniques whether or not we choose to rely on controls.

14.20   During the course of our audit we may rely upon computer-produced information as part of our normal procedures and we must take care to ensure that the computer has operated properly when producing it. This may be achieved by using CAATs or manual tests.

14.21   Unlike a manual system, a computer system can be relied upon to process similar items identically. This means that given no change in surrounding circumstances much smaller samples may be used when testing procedures which are carried out by the computer. For example, if the control environment is good when testing sales pricing, instead of using substantive procedures we may obtain the same level of assurance in less time by:
(a) documenting and testing controls over standing data (which may also give assurance in other areas, for example, turnover);
(b) testing that standing data includes correct prices; and
(c) testing that a small number of items have been priced correctly.

14.22   The number of items to be tested will vary depending on the general control environment and in particular whether more than one copy of a program has been used, during the period under review, to process particular transactions. If we test transactions processed by one copy it will not give us any assurance that transactions processed using another copy will have been recorded correctly. For example, where standing data is maintained on a hard disc in the computer, the sample can be reduced to a minimum. If standing data is on 'floppy discs' the sample will need to cover a spread of items throughout the period to gain assurance that the transactions have been processed against the correct standing data.

Differing Approaches for Simple or Complex Systems

14.23   The effect of computers on the audit approach will vary depending upon the complexity of the system and the control environment. In general, however, the following apply:

On simpler systems it is often sufficient to record the system, assess computer controls as part of our risk assessment and use a substantive (round the computer) approach to testing;

On more complex systems:
(a) we may, in addition, need to perform an extensive review of application controls and general controls;
(b) there are more likely to be controls upon which it is cost effective to rely to reduce our substantive testing;

(c) relying upon computer controls may be the only cost–effective way to achieve the necessary audit assurance; and

(d) the use of CAATs is more likely to be efficient.

Part B Techniques

15   Recording systems

This chapter explains the methods we use to record accounting systems.

15.01   Before any audit tests can be designed, it is necessary to understand the accounting records kept and their format and the way in which items are processed through the accounting system. This is necessary whether or not internal controls are likely to be relied upon since, without this knowledge, we are unable to decide upon the most efficient way of carrying out the audit or appropriate audit tests. So, for example, unless we know the source from which sales invoices are prepared, the way in which goods received are recorded or how the wages are made up, we are unable to design appropriate audit tests. We are also unable to tell whether all transactions and balances have been captured in the accounting records.

15.02   With existing clients it is necessary only to update the record of the systems on the permanent file. For a new client, or client whose systems have changed substantially, unless the company has prepared or is willing to prepare a suitable record, we need to ascertain and prepare our own record of the system.

15.03   We use two main methods of recording systems — flowcharts and narrative notes. Flowcharts are the best way of recording any system which involves the movement of documents from one person to another. They are vital where we hope to rely on any controls in the system. Narrative notes are preferable for very simple systems where all the paperwork is handled by one person. They are also helpful to amplify particular procedures on flowcharts.

15.04   Flowcharts have a number of advantages over narrative notes. They are easy to follow — it is usually clear what happens to each document and each copy of it; omissions are usually obvious, and they assist in identifying key controls. Flowcharts are easy to amend for changes in the system and they help to ensure that all parts of the system are recorded. With practice, they are quick to draw. In narrative notes it is easy to leave out a document completely or not explain what happens to it. It is strongly recommended that flowcharts be used wherever possible.

Example 17

J Stephens Ltd	Prepared by:	ABC
Accounts to 30 June 1990	Date started:	17.5.90
Sales walk-through test	Date finished:	17.5.90

Customer order

date:	5.4.90
no:	12345
goods description:	product x
quantity:	3 boxes
agreed price:	£15

Despatch note

date:	4.4.90
no:	23456
Goods agreed to order:	✓
Quantity agreed to order:	✓
Evidence of check by gate staff:	✓

Invoice

date:	4.4.90
no:	34567
Goods agreed to order and despatch note:	✓
Quantity agreed to order and despatch note:	✓
Price agreed to price on order:	✓

Checked

Invoice correctly entered in:	
SDB:	✓
S/L:	✓

Conclusion

The system is correctly recorded on the flowchart.

15.05 Whatever method of recording the system is used its accuracy must be confirmed. This is done by means of a 'walk-through test', which consists of following one transaction right through the system from start to finish. Any 'error' indicates that the system has not been recorded correctly and this must be put right before any audit tests are designed. It is also usually a good idea to agree flowcharts with the client. The walk-through test and the client's confirmation of the system should be documented on the current working paper file (see *Example 17* for an example of the documentation of a walk-through test).

Flowcharting

15.06   There are three methods of flowcharting which may be used:
(a) document flowcharts;
(b) information flowcharts; and
(c) overview schematic flowcharts for computer systems.

15.07   Document flowcharts are the most commonly used because they are easy to prepare. All documents are followed through from source to destination and all operations and controls are shown. Hence, they may contain more information than we need but there is little risk that important facts have been missed.

15.08   Information flowcharts are prepared 'back to front', that is starting with the entry in the general ledger and working back to the actual transactions. They concentrate on the important information flows and ignore any unimportant documents or copies of documents. Hence, they are much more compact than document flowcharts. Information flowcharts help in identifying key controls. They are simple to understand and review but their main drawback is the skill and experience needed to draw them. Information flowcharts of this sort are not dealt with in this *Guide*.

15.09   A schematic overview flowchart is often used to record a computerised system in those cases where we are not planning to rely on controls. It gives a one-page overview of the system and provides a basis for the design of tests (see **15.34** below).

Preparing a Document Flowchart

15.10   A document flowchart records a system by showing the progress of documents through all stages of processing. Every document or copy of it which is shown on the chart must come from somewhere and go to somewhere.

15.11   It is easy to draw a flowchart mechanically, without thinking about the strengths and weaknesses of the system being recorded. However, such an approach greatly reduces its value. When drawing a chart, we should always be conscious of the controls we expect to see at each point and ask ourselves 'are important controls missing?' or 'are unnecessary controls present?'.

15.12   To prepare a flowchart use:
(a) a flowcharting template to ensure the symbols are neatly drawn;
(b) a sharp pencil, rather than a pen, to facilitate corrections, and alterations; and
(c) A3 paper.

15.13   Separate columns are used for:
(a) the narrative;
(b) the operation number; and
(c) each individual or department that performs a check or operation on a document. This emphasises the division of responsibilities which is a part of the system of internal control. Wherever possible, these columns should be in the order in which operations or checks take place. This simplifies the chart, but some backtracking is unavoidable in many complex systems.

Example 18

A B Wilkes Ltd

		Prepared by:	ABC
		Date started:	20.8.90
		Date completed:	20.8.90

Sales system flowchart

Narrative	Operation number	Sales Mr Smith	Warehouse Mr Green

It may sometimes be necessary to record the work of individual members of a department in separate columns if they are carrying out separate operations or controls.

15.14   All narrative is written in the left-hand column; we do not write on the chart itself. The narrative should be written opposite the operation or check to which it relates. It should comprise a brief explanation of each operation or check and give the name of the person who performs it (unless this is obvious from the chart). If it is necessary to give a lengthy explanation, the flowchart is almost certainly inadequate or faulty in some respect (perhaps we have combined several operations or checks).

15.15 Each operation or check should be numbered and the number entered in the operation number column. Again, we do not write on the flowchart itself. The numbering will prove helpful for cross referencing; for example, we can give the number of a control when we refer to it in the working papers.

15.16 All symbols used on flowcharts should be explained in a key unless they are both standard and obvious from the flowchart itself. The standard symbols used in the firm are:

Document

3-part document

Book of account

Operation

Check

File

Page connector

'Ghost' – document brought forward from another page

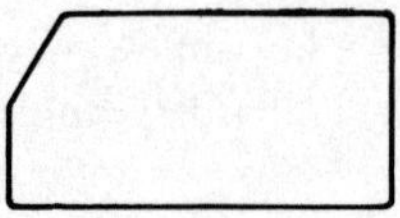

Punched card

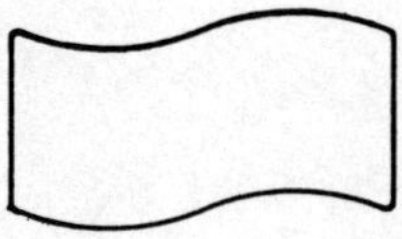

Paper tape

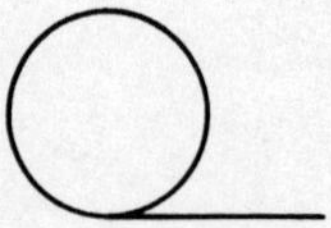

Magnetic tape

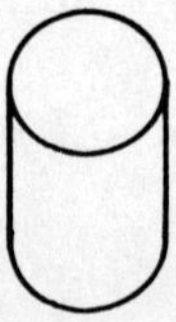

Magnetic disc

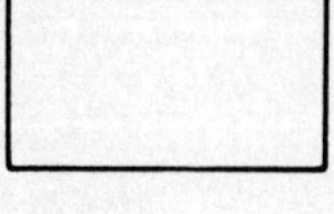

Computer process

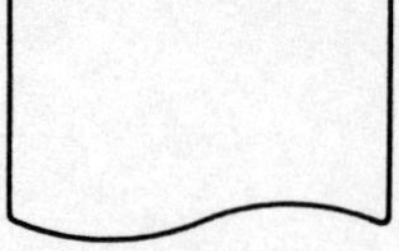

Print-out

On-line transmission

Each symbol must be labelled to show exactly what it is. If initials or abbreviations are used, a key must be provided.

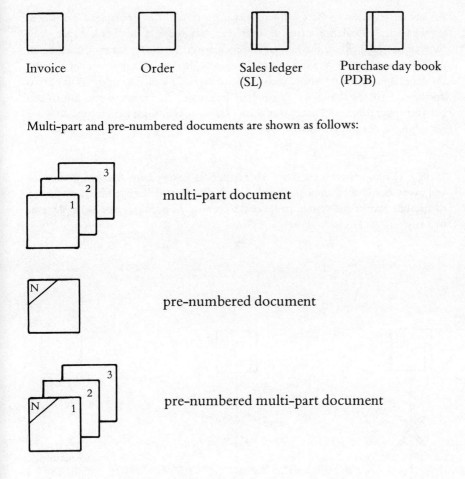

| Invoice | Order | Sales ledger (SL) | Purchase day book (PDB) |

Multi-part and pre-numbered documents are shown as follows:

multi-part document

pre-numbered document

pre-numbered multi-part document

15.17 Different symbols are used to record an operation and a check:

operation   check

An operation occurs where information is processed. For example, a document is prepared, a calculation made or an invoice entered in a day book. Operations show what happens to the accounts information. A check, on the other hand, does not involve the creation of anything new. It is an accounting control over the processing of information, such as a sequence check or the comparison of two documents to see that they agree. It is important to maintain the distinction between operations and checks. It is checks, not operations, that we are looking for when we seek key controls.

15.18   The flowchart must show what happens to every copy of every document and every book of account recorded. Eventually they are either filed, transferred to another part of the system or leave the company's premises (for example, sent to a customer). They are shown as follows:

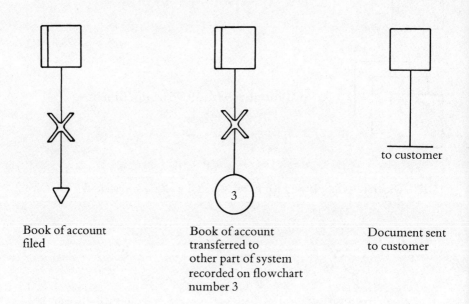

Book of account   Book of account   Document sent
filed   transferred to   to customer
                         other part of system
                         recorded on flowchart
                         number 3

Letters are usually added alongside the inverted triangle denoting a file, in order to explain the sequence of the documents (the letter is preceded by a 'T' if the filing is temporary).

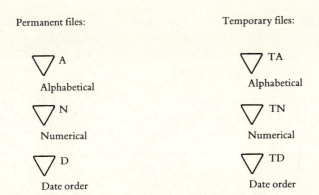

Permanent files:

▽ A

Alphabetical

▽ N

Numerical

▽ D

Date order

Temporary files:

▽ TA

Alphabetical

▽ TN

Numerical

▽ TD

Date order

15.19 The chart shows the flow of documents and describes any operations or checks which are carried out on them. Consequently, the chart begins with the first document in the system — this is often a purchase requisition or order, a sales order or clock card.

Example 19				
A B Wilkes Ltd			Prepared by: ABC Date started: 20.8.90 Date completed: 20.8.90	
Sales system flowchart				
Narrative	Op	Sales Mr Smith	Warehouse Mr Green	Invoices
Customer order received	1	Order		

15.20 The flow of a document is indicated by a continuous line. Vertical flow-lines show the passing of time, therefore, the direction of the chart is down the page. Horizontal flow-lines show the passing of documents from one area of responsibility to another. Lines flow usually to the right but sometimes, if a document backtracks, they flow to the left. Diagonal flow-lines are never used. Arrows may be added if necessary to aid clarity.

Example 20

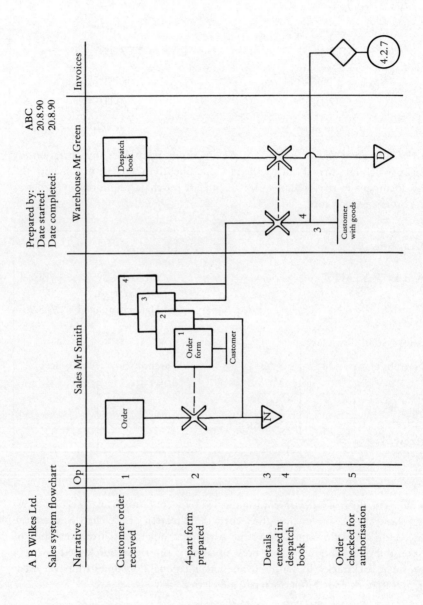

Example 20 — *contd.*
This chart shows that Mr Smith receives written customer orders from which he prepares a four part order form. The customer's order together with copy 2 of the order form set is filed in numerical order by Mr Smith. Copy 1 of the order form set is sent to the customer as an acknowledgement of his order. Copies 3 and 4 of the order form set are passed to Mr Green in the warehouse and the details are entered in the despatch book. Copy 3 of the order form set is then sent with the goods (the chart only shows the flow of documents — it does not show the movement of goods). The despatch book is retained in the warehouse — it is written up and maintained (filed) in date order. Copy 4 of the order form set is passed to the invoice department where it is checked for authorisation; the remainder of its processes are dealt with on the next flow-chart, reference 4.2.7.

15.21 Sometimes different documents travel together through a system. If they are attached to one another, for example a despatch note is attached to a copy order, then two flow-lines are joined. If, however, they are not attached, the lines are kept independent of one another.

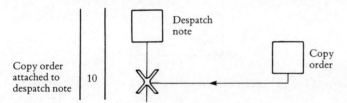

15.22 Books of account are permanent records in an accounting system. They usually remain within a particular department and do not 'flow' with the documents. They are introduced into the chart in the appropriate department and shown as remaining (being filed) there.

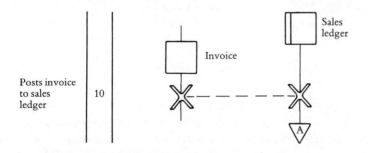

15.23 Sometimes systems allow for alternative procedures. For example, export and home sales invoices may be dealt with identically for much of the system but separately for, say, credit checks. One of two methods can be used:
(a) where the alternative is simple, it can be dealt with by narrative notes; or

(b) where the alternative is more complicated, it is dealt with in a subsidiary
flowchart or as a loop.

A similar problem arises on 'checks' where items are found to be incorrect. If
they are corrected immediately that fact can be referred to in the narrative. If
not, an error procedure can be dealt with by a more detailed narrative note, by
a subsidiary flowchart or by a loop.

15.24   Where a document is brought forward from one chart to another (or
sometimes from one column to another), it is good practice to re-draw it. This
is done by using a 'ghost' document symbol which is drawn in dotted lines instead
of continuous lines.

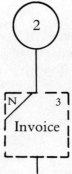

Copy 3 of invoice set brought forward from flowchart 2

15.25   Where two document lines cross, the 'hump-bridge' symbol is used to
avoid confusion.

document flow-lines

15.26   A broken line (which must be horizontal and never vertical) is used to
indicate the flow of information. Some common examples are the preparation of
one document from the information contained on another, the posting of a ledger
and the checking of one document with another. Wherever possible, the flow of
information is from left to right.

In the above example, information on one document is checked against another —
hence information 'flows' from one document to the other.

15.27   Where a document is prepared from another it is shown in parallel to the
flow-line of the document from which it is prepared. Each document has a
separate flow-line.

15.28   Finally, remember that all symbols are placed on vertical flow-lines.
Operations are not usually carried out on a document while it is being transferred
from one person or department to another.

15.29   Computer systems often pose a problem in flowcharting, particularly if
we are to avoid a 'black box' approach. Computer application controls should
be recorded on the flowchart in the same way as manual processing controls. We
should look for controls over data input to and output from the computer,
controls over the processing of data and controls over the maintenance of files.
Where an operation is performed by the computer, the narrative description
should include details of any controls internal to the computer.

15.30   Computer systems involve additional types of records and processes.
Additional symbols are used to depict these.

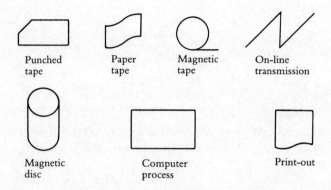

15.31 Examples of complete flowcharts are shown in:
(a) *Example 21* — Machine Parts Ltd; and
(b) *Example 22* — Micros Ltd.

Example 21

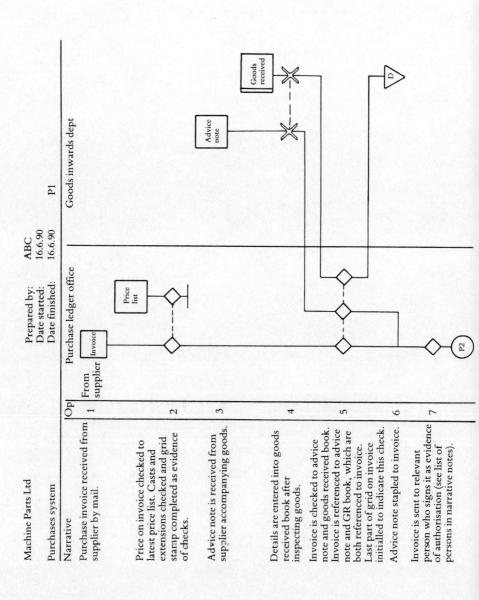

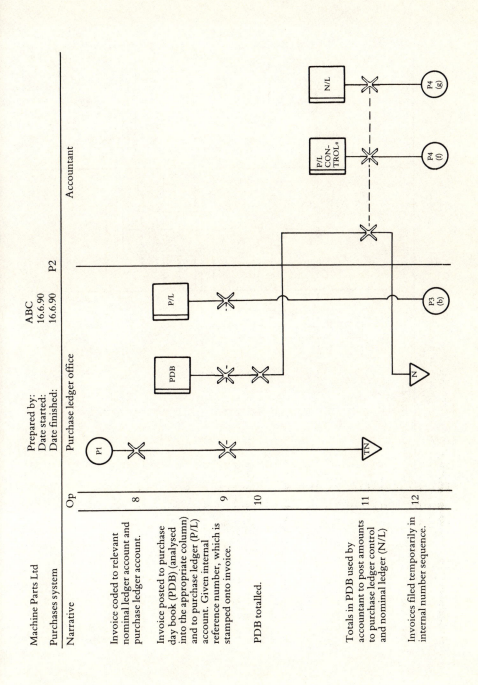

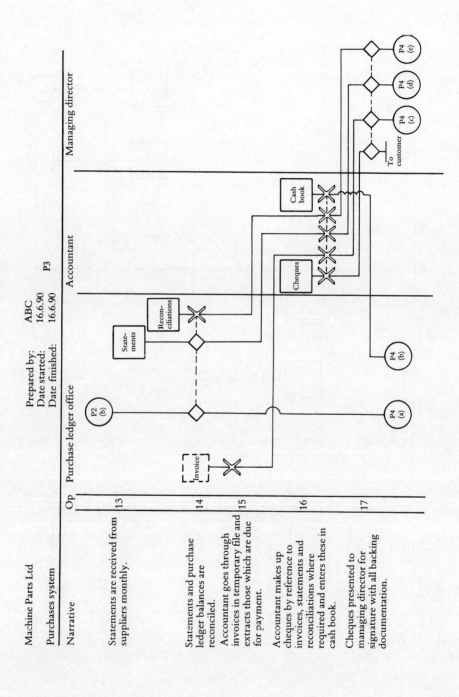

Machine Parts Ltd

Purchases system

Prepared by: ABC
Date started: 16.6.90
Date finished: 16.6.90   P3

Op	Purchase ledger office	Accountant	Managing director

Narrative

13 Statements are received from suppliers monthly.

14 Statements and purchase ledger balances are reconciled.

15 Accountant goes through invoices in temporary file and extracts those which are due for payment.

16 Accountant makes up cheques by reference to invoices, statements and reconciliations where required and enters these in cash book.

17 Cheques presented to managing director for signature with all backing documentation.

Invoice

Statements

Reconciliations

Cheques

Cash book

P2 (b)

P4 (a)

P4 (b)

P4 (c)

P4 (d)

P4 (e)

To customer

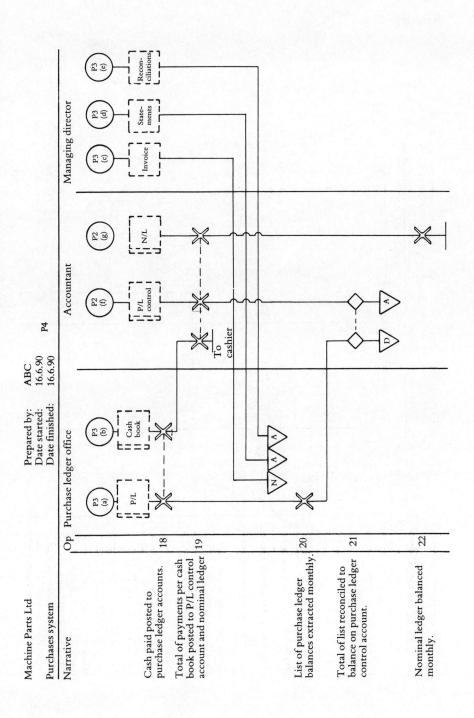

Example 22

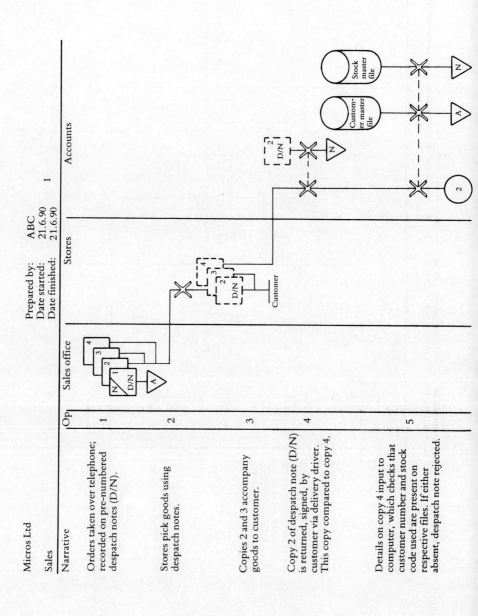

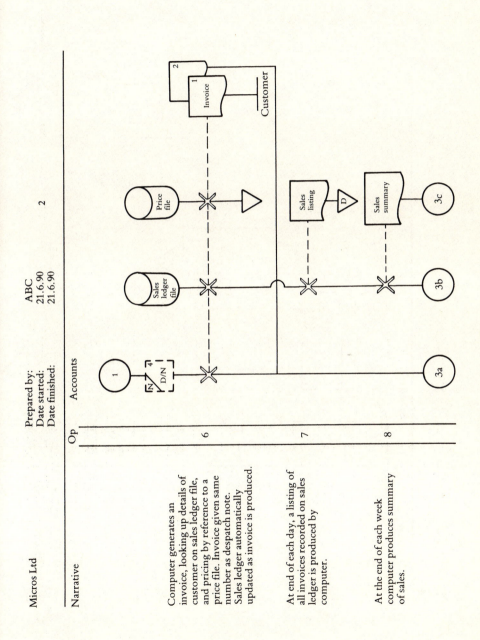

Micros Ltd

Prepared by: ABC
Date started: 21.6.90
Date finished: 21.6.90   2

Narrative

Op   Accounts   Sales ledger file   Price file   Customer

6   Computer generates an invoice, looking up details of customer on sales ledger file, and pricing by reference to a price file. Invoice given same number as despatch note. Sales ledger automatically updated as invoice is produced.

7   At end of each day, a listing of all invoices recorded on sales ledger is produced by computer.

8   At the end of each week computer produces summary of sales.

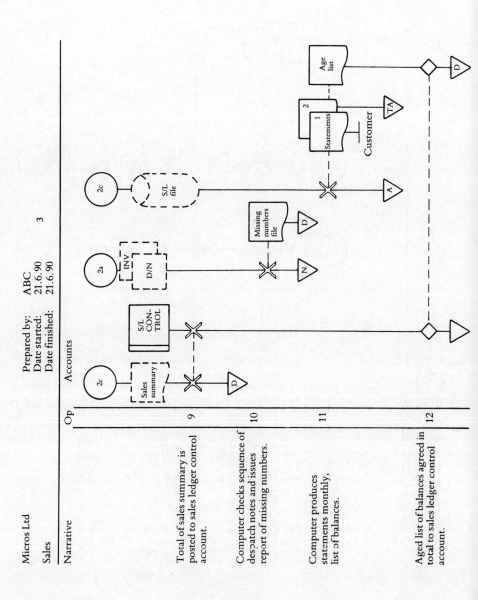

Micros Ltd

Sales

Prepared by: ABC

Date started: 21.6.90

Date finished: 21.6.90   3

Op	Narrative
9	Total of sales summary is posted to sales ledger control account.
10	Computer checks sequence of despatch notes and issues report of missing numbers.
11	Computer produces statements monthly, list of balances.
12	Aged list of balances agreed in total to sales ledger control account.

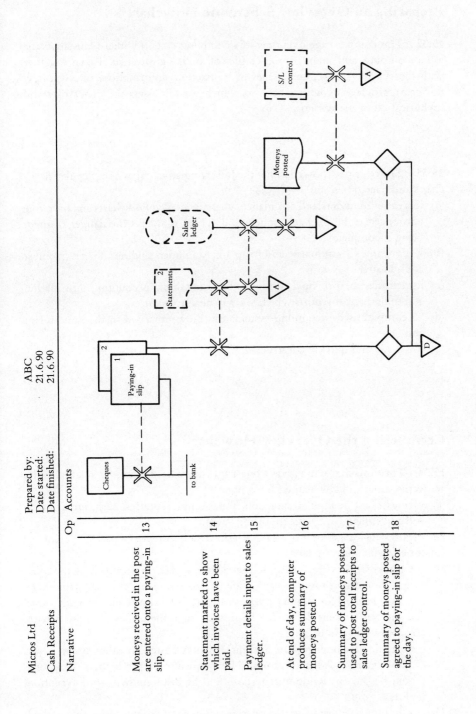

Micros Ltd   Prepared by: ABC
Cash Receipts   Date started: 21.6.90
    Date finished: 21.6.90

Narrative	Op	Accounts
Moneys received in the post are entered onto a paying-in slip.	13	
Statement marked to show which invoices have been paid.	14	
Payment details input to sales ledger.	15	
At end of day, computer produces summary of moneys posted.	16	
Summary of moneys posted used to post total receipts to sales ledger control.	17	
Summary of moneys posted agreed to paying-in slip for the day.	18	

Preparing an Overview Schematic Flowchart

15.32   This is a one-page overview of a computer system which summarises the inputs, outputs, and main computer files of audit significance. Taken together with the types, volumes and values of transactions information, the overview flowchart provides us with a basis on which we can assess the materiality and sophistication of the systems.

15.33   The overview flowchart has the following advantages over detailed flowcharts and narrative notes:
(a) it is easier to understand at a glance whereas detailed flowcharts and narrative notes need to be read and understood. There is always the danger of them being incomplete;
(b) it is possible to summarise and form a broad understanding of even the most complicated of systems;
(c) it identifies the principal computer files containing accounting information and the principal reports which we will need to audit;
(d) all computerised accounting systems can be summarised in the same form; and
(e) it is easily and quickly constructed.

Completing the Overview Flowchart

15.34   The flowchart is drawn as a one-page summary flowing from left to right across the page, and covers the following:
(a) various types of input transaction, for example invoices, cash, credit notes and adjustments in a basic invoicing system;
(b) the principal stages of processing (*not* the detail) shown as separate operations, for example, edit, update;
(c) the principal files; for example the reference data masterfile and the sales ledger should be shown at each stage of processing. At the edit stage these files may be used for enquiry purposes by the programs to check credit limits and the outstanding debts. At the update stage these files are posted with accepted transactions; and
(d) output; this includes reports and information posted to other systems, for example general ledger postings. The frequency of production of reports should be shown. Routine reports should be distinguished from exception reports.
The symbols used in producing an overview flowchart are the same as those used in other flowcharts. They are illustrated in paragraph **15.30**.

15.35 The first example in Appendix 9 is an overview flowchart of a purchase ledger where details of invoices, cash, adjustments and reference data are held. Input is by VDU terminals from the Accounts Department. The reference data includes supplier names and addresses and payment terms. Transaction data comprises open items (i.e. transactions still active, for example, those currently making up the balance on the purchase ledger) stored on a purchase ledger. Cash is allocated to specific invoices on input and invoices are then removed from 'outstanding' status.

15.36 The example also shows an edit stage. Reasonableness checks and confirmation of batch totals are carried out and the day books (more commonly called edit/transaction listings) are produced.

15.37 Those items completely rejected at this stage must be re-input. Accepted items are held on a 'holding' file awaiting the main update run (often carried out overnight). This is shown on the flow-line as a temporary file awaiting release to update the masterfiles. It is at the update stage that the purchase ledger and relevant masterfiles are actually posted.

15.38 The update process is shown as a separate step. There are some systems where masterfiles are updated immediately following edit and acceptance. In such cases the overview flowchart should show the edit and update as a one-stage process. Following update of the masterfiles various reports are produced. Some are not produced daily, for example the complete purchase ledger printout. Others are produced more frequently, for example the purchase ledger and nominal ledger update reports showing totals and amounts posted to masterfiles. The frequency of each should be noted on the flowchart.

Less Simple Systems

15.39 The overview flowchart need not be complicated, even if the system is relatively sophisticated. The more sophisticated a system is, the more checking the computer should be doing at the edit stage, for example, referring to stock records to check that sufficient quantity is in stock when an order is placed. The number of masterfiles to be updated and computer reports should also increase.

Narrative Notes

15.40   Like any written work, narrative notes should be accurate, brief and clear. For each system, they need to deal with:
(a) who does what;
(b) how it is done;
(c) what documents are used;
(d) where documents come from;
(e) where documents go to;
(f) what books and files are kept;
(g) where are they kept; and
(h) in what sequence are documents filed.
In only the simplest of systems is it likely that all of this can be done accurately and clearly. Furthermore, making changes to narrative notes is difficult (although they become easier if the notes are prepared and maintained on word processing systems). It is strongly advised, therefore, that narrative notes only be used where there is no or very little flow of documents and changes are unlikely.

15.41   Narrative notes can be used to support flowcharts. They can be used effectively to explain error procedures or uncomplicated alternatives to standard procedures. They may also be used to provide additional information on operations or checks — for example, narrative notes could be used to describe the sources used by a credit controller when carrying out credit-worthiness checks.

16 Some analytical review procedures

Chapter 4 explains the meaning and purpose of analytical review. This chapter discusses some of the procedures which may be used in reviewing the profit and loss account and balance sheet and suggests some client specific procedures. The procedures may be used while planning the audit, during the audit and at the final review stage.

Sales

16.01 The key figure in any profit and loss account is sales. Changes occur because:
(a) prices are increased or decreased;
(b) trade discounts, rebates etc are increased or decreased;
(c) volumes have changed;
(d) the mix of products has changed.
Explanations should be sought, reviewed and interpreted in these terms.

16.02 The revenue cycle ideas list includes some ideas on ratios and statistics which may be examined when reviewing or auditing the sales figure. Those which are most appropriate to the circumstances of the business should be chosen (often they are the same as used by management). As many companies judge their success by their ability to make sales, there may well be a detailed sales analysis available (even if there are no other management accounts), which can be used as the starting point of the review. It may already highlight volume and mix changes and, possibly, the effects of price changes.

16.03 The audit working papers should always include an explanation of the reasons for any changes in sales from one period to the next, from budget to actual, and from our expectations to actual.

Example 23

An increase in the sales by a chain of restaurants from £10,325,000 to £13,480,000 (30%) may be explained as follows:

(a) 15% increase in covers served;

(b) increase in average cover value from £8.60 to £9.77 (13.6%) due to a 5% increase in standard prices and an 8.2% increase as a result of introducing 'speciality dishes' at higher prices.

These reasons could be verified by:

(a) examining a sample of till rolls to identify the increase in covers served;

(b) agreeing the increase in prices to menus; and

(c) checking the introduction and prices of speciality dishes to menus for prices and a sample of till rolls to indicate approximate numbers of these dishes served.

Cost of Sales/Gross Profit

16.04   Depending on the nature of the business, cost of sales may comprise:

(a) the purchase price of goods bought for resale, adjusted for opening and closing stocks;

(b) the purchase price of raw materials, production wages and relevant manufacturing overheads (including depreciation), adjusted for opening and closing stocks and work in progress;

(c) wages and other costs involved in providing a service, adjusted for opening and closing work in progress; and

(d) the total costs, including materials, wages, overheads and depreciation of carrying out construction projects, adjusted for opening and closing work in progress.

16.05   Even within each of the above there may be substantial variations in approach. For example, one manufacturing company may have a standard costing system which is used to record all transactions and movements of raw materials, work in progress and finished goods. Another manufacturing company may not attempt to record transactions and movements in such detail; it may limit itself to charging all the costs to the profit and loss account and valuing stocks by reference to selling prices less a margin.

16.06   These wide variations in practice mean that it is essential to tailor our analytical review procedures (and our later audit tests) to meet the requirements of the business. The expenditure and stock cycle ideas lists suggest some procedures which may be used in appropriate circumstances.

16.07   One procedure which is almost always followed is to calculate gross profit or gross margin as a percentage of sales. It is calculated as follows:

$$\frac{\text{gross profit (margin)}}{\text{turnover}} \times 100\%$$

Even with this common and straightforward ratio, problems can arise from different accounting methods. Extreme care is needed if stocks are valued at selling price less a gross profit percentage — the percentages may be self-fulfilling. With a standard cost system, it may be better to use the standard margin rather than the actual gross margin if variances are recorded at a time other than that of the sale.

16.08   These considerations apart, variations in gross profit may result from such genuine reasons as:
(a) changes in sales mix;
(b) cost reductions or increases;
(c) a policy of price cutting, or absorbing increased raw material costs to increase or maintain market share; and
(d) changes in productivity.
Variations may also suggest errors — for example that sales and stock are overstated or liabilities understated.

16.09   A higher than expected ratio can also arise in times of rising prices. If a company is basing its selling prices on up-to-date costs, the gross profit may benefit from buying at lower prices. This means that the gross profit percentage falls if prices stop rising and increases if prices increase more rapidly.

Example 24

A company has a tight system of control over its pricing and is able to react quickly to cost increases. It aims to achieve a 25% gross profit on sales. It holds stocks of a particular product which it bought for £1.50 each. Immediately on learning of a cost increase to £1.80 each, it increases its selling prices, to maintain a 25% margin, to £2.40 (from £2.00). When it sells the items it held in stock and which it bought for £1.50, it earns a gross profit of 90p per unit or 37.5%.

16.10   The working papers should always include a quantified and verified explanation of movement in gross profit (even if the movement is small in percentage terms, it may have a substantial effect on net profits).

Overheads and Expenses

16.11   Actual overheads should be compared with our expectations based on our understanding of the business and any budgets, profit forecasts etc that are available, and previous years. Explanations should refer to:

(a) specific price changes, such as rent reviews, increases by gas and electricity companies, wage increases, etc. It is not sufficient to explain increases as 'inflation', since inflation affects different items in different ways; and

(b) volume changes which arise from specific causes, such as moving to new premises, changing levels of production, promotional campaigns for new products, and so on.

Example 25

An increase from £150,000 to £190,000 in the gas charges borne by a manufacturing company could be explained as arising from:

(a) a 25% increase half way through the year arising from the installation of new plant (£19,000);

(b) a price increase of 12% during the first month of the year (£21,000).

16.12   In reviewing overheads and expenses, we should not express all of them as a percentage of sales. Often there is no reason to expect any direct relationship between sales and the overheads and expenses. Only items such as cost of sales and salesmen's commission are likely to vary in the short term with sales and should be compared with them. Even things like advertising rarely have a relationship with sales (although management may well assess the success of its campaign by relating advertising expenditure to an increase in sales or market share). Expenses should be compared with items with which they are connected, for example interest charges should be compared with the bank overdraft (or other borrowing), depreciation with fixed assets, and so on.

16.13   A mistake which is easy to make with overheads and expenses is to produce detailed schedules setting out the component parts of the account balance without any attempt to explain the change or any variation in it. This analysis of profit and loss items may be required for some other purpose, such as the tax computations, in which case it should be limited to where it is strictly necessary. Instead of analyses of expenditure, the working papers should include explanations of the charge and of changes (or lack of changes).

Net Profit as a Percentage of Turnover

16.14   This is a commonly calculated percentage and is:

$$\frac{\text{net profit before tax}}{\text{turnover}} \times 100\%$$

The net profit percentage indicates the proportion of sales available to pay dividends or provide for growth in the business. Variations in the ratio may, for example, result from:

(a) any of the reasons for a change in gross profit; and

(b) any changes in the relationship of overheads and expenses to sales.

This percentage should, however, be viewed with extreme caution. In arriving at net profit, substantial sums have been charged for overheads and expenses which may have no short-term relationship with sales. Nevertheless, it is useful to calculate the ratio as a quick check that everything appears as expected in the light of our knowledge of any improvements in productivity, cost reduction programmes and so on. It may also be useful when making comparisons with other companies in similar businesses.

Debtors' Collection Period

16.15   This is:

$$\frac{\text{debtors}}{\text{average sales per day}}$$

Sales should exclude cash sales but include VAT (alternatively the VAT element of debtors should be deducted from debtors and compared with sales excluding VAT). Where the trade is seasonal, it may be better to work backwards from the period end accumulating sales for each day, week or month until the debtors' figure is reached.

16.16   Changes in the collection period may be genuine; for example, an increase may be caused by a lengthening of credit period to encourage sales. Alternatively they may suggest error — the overvaluation of debtors or an understatement of turnover. Changes may be genuine, but a sign of commercial and audit problems — for example, the period may have been extended because the business is having to give greater credit to make its sales targets in difficult times; this may mean we have to spend more time considering the possibility of bad debts.

Example 26

A business has debtors of £100,000 at the year end and sales of £450,000 for the year. Adjusting for VAT, debtors represent 70 calendar days' sales.

If, however, we know the business is seasonal and that the year end is at a low point in the year, we find it more helpful to work backwards from the year end:

	Sales including VAT £	Days
Month 12	20,000	31
Month 11	21,000	30
Month 10	16,000	31
Month 9	22,000	30
Month 8	45,000	31

On this basis debtors represent the last 136 calendar days' sales, which gives a different picture to that first obtained.

Example 27

A company has the following figures:

	1990 £	1989 £
Turnover (including VAT)	1,200	1,100
Trade debtors	171	108
Debtors' collection period (days)	52	36

The company has adequate controls over despatch and invoice procedures to ensure that despatches are invoiced and correctly recorded and the trade is not significantly seasonal.

The increase in debtors' collection period may reflect the lengthier credit taken by or given to customers. Alternatively, it may indicate that debtors are overstated. Possible causes are:
(a) goods despatched to bad credit risks and an underprovision for bad debts;
(b) breakdown in cash collection procedures;
(c) cash being received but not banked or credited to customers' accounts.

Only a knowledge of the company will enable us to narrow down the choice of possible causes and design appropriate tests.

Creditors' Payment Period

16.17 This is:

$$\frac{\text{trade creditors}}{\text{average purchases per day}}$$

Again, VAT must be treated consistently; in the accounts, creditors include VAT whereas purchases usually exclude VAT. Either purchases or creditors can be adjusted. A further problem with this ratio is deciding which purchases and, in particular, which overheads and expenses to include. Again, the aim should be consistency. Care is also needed to iron out the effects of any seasonal trade.

16.18 The creditors' payment period can be used to tell us whether trade creditors and purchases appear correctly stated. A decrease in the payment period may reflect an understatement of creditors (arising perhaps from the failure to record invoices) or an overstatement of purchases. In the same way as with debtors, the reasons may be genuine — the business could be paying more promptly in order to gain the benefit of lower prices or cash discounts. Conversely a rise in the creditors' payment period could indicate cash flow problems, the financing of the business being more dependent on late payments to creditors.

Stock Turnover

16.19 This is usually measured in terms of the number of days' worth of sales available in stock and is:

$$\frac{\text{average stocks}}{\text{cost of goods sold}} \times 365$$

Care is needed to ensure that distortions caused by seasonal business are eliminated. We should also ensure that 'cost of goods sold' includes the same costs as included in the stock valuation. In addition, it may be necessary to eliminate the effects of writing stocks down to net realisable value because this can distort the result.

16.20 A decrease in the number of days it takes stock to turnover may be a sign that:
(a) the business is understocked, and is running the risk of losing business;
(b) a switch in the sourcing of products (for example from frozen goods to fresh produce in a restaurant);
(c) management has successfully implemented a plan to reduce stock levels;
(d) turnover is understated (possibly a cut-off error at the balance sheet date);
(e) stock is undervalued in that quantities are understated or it is underpriced; or
(f) cost of goods includes costs which are not included in the cost of stocks.

An increase in the number of days it takes stock to turnover may indicate the opposite of any of the above. We must satisfy ourselves as to the right answer. If we receive and verify explanations early enough in our audit, we can take that fact into account in deciding the levels of our tests on stocks.

Current Ratio

16.21   This is:

$$\frac{\text{current assets}}{\text{current liabilities}}$$

where current assets are stock and work in progress, debtors, cash and cash investments and current liabilities are trade creditors for purchases, overheads and expenses and any creditors for capital expenditure, tax, dividends and interest payable within one year.

16.22   This ratio can reinforce the conclusions on debtors, creditors and stock ratios. For example, if a reduction in the debtors' ratio is attributed to faster settlement by customers, this should be confirmed by the current ratio which should not change — debtors have been converted into cash, both of which are included in the ratio. If the creditors' ratio has increased because the company is delaying payment, then this should be compensated for by an increase in cash balances or reduction in the overdraft.

16.23   Changes in the current ratio tend to indicate:
(a) increased stock and debtors financed by long-term funds (or conversely, a reduction in stock and debtors has been used to pay off loans);
(b) working capital balances used to finance fixed assets (or conversely, the disposal of fixed assets has increased the funds available for working capital);
(c) errors in the valuation of stock, debtors or creditors.
A high ratio may indicate an overvaluation of stocks or debtors (or an excessive level of stockholding) or that liabilities have been understated. A low ratio may indicate a shortage of working capital.

16.24   The liquidity ratio is a variant on the current ratio and is defined as:

$$\frac{\text{current assets less stocks}}{\text{current liabilities}}$$

This ratio concentrates on those assets which can be turned into cash quickly. A high ratio may indicate that liabilities can be met, whereas a low ratio may indicate liquidity, and hence going concern, problems. The cash inflows and outflows of a business should also be reviewed as these may give an early warning of trouble which may not be obvious from elsewhere in the accounts.

Quantities and Volumes

16.25 A review of the accounts should include a review of quantities and volumes of products sold, purchased etc, and not merely a review of monetary amounts. For example, if the monetary value of purchases and sales has remained reasonably constant from one year to another, we may initially conclude that the figures were reasonable. However, if we review the number of purchase invoices and find a significant increase, we would wish to explore the causes and consider the possible effects of a change in the pattern of purchases.

16.26 We can try to reconcile quantities sold and quantities purchased. We can also look at certain expense items, such as consumable stores or products and fuel, which can be expressed in quantity terms, and compare them with production or sales volumes (as appropriate).

> **Example 28**
>
> The value of considering volumes was demonstrated in a press report of a receivership of a large piggery in Ireland. A review of cost of sales indicated that the quantity of pig food consumed was excessive in comparison to the number of pigs being fattened. Further investigations showed that approximately 2,000 pigs not belonging to the company were being fattened in the piggery at the company's expense.

Ratios Specific to the Business

16.27 The above ratios are useful for many businesses. We should however always use the appropriate ratios for each business. We should find out what figures or ratios a competent managing director uses himself to control the business on a day to day basis.

16.28 In the hotel business, for example, management uses room occupancy percentage; this is the ratio of actual income from room letting to the maximum potential room sales figures. It is defined as:

$$\frac{\text{actual room income}}{\text{rate per room } (\pounds) \quad \times \quad \text{total number of rooms}}$$

A fall in the percentage could reflect a genuine shift by customers to cheaper rooms or a decline in the number of room sales. It may indicate audit problems in that all sales are not billed or recorded. Alternatively, it may be genuine but still warrant some attention; the front desk may be selling the cheaper rooms in preference to the more expensive ones and so costing the business revenue; this should be reported to management quickly.

16.29   In a transport company, the repairs and renewals per vehicle may be an important ratio. Where the level is high or rising, it may indicate that the fleet is old and we may need to direct special audit effort at ensuring the depreciation charge is adequate. If the business is suffering from cash flow problems and repairing vehicles rather than renewing them, we may have to question the validity of the going concern basis. Another important statistic in such a business is the amount of fuel consumed in relation to the mileage driven. Excessive fuel consumption may reflect under-recorded income, 'cheating' by drivers, old vehicles or inefficient route planning.

16.30   In retailing, an important measure is the sales per square meter of shop space. Poor figures (possibly coupled with poor gross margins) may indicate that sales are being under-recorded. It could also reflect that the shop is in a bad position with a sales mix biased towards the items with low profitability. As auditors, we should satisfy ourselves on the right answer — and record the results of our enquiries in our working papers.

17 Error rate sampling

This chapter explains the firm's approach to error rate sampling and suggests when and how we should use it.

17.01 Error rate sampling (ERS) is a technique which is used to provide us with information about the number of errors in a population. For example, it can be used to tell us something about the number of occasions sales invoices are not being raised correctly from despatch notes. It contrasts with monetary unit sampling (MUS) (Chapter 18) from which we can glean information on the value of errors in a population — for example, that (with certain levels of assurance) debtors are not in error by more than £50,000.

17.02 As the primary purpose of our audit work is to express an opinion on the accounts, which are expressed in money terms, we should wherever possible use MUS. There are, however, many occasions when it is not possible. In a test to check for the understatement of sales, we usually cannot select a monetary unit sample of despatch notes because they are not evaluated. On some tests for the overstatement of expenditure, MUS is difficult; it may be a laborious and time consuming exercise to select such a sample.

17.03 In those cases where MUS is not possible, our approach is to use ERS to reach a conclusion on the number of errors in the population. We do this for compliance tests and for some substantive tests of transactions. If the number of errors is within an acceptable level, we accept this as evidence that the value of errors is not material. We receive additional assurances about this from our analytical review procedures and other related tests — for example our review of gross margins, sales and stocks reinforces our conclusion that all despatches are being invoiced. As soon as we discover that the error rate is unacceptable (and it may be before the scheduled end of our test), we stop the test and switch our emphasis to try and find the extent of any material monetary error. This may involve the company carrying out detailed checks or it may require us to adopt different procedures.

17.04 The ERS we use is based on a form of attribute sampling called 'discovery sampling'. This recognises that the error rates found in accounting populations are usually low. It also minimises sample sizes but, as a consequence, a satisfactory result is only achieved if no errors occur in the sample. Where, however, we discover only 1 or 2 errors, we check that they are not 'isolated' before we reject the sample and, hence, the population.

17.05 Ideally we should base our sampling methods and evaluation on what statisticians call the 'hypergeometric distribution' which is suitable for cases of sampling without replacement from a finite population. Unfortunately, the formulae based on the hypergeometric distribution are difficult to use for large samples and population sizes. Hence our methods are based on the 'poisson distribution' which is a good approximation as long as the population is reasonably large (greater than 5,000 items) and free from error and the sample size is reasonably large but not a significant proportion of the population.

17.06 The 'poisson distribution' makes the use of R-factors a very convenient method of determining sample sizes (R-factors are described in Chapter 9) because:

$$n = \frac{R}{P}$$

where n is the sample size, R the R factor and P the population error rate or precision expressed as a decimal.

Example 29

If we want all our audit assurance on the understatement of sales from one test (so that the required R-factor is 3) and the acceptable error rate is 2%, the sample size is calculated as follows:

$$n = \frac{R}{P} = \frac{3}{0.02} = 150$$

If we test 150 items and find no errors, we conclude that the error rate did not exceed 2% (at a confidence level of 95%). If we find an error we check to see whether or not it is isolated and, if it is not, we have to reject the conclusion.

Precision

17.07 The aim of all audit work is to establish that material error does not exist in the accounts. In ERS, material error is referred to as 'precision' (or sometimes as 'maximum potential error rate' [MPER]). For substantive testing, precision is the relationship between the preliminary estimate of materiality for the accounts as a whole and the value of the population to be tested. For the purposes of the sample size formula in paragraph **17.06**, precision needs to be expressed as a decimal.

Example 30

If the preliminary estimate of materiality is £20,000 and we are testing sales of £1,000,000, precision is:

$$\frac{20,000}{1,000,000} \times 100 = 2\% \text{ of sales}$$

or 0.02 as a decimal.

17.08   For all ERS for substantive tests, except where the test is likely to provide the only assurance on the area under review (which is extremely unlikely), the materiality level used in the calculation of precision should not be smaller than 3% of sales.

Example 31

A company's profit and loss account contains the following amounts:

	£	£
Sales		100,000
Cost of sales	40,000	
Wages	20,000	
Overheads	30,000	
		90,000
Profit before tax		10,000

All the items are to be tested by means of ERS. Precision is calculated by dividing £3,000 (3% of sales) by the population value. So precision and sample sizes (at an R-factor of 3) would be:

	Precision	Sample size
Sales	0.03	100
Cost of sales	0.075	40
Wages	0.15	20
Overheads	0.1	30

Hence for substantive tests of transactions, the sample size is normally limited to a maximum of 100 for sales. The sample size for other transaction tests will depend on the size of the population, relative to sales, again with an overall restriction of 100.

17.09   The factors which have been taken into account in deciding upon this restriction, include the fact that if there are significant errors in the population, they should already have been highlighted by other audit procedures by the time the restricted sample size is tested. We have also recognised that accounting errors are rarely 100% errors (for example, despatches may be invoiced wrongly — but it is rare for them not to be invoiced at all). Finally, it is often the case that there is a better and more cost-effective way of achieving the same level of assurance about a population than checking a large sample using error rate techniques.

17.10   For compliance tests only, precision is further restricted to 5% for significant controls and 10% for less significant controls. In normal circumstances given an R-factor of 3, the sample size for a compliance test should never be more than 60 and should in many cases only be 30.

17.11   Where there is a higher than normal risk of error for a particular transaction test, it is unlikely that R-factor reductions for analytical review and internal controls are possible. Furthermore, it may not be reasonable to restrict the sample size as suggested in paragraph **17.08**. We should consider whether to calculate the sample size on the same basis as for tests of balances, that is by calculating precision by reference to the relationship between materiality and the population value.

Small Populations

17.12   Before using any sample size, it must be checked for reasonableness. If it is more than 20% of the number of items in the population, it is probably unnecessarily large. This is only likely to happen where the population is small, for example where there are only 300 transactions in that cycle in the year.

Sample Selection

17.13   The sample for ERS must be selected randomly, or using a method which is as near to being random as is possible in the circumstances. The objective is to ensure, as far as possible, that every item in the population has an equal chance of being selected.

17.14   A truly random sample is selected by taking a series of random numbers (which then may be sorted into ascending numerical order to simplify selection). This method may be costly, although it may be used where the random numbers can be easily generated and sorted by computer or where a very small sample is to be selected.

17.15   A more common method of selection is systematic sampling with a random start. The number of items in the population is divided by the sample size to give the sampling interval. A random number is chosen between 0 and the sampling interval (inclusive). The first item to be selected is based on the random number; the second and subsequent items are selected by repeatedly adding the sampling interval.

Example 32

We need to select 43 despatch notes from a population numbered 1068 to 9052. The sampling interval is:

$$\frac{9052 - 1068}{43} = 185 \text{ (rounded down)}$$

We select a random number between 0 and 185 (inclusive) — say 77. The first invoice we select is number 1145 (that is 1068 plus 77). The next invoice is 1330 (1145 + 185) and the next 1515 (1330 + 185) and so on.

This method must be used with care if the population is arranged in a repeating pattern. For example, a sample of 30 items from the first 30 weeks' wages records might pick the same employee every week. If this situation is likely to arise, one of the other selection methods must be used.

17.16   A third method of selection requires random numbers but does not need the random numbers to be sorted into order. The sampling interval is calculated as in systematic sampling. Random numbers are then generated between 0 and twice the sampling interval. The first random number gives the first selection point, the second random number is added to the first to give the next selection point, the third is added to the sum of the first two to give the next selection point and so on. This method can be almost as quick as systematic sampling and does not suffer from the same drawback where the population is arranged in a repeating pattern.

Example 33

Using the same data as in *Example 32*, we select a random number between 0 and 370 (that is, twice 185) — say 22. The first invoice selected is 1090 (that is 1068 + 22). We then select another random number between 0 and 370 — say 225 — and the next selection is 1315 (1090 + 225). We repeat the process again — the random number is 247 — the next selection is 1562 and so on.

Random Numbers

17.17   Random numbers can be obtained from a computer program or a suitable pocket calculator; it is then a simple matter to select any number of random numbers over any given range. If neither of these methods is practicable, then random number tables may be used. To use such tables properly, start at an arbitrary point in the table (not necessarily at the start of a page) and, if more than one number is required, work through the table in an arbitrary direction (for example, work up a column, work diagonally down the table etc.). This avoids using the same 'random' numbers for every test.

17.18   Alternatively, if none of these methods is possible and only one random number has to be selected, the last three or four digits of a bank note may be used, or the last three or four digits of the square root of an arbitrary number put into a calculator. For example, the square root of 2.5146534 is 1.5857659. The random number is 7659.

Haphazard Selection

17.19   A fourth method of selection, 'haphazard selection', may be used if none of the other methods is possible. This method involves, for example, picking invoices out of a loose binder or selecting stock items from the warehouse floor as randomly as possible. The method has two drawbacks. First, it is not possible to be truly random and some bias inevitably gets into the sample. Secondly, unlike the other methods of selection, it does not ensure the completeness of the population (see *Example 34*).

Example 34

A sample is to be selected from despatch notes numbered 4003 to 5112. A random sample will select, say, items 4007, 4009, 4093 etc. If any of these invoices cannot be found in the invoice file, then action will be taken to investigate the missing invoices. If, instead, a haphazard sample is selected by picking the invoices out of the files, any invoices which are missing from the files cannot be selected. Thus a separate sequence test must be done to ensure there are no missing invoices. For these reasons, great care should be exercised in extracting a haphazard sample and interpreting the results.

Sample Results

17.20   Having selected the sample and carried out the test, we can express the results in statistical terms — for example that we are 95% confident that error rates do not exceed 3%. Where the test has been carried out and no errors have been found, the objective of the test has been met. We should express our conclusion not simply in statistical terms, but also in audit terms — that, for example, we are satisfied that despatches are being invoiced. In addition, where ERS is used for compliance tests, the conclusion should state the effect on the appropriate substantive test (presumably that the sample size can be reduced).

17.21   Where the test has been carried out and errors have been found, we have a choice of:
(a) abandoning the test (and reverting to full substantive testing, in the case of a compliance test);
(b) proving that the errors are isolated and that the population error rate is at an acceptable level; or
(c) using alternative audit procedures.

17.22   This decision process is exactly the same as if we were using non-statistical sampling methods. The first step we usually take is to investigate the errors and find out whether there is anything special about them. Did they arise when the person who usually does the job was on holiday or ill? Were the transactions unusual in some way which meant that the laid-down procedures could not cope? We may find that the problems only arose at certain times or on certain types of transactions and we may be able to conclude that material error did not arise at other times or on 'usual' transactions.

17.23   If we find many errors — particularly early in the test — we do not carry on to the end of the sample and then conclude that the error rate is unsatisfactory.

Instead, as soon as we realise that the error rate is going to be unacceptable, we stop the test and decide the best way to proceed. It may be to ask the company to do detailed checks — it may be that the company wants us to carry out some special error search techniques — it might be that we have to look for other ways to find our audit assurance.

17.24   Where errors are found it is possible, using statistical tables, to work out an estimate of the population error rate. For example, discovering 3 errors in a sample of 100 items implies a maximum potential error rate of 7.7% (assuming an R-factor of 3 was used in setting the sample sizes). Apart from being an estimate which becomes less accurate the more errors are found, this is a fairly useless piece of information in many cases. What really matters is whether we can rely on the control or, given that the error rate in the sample is unacceptably high, what is the likely money value of any errors in the accounts. In other words, error rates give us assurance that everything appears alright or put us on warning that it is not; if we receive that warning we need to find out what happened in money terms.

18 Monetary unit sampling

This chapter explains the firm's approach to monetary unit sampling and suggests when and how we should use it.

18.01 Monetary unit sampling (MUS) is used to tell us about the value of errors in a population — for example, that (with certain levels of assurance) debtors are not in error by more than £50,000. As the primary purpose of our audit work is to express an opinion on the accounts, which are expressed in money terms, MUS is a much more useful technique than error rate sampling (ERS).

18.02 MUS is a variation of attribute sampling in which the population is taken to consist of the individual £ units making up each item of the population. Hence, debtors of £150,000 are regarded as 150,000 £1 units. The basis for our approach to MUS is similar to that for ERS in that it relies on the poisson distribution as an approximation for the hypergeometric distribution.

18.03 The advantage of MUS from an audit viewpoint is that the conclusion from the test can be expressed in money terms rather than error rates. A typical test conclusion might be that we are 95% confident that stocks are not overstated by more than £20,000 — our materiality level. We have thus established that the risk is 5% or less of an undetected material error caused by overstatement of stock.

18.04 The major disadvantage of MUS is that it is conservative, in some cases by a substantial amount. The degree of conservatism depends on the nature of the population being sampled and cannot be evaluated unless a detailed statistical examination of the population is carried out. This would certainly not be cost effective so that when using MUS a degree of over-auditing inevitably occurs.

18.05 It is difficult to see how this over-audit can be reduced. Use of non-statistical methods means even greater uncertainty as to achieved precision and often leads to larger sample sizes. In practice we must acknowledge the problem and recognise that, when we state a conclusion on an MUS test in terms of a specific monetary precision, the actual precision achieved is always better than that stated.

18.06   MUS does not produce a useful estimate of the total population error. A best estimate of the population error (or 'most likely error') is obtained by extrapolating the errors found over the whole population. However, no indication is given of the accuracy of this estimate. Unless a large number of errors is found, the estimate is likely to be extremely inaccurate and it should not be used to adjust the accounts.

Sample Size

18.07   The sample size for MUS is determined in the same way as for ERS, that is:

$$n = \frac{R}{P}$$

Where n is the sample size, R the R-factor and P the precision.

Example 35

We are testing debtors of £300,000 and our preliminary estimate of materiality is £50,000. We have assessed risk as normal and have carried out a satisfactory but limited analytical review. Hence, we require an R-factor of 1.5 from our test of debtors.

Precision is $\dfrac{50,000}{300,000}$

The sample size is: $n = \dfrac{R}{P} = \dfrac{1.5}{0.1667} = 9$

18.08   The sample size is the number of £ units we test. However, we test the whole balance (or transaction) which includes each one — it is impossible to test single £ units. Furthermore, as some of the £ units may be in the same balance or transaction, the number of balances or transactions tested may be less than the sample size.

Sampling Interval

18.09   For MUS it is, however, unnecessary to calculate the sample size. It is easier and sufficient to calculate directly the sampling interval. The sampling interval is the population value divided by the sample size. So, as precision, in the formula in **18.07** above, is materiality divided by the population value, we can substitute in the formula so that:

$$\text{Sampling interval} \quad = \quad \frac{\text{Materiality}}{\text{R-factor}}$$

Example 36

Continuing *Example 35*, if we work out the sampling interval from the sample size, we arrive at a figure of £33,333 (that is £300,000 divided by 9).

A shorter route, using the formula in **18.09**, is:

$$\frac{50,000}{1.5} \quad = \quad £33,333$$

Sample Selection

18.10   Monetary unit samples are selected by methods based on systematic selection with random start (see paragraph **17.15**). The normal method of selection is as follows:
(a)   choose a random number between 0 and the sampling interval (inclusive);
(b)   add through the population until the cumulative total first exceeds the random start;
(c)   select the last item to be added on as the first sample item; and
(d)   continue adding through the population, selecting the items corresponding to the random start plus the sampling interval, random start plus twice the sampling interval and so on (see *Example 37* overleaf).

18.11   Where cumulative totals are not available but frequent sub-totals or page totals are, there is a quicker method of MUS sample selection called 'sub-sampling'. This is effectively a two-stage application of the previous method, first extracting a sample of pages and then selecting individual items from each page. The method can also be used when we want to test part of a balance rather than the whole balance — for example, when circularising details of invoices rather than debtor balances (see *Example 38* overleaf).

Example 37

A sample is to be selected from a list of debtor balances. The sampling interval is £1,000.

A random number is selected between 0 and 999. It is 206.

Balances £	Cumulative total £	Target totals £	Selected?
400	400	206	✓
900	1,300	1,206	✓
300	1,600	2,206	X
1,700	3,300	2,206/3,206	✓
600	3,900	4,206	X
900	4,800	4,206	✓

✓ = selected   X = not selected

Example 38

If we want to carry out a circularisation of individual unpaid sales invoices rather than debtor balances, we need to select invoices from within the balances. So, if the sampling interval is £16,000 and the random start is £15,904, we first select balances:

Balance £	Cumulative total £	Target totals £	Selected?
5,642	5,642	15,904	X
17,825	23,467	15,904	✓
9,300	32,767	31,904	✓
84,987	111,754	47,904/111,904	✓
9,632	127,386	127,904	X

Then we select invoices within the balances as follows (taking the third balance as an example):

Invoices £	Cumulative total £	Target totals £	Selected?
	23,467	31,904	X
589	24,056	31,904	X
1,748	25,804	31,904	X
5,310	31,114	31,904	X
1,438	32,552	31,904	✓
215	32,767	47,904	X

✓ = selected   X = not selected

18.12   A third method of selection may be used, if neither of the others is possible, provided that all population items are relatively small. It is again a two-stage approach, the first stage being a numerical rather than monetary selection. The following example illustrates the method.

Example 39

Population value £3,000,000 made up of 10,000 items. Those items greater than say £500 are extracted and either examined 100% or tested using a standard MUS approach.

Sample interval is £60,000.

Stage 1
Give every item a deemed value of £500 and select, on average, every 120th item from the population (£60,000/£5000   =   120). This sample contains 84 items (10,000/120).

Stage 2
Using the sample of 84 items selected in *Stage 1* as the population, sample through using MUS with a fixed sampling interval of £500.

In practice, the two stages can be combined. Each *Stage 1* selection is entered into a calculator as it is selected and the running total used to select items for *Stage 2*.

Monetary Unit Sampling for Understatement Tests

18.13   MUS may be used to test for understatement by sampling from a 'reciprocal' population such as for creditors, after date cash payments or a list of the purchases from each supplier. In this case it is easier and safer to work out first a sample size and then calculate the sampling interval because the former is based on the expected amount of the liabilities and the latter on the reciprocal population. Another way of dealing with this problem is to select the items from a related test — for example, we can test for understatement the balances of those suppliers whose invoices we checked in our overstatement test of purchases.

Evaluation of Monetary Unit Sampling

18.14   The statistical evaluation of a monetary unit sample assumes that errors whose cause is known have been separately investigated and removed from consideration. For example, if errors are known to have occurred during a week in which the computer was not working, this week is tested in depth to establish the total error in this period. When evaluating any errors found in other periods, the week examined in depth is treated separately.

Example 40

Assume we are testing trade creditors using MUS on cumulative purchases for each supplier and total recorded creditors are £4,900,000, materiality is £85,000, the R-factor is 2 and total purchases for the year £32,000,000. We might adopt the following procedures.

To allow for possible understatements, creditors are taken as £5,000,000.

$$\text{Precision} \quad = \frac{85,000}{5,000,000} = \quad 1.7\%$$

$$\text{Sample size} \quad = \frac{2}{0.017} = \quad 117.6471$$

$$\text{Sampling interval} \quad = \frac{32,000,000}{117.65} = \quad £272,000$$

The sample is then extracted by sampling through the bought ledger using the 'year's turnover' column rather than the balance column.

18.15   A special MUS error evaluation form can be used (see *Example 41* opposite) to give an indication of the most likely amount of monetary error in the population and the maximum possible net overstatement error at the R-factor for the test. No value is calculated for the maximum potential understatement because MUS is not a satisfactory technique for dealing with substantial understatements. A significant number of understatement errors indicate that MUS is inappropriate and that alternative procedures should be used.

Example 41

Example of error evaluation schedule

Client: XYZ Ltd

Accounts to: 31 December 1990

Cycle: REVENUE - Debtors

Prepared by	AMH	Sch. No.
Date started	15.3.91	
Date finished	20.3.91	H3.2
Reviewed by		
Date		

MONETARY UNIT SAMPLING — ERROR EVALUATION

Test H3.3

Materiality £ 95,000

R-factor 1.5

Sample interval £63,000

(A)	(B)	(C)	(D)	(E)	(F)	(G)	(H)
				Where item value less than sample interval			
Item	Item value	Amount of over/(under) statement	Where item value exceeds sample interval	Tainting (C ÷ B)	Rank of tainting	Adjustment factor	Adjusted tainting
4	4,181	(289)		(0.069)	N/A	N/A	(0.069)
7	765	33		0.043	2	1.26	0.054
8	2,500	250		0.1	1	1.35	0.135
11	67,700	370	370	–	–	–	–
26	189	2		0.011	3	1.22	0.013
Totals	–	366	370	0.085	–	–	0.133

	Most likely error	Maximum potential error
	£	£
Materiality		95,000
Top stratum errors (column D)	370	370
lower stratum errors		
— Column E x sampling interval	5,396	
— Column H x sampling interval		8,379
	5,766	103,749
Client adjustments	366	366
Total after client adjustments	5,400	103,383

Conclusion

Maximum potential error is only marginally greater than materiality indicating that a material error is unlikely to occur. The most likely error should be considered with other errors at the final review stage.

18.16 One major difference between MUS and ERS is that with the former we can take account of partial errors. The degree to which a monetary amount is in error is called the 'error tainting'. An amount of £100 which is incorrectly stated as £110 has an error tainting of:

$$\frac{10}{110} \quad = \quad 9\%$$

An item of £100 stated as £300 has an error tainting of:

$$\frac{200}{300} \quad = \quad 67\%$$

18.17 The approach to be adopted for evaluating monetary unit samples is as follows (using the form in *Example 41*):
(a) for all items which contain errors, enter the amount of the selection or sub-selection in column (B) and the amount of the over- or understatement in column (C);
(b) enter any errors which have been found in selections of greater than the sample interval in column (D) — this is because the sampling process automatically selects all items which exceed the sampling interval; no further calculations are required for these items;
(c) for errors in items of less than the sampling interval, calculate the error tainting per paragraph **18.16**;
(d) next, rank all taintings for overstatements in descending order of magnitude (no ranking is required for understatements);
(e) enter the adjustment factors in column (G) from *Table 8*. Adjustment factors are needed when calculating the maximum possible overstatement because the existence of errors tends to worsen the precision achieved by an MUS test. Ranking the error taintings in order of size ensures that a prudent result is achieved;
(f) enter the adjusted tainting in column (H); it is column (E) multiplied by column (G);
(g) the totals for taintings in columns (E) and (H) are then used, together with the total errors in column (D), to calculate the most likely error and the maximum potential error respectively.

18.18 The most likely error comprises:
(a) the total top stratum error, plus
(b) the estimated lower stratum error.
From this may be deducted the total of any adjustments made by the client. The estimated error in the lower stratum is calculated by extrapolating the total error tainting found in the sample (excluding errors found on items greater than the

sampling interval) to the total population. It is the total (unadjusted) taintings multiplied by the sampling interval.

18.19 The maximum potential error is slightly more complicated. Again, the total value of top stratum errors is included. To this figure is added:
(a) the materiality for the test. This is the original amount of uncertainty in the test results;
(b) the total adjusted tainting multiplied by the sampling interval. This is a combination of two factors; the likely error in the lower stratum together with the worsening of precision due to the errors found.
Again, the total of any adjustments made by the client may be deducted.

Table 8

Table of adjustment factors for overstatement tainting in monetary unit sampling

Rank of errors	R-factor				
	1.0	1.5	2.0	2.5	3.0
1	1.15	1.35	1.51	1.64	1.75
2	1.11	1.26	1.37	1.47	1.55
3	1.10	1.21	1.31	1.39	1.46
4	1.08	1.19	1.27	1.34	1.40
5	1.07	1.17	1.24	1.30	1.36
6	1.07	1.15	1.22	1.28	1.33
7	1.06	1.14	1.21	1.26	1.30
8	1.06	1.14	1.19	1.24	1.29
9	1.06	1.12	1.18	1.23	1.27
10	1.05	1.12	1.18	1.22	1.26
11	1.05	1.11	1.16	1.21	1.24
12	1.05	1.11	1.16	1.20	1.24
13	1.05	1.11	1.15	1.19	1.22
14	1.04	1.10	1.15	1.18	1.22
15	1.04	1.10	1.14	1.18	1.21

18.20 When using MUS we are only concerned whether the total per the accounts is likely to be overstated by a material amount. If the maximum potential error is less than the materiality level, then there is little chance of a material overstatement. If the maximum potential error is greater than materiality by less than about 10%, we can probably conclude there is little chance of material overstatement (remember that our materiality limit is a band rather than a point) and that we may have used a lower materiality level for our tests than for adjusting — see **8.15**. If the maximum potential error is much greater than the materiality level, there is a good chance of material error and further investigation is required.

Transaction Tests

18.21   Where a transaction test is carried out using MUS, it is necessary to calculate the sampling interval in order to extract the sample. The sampling interval is the total population value divided by the sample size. For this purpose, the sample size should be used before rounding — the sampling interval may then be rounded if required. In appropriate cases we also restrict precision to 3% of sales, as explained in **17.08**.

Example 42

Assume a test of purchases where the total value of purchases is £1.9m and the R-factor for the test is 2.5 (assurance obtained from a limited analytical review). If we use the same limit to precision as for ERS (see paragraph **17.08**) and the total value of sales is £3.5m, then:

$$\text{Precision} \quad = \quad \frac{105,000}{1,900,000} \quad = \quad 0.055$$

$$\text{Sample size} \quad = \quad \frac{R}{P} \quad = \quad \frac{2.5}{0.055} \quad = \quad 45.45$$

$$\text{Sampling interval} \quad = \quad \frac{1,900,000}{45.45} \quad = \quad £41,804$$

Part C   Appendices

Appendix 1   Ideas lists

Ideas lists are what their title implies. They are ideas on what objectives to test, what tests to perform, what controls to look for, what analytical review procedures to use and what things to consider when trying to understand the business and its accounting systems. They are not checklists — they may be used as the basis for an audit programme — in some cases they may be 'answered' and filed with the working papers.

The *revenue cycle* ideas list in this appendix might be used in the following way:

(a)   The section on understanding the business forms the basis for notes in the permanent audit file; these notes help speed up the understanding process each year. This goes into the cycle in greater depth than the business review and should be used in conjunction with the information contained in our risk assessment.

(b)   Before starting the cycle, the senior in charge and all the assistants who will be doing the work run through the 'understanding the business' points and check their understanding of this particular revenue cycle (they do not 'answer' the points on the list, nor need they write notes in answer to them although they may if they wish; the vital thing is that they understand how the cycle works at the company they are auditing — it is not vital that they write out their knowledge).

(c)   The sections on accounting policies and the recording of transactions are used in a similar way to the 'understanding the business' section. They form the basis of permanent file notes (so that each year's audit team can quickly gain an understanding) and they are a 'check' on each person's understanding.

(d)   The senior and the assistants use the 'analytical review' section to help them choose those procedures which are relevant in their case. They also need to decide when the procedures can be carried out.

(e)   The 'substantive tests' section provides ideas which point the audit team to the tests which need to be carried out.

(f)   The final section on 'compliance tests' is only used where there are key internal controls upon which we find it cost effective to place reliance. The senior may, when preparing the audit programme, run down the key control questions as a check to see whether there are any controls in the system under review. Again, he need not answer all the questions but should prepare an internal control evaluation form (see Appendix 4) for those key controls which are identified as being worth relying upon.

This guidance manual is supported by ideas lists on all the major cycles as well as on particular tasks and topics such as risk, audit planning, computer systems and so on. There are also ideas lists for individual audit techniques within each cycle — for example, attendance at stocktakes and the circularisation of debtors and creditors.

The *revenue cycle* and *stocktake attendance* ideas lists are reproduced as part of this appendix.

Revenue Cycle — Ideas List

This cycle deals primarily with sales, trade debtors and cash receipts. In addition, it may include:

(a)   sundry debtors;
(b)   prepayments;
(c)   loans and quasi-loans to and credit transactions with directors and their connected persons;
(d)   bills receivable;
(e)   other current asset receivables.

The ideas list has been written for a company selling goods on credit. The tests require tailoring to match the company's particular procedures and transactions. They must also be modified for cash businesses (retailers, hotels, casinos, etc.) and for those companies which supply services or whose prime source of income is interest, rent, etc.

The cycle must not be looked at in isolation. Before carrying out any tests, consideration should be given to any matters arising from the risk assessment, the results of work on other cycles, any analytical review already completed and our experience in prior years. Sometimes these give us audit assurance or point to errors on this cycle.

Wherever possible, tests and samples should be combined. This applies not only *within* the cycle but also *across* the cycles. For example:

(a)   the same sample of despatch notes can be used as the basis for tests on the preparation of invoices, the pricing, calculations and casts of invoices and the recording of the invoice in the sales day book and sales ledger;

(b) the same sample of debtor balances can be used for checking to the sales ledger cards, for the circularisation and for reviewing the bad debt provision;

(c) the cut off tests (despatch notes to invoices and vice versa) at the year end should be combined with similar tests for the expenditure and stock cycles;

(d) tests of the procedures for handling cash receipts should include all possible types of receipts (e.g. sales ledger, sales of fixed assets, interest and rents received etc.);

(e) where goods are purchased only on the receipt of a sales order, the tests of purchases and sales should be combined.

Understand those aspects of the business relating to sales, debtors and cash receipts

Products

What does the company sell? Are the products up to date? What is the risk of obsolescence in current products? Is the sales cycle seasonal?

How do the company and the market determine selling prices? Are prices affected by any regulations?

Does the company pay or receive royalties in connection with the product?

Does the company offer any special guarantees or warranties? Are many items returned as defective or for warranty repairs?

Does production restrict the company's ability to meet orders or develop new products?

Does the company know the profitability of its major products? What percentage of sales is attributable to each major product or product group? Are there any trends?

Are there any special legal regulations affecting the products? How are they treated for VAT purposes? Are there any duties payable?

What is the company's approach to developing new products? Are the products changed frequently?

CUSTOMERS

What types of customers does the company sell to? Are there a few large customers or are there many small customers? Who are the major customers?

What is the current financial and trading position of major customers and the economic outlook for the industries to which the company sells?

Are customer complaints a problem? Is there a pattern of customer complaints?

Are goods sold on sale or return or on consignment or subject to reservation of title?

Does the company know the profitability of its major customers and markets? What percentage of sales is attributable to each market? Are there any trends?

COMPETITION

Does the company face competition from many similar companies or from only a few large companies? Is the competition local, national or international? What is the company's market share? Are there any trends?

Is the competition mainly in terms of price or is it in terms of service, quality, credit or other factors?

SELLING AND MARKETING

Who sells the goods? How are sales people and agents remunerated? Is there any unusual relationship between sales revenue and the number of sales people, agents etc. and their remuneration?

Are sales limited by the company's ability to produce or by its ability to sell?

What types of advertising and sales promotion does the company use? Are the results evaluated? How is expenditure controlled?

Does the method of remuneration encourage sales of the most profitable products and sales to the most profitable markets?

What are the usual terms of trade? Does the company offer trade discounts, bulk rebates, loyalty bonuses etc.? How important are they? Does the company offer cash discounts? How important are they?

How does the company market its products?

DISTRIBUTION

How does the company distribute its goods? Does it use its own vehicles or sub-contractors or do customers collect the goods?

Does the company use returnable containers?

Does the company charge separately for carriage costs, returnable containers etc?

DEBTORS AND CASH RECEIPTS

What proportion of sales are for cash? Are any other receipts from debtors in the form of cash?

How significant are debtors? Are there any special circumstances affecting any of the debtors?

Does the company send out statements regularly and promptly? Does it chase slow payers?

What is bad debt history and experience in the industry?

Are the customers based in unusual areas or countries?

Does the company insure or factor its debtors?

Does the company accept bills of exchanges or other documents of credit in settlement of debtors? If so, in what circumstances? Are they discounted?

Understand the accounting policies relating to sales, debtors and cash receipts

When is revenue recognised in the accounts? How is this affected where goods are sold on sale or return, or on consignment or subject to reservation of title?

What are the requirements of company law, accounting standards, professional or other regulations for accounting for revenue in this business?

Is the company affected by accounting rules of another country? If so, how do they affect the company's accounting for revenue?

In what areas are estimates or judgements used (e.g. percentage completion, provisions for bad and doubtful debts, provisions for returns or warranty claims etc)?

How does the company ensure it matches revenue and related costs?

How are intercompany profits on stock identified and eliminated in the consolidated accounts?

Are there any unusual accounting policies?

Understand how sales transactions (including cash receipts) are recorded

The revenue cycle normally includes the following operations:

(a)   receipt of an order from the customer;
(b)   checking credit limit of the customer and authorisation of order;
(c)   picking of goods and checking to order (see also stock cycle);
(d)   raising a despatch note and checking goods to the despatch note before sending to the customer (see also stock cycle);
(e)   raising an invoice from the despatch note;
(f)   recording the invoice in the sales day book and the sales ledger;
(g)   receipt and banking of monies from a customer;
(h)   recording monies in rough cash book, main cash book and paying-in-slips, or in a cash business on the till roll or till slips;
(i)   posting receipts to the sales ledger;
(j)   preparation of a monthly statement for sending to customers;
(k)   summarising till receipts for posting to nominal ledger in a cash business;
(l)   posting the totals of invoices and cash receipts to the sales ledger control and the nominal ledger;
(m)   reconciliation of till rolls to cash received in a cash business;
(n)   reconciliation of the balances on the sales ledger with the sales ledger control account;
(o)   reconciliation of the cash book to the bank statements.

How does the computer fit into the revenue cycle? How will it affect our audit?

To obtain a full understanding of the system, it is useful to prepare a flowchart showing:

(a)   the inputs to the system;
(b)   the controls which enable management to be satisfied that all transactions are input into the system and not lost in processing;
(c)   the flow of documents and other paperwork;
(d)   the documents and records that are output from the system;
(e)   any intermediate records which are prepared;
(f)   any reconciliations, error reports etc which are prepared;
(g)   what types of calculations are performed;
(h)   what permanent information (master files, price lists) is used and how it is updated;
(i)   who performs the various operations and checks.

Analytical review procedures

Analytical review procedures help to:

(a)   identify areas of the accounts which are important because of their size;
(b)   highlight unusual or unexpected figures or relationships in the accounts;
(c)   design audit tests which concentrate on the important and unusual items;

(d)   obtain sufficient audit assurance to allow the reduction or even elimination of detailed testing.

The procedures listed below (and any others which are appropriate) may be used when planning the audit as a whole, identifying objectives, as part of the audit evidence or at the final review stage. In appropriate cases, comparisons should be made with prior years, budgets, expectations and other businesses in the same industry.

Some of the ratios and statistics which can be considered for the revenue cycle include:

(a)   sales and debtors for each product group and market;
(b)   proportions of cash and credit sales;
(c)   volumes of products sold;
(d)   sales revenue per sales person, branch, region, square foot etc;
(e)   average sales per customer and per invoice;
(f)   sales per quarter or per month;
(g)   returns and allowances as percentage of sales;
(h)   number of days sales in debtors;
(i)   debtors as a percentage of current assets or total assets;
(j)   debtors in excess of normal credit terms;
(k)   debtors in hands of solicitors, collection agencies etc;
(l)   gross profit as a percentage of sales for each product group and market;
(m)   commission payable as a percentage of sales;
(n)   selling and distribution costs as a percentage of sales;
(o)   bad debts as a percentage of sales;
(p)   unfulfilled orders;
(q)   VAT and other sales taxes as percentage of total sales revenue;
(r)   number of sales invoices, credit notes, cash receipts etc;
(s)   pilferage rates (especially in a cash business).

Substantive tests of transactions and balances

Normally our objectives on this cycle are to ensure that:

(a)   sales are not understated;
(b)   debtors are not overstated; and
(c)   sales and debtors are properly disclosed.

Additional objectives may be required to deal with other income and other receivables.

To make easier the choice and design of audit procedures, the objectives may be subdivided. This may be done best by considering the type of errors which may occur.

The audit programme must specify the audit evidence which will be obtained for each objective. The evidence may take the form of analytical review procedures, tests in total and substantive tests of detail. The programme should state precisely the nature and direction of the test, as well as the number of items to be tested. It should specify how any samples, whether statistical or non-statistical, are to be determined.

The programme should also show where the level of substantive tests of detail may be reduced by placing reliance on:

(a)   analytical review procedures;
(b)   results of risk assessment;
(c)   key controls which have been subject to compliance tests;
(d)   other factors (e.g. the consistent operation of the computer).

The tests chosen must take into account the significance of the transactions or balances under review, the risk of material error in those transactions and balances and the likely effectiveness of the tests. There is no value in carrying out so-called 'standard tests' where they are irrelevant, where the balances or transactions are insignificant or where the tests are unlikely to provide relevant or reliable audit evidence.

The lists on the following pages show possible tests for the three primary objectives on the revenue cycle. They require adaptation to match the company's procedures and transactions, for cash businesses, for those companies which supply services or whose prime source of income is rents, interest etc. and for other income and receivables dealt with under this cycle.

OBJECTIVE: To ensure that sales are not understated

Type of error	*Substantive tests*
Goods are despatched but an invoice is not raised for every despatch in that period.	Observe procedures for checking that all despatches have been documented (e.g. gate controls, security over stock etc.). Select .... despatches from stock records or goods outward records and trace to invoice. Check that invoice agrees as to customer name and quantity and description of goods. Select .... despatches in last .... days of accounting period and check that: — excluded from stock, and — accurate sales invoices have been raised and processed so as to be included in sales and debtors at the year end.
An invoice is prepared inaccurately.	For .... invoices, check pricing to price lists etc, calculations and casts.
Invoices are omitted from or not entered accurately in the sales day book.	For .... invoices, check that recorded correctly in sales day book.
Invoices are omitted from or not posted to the nominal ledger (sales ledger control account).	Check .... casts of sales day book, postings of totals to sales ledger control account and sales account in nominal ledger.
Fictitious or incorrect entries are made for credit notes, journals, or other debits to sales.	Select .... credit notes, journals or other adjustments debited to the sales account and check that they are valid by reference to correspondence, goods returned records, authorisation procedures, remittance advices, paying in slips etc.
Sales for cash are not recorded.	Observe procedures to ensure that a sale is recorded for all goods sold (e.g. recording on till slips at point of sale). For .... till slips, check numerical sequence ensuring that all copies of cancelled slips are retained. Agree dates to daily summaries. Ensure that a till total is recorded for each till for .... days.

Type of error	*Substantive tests*
	Reconcile till totals for each day to cash book and the credit of the appropriate account in the nominal ledger.
Sundry income is not recorded.	Consider the disposal of fixed and other assets and ensure that the income arising has been accounted for.
	Review the cash book for unusual receipts and ensure they have been correctly analysed as revenue when appropriate (i.e. not as creditors or other credits).

Objective: To ensure that debtors are not overstated

Type of error

There are fictitious or incorrect entries on the list of sales ledger balances or the list is incorrectly cast.

The total on the list cannot be agreed to the balance on the sales ledger control account.

Substantive tests

Using client's list of balances, check extraction and casts of .... balances to sales ledger account. Check cast of list and agree to balance on sales ledger control accounts, confirming that reconciling items are properly supported.

The sales ledger balances do not represent genuine customers, or the customers do not agree with the balance. Debit entries in the sales ledger are fictitious or incorrect or relate to despatches made after the year end.

Carry out a debtors circularisation (see separate ideas list) using monetary unit sampling on the list of balances at .... Select .... sales invoices recorded in sales ledger and sales day book in last .... days of accounting period and check that:
— entry is supported by despatch note
— goods excluded from stock
— goods despatched prior to year end.

Invoices are omitted from or posted inaccurately to individual sales ledger accounts.

Check that each invoice selected in the sales understatement test has been posted to the correct sales ledger account.

Credit notes are not issued and recorded for goods returned/complaints etc. arising during the year.

Review .... goods inwards records, returns records, correspondence etc. for returns or disputes relating to goods despatched during period under review and ensure that credit note is prepared correctly and recorded in the year.

Review .... credit notes issued after year end and check that provision is made for any relating to the period under review.

The analysis of debtors by age is incorrect. The company does not make adequate provision for doubtful debts.

For .... debtors (use monetary unit sampling, where appropriate):
— agree analysis by age
— check cash received since verification date per cash book through to the ledger cards and cash receipts records, remittance advices etc.

Type of error	*Substantive tests*
	Check adequacy of doubtful debt provision by considering:
	— debtors over .... days old and balances at random
	— non-replies to circularisation requests
	— correspondence and other documents in client's files including details of accounts in hands of debt collection agencies and solicitors, and
	— published or statutory accounts of debtors or other information available from credit reference agencies etc.
Monies received are not correctly entered in the cash book, e.g.	Observe procedures for handling of cash receipts and check that recorded and banked promptly and accurately.
— monies received are not fully recorded at point of receipt, or	
— these original records do not agree with the bank paying-in slips.	Check .... postings of receipts from initial record to paying-in book and cash book.
Cash receipts are not posted to or are incorrectly posted to the sales ledger or sales ledger control in the nominal ledger.	Check .... casts in cash book and postings of totals of receipts per cash book to sales ledger control account in the nominal ledger. Check .... postings of receipts from cash book to individual sales ledger accounts.
The receipts per the cash book are not reflected on the bank statements.	Check .... receipts in cash book to bank statements. Check reconciliation at year end. (See also cash and bank cycle.)

Sundry debtors and prepayments

Sundry debtors are not valid receivables.	Obtain positive confirmation or check to loan agreements etc. for .... balances.
Sundry debtors are not recoverable.	Select .... balances and check:
	— terms of repayment and interest are complied with
	— cash received after balance sheet date
	— correspondence with debtor
	to ensure that adequate provision has been made for bad and doubtful debts.

Type of error	*Substantive tests*
Prepayments are wrongly calculated.	Compare amounts over £............ with those at previous balance sheet date and obtain explanations for significant change.
	Vouch items over £............ and check calculations.
Sundry debtors and prepayments listings do not agree to nominal ledger.	Agree lists of debtors and prepayments to nominal ledger.

OBJECTIVE: To ensure that sales and debtors are correctly disclosed

Type of error	*Substantive tests*
Accounts receivable in more than one year are not identified.	Review credit terms, agreements etc. and check that for all categories of debtors, amounts receivable in more than one year from the balance sheet date have been identified and shown separately.
The analysis of sales by class of business and geographical market is incorrect.	For each class of business and geographical market, check that sales are correctly identified as such in the accounting records and shown separately in the notes to the accounts.
Sales and debtors are shown under the wrong headings in the profit and loss and balance sheet formats.	Check that amounts on company schedules/our working papers are correctly transferred to lead schedules and accounts. Ensure lead schedules include all format items relevant to the company. Ensure items are correctly classified, in particular: — credit balances are separated and treated as creditors — inter-company balances and balances with related companies are disclosed separately — amounts due after more than one year are shown.
Items requiring separate disclosure are not identified.	Review the treatment of credit balances on the debtors ledger and ensure that, where material, they are treated as creditors. Identify items requiring separate disclosure (using disclosure checklists if necessary). Review our working papers and schedules and ensure items requiring separate disclosure are incorporated, in particular: — turnover and profit for each major class of business — turnover analysed geographically — debtors due after more than one year — balances with group and associated undertakings — loans, quasi-loans and credit transactions with directors (and their connected persons).

Determine compliance tests which reduce the level or change the nature of substantive tests

Compliance tests are carried out on key controls upon which we wish to rely. We test for evidence that the controls have been properly operated. Compliance tests are only carried out where the time costs saved on the substantive test are greater than the time costs of the compliance test.

Key controls are those which prevent (or would detect promptly) material errors in the accounts and whose failure would not be compensated by any other control. By definition, therefore, key controls only arise in significant audit areas.

KEY CONTROL QUESTION	TYPES OF KEY CONTROL	POSSIBLE COMPLIANCE TESTS
Can goods be despatched but not invoiced?	Reconciliation on regular basis of stock per physical count to records investigating differences.	Check for evidence of regular reconciliations, ensuring that they appear reasonable with no unexplained differences.
	Goods despatch note and invoice part of same set, or cross-referenced to each other. Filed together sequentially, with regular sequence checks.	For ——— despatch notes, check cross-referenced to invoice and check for evidence of sequence test.
Can invoices be raised but omitted from the sales day book?	Evidence on invoice, e.g. grid stamp, to indicate posted to sales day book.	For ——— invoices, check for grid stamp.
	Sequence check on sales day book to ensure all pre-numbered invoices are entered.	Check for evidence of sequence check.
Can invoices be raised but not recorded in the sales ledger or the nominal ledger?	Regular reconciliations of balances per sales ledger accounts and sales ledger control account.	Examine reconciliations regularly and ensure appear reasonable with no differences brought or carried forward.
Can invoicing errors occur?	Evidence on invoice, e.g. grid stamp, to indicate checks of quantities, prices and calculations (including VAT).	For ——— invoices, check for grid stamp and initials or signatures of appropriate person.

KEY CONTROL QUESTION	TYPES OF KEY CONTROL	POSSIBLE COMPLIANCE TESTS
Can debtors be improperly credited by fictitious or incorrect credit notes, journals, bad debt write offs, cash receipts etc.?	Evidence of authority for credit notes, journals, bad debt write offs. Regular reconciliations of balances per sales ledger control account and regular bank reconciliations both at the same date with differences investigated.	For ⸻ credit entries in the sales ledger, check for evidence of authority. Examine ⸻ reconciliations and ensure that carried out regularly at same date and appear reasonable with no differences brought or carried forward.
Can cash be received but not banked?	Segregation of duties between those responsible for receiving receipts and recording them in the cash book and those writing up the sales ledger.	Observe procedures. Inquire into what changes take place during holidays, illness, etc.
	Independent agreement of initial record of cash receipts with cash book.	For ⸻ records, check for evidence of independent check.
	Regular bank reconciliations reviewed by senior officer of the company.	Check that reconciliations are carried out regularly and for evidence of review by senior officer. For reconciliations, check that they appear reasonable with no differences brought or carried forward.
Can goods be despatched to bad credit risks?	Checks of credit limits etc. before goods are despatched.	For ⸻ despatches, check for evidence of credit check.
Can debtors be over-stated by including despatches made after the year end and excluding credits due for goods returned/complaints arising during the year or cash received?	Statements sent regularly to customers, with queries etc. followed up.	For ⸻ customers, ensure there is statement for selected months. Peruse correspondence files for references to statements as evidence these are sent out.

KEY CONTROL QUESTION	TYPES OF KEY CONTROL	POSSIBLE COMPLIANCE TESTS
	Debit entries in sales ledger are referenced to valid invoice numbers.	For ——— entries in the sales ledger, check they are referenced to valid invoice numbers.
	Regular bank reconciliations reviewed by senior officer of the company.	Ensure bank reconciliations are prepared regularly and for ——— of them, ensure: — balance corresponds to cash books — there are no differences/adjustments brought/carried forward, and — the balance is agreed to bank statement.

Stocktake Attendance — Ideas List

The ideas list has been written for a company holding physical stocks. The tests require tailoring to match the company's particular procedures and transactions. They must also be modified for service companies and for those companies which have large quantities of work in progress (whether manufacturing or construction projects) or those which operate some form of continuous process.

The ideas list should be read in conjunction with that for the stock cycle as a whole. In particular, anybody attending a stocktake should understand:
(a)   those aspects of the business relating to stock;
(b)   the accounting policies relating to stock;
(c)   how stock movements are recorded and valued; and
(d)   how attendance at the stocktake fits in with the audit objectives and the audit programme.

The stocktake attendance must not be looked at in isolation. There is a close relationship between the revenue and expenditure cycles and stock, particularly when considering cut-off. Anybody involved in attending the stocktake may need to study the ideas lists and working papers for the revenue and expenditure cycles.

The principles of sampling as set out in the *Audit Guide* apply to attendance at stocktakes as to other audit procedures. Because the stocktake is concerned with quantities rather than values and because the attendance is at the same time as the count, monetary unit sampling techniques are difficult to apply. Nevertheless, they should be used to give a rough idea of the number of items to be checked.

Review of stocktake instructions

The following are possible factors which need to be considered when reviewing the adequacy of stocktake instructions which should also be reviewed at the time of the count
(a)   the timetable for the count;
(b)   how stock is arranged for the count, including proper segregation of different stocks and the return of excess materials to stores;
(c)   how third party stocks are separated and excluded from the count;
(d)   how stocks held subject to reservation of title are identified;
(e)   the identification of stocks and high value items in particular;
(f)   the procedures for dealing with sealed boxes and containers;
(g)   cut-off arrangements to ensure goods in stock are included in purchases and excluded from sales;
(h)   whether there are any stock movements during stocktake and, if so, how they are controlled;

(i)   the methods of measuring stocks, for example counting, weighing, dipping etc.;

(j)   control over counting to ensure all stock is counted accurately, and correctly recorded only once;

(k)   the method used to record the details of the stock count, including any pre-ticketing;

(l)   how work in progress is identified and correctly recorded after assessing its state of completion;

(m)   the identification of intra-group stocks;

(n)   the name, duties, experience and independence of the people taking part in the count;

(o)   controls over stock sheets/tickets (for example are they pre-numbered?, how does the company ensure no stock item sheets or tickets are improperly added, deleted or amended later?);

(p)   method of identifying damaged/obsolete/slow-moving items;

(q)   whether any changes from previous years;

(r)   where adequate stock records are maintained, the reconcilation to such records and the follow up of differences;

(s)   how stock held at outside locations under the control of third parties is to be dealt with;

(t)   any restrictions on our handling goods caused by union rules, customer requirements or safety regulations;

(u)   who is responsible for answering technical queries;

(v)   who is responsible and what are the procedures for dealing with discrepancies or other problems during the count.

Substantive tests

The following list shows possible tests which help determine that stock quantities have been properly computed. They require adaptation to match the company's procedures and transactions:

(a)   Attend oral briefing of client's staff. Ascertain whether there have been any last minute changes in procedures. Check that all client's staff scheduled to take part are present.

(b)   Obtain control lists of stock sheets, tickets issued.

(c)   Make a tour of areas in which stocks are located and ensure that the nature of each category is understood and categorised.

(d)   Observe the client's staff performing the stocktake and ensure that they are following the prescribed procedures effectively.

(e)   Test .... items from the rough stock sheets and check that they have been accurately counted/weighed/measured and described.

(f)   Test .... items from the floor and check that they have been accurately recorded on the rough stock sheets. Ensure that they have been counted/weighed/measured and described correctly.

(g)   During test counts open .... cartons to ensure the contents are correct.

(h)   Where there are discrepancies between our count and the counters' figures, resolve the matter before the end of the count.

(i)   Note the condition of stocks and ensure a full record is made (for follow-up) of:
   (1) damaged or deteriorated stocks;
   (2) slow-moving stocks;
   (3) discontinued or obsolete stocks.

(j)   Note details of the last goods received and despatch documents for subsequent tests on cut-off.

(k)   Record details of any movements of stock during count.

(l)   Where there are goods-in-transit (between locations), take details of goods despatched/received in last few days to ensure at a later stage that these were included in stock and included only once.

(m)   Test check sequence of stock sheets/tickets for completeness.

(n)   Where stock records are up to date, compare quantities counted with records to ensure count seems accurate. Where possible resolve any discrepancies before the end of the count.

(o)   At the end of the count, consider retaining full record (for example, photocopy of rough sheets) or full details of all high value items and serial numbers of stock sheets/tickets issued for later checking to final stock sheets to ensure final record:
   (1) does not contain stocks which were not counted;
   (2) has not omitted items of stock which were counted.

(p)   At the end of the count, check that all items have been counted.

Appendix 2   Example of lead documentation for each cycle

The lead documentation for each cycle comprises:
(a)   a lead schedule summarising the balances and transactions in the cycle;
(b)   a schedule summarising the important ratios and other statistics in the cycle, together with an explanation of significant changes;
(c)   a checklist of the main audit steps to be followed.

The top memo (see paragraphs **11.16** et seq and *Example 15*) should be filed between the ratios schedule and the checklist.

Both the lead schedule and the schedule of important ratios and significant changes:
(a)   include certain preprinted items; these must be added to or deleted in appropriate circumstances;
(b)   provide for four years' figures; a minimum of two years should be shown — four may be desirable to disclose trends. Alternatively, columns may be used for budgeted or forecast figures.

Client _____	Prepared by		Sch No
	Date started		
Accounts to _____	Date finished		
	Reviewed by		
Cycle _____ Revenue _____	Date		

LEAD SCHEDULE

	Sch. No.	19	19	19	19
Trade debtors					
Other debtors					
Prepayments and accrued income					
The above includes the following amounts due after more than one year:					
Trade debtors					
Other debtors					
Prepayments and accrued income					
Turnover					

Client _____	Prepared by		Sch No
	Date started		
Accounts to _____	Dates finished		
	Reviewed by		
Cycle _____ Revenue _____	Date		

KEY RATIOS AND EXPLANATIONS

	19	19	19	19

Key ratios:

1 $\dfrac{\text{Net debtors}}{\text{Average Sales per day}} \times 365 \text{ days}$

2 $\dfrac{\text{Bad debt provision}}{\text{Gross trade debtors}}$

3 $\dfrac{\text{Gross profit}}{\text{Turnover}}$

Explanations for significant changes in debtors and key ratios

Client _____	Prepared by		Sch No
	Date started		
Accounts to _____	Dates finished		
	Reviewed by		
Cycle_____Revenue_____	Date		

	Sch. ref.	Initials

Planning

1. Examine and review current year planning memorandum and risk assessment, together with permanent file notes, results of other audit work and discussions with client and last year's file. Ensure any necessary amendments have been made to the systems notes for the cycle and carry out walk–through tests to confirm our understanding of it.

    As a result, ensure you understand:
    (a) those aspects of the business relating to sales, debtors and receipts;
    (b) relevant accounting policies;
    (c) how transactions take place and how they are recorded;
    (d) the financial statement representations and the type of errors which could occur together with the risk of those errors occurring.

2. Taking into account the specific risks and related audit procedures identified in the risk assessment, design substantive tests of transactions and balances. These may comprise analytical review procedures, tests in total, tests of detail or any combination thereof. The tests should ensure that:
    (a) sales are not understated;
    (b) debtors are not overstated;
    (c) sales and debtors are properly disclosed.

3. Design compliance tests (to check the operation of key controls) and identify analytical review procedures which enable us to reduce the level of specific substantive tests of detail and where it is cost effective to adopt such an approach.

Client _____	Prepared by		Sch No
	Date started		
Accounts to _____	Dates finished		
	Reviewed by		
Cycle _____ Revenue _____	Date		

	Sch. ref.	Initials
(Note — the analytical review procedures identified at this stage may already have been carried out while planning the audit or been planned as part of the substantive tests in 2 above).		
4. Review transactions and balances to ensure that procedures and tests cover unusual and related party items (if material).		
Review		
5. Ensure all working papers contain the appropriate audit evidence and that all audit evidence is recorded.		
6. Consider the significance of errors, noting the action taken.		
7. Draft appropriate paragraphs of management letter and letter of representation.		
8. Ensure that accounting policies and notes in the financial statements correctly reflect the transactions and balances in the cycle.		
9. Update analytical review and complete lead schedule, key ratios and significant changes.		
10. Prepare 'top memo' summarising the work performed, any audit problems encountered, important audit and accounting judgements and audit conclusions.		

Before handing the section for review ensure
that all working papers, lead schedules and
the financial statements are in agreement and
properly cross–referenced and that no work
which could have been completed has been
left undone.

Client _____	Prepared by		Sch No
	Date started		
Accounts to _____	Date finished		
	Reviewed by		
Cycle _____ Stock _____	Date		

STOCKTAKE ATTENDANCE

Location _____

Date, start time and estimated duration _____

Approximate value of stock　　£ _____

	Sch. ref.	Initials
1 Examine and review permanent file notes, results of other audit work and discussions with client, last year's file, planning notes and current financial and non-financial information. As a result, ensure that you understand:		
(a) those aspects of the business relating to all categories of stock (for example raw materials, work in progress, finished goods) including their nature and location;		
(b) how transactions and movements take place and how they are recorded;		
(c) the type of errors which could occur during the stocktake and the risk of those errors occurring.		
2 Obtain and review a copy of the client's stocktaking instructions and find out when they will be issued to the client's staff and the nature of any oral briefing. Make any recommendations to the client for improvements in the instructions or arrangements.		
3 Determine what audit work will be carried out during the stocktake attendance. Ensure that all unusual and high value items are verified.		
4 During the stocktake attendance, carry out agreed procedures, deal with any changes or problems as they arise and record details of work done.		
5 After the stocktake, write a report stating our conclusions on the count and any recommendations for further or reduced audit work this year or in the future.		

Appendix 3   Audit programme

This appendix shows what the programme for an individual cycle might look like. It includes columns for:

(a)   describing the substantive test
(b)   noting when the test is to be carried out
(c)   cross referencing to the detailed test schedule and the management letter
(d)   summarising the results of the test.

The description of the test must be specific to the types of documents and records maintained by the client and to the direction of the test. It may also show how the sample size is to be calculated by setting out the materiality level and R-factor; this information may, however, be included on the detailed test schedule.

Detailed test schedules should not repeat information contained on the programme. They should show how items have been selected for testing and should contain sufficient information to enable a reviewer to see precisely what work has been done.

The following two pages show extracts from the audit programmes on the revenue and expenditure cycles of **Top Products Ltd**.

Client	Top Products	Prepared by	ABC	Sch No
		Date started	16.4.90	
Accounts to	30 June 1990	Date finished		
		Reviewed by		
Cycle	Revenue	Date		

AUDIT PROGRAMME

OBJECTIVE   To ensure that sales are not understated

Substantive tests	Interim/ final	Sch. No.	Conclusions	Management letter	Initials
1. Select 50 order acknowledgement forms and check: (a) details to despatch book; (b) description and quantity of goods to invoices; (c) prices on invoices to price list; (d) casts and calculations; (e) invoices to sales day book listing and individual sales ledger accounts; (f) total of sales day book listing is posted to the nominal ledger (sales account and sales ledger control account).	Interim				
2. Select 5 sales day book listings and check casts.	Interim				
3. Select 10 credit notes and 5 journals posted to the credit of sales ledger accounts and check to supporting documentation for accuracy and authorisation.	Interim				

Client	Top Products	Prepared by	ABC	Sch No
		Date started	16.4.90	
Accounts to	30 June 1990	Date finished		
		Reviewed by		
Cycle	Expenditure	Date		

AUDIT PROGRAMME

OBJECTIVE   To ensure that creditors are not understated

Substantive tests	Interim/ final	Sch. No.	Conclusions	Manage- ment letter	Initials
1. Using the 'turnover per year' column on the purchase ledger cards, select a sample of suppliers using monetary unit sampling, materiality of £40,000 and an R-factor of 1.5 (see E1.2 — not reproduced) and check: (a) to listing of purchase ledger balances (b) to suppliers' statements (circularise the suppliers for whom statements are not available) (c) that all differences and reconciling items have been correctly dealt with.	Final				
2. Check the casts on the list of purchase ledger balances and agree the total to the purchase ledger control account in the nominal ledger. Check that differences and reconciling items are dealt with correctly.	Final				

Appendix 4 Internal control evaluation form (ICE)

For those substantive tests where we hope to place reliance on internal controls, we must complete an evaluation form. The first column lists the appropriate key control questions (for example, if we have decided we would like to rely on internal controls to reduce the level of our test from despatch records to invoices, the key control question is 'can goods be despatched but not invoiced?'). It is only necessary to list these questions where we hope to rely on internal controls.

The next column allows us to record the key control in the system which satisfies the key control question. In practice, it may be necessary to consider the effects of various strengths and weaknesses before identifying the key control — these may be listed on the ICE, provided a system is used to distinguish between key and non-key controls and that only key controls are tested.

The third column is used to describe the nature and the extent of the compliance test. This is followed by a column for the test conclusion — this must specify which substantive tests are affected.

The ICE should be cross referenced to the flowchart, the supporting working papers and any appropriate paragraphs in the management letter.

	Prepared by		Sch No
Client _____	Date started		
Accounts to _____	Date finished		
Cycle _____	Reviewed by		
	Date		

INTERNAL CONTROL EVALUATION

Audit Programme	Key Control Question	Key Control			Nature and extent of compliance tests	Sch. No.	Errors?	CONCLUSIONS:— specifying the substantive tests for which reliance is or is not possible.	Management letters	Initial
		Strengths/ Weaknesses	Flow-chart	Key/ non-key						

Appendix 5 Audit planning documentation

As explained in Chapter 10, the audit plan must be documented. The three examples in this appendix demonstrate how the form and size of the written plan varies to suit the audit.

A Jones (Newsagents) Ltd shows how the audit plan for a very small incorporated business can be documented. The 'audit' involves preparing the statutory accounts from the client's records as well as verifying them. Very little information is available before the start of the job — but the manager knows the client well and uses the planning document to pass on some of the information to the assistant doing the job (in practice, the document may well be written out by the assistant as notes of a briefing discussion). The plan is supported by a detailed accountancy and audit programme (which has not been reproduced).

J L Computers Ltd is an example of an audit plan for a small but growing company. It is in note form and may be hand written. Nevertheless it addresses all the points mentioned in Chapter 10 and helps the audit team to concentrate its efforts on the important areas. The written plan is supported by a written audit programme (which has not been reproduced).

The Real Cider Brewery Co Ltd example shows how the audit plan should be documented for a larger company where there are, generally speaking, reliable accounting systems and there is up-to-date and accurate management information. The audit is carried out to a reasonably tight deadline.

The written plan addresses all the points in Chapter 10 in much more detail than the J L Computers Ltd example. A separate section deals with the audit approach to each cycle (the example has been abbreviated by excluding the information on all the cycles — the revenue and payroll cycles are shown in order to demonstrate the different approaches to different cycles).

The written plan includes the key figures and ratios from an initial analytical review. These are supported by copies of the management accounts and stock reconciliations which are themselves backed up by written explanation of the figures.

A detailed audit programme, risk assessment, a budget and a timetable support the written plan (of these only the risk assessment has been reproduced).

The audit plan is typed. The basic framework is kept on a disc in the word-processing system so that it can be quickly updated each year. It is, however, vitally important that the content is considered and revised, where appropriate, each year.

	Prepared by		Sch No
Client A Jones (Newspapers) Ltd	Date started		
	Date finished		
Accounts to 31 March 1991	Reviewed by		
	Date		

AUDIT PLAN

1 Terms of the engagement including reports required and client expectations.

Normal Companies Act report — we write up the nominal ledger and prepare draft statutory accounts from client records — abbreviated accounts to be filed at Companies House.

2 The company and its business.

Old established confectioners, tobacconist and newsagents with main shop in High Street and branch in Kings Road Estate.
Turnover about £200,000.

3 Special audit problems.

Review gross margins and drawings to ensure that both appear reasonable in light of other evidence, the nature and location of the business and the proprietor's standard of living.

4 Results of analytical review procedures.

No information available—we expect gross margins of 26% (newspapers), 10% (tobacco) and 20% (confectionery). Normally sales mix (based on purchases) has been approximately 5:3:2

5 Evaluation of audit risk.

Our risk assessment indicates normal audit risk except on the understatement of income/stock where there is a higher than normal risk.

6 Preliminary estimate of materiality.

Accounting — all postings etc to be accurate — wherever possible work to nearest £ or £10.
Auditing — £1,000 based on approximately $\frac{1}{2}$% turnover and 5% of profits.

7 Audit approach.

No reliance is to be placed on internal controls or analytical review. Generally a vouching approach will be adopted.

Prepared by		Sch No
Date started		
Date finished		
Reviewed by		
Date		

Client A Jones (Newspapers) Ltd

Accounts to 31 March 1991

7 Audit approach (contd)

As far as the risk of understatement of sales is concerned, we will check from till rolls to the cash book, estimate the sales mix from the purchases mix and predict a gross margin. We will also review cash movements in ten weeks at random and check that they appear reasonable. For other procedures, see accountancy and audit programme (not reproduced).

8 Other matters.

None.

9 Budget and fee.

£800.

10 Timetable and staffing.

Accounts to be ready for discussion with client on 6 July 1991

Audit plan approved   Date

   Manager _____   _____

   Partner _____   _____

	Prepared by		Sch No
	Date started		
Client J L Computers Ltd	Date finished		
	Reviewed by		
Accounts to 3oth June 1991	Date		

AUDIT PLAN

1 Terms of the engagement including reports required and client expectations.	Normal Companies Act report — we write up nominal ledger and prepare draft statutory accounts from client records.
2 The company and its business.	New company set up in 1989 to retail microcomputer systems and related software packages — provides some consultancy services. Financed mainly by proprietors and overdraft until £100,000 new capital injected by Venture Capital Ltd in January 1991. Turnover about £1,000,000 (£270,000 last year).
3 Special audit problems.	Possible obsolete stock due to changes in technology; XL40 software may be unsaleable. Billing of sales is likely to give rise to errors — new systems are invoiced in advance of delivery; consultancy work is billed retrospectively and there is little by way of 'work in progress' records.
4 Results of analytical review procedures.	Client produces management accounts comprising sales analysis and cash flows (not reproduced); these are in line with the forecasts done in the report to Venture Capital Ltd.
5 Evaluation of audit risk.	In view of the rapid growth of the business, the importance placed on the accounts by Venture Capital Ltd and the problems in recording sales, this audit should be treated as higher than normal risk. The detailed assessment of risk is set out in E1.3 (not reproduced). Procedures required for specific areas of risk are set out in E1.2 point 7.
6 Preliminary estimate of materiality.	£36,000 based on estimate of turnover of £1,000,000 and likely profit of around £50–100,000.

Prepared by		Sch No
Date started		
Date finished		
Reviewed by		
Date		

Client J L Computers Ltd

Accounts to 30th June 1991

AUDIT PLAN

7 Audit approach.

Due to the whole audit being identified as being high risk we will not rely on internal controls, or analytical review to reduce sample sizes. The following specific procedures will be carried out:

(a) reconcile purchases and sales of computer systems and check that cut off is correct and in particular that no undelivered systems are included in sales, bearing in mind that it is the company's practice to invoice before delivery;

(b) review consultants' diaries for the last three months to check that all assignments are included in work in progress or billings; and

(c) ensure that all XL40 software is identified and that provision is made except where it is covered by definite orders.

For other procedures and objectives, see audit programme which has already been prepared (not reproduced).

8 Other matters.
(e,g, Taxation—see V10)

The company moved to new leasehold premises in April; we need to pay particular care that leasehold improvements are treated correctly (see attached letter — not reproduced).

9 Budget and fee.

Budget £5,500, excluding tax.

10 Timetable and staffing.

A J Taylor and S Smith — complete by 6.9.91.

Audit plan approved   Date

Manager _____   _____

Partner _____   _____

REAL CIDER BREWERY COMPANY LIMITED PLANNING MEMORANDUM — YEAR ENDING 31 DECEMBER 1990

Prepared by S Senior, 15 October 1990

1   Terms of the engagement; reports required; client expectations

We are required to carry out an audit under the Companies Act 1985. The client produces draft accounts but we have to convert them into the statutory form.

We also prepare and submit the tax computations, together with supporting schedules. We therefore need to carry out sufficient analysis of expenditure to identify disallowable items. We need not prepare detailed schedules provided the add backs in the computation can be readily traced back through the accounting records.

It has been agreed by the client that we should draw management's attention to areas of waste and inefficiency in the recording of accounting transactions and the preparation of accounts in areas which are incidental to our audit work.

2   Analytical review

2.01   We have reviewed the management accounts for the 9 months to 30 September 1990 and the key figures and ratios are summarised below. We have also reviewed the reconciliations of physical quantities of production, sales and stock (and purchases in the case of soft drinks) and have confirmed that all differences have been investigated and dealt with properly.

2.02   Cider brewing and soft drink sales have not been as adversely affected by the current economic recession as certain other parts of the drinks trade. One reason for this is the relative price advantage over beer and spirits. The figures available for the nine months to 30 September 1990 indicate that the company has not only managed to maintain its level of activity and share of the market, but to increase both. This is due to aggressive marketing and selling of Green Griffin and the recent press publicity given to 'real' cider.

2.03   We have also examined the forecast for the year to 31 December 1990 and the key figures and ratios are summarised below. As usual, the final quarter shows lower sales than the summer quarter and only a small increase in cumulative profits.

2.04   *Key figures and ratios*

	9 mths to 30.9.90 £000	9 mths to 30.9.89 £000	Forecast Yr ended 31.12.90 £000	Yr ended 31.12.89 £000	Yr ended 31.12.88 £000
Turnover	7,134	5,096	8,400	6,104	5,126
Cost of sales	4,436	3,334	5,250	3,870	3,678
Gross margin	2,698	1,762	3,150	2,234	1,448
Overheads	1,304	864	1,580	1,058	1,014
Depreciation	170	148	220	196	148
Finance charges	144	152	200	194	86
Profit before tax	1,080	598	1,150	786	200
Stock	830	604	800	542	453
Trade debtors	1,784	1,268	1,600	1,150	920
Trade creditors	1,080	644	800	646	379
Bank balance	304	498	200	474	315

	9 mths to 30.9.90	9 mths to 30.9.89	Forecast Yr ended 31.12.90	Yr ended 31.12.89
Gross margin as % of turnover	37.8	34.6	37.5	36.6
Net profit as % of turnover	15.1	11.7	13.7	12.9
Stock as % of turnover	11.6	11.8	9.5	8.9
Trade debtors as % of turnover	25.0	24.9	19.0	18.8
Trade creditors as % of purchases	32.9	35.7	28.0	27.1
Debtors' collection period (months)	3.0	2.99	2.28	2.26
Creditors' payment period (months)	3.95	4.28	3.36	3.25

2.05   *Turnover*

Turnover has increased by over one third compared with last year. We need to pay particular attention to:

(a)   sales cut-off;

(b)   results of debtors' circularisation; and

(c)   correspondence with debtors;

to ensure that sales are not overstated. We can, however, rely on the check of physical quantities of production, sales and stock in order to reduce the level of our substantive tests of detail.

2.06   *Debtors*

The debtors' collection period remains at close to 3 months (although it tends to fall in the last quarter). The Chief Accountant is dissatisfied with this as credit terms are one month only. His efforts to reduce the balances outstanding have been countered by the marketing effort on Green Griffin. We need to pay special attention to possible bad debts, particularly as there are about 150 new off-licence customers.

2.07   *Gross margin*

The improvement in gross margin is attributable to the launch of Green Griffin, which the company is able to sell at a premium price:

	Sales £000	Gross margin £000	Gross margin %
9 months to September 1989			
Scrumptious	3,678	1,536	41.8
Green Griffin	—	—	—
Soft drinks	1,418	226	15.9
Total	5,096	1,762	34.6
9 months to September 1990			
Scrumptious	3,764	1,524	40.5
Green Griffin	1,740	922	53.0
Soft drinks	1,630	252	15.5
Total	7,134	2,698	37.8

These margins have been checked to selling prices and the costings and appear reasonable. The forecast gross margin for the full year assumes a drop in the percentage in the final quarter. From discussions with the Marketing Director this is unlikely and the forecast margin may be exceeded by about 0.4%.

2.08   *Cash flow*

The company's cash flow projections predict a healthy bank balance, despite extra purchases for stock and the high level of debtors. The company is unlikely to have a problem in this area although funds will be required to develop Merlin.

2.09   *Conclusion*

The strength of the client's management accounting system has allowed us to carry out an extensive analytical review. We have been able to explain any significant variations and will attribute an R-factor of 1 to analytical review.

3   Evaluation of audit risk

A detailed evaluation of risk is included on E2, risk assessment (see *Appendix 6*). The main points arising are:

(a)   The Cox family takes an active role in the business and has tended to be prudent in its accounting. There is the remote possibility of a Stock Exchange quote, although at present the company has adequate financing and a healthy cash flow.

(b)   There has been a rapid expansion during the current year. Generally, there have been adequate resources to cope with the accounting consequences. However, an area of concern is the possibility of doubtful debts as less thorough checks have been carried out on new customers (see also d and e).

(c)   Higher than expected provisions have been made against debtors and stocks. This mitigates the risk identified in (b) to some extent, but we need to ensure that the current year charges are not overstated.

(d)   Another effect of the growth of the business has been the need to take on extra staff. Many of these temporaries have been paid in cash and there may be some lack of control over payments and deductions. However, this is unlikely to give rise to a material error and this is to be reviewed at the interim.

(e)   Temporary staff have been used in the production and accounts departments. In the latter, this has led to some problems over recording sales. However, a check is run by the computer on any gaps in the numerical sequence of advice notes so it is unlikely to lead to a material understatement of sales.

(f)   In the past cheques have been held back at the year end by directors. There is no anticipated problem with bank balances at 31 December 1990 so this is not expected to be an issue this year.

We have concluded that overall risk is normal. It is therefore appropriate to place reliance on risk assessment to reduce the extent of our other audit procedures, by attributing an R-factor of 1 to it, except in the areas noted above where specific risk has been identified i.e. the testing of provisions (bad debts and stock), clearance of cheques and temporary staff payroll (depending upon results of interim work).

4   Materiality

Based upon the management accounts for the 9 months to September and the forecasts for the full year, a materiality level of £80,000 should be used for the purpose of assessing adjustments and £72,000 for testing. These figures should be reviewed before the start of the final audit.

The level is approximately 1% of turnover, 2% of total assets and about 7% of profit before tax.

5   Audit approach and audit problems

Having attributed R-factors of 1 to both analytical review and risk assessment for most cycles (see 3 above) we can reduce our procedures to a minimum consistent with firm policy and Auditing Standards where appropriate.

5.01   The important cycles to our audit opinion are revenue, expenditure and stock. Sample sizes for transactions work should be chosen to cover the period up to the time of our interim visit and, in the case of sales, spread over the different products in proportion to sales value.

5.02   *Revenue cycle*
The computer audit department has reviewed and updated the records of the sales system and has reported on the reliability of general and application controls (not reproduced). They have also suggested ways in which the enquiry facility supplied as part of the manufacturer's software can speed up the selection of debtors and sales transactions for verification (not reproduced).

Our flowcharts indicate that adequate controls exist over this entire cycle. The only problem which has been encountered in the past has been to ensure that all advice notes were accounted for. This has now been rectified by regular checks; if these are working we will be able to rely on them to reduce the level of our substantive tests of detail.

We need to check that:
(a)　all despatches are recorded on advice notes;
(b)　correct invoices are raised for all advice notes;
(c)　all invoices are recorded in the nominal ledger and sales ledger;
(d)　debtors represent amounts due from customers;
(e)　the provision for doubtful debts is adequate.

We will also seek to rely on analytical review procedures for the first four objectives. We will examine the detailed sales analysis prepared by the company together with the reconciliations of physical quantities of cider production, sales and stocks. These should contribute an R-factor of 1.

The company does not carry out formalised credit checks which could be tested and relied upon. In addition, the rapid expansion of the trade has increased the risk of bad debts. We probably will not be able to rely on analytical review procedures, although we should reassess the situation before the final audit. We will review this area during our interim visit and finally decide on our approach when we have carried out this assessment.

We will use error rate sampling, based on a precision of 3% and the appropriate R-factors, for the transactions work. We will use monetary unit sampling for our tests on debtors and the doubtful debt provision.

A debtors' circularisation is to be carried out as at 30 November 1990. The list of balances will be available on 5 December 1990 and a member of staff will visit the client on 6 December to carry out the circularisation. We have sent the client a sample of the standard letter and copies will be ready, signed, for us on 6 December. The balances for circularisation will be selected using the software enquiry facility (not reproduced) and monetary unit sampling.

The client has agreed to investigate all differences arising on the circularisation replies as well as to extract our samples of advice notes and invoices.

5.03　*Expenditure cycle*
(not reproduced).

5.04　*Stock cycle*
(not reproduced).

5.05　*Payroll cycle*
Total payroll is about £500,000 with the result that wages are not a significant

area. As management is very closely involved in the day-to-day running of the business and each employee is personally known, there is therefore only a normal risk of material error.

However, the use of temporary staff, who are paid in cash, has led to a lack of control, especially over deductions. There are about 20 such workers who have been paid about £40,000 during the year. This is posted via a separate journal to the wages account in the nominal ledger.

We will therefore eliminate detailed testing for permanent staff and carry out tests of total by means of a week-by-week review for twelve weeks this year for:
  Gross pay
  Overtime
  PAYE
  NI
  Net pay.

We will also check the cumulative PAYE calculations for 5 employees as at the last payroll before the interim audit.

For temporary staff we may need to carry out some detailed testing. The matter will be reviewed during an interim visit to determine the extent of the problem.

5.06   *Fixed assets cycle*
(not reproduced).

5.07   *Other areas*
(not reproduced).

6   Budget and fee
This is attached (not reproduced). All time and expenses should be charged to 0999–0007.

7   Timetable

Our interim visit has been arranged for two weeks commencing on 12 November 1990. The team consists of a senior (grade 55) and an assistant (grade 70) (J Junior).

The final visit has been arranged to start on 14 January 1991 for three weeks. The visit will involve a senior (grade 55) for three weeks and an assistant (grade 70) for two weeks. We will adhere strictly to client's normal hours of work, although overtime is likely to be required and has been budgeted for in the final week.

8   Other matters

8.01   *Management letter procedures*
Two management leeters will be sent, one following each of our visits.

Management letter points should be noted as soon as they arise, so that they may be incorporated into the main letter. The manager will discuss the draft letters with the Chief Accountant at meetings immediately following the completion of the interim and final audits.

8.02   *Queries to client*
We should collect all our queries for the Chief Accountant and discuss them with him twice weekly. Any such queries which cannot be resolved should be dealt with by the manager or partner.

8.03   *Computer installation*
A computer (an IBM AS400) was installed in February 1989 to deal with sales invoicing and sales ledger. The computer issues invoices, from advice note details, on the basis of the prices it holds as standing data. The computer print-out of invoices acts as the sales day book; the totals are posted to the sales ledger and control account automatically. However, the nominal ledger and stock records are not linked and these are dealt with manually (it is planned to computerise this part of the system in 1991).

S Senior
15 October 1990

	Signature	Date
Approved by manager	_____	_____
Approved by partner	_____	_____

Appendix 6 Audit planning — risk assessment

Client Real Cider Brewery Company	Prepared by		Sch No
	Date started		
	Date finished		
Accounts to 31st December 1990	Reviewed by		
	Date		

AUDIT PLANNING — RISK ASSESSMENT

Our assessment of the risk of material error is based on our knowledge of the business, formally documented in the Business Review Report E2.1 and a review of the accounting system via the Accounting Systems Checklist E2.2. This work will also highlight specific areas of risk, for which we must adapt our audit approach.

SUMMARY OF CONCLUSIONS

1. Business Review
   Have you assessed the risk inherent in the way the business is structured and operated?   E2.1   YES/NO

   Have you assessed the risk inherent in the control environment?   E2.1   YES/NO

2. Accounting Systems Checklist
   Is our documentation of the accounting system up to date?   YES/NO

   Have you completed the Accounting Systems Check-list?   E2.2   YES/NO

   Have you completed the Computer Controls Summary?   E2.2   YES/NO

   Have you assessed the risk inherent in the way the accounting system operates?   YES/NO

OVERALL ASSESSMENT OF RISK
We have concluded that overall risk is normal. It is therefore appropriate to place reliance on risk assessment to reduce the extent of our other audit procedures, by attributing an R-factor of 1 to it, except in the areas noted above where specific risk has been identified i.e. the testing of provisions (bad debts and stock), clearance of cheques and temporary staff payroll (depending upon results of interim work).

Partner: _____   Manager: _____
Date: _____   Date: _____

Prepared by	
Date started	
Date finished	
Reviewed by	
Date	

Sch No

Client Real Cider Brewery Company

Accounts to 31st December 1990

BUSINESS REVIEW	Risks	Mitigating Factors	Mitigated? Yes/No	Cycle affected	Audit Procedures and Programme Reference	MLP
The business, its structure and ownership	Possibility of attempts to overstate results in run up to stock market quote.	Strength of accounting systems and conservative nature of management.	Yes	—	—	
Industry, markets and products	The rapid expansion of the customer base, resulting in fewer credit checks could lead to problems with bad debts.	A net material bad debt is unlikely as bad debt provisions are usually high (see Control environment).	No	Revenue	Bad debt review including circularisation and after date cash checks. H4.1	
	Lack of control over wages of short term contract workers.	None, but unlikely to be material.	No	Payroll	Review area at the interim audit to assess materiality. Perform sample checks of payments to contract workers. L4.1	
Financial position	The business is vulnerable to going-concern problems if production was halted due to disruption by suppliers on which the company is dependent.	There is some diversification away from supplier-dependent products.	Yes	—	—	

Client Real Cider Brewery Company

Accounts to 31st December 1990

Prepared by	MLP
Date started	
Date finished	
Reviewed by	
Date	
Sch No	

BUSINESS REVIEW	Risks	Mitigating Factors	Mitigated?	Cycle affected	Audit Procedures and Programme Reference
Control environment	Stock and debtor provisions reflect an unduly pessimistic view and may therefore be unjustifiably large.	None	No	Stock	Review of stock provisions, movements of stock after the year end. J4.1
				Revenue	Review of bad debt provision and specific bad debts recovered after the year end. H4.1
	Problems may occur in the recording of sales due to the use of temporary staff.	Sequence checks done by computer ensures no sales are wrongly recorded.	Yes	—	—

Client Real Cider Brewery Company

Accounts to 31st December 1990

	Prepared by	
	Date started	
	Date finished	
	Reviewed by	
	Date	

	Risks	Mitigating factors	Mitigated ? Yes/No	Cycle affected	Audit Procedures and Programme Reference	MLP
ACCOUNTING SYSTEMS REVIEW	Cheques may be held back at the year end leading to under-statement of credi-tors (and cash).	No cash problem at the year end so no need to hold pay-ments back.	No	Cash Creditors	Ensure cheques issued before year end have cleared within a reason-able period. S4.1	
	Casual labour tax and NI may not be deducted properly and no real checks carried out on this.	Unlikely to be material.	No	Payroll	See above.	Yes
COMPUTER CONTROLS SUMMARY	No separation of functions between applications develop-ment and pro-gramming functions.	No one has the knowledge to amend programmes/data.	Yes	—	—	Yes

	Prepared by		Sch No
	Date started		
Client Real Cider Brewery Company	Date finished		
	Reviewed by		
Accounts to 31st December 1990	Date		

BUSINESS REVIEW REPORT

Have you considered the following areas, and documented the information obtained:

The External Environment   Initials

1.   The business, its structure and ownership

2.   Industry, markets and products

3.   Financial position

4.   Initial results review

The Control Environment

1.   Control environment

2.   Departmental review

Other Risks

BUSINESS REVIEW — IDEAS LIST
THE BUSINESS, ITS STRUCTURE AND OWNERSHIP   Considered ?

Who owns the company? (e.g. family business, subsidiary of private group etc.) Describe the concentration of ownership, including approximate number of shareholders, any significant shareholders, whether shares are actively traded, extent of management's ownership interest.   YES/NA

Is the company a subsidiary or associate of another company? Is the company UK or foreign? Does the company have subsidiaries, UK or foreign? What are the percentage holdings in each class of shares?   YES/NA

Is it a manufacturer or distributor, a wholesaler or retailer? Does it sell goods or services? Does it buy to meet specific orders or does it hold stocks in expectation of orders?   YES/NA

If it is a manufacturer, is it producing in bulk, in batches, by means of a continuous process or does it deal with individual jobs? Does it manufacture from basic raw materials or does it buy in components and assemble finished goods?   YES/NA

If the business is that of a distributor or wholesaler, how wide is the range of suppliers, goods and customers?   YES/NA

What product groups does a retailer deal in — and is it for cash only?   YES/NA

If it is a service company, how does it provide the service — is it based on people or assets? Is the business trading entirely on its own account — are franchises or licences involved in some way?   YES/NA

What are the major products of the business and for which 'market' are they intended?   YES/NA

What is the extent of the company's dependence on major suppliers/customers?   YES/NA

How long has the company been in existence? What is the history of its major businesses (including the development of the businesses before they were acquired by the company)?   YES/NA

What are the principal activities of other group companies?   YES/NA

Who audits other group companies? Does the audit of foreign subsidiaries comply with UK standards?   YES/NA

Have branches, depots or subsidiaries been acquired or sold?   YES/NA

What are the directors' plans for the future? Are there any intentions to seek a listing? Are future plans influenced by agreements with providers of finance? Are the directors/shareholders hoping to sell up and retire? Are there any plans to change the group structure? What progress has been made to date in achieving the directors' aims?   YES/NA

Do the directors intend to run down/dispose of unprofitable activities or subsidiaries? Do they hope to improve profitability by greater efficiency/lower overheads at the same level of output?   YES/NA

Client Real Cider Brewery Company

Accounts to 31st December 1990

BUSINESS REVIEW REPORT

The Business, its Structure and Ownership
RCBC Ltd is a private company which is controlled by the Cox family and has been established for over 15 years. The ownership is as follows:

A Cox	— 20%)
P Cox	— 20%) Directors
S Cox	— 20%)
Other Cox's	— 40%

The company produces and markets a number of 'real' ciders and also bottles and sells soft drinks. The current range of products consists of one bottled cider (launched March 1990) and one draught cider, as well as bottled soft drinks. Another draught cider is being developed.

Production is in batches with raw materials being brought in from apple growers between September and December each year. There is considerable dependence on two suppliers as Scrumptious can only be made from a particular type of apple. Green Griffin is not so dependent on particular apple types and this diversification should help reduce dependence on suppliers. The company depends on Squashara for supplies of the soft drink raw material. The company is not dependent on any one customer.

The owner/directors have close involvement in the day-to-day running of the business. Neither Mr A Cox nor Mr P Cox intend to retire in the near future and are committed to expanding the company. There is a remote possibility that the company will be looking for a stock market quote in the next 3–5 years.

The business is managed from the Taunton site, where all records are kept. Mr A Cox is in charge of operations at the Exeter factory.

Risk Factors Identified and any Mitigating Factors
Possibility of attempts to overstate results in run-up to stock market quote.

INDUSTRY, MARKETS AND PRODUCTS	Considered ?

What stage of development has the industry reached? Is it in a period of rapid expansion?, decline? etc.   YES/NA

Is the industry international? Regional? Where are its main markets? Is the industry dominated by particular companies?   YES/NA

Can new businesses enter the industry easily or are there barriers to entry?   YES/NA

Is there scope for our client to expand further? Can our client cope with expansion?   YES/NA

Is our client one of the market leaders?   YES/NA

Is there strong competition? Are many companies failing?   YES/NA

What general economic factors affect the industry (e.g. interest rates, foreign exchange)?   YES/NA

Is the trade seasonal or spread evenly over the year?   YES/NA

Who are the major customers of the business?   YES/NA

Does it sell and buy in cash or credit?   YES/NA

Is research carried out to identify new opportunities and are management responsive to new ideas.   YES/NA

Are the directors seeking to expand sales of existing products in existing markets or by developing new products or new markets? Do the directors have a policy of expansion by acquisition?   YES/NA

Legal and Professional Requirements

Are there any special laws or rules that apply to the industry (e.g. pollution control)?   YES/NA

Is the company registered under the Financial Services Act?

Are there any special accounting requirements/problems in the industry? Is the industry covered by a SORP?   YES/NA

Are there any particular audit problems in the industry (e.g. valuing stocks at a jewellers)? Is the company covered by an industry Auditing Guideline?   YES/NA

How is the industry treated for VAT purposes?   YES/NA

Client <u>Real Cider Brewery Company</u>

Accounts to <u>31st December 1990</u>

BUSINESS REVIEW REPORT

Industry, Markets and Products
The cider industry is a well-established one, relying on traditional products of good quality, especially for companies of Real Cider Brewery's size. The larger companies which dominate the industry include Bulmers, Coates and Taunton who rely on mass production.

The company's major competitors are therefore comparable sized companies offering the 'traditional' ciders and include Whole Apple Cider Company and Quick Brew Cider Company.

Currently, RCBC's main market is the South West although the launch of a new cider has increased sales outside the area. Customers include:
(a)   pubs and off-licences (35–40% sales)
(b)   major breweries (45%)
(c)   industrial and transport caterers (15%).
Trade is seasonal, with most sales occurring during the summer months.

The directors have put considerable resources into developing new products and recognise the need for diversification away from Scrumptious which relies on supplies from two growers. During the year Green Griffin was launched. It has met with considerable success to date and demand is high, resulting in the bottling plant working at full capacity. Another new draught cider, Merlin, has been developed but is not yet in production.

Green Griffin has expanded the customer base of the company with many orders from independent off-licence customers who had not previously bought from RCBC.

To date the expanded product range and increased production have been managed well. The directors planned the launch of Green Griffin after commissioning trials of the cider in order to gauge demand. Demand has subsequently met expectations. The directors have taken on short term contract workers to deal with the extra production, although the aim is to take on full time workers if demand continues at current levels.

Legal and Professional Requirements
There are no special problems relating to the industry. The accounting arrangements for determining excise duty have generally been adequate. Customs & Excise officials pay regular visits.

Risk Factors Identified and any Mitigating Factors
The rapid expansion of the customer base could lead to problems with recoverability of debts, as fewer credit checks are possible due to time pressure. However, this is unlikely to have a net material effect on the accounts as provisions for bad debts are usually quite high (see Control Environment).

There may not be adequate control over the wages of the short term contract workers. The payroll clerk is not used to dealing with wages for these people and errors may therefore arise.

FINANCIAL POSITION	Considered ?

How is the business financed? Have there been any recent changes   YES/NA
in financing arrangements?

Are the agreed borrowing/overdraft facilities adequate for immedi-   YES/NA
ate and future needs? Have they been exceeded during the year?

Are cash flow requirements for seasonal trade catered for adequately?   YES/NA

Is there consideration of various forms of financing prior to imple-   YES/NA
menting projects e.g. lease or buy?

Are cash surpluses identified quickly and placed on deposit?   YES/NA

Has there been a recent decline in turnover or profitability? Can we   YES/NA
identify reasons for this? Is the decline in line with the industry as a
whole or are special factors involved?

Is the company suffering liquidity or longer term financing diffi-   YES/NA
culties?
- Is cash flow and working capital declining or inadequate for the
  needs of the business?
- Have fixed assets or long term projects been financed out of
  short term borrowings?
- Is the debt to equity ratio high and increasing?
- Are debtor or stock turnovers decreasing significantly?
- Is the company near to, or in breach of, debenture trust deeds,
  loan covenants, overdraft limits etc?
- Have approaches to financial institutions for further funds been
  unsuccessful?
- To what extent does the company rely on 'off balance sheet'
  financing?
- Does the company finance out of overdue suppliers and other
  creditors?
- Are old fixed assets used because the company cannot afford to
  purchase new ones?

Is the company able to withstand possible adverse events such as:
- change in economic conditions, affecting demand for products,
  exchange rates, input prices, etc
- potential losses on long term contracts
- loss of a major supplier or customer
- loss of key personnel
- computer breakdown or restriction under the Data Protection
  Act
- obsolescence of key products?   YES/NA

Have any of these events occured during the year?   YES/NA

Client Real Cider Brewery Company

Accounts to 31st December 1990

BUSINESS REVIEW REPORT

Financial Position
The business is financed by bank overdraft facilities, a mortgage for the Exeter factory from Bristol Venture Capital Co and interest-free loans from two of the directors. The company has not exceeded its agreed facilities at any time. The directors are aware that before they can launch Merlin cider they will need to raise further external medium term finance and are currently negotiating this with X bank.

Extra funds were raised last year in order to purchase the new factory and this has increased interest payment commitments. The company chose to negotiate a fixed-interest loan as a hedge against increased interest rates.

The company is currently in a stable financial position. However, there are two main factors on which the business depends — the involvement of the Cox brothers and the Scrumptious apple suppliers. There is little dependence on any one customer. The company has adequate funds to finance fluctuations in working capital needs.

Risk Factors Identified and any Mitigating Factors
Dependence on suppliers may lead to lack of control over costs and severe production problems if supplies were withdrawn. However, the diversification away from Scrumptious should help this.

INITIAL RESULTS REVIEW	Considered ?
What are the financial trends for the last few years?	YES/NA
Has turnover and profits increased or decreased?	YES/NA
Has there been a change in cash flow or liquidity?	YES/NA
Has the level of gearing increased? Is the current level unusually high or low?	YES/NA
How do the anticipated figures for the current period fit in with these trends?	YES/NA
How do the above figures reflect changes in product range, markets, financial structure, etc? Are the changes what we would expect? Are there any unexplained changes?	YES/NA
Has initial analytical review been completed?	YES/NA
Have you identified any factors which would indicate material error or which require further investigation?	YES/NA

Client <u>Real Cider Brewery Company</u>

Accounts to <u>31st December 1990</u>

BUSINESS REVIEW REPORT

Initial Results Review

	Forecast 31.12.90 £000	31.12.89 £000	31.12.88 £000
Turnover	8,400	6,104	5,126
Profit before Tax	1,150	786	200
Debtors collection (months)	2.28	2.26	2.15
Creditors payment (months)	3.36	3.25	3.14
Stock Turnover	56 days	51 days	45 days

Turnover and profits have increased due to the successful introduction of Green Griffin at a higher margin than Scrumptious and careful control over the costs involved in its launch and production.

The company has not experienced severe cash flow problems although the directors would like to raise further funds before developing Merlin cider further.

Gearing has increased from 2% to 20.4% due to the £350,000 mortgage taken out to buy the new factory.

Risk Factors Identified and any Mitigating Factors
None.

CONTROL ENVIRONMENT

The attitude of management affects our assessment of risk because they may have the ability to override controls and to influence the figures shown in the accounts, for example, to meet profit targets. If we suspect this is happening we should try to assess how this is likely to affect the accounts, and direct our tests accordingly. The level of expertise of management can also affect the business as a whole, and its ability to continue as a going concern.

	Considered ?
Is control exercised in a formal/informal way or does control rely on owner/manager controls?	YES/NA
Describe the makeup of the board of directors, including number of directors, background of non-executive directors, duties of each director and length of service.	YES/NA
Describe any specific authorities retained by the board or its committees. Describe the terms of reference and composition of any committees, how often they meet and state whether minutes are taken of all meetings and retained.	YES/NA
Is there a clearly defined management responsibility structure?	YES/NA
Is the quality and ability of management appropriate to the business?	YES/NA
How dependent is the company on one or a limited number of key personnel?	YES/NA
Are any key officers or employees related? State relationships and duties.	YES/NA
Are outside specialists employed to supplement internal expertise?	YES/NA
Are employees who handle cash, securities and other valuable assets insured?	YES/NA
Does management hope to maximise or minimise reported profits?	YES/NA
Does management require a certain level of profits in order to raise finance, sell the business, meet a profit forecast etc?	YES/NA
Is this level of profits achievable, based on past performance and present trading conditions?	YES/NA
Is management generally conservative in its business decisions, or is it prepared to accept substantial risks?	YES/NA
Does management raise external expectations of profits?	YES/NA
Does management make use of budgets and management accounts?	YES/NA
Does management pay attention to cash flow as well as profitability and sales? Does management make use of formal business plans?	YES/NA
Where major expansion is planned or in progress, is there a danger that management is moving outside its areas of competence?	YES/NA

Client Real Cider Brewery Company

Accounts to 31st December 1990

BUSINESS REVIEW REPORT

Control Environment
Control is exercised in a fairly informal way and is largely dependent on the close involvement of the directors. The directors and their major duties are:

> Mr A Cox — Managing Director and Sales Director
> Mr P Cox — Production Director
> Mr S Cox — Finance Director

All of the above have been involved with the company since it was set up and therefore are very familiar with all aspects of the business. The directors aim to keep their responsibilities separate but this is not always possible. Formal board meetings are rare.

Due to the directors' depth of knowledge of the business, the company is dependent on their continued involvement. However, the directors are gradually passing more responsibility on to their management team, especially A. Wall in Sales and P. Door in Production.

There is little use of external expertise, although consultants were used for some of the initial research into Green Griffin.

The Cox's are generally conservative in their approach and have always taken the prudent course.

Risk Factors Identified and any Mitigating Factors
The lack of formal controls is offset by the strong informal control exercised by the brothers.

If one of the Cox's was absent due to illness or accident there would be a large gap in the management. This is mitigated by the fact that some control is being passed down to the other (non-Cox) managers and by the ability of the brothers to cover for each other at least in the short term.

CONTROL ENVIRONMENT continued   Considered ?

Is management more than usually concerned about reducing taxes? Has its relationship with the Inland Revenue, Customs & Excise and other regulatory authorities been good in the past?   YES/NA

Does the company change its advisers frequently? Does it have a good relationship with, for example, its brokers/merchant bankers?   YES/NA

Is management prepared to accept the spirit of SSAPs and legal accounting requirements or does it attempt to circumvent such rules?   YES/NA

Has a change in accounting policy been made primarily to improve reported results?   YES/NA

Are accounting estimates, such as provisions for bad debts, stock obsolescence etc, based on an unusually optimistic (or pessimistic) view of the future?   YES/NA

Do the majority of errors found in previous audits affect profit in the same direction?   YES/NA

Are the directors more than usually involved in the detailed accounting functions, for a company of its size? Do they sometimes short cut accounting controls?   YES/NA

Have the directors been involved with any unsuccessful enterprises in the past, or are they known for their successful track records?   YES/NA

FINANCIAL CONTROLS

Are management reports timely and are they acted upon?   YES/NA

Is there an accounts department with resources appropriate to its size? How well qualified and experienced are key members of staff? Are many staff employed on a temporary basis? Is there a high turnover of accounting staff? Are there frequent problems with or breakdowns of the computer system?   YES/NA

Are management accounts submitted at regular intervals to:
    the board of directors?   YES/NA
    the audit committee?   YES/NA

Do they show comparisons with:
    prior periods?   YES/NA
    budgets or forecasts?   YES/NA

Are they accompanied by an analytical review?   YES/NA

Do they include a balance sheet?   YES/NA

List the principal operating analyses used, e.g. analysis of sales, cost of sales. Describe contents and indicate frequency of preparation.   YES/NA

Are the same accounting and cut-off procedures followed at interim dates as at the year end? If not, describe how gross margins are calculated.   YES/NA

Client <u>Real Cider Brewery Company</u>

Accounts to <u>31st December 1990</u>

BUSINESS REVIEW REPORT

Control Environment continued
The company has a good relationship with the Customs & Excise and taxation authorities and with its bankers and lawyers. The directors are willing to follow the spirit of both the law and accounting requirements. However, a pessimistic view is often taken by the directors and large provisions for stock and debtors are made.

Mr S Cox deals with accounting records and controls and this is one area where the other two directors have little involvement on a day-to-day basis.

Financial Controls
Mr S Cox produces monthly management accounts and an annual budget. The directors aim to meet to discuss the monthly management accounts, but in many months this does not happen due to time pressure.

Because of the directors' close involvement problems are generally spotted quickly and dealt with promptly.

Sales and costs are analysed by product type. Mr A Cox keeps detailed information analysed by customer type and market area.

Mr P Cox prepares detailed production plans on a monthly basis and keeps tight control over purchasing costs.

The Finance Department comprises Mr S Cox as well as a part-qualified accountant and three clerical staff. This seems adequate given the size of the business.

Risk Factors Identified and any Mitigating Factors
There is little check on what Mr S Cox does and he is in a position to override controls, but only in relation to cheques less than £5,000.

Stock and debtor provisions may reflect an unduly pessimistic view and therefore be unjustifiably large.

CONTROL ENVIRONMENT continued   Considered ?

Financial Controls
Who reviews and approves financial information for distribution to
shareholders and analysts?   YES/NA

Are accounting policies, procedures and nominal ledger accounts
formally recorded in an accounting manual or similar document?   YES/NA
Is it updated for any changes?   YES/NA

Are all journal entries supported by full explanations and/or documentation and required to be authorised by a responsible official not
involved with the origination of the entries?   YES/NA

Budgets
Does the company use budgets to plan and control its performance?   YES/NA

Is there a system of budgetary control?   YES/NA

Do budgeting procedures cover all divisions and departments?   YES/NA

Do budgets and forecasts cover:
    revenue
    costs and expenses
    capital expenditure
    cashflow?   YES/NA

Are budgets and forecasts submitted to management on an established timetable?   YES/NA

Are forecasts updated on a regular basis during the year?   YES/NA

Are budget variances reported and analysed?   YES/NA

Internal Audit
Describe the normal duties of the internal auditors and evaluate
their competence and objectivity. Consider:
    Size and organisation of the staff
    Prior experience of staff
    Number of qualified accountants
    Extent of supervision of junior staff
    Flexibility/adequacy of audit documentation
    Scope restrictions?   YES/NA

Is the scope of internal audit activities planned in advance with:
    Senior Management?   YES/NA
    Board of Directors?   YES/NA
    External Auditors?   YES/NA

Do internal auditors have direct access to senior management and
the board of directors?   YES/NA

Do internal auditors prepare and follow written audit programmes?   YES/NA

Client <u>Real Cider Brewery Company</u>

Accounts to <u>31st December 1990</u>

BUSINESS REVIEW REPORT

Control Environment continued
Mr S Cox and his part-qualified assistant keep tight control over the accounting system. All journals are supported by documentation and signed by S Cox. During the second part of this year, however, the department has been very busy trying to keep up with the extra work generated by Green Griffin sales. In particular, the sales ledger clerk has been assisted by a temp since September.

Budgets
Budgets covering all areas are produced annually. A formal directors' meeting is held to discuss and agree them. In previous years these budgets have proved to be fairly accurate.

Risk Factors Identified and any Mitigating Factors
Problems may occur in the recording of sales due to the use of temporary staff.

CONTROL ENVIRONMENT continued   Considered ?

Internal Audit

Do internal auditors document, evaluate and test the accounting
system, including computer controls?   YES/NA

Are internal audit reports prepared and issued on a timely basis for
all assignments?   YES/NA

Are the reports issued to appropriate staff?   YES/NA

Are responses to recommendations documented?   YES/NA

Is implementation of internal audit recommendations monitored?   YES/NA

Audit Committee

Is there an audit committee?   YES/NA

How many members serve on it?   YES/NA

How many are outside directors?   YES/NA

How often does the committee meet?   YES/NA

Are minutes kept?   YES/NA

Client <u>Real Cider Brewery Company</u>

Accounts to <u>31st December 1990</u>

BUSINESS REVIEW REPORT

Control Environment continued

Internal Audit and Audit Committee
There is no internal audit function or audit committee.

Risk Factors Identified and any Mitigating Factors
None.

DEPARTMENTAL REVIEW
The purpose of a departmental review is to gain an understanding of the way different functions are organised and operated within a business. In an owner-managed business this may not be applicable but it is still necessary to describe the approach taken by the directors to each of the areas.

	Considered ?
Obtain copies of:	
Corporate structure chart	YES/NA
Personnel organisation chart.	YES/NA
If none, prepare charts for permanent file.	YES/NA
Do the charts clearly reflect areas of responsibility and lines of reporting and communication?	YES/NA
Are there formal job descriptions for administrative and financial personnel?	YES/NA
Do they clearly set out duties and responsibilities?	YES/NA

Personnel Policy

Is the recruitment and selection process for new employees in the administrative and financial areas properly carried out, and a review of past employment and achievements carried out and references obtained?	YES/NA
Are personnel policies documented and communicated to employees?	YES/NA
Is there a requirement to declare possible conflict of interests? Provide details, describing the system used to monitor compliance with the policy.	YES/NA
Are there formalised recruitment procedures?	YES/NA
Is there an operating manual for day-to-day activities, and a recognised complaints/disciplinary procedure?	YES/NA
Is there a high level of turnover among any particular sector of the work force?	YES/NA
Are staff generally competent?	YES/NA
Is job performance periodically evaluated and reviewed with each employee?	YES/NA
Are there training programmes for administrative and financial personnel?	YES/NA
Describe the major training programmes.	YES/NA

Client <u>Real Cider Brewery Company</u>

Accounts to <u>31st December 1990</u>

BUSINESS REVIEW REPORT

Departmental review
Copies of corporate structure chart on permanent file. There are no formal job descriptions for administrative or financial personnel.

Personnel Policy
References are always obtained for administrative and financial staff.

Recruitment is carried out by any of the directors, depending on what staff are being sought.

Personnel policies (staff handbook) are detailed on a brief document (attached).

The company has not experienced high turnover of staff. Most staff have been with the company for a number of years and are competent at their jobs.

Training is not formalised, but tends to be on-the-job.

Risk Factors identified and any Mitigating Factors

None.

DEPARTMENTAL REVIEW continued   Considered ?

Production and Purchasing
Are there established quality control procedures and reviews?   YES/NA

Does the business depend on one or two major suppliers or customers
and how vulnerable is it in negotiating terms with these people?   YES/NA

How is pricing controlled/monitored?   YES/NA

Are there written policies for purchasing of stock and are these
policies followed?   YES/NA

Does production planning take account of, and cope adequately
with, seasonality?   YES/NA

Marketing and Selling
Is there a specialist department dealing with this area?   YES/NA

Is there a monitoring programme, following customers' needs?   YES/NA

Is management responsive to results obtained from research?   YES/NA

Can the business cope with shifts in customer loyalty?   YES/NA

Is product development work carried out in conjunction with production departments?   YES/NA

Are products up to date? How often is the product updated?   YES/NA

Client Real Cider Brewery Company

Accounts to 31st December 1990

BUSINESS REVIEW REPORT

Departmental Review continued

Production and Purchasing
Quality control is undertaken by the production director who deals with all purchasing of raw materials. Scrumptious Cider is produced from particular apples, therefore there is little room for negotiating discounts from the suppliers who grow those particular types.

Production is at its greatest in the early months of the year and Mr P Cox usually employs local people to help top up his regular workforce at this time.

Marketing and Selling
Mr A Cox deals with the sales function. He knows most of his customers well and maintains close contact with them. However, this year the introduction of Green Griffin has meant rapid expansion of the customer base with the result that fewer credit checks have been done on new customers.

A Cox is currently working on the plans for the further development of Merlin. This work is done in close conjunction with P Cox in production.

A Cox is happy with the expansion in the range of products as it has enabled him to increase his customer base outside the South West.

Risk Factors Identified and any Mitigating Factors
Control over wages may not be good when temporary staff are employed.

'OTHER RISKS'	Considered ?
Is there any likelihood of material errors in particular cycles?	YES/NA
– Have our previous audits revealed errors of a particular type?	YES/NA
Do any overall risks affect the risk of specific types of error? (e.g. where management are seeking to maximise profits, under-statement of turnover is unlikely, but the risk of overstatement of stocks or debtors is higher than normal).	YES/NA
– Are there any transactions of an unusually large value?	YES/NA
– Are there any unusual transactions near the end of the accounting period?	YES/NA
– Are there substantial transactions with related parties?	YES/NA
– Are any unusually large payments made to consultants, agents, brokers or employees?	YES/NA

Client <u>Real Cider Brewery Company</u>

Accounts to <u>31st December 1990</u>

BUSINESS REVIEW REPORT

'Other Risks'
The company has had problems in the past ensuring that all sales are recorded.
This year, however, a system of control within the client's computer has been set
up that automatically runs a check on advice note sequences.

Risk Factors Identified and any Mitigating Factors

None.

Client Real Cider Brewery Company	Prepared by		Sch No
	Date started		
	Date finished		
Accounts to 31st December 1990	Reviewed by		
	Date		

ACCOUNTING SYSTEMS REVIEW

The Accounting Systems Review is designed to help us to perform an overall review of the client's accounting system when planning the audit and to help identify areas of weakness that may lead to errors in the financial statements. It sets out a number of procedures and controls which should be present to ensure protection of a company's assets and correct recording of transactions.

The checklist is not designed to be all-embracing. It may be necessary to adapt it according to the nature of the client's business. Where the client has a computerised system, the Computer Controls Summary should also be completed. This deals with the areas in the data processing function where control is necessary.

The knowledge we obtain by performing the review of a client's accounting system contributes to our assessment of inherent risk.

Once the checklist is complete, we record our conclusions on the Risk Assessment Summary (E2).

	Yes/No	Comments

REVENUE CYCLE

Have there been any changes to the system for recording revenue?

The system should usually include controls to ensure that:

— *all goods and services supplied have been properly invoiced and included in sales*
— *no unauthorised credit notes are issued*
— *debtor balances are correct and are collectable.*

(See Ideas List for operations involved in the revenue cycle.)

1. *Goods Outwards*
Are records of goods shipped or services performed:

(a) prepared for all goods leaving the premises/work done
(b) matched to sales invoices
(c) reviewed regularly to ensure invoices are raised promptly?

2. *Recording*
Is there a system (e.g. sequential pre-numbering) to ensure control over:

(a) sales invoices
(b) credit notes
(c) other adjustments such as contras?

3. *Authorisation*
Does someone other than the person preparing them approve:

Yes — Amendments to procedures on unmatched advice notes — computer carries out sequential check.

(a) **Yes**
(b) **Yes**
(c) **Yes**

(a) **Yes** — Sequential numbering used but not always reviewed.
(b) **Yes**
(c) **No** — But usually journals agreed with director (S Cox) — MLP.

	Yes/No	Comments
(a) invoices for sales, prices/ discounts allowed	Yes	Prepared by clerks and agreed by B Williams (accountant).
(b) credit notes issued	Yes	Prepared by B Williams, agreed by S Cox.
(c) bad debts written off/other adjustments (e.g. contras)?	Yes	As for credit notes.
Are customers reviewed for poor credit risk?	No	No formal review, initial decision to take on customer left to directors but it is thought that directors are not giving as much consideration to this as in past.

4. *Sales Ledger Control*
Is a list of debtors regularly:

(a) prepared		
(b) aged	Yes	On a monthly basis.
(c) reviewed		
(d) reconciled to the sales ledger control account?		
Are statements regularly sent to customers?	Yes	On a monthly basis.

5. *Receipts*
Are there appropriate procedures for:

(a) opening of mail	Yes	Carried out by two clerks, one makes entries in appropriate ledgers, the other watches.
(b) recording of receipts?		
Are initial records of receipts checked to bankings?	Yes	By B Williams.

6. *Cash Sales*

(a) Is each sale recorded at the time it is made?		
(b) Is the list of sales controlled in such a way that no transaction can be omitted?	N/A	No cash sales.
(c) Is the list reconciled daily with the cash received?		

	Yes/No	Comments
(d) Is the cash banked intact daily?	N/A	

STOCK

	Yes/No	Comments
Have there been any changes to the stock system?	No	
7. Does someone regularly scrutinise the stocks to:		
(a) ascertain what is in stock	Yes	Stock production levels are closely monitored by P Cox as part of the production plan.
(b) discover damaged or obsolete items	Yes	There are various quality control tests during the production process. Very little damage occurs.
(c) check pilferage rates are not excessive	Yes	Pilferage rates reviewed.
(d) ensure stock levels are kept under control?	Yes	See (a).

EXPENDITURE CYCLE

	Yes/No	Comments
Have there been any changes to the system for recording expenditure?	No	

The system should usually include controls to ensure that:

— *all liabilities incurred by the company are recorded and analysed properly*
— *expenses are included only in respect of goods or services authorised and received.*

(See Ideas List for operations involved in the expenditure cycle — not reproduced.)

8. *Purchase Orders*
(a) Are written orders used for all purchases?

	Yes/No	Comments
(b) Does the company keep a copy of all orders? (c) Are all orders used accounted for (e.g. by pre-numbering)? (d) Are all orders formally approved?	Yes	Pre-numbered written order which is authorised by accountant (up to £1,000) or director.

9. *Receipt of Goods*
Are delivery notes (or goods received notes):

(a) checked to the goods (b) checked to the order?	Yes	Filed with order.

10. *Invoices for Goods*
Are invoices received checked for:

(a) agreement to delivery note/goods received note (b) agreement of prices (c) extensions and additions?	Yes	Filed with GRN/order.

11. *Invoices for Services*
Are invoices received checked for:

(a) evidence of performance of service (b) agreement of prices (c) extensions and additions?	Yes	Given size of operation, director/accountant, who sign cheques, know what services have been performed.

12. *Wages*

(a) Are the wages records reviewed before signing the cheque?	Yes	By accountant.
(b) Are amendments to pay rates, tax codes, etc approved?	Yes	By accountant.
(c) Are cheques drawn for the exact amount of wages?	Yes	Paid through bank for permanent staff but temps may be paid in cash, and deductions may not be made properly.

		Yes/No	Comments
(d)	Are payments for PAYE and NI agreed to the wages records?	Yes	Agreed by director.
13.	**Returns**		
(a)	Are pre-numbered credit-requests raised?	Yes	Very few raised.
(b)	Are credit notes matched to credit requests on receipt?	Yes	By accountant.
(c)	Are outstanding credit-requests followed up?	Yes	By accountant.
14.	**Creditors' Balances**		
(a)	Are accounts reconciled regularly with suppliers' statements?	Yes	By clerks.
(b)	Is the control account reconciled regularly with the individual balances?	Yes	On monthly basis.
(c)	Are these reconciliations reviewed?	Yes	By accountant.
15.	**Payments**		
(a)	Are all major payments made by cheque or credit transfer?	Yes	
(b)	Are all cheques sent out immediately?	No	Sometimes held back by directors.
(c)	Is the use of cheques controlled (e.g. no blank cheques allowed, cheques over a set limit countersigned)?	Yes	Accountant and a director (usually S Cox) have to sign all cheques up to £5,000, over this 2 directors sign.
(d)	Are all payments checked to supporting documentation?	Yes	
(e)	Is supporting documentation cancelled when paid?	Yes	
(f)	Is petty cash book and vouchers reviewed before the fund is reimbursed (e.g. by use of an imprest system)?	Yes	By accountant.

	Yes/No	Comments
(g) Are paid cheques returned and reviewed?	No	Cheques no longer returned by bank — consider requesting a sample — MLP.

OTHER MATTERS

16.   *Bank Reconciliations*

(a) Are the bank statements sent to someone independent of the payments function?	No	Sent to accountant — possible MLP.
(b) Are reconcilations prepared regularly?	Yes	
(c) Are all reconciling items explained and reviewed?	Yes	

17.   *Financial Data*

Is regular financial data prepared and reviewed on:

(a) cash levels	} Yes	Monthly management accounts prepared and compared with budget.
(b) sales		
(c) expense levels?		

18.   *Insurance*

Is the adequacy of the company's insurance cover and security of assets regularly reviewed?	Yes	On a yearly basis when policy renewed.

Risk Factors Identified and any Mitigating Factors

— Cheques may be held back at year end leading to understatement of creditors but cash will similarly be understated.	No cash problems anticipated at year end — balance of £200,000 so no need to hold payments back.
— Casual labour tax and NIC may not be deducted properly and no real checks carried out on this.	Unlikely to be a material amount. MLP.
— New customers' credit not always thoroughly checked.	

COMPUTER CONTROLS SUMMARY	Yes/No/NA	Comments

ORGANISATION AND ADMINISTRATION OF THE PROCESSING ENVIRONMENT

1. *Separation of Functions*

— Does the size of data processing allow for separation of the applications development and programming functions?	No	Programming and development not carried out in-house.
If so, is this objective achieved?		
If not, is the client over reliant on or at risk from tasks carried out by key personnel?		Software house will provide this service — no reliance on key personnel within RCBC.
— Are data processing staff prohibited from having incompatible responsibilities in user departments?	NA	

2. *Documentation*

— Is there adequate documentation supporting data processing functions and procedures?	Yes	
— Is user documentation adequate?	Yes	Copy of user guide in PAF.
— Are there adequate controls over access to application and program documentation to ensure it is not used to facilitate unauthorised changes to programs and/or data files?	Yes	Only copy on site kept in S Cox's office (locked away). Staff would not be capable of changing programs/data files.

3. *Management*

— Are appropriate management and staff actively involved in the development of new or major changes to existing systems?	Yes	Development work carried on by outside consultant. Board is kept informed and has to authorise expenditure.

COMPUTER CONTROLS SUMMARY	Yes/No/NA	Comments
— Does there appear to be reasonable liaison between user and data processing departments, where appropriate?	NA	

ACCESS TO COMPUTER FACILITIES

1. *Computer Room*

— Is access to the computer adequately restricted to appropriate authorised individuals?	No	No restrictions over physical access — possible MLP.
— Are programmers and non-operational staff restricted from facilities which can access or amend live programs other than where authorised?	Yes	Programmers not on site.

2. *Data Files*

— Are there adequate controls to restrict the use of data files to authorised individuals and programs for example, physical library, internal label checking, passwords or user identification codes?	Yes	Passwords

3. *Programs*

— Is access to programs restricted to authorised individuals for example, separate test and production libraries, passwords, review of console log?	Yes	Passwords (different from access to data files).

4. *On-Line Terminals*

— Is on-line access restricted to appropriate authorised users?	Yes	
— Are passwords changed on a regular basis?	Yes	Every two months.
— Once access to the system has been gained, do controls prevent unauthorised access to programs and data files?	Yes	Different level passwords.

COMPUTER CONTROLS SUMMARY	Yes/No/NA	Comments
— Is there a mechanism for detecting unauthorised entry to the system after it has occurred?	Yes	Log print out will show who has accessed system but not reviewed regularly.

5. *After-Hours Processing*
— Are DP operations carried out after normal office hours properly supervised and controlled?   Yes

6. *Connections with Third Parties' DP Facilities*
— If the computer is linked to any third parties' DP facilities (e.g. using SWIFT for inter-bank transfer, BACS for payroll settlement and payments etc) is control over access adequate?   NA

OPERATORS

1. *Computer Room*
— Are production workflows monitored so that deviations from planned processing can be monitored on a timely basis?   NA

DISASTER PLANNING AND HOUSEKEEPING

1. *Key Personnel*
— Is any member of data processing a key member of the organisation?   Yes   S Cox may use computer.

— Is the client adequately covered by insurance for supporting staff and documentation in the event of the demise or departure of a key person?   No   MLP

2. *General Housekeeping*
— Do there appear to be good housekeeping procedures, for   Yes   Regular back-ups.

COMPUTER CONTROLS SUMMARY	Yes/No/NA	Comments
example, back-up and recovery procedures, arrangement of the computer room?		
3. *Disaster Plan*		
— Is there a formal contingency plan and disaster recovery procedures to ensure continued operation of the business in the event of a significant disruption to processing?	Yes	Back-ups taken every week and one copy kept off site.
— Are staff aware of their duties in the event of a major disruption?	Yes	

Risk Factors Identified and any Mitigating Factors

— No separation of functions.		This is not seen as a risk as no-one has the knowledge to amend programs/ data.

Appendix 7   Interim notes

As explained in paragraphs **12.8** and **12.9**, when a separate interim audit visit is made, the senior should prepare some notes linking the interim and final visits. The following example, for the *Real Cider Brewery Co Ltd*, shows how such notes can be set out (they have been abbreviated by including only the information on two cycles).

25 November 1990

REAL CIDER BREWERY COMPANY LIMITED
INTERIM NOTES — YEAR ENDING 31 DECEMBER 1990

1   Work outstanding from interim visit

The following work is outstanding:

(a)   revenue cycle — completion of substantive transactions work to check that all despatches are recorded on sales invoices;

(b)   expenditure and stock cycles — (not reproduced);

(c)   payroll cycles — completion of test in total for one week in each of November and December;

(d)   other cycles and areas — (not reproduced).

2   Proposals for reduction in work at final visit

Payroll cycle
Our risk assessment identified a potential problem regarding the statutory deductions made for temporary staff. This was reviewed at the interim visit and it was found that the total amount paid to temporary staff was £45,000 and that out of a sample of 5 payments, only one had not had deductions made. The likely error is therefore considered immaterial. The client has been informed and is reviewing this area. A small provision will be made to cover any liability based upon this review. No further work is considered necessary other than a review of the client's findings.

Other cycles
(not reproduced)

3   Problems identified during interim visit

Revenue cycle
We confirmed by enquiry that credit checks have not been carried out in practice.
We will pay particular attention to:
(a)   any increase in ratio of debtors to turnover;
(b)   the age analysis and comparisons to prior year;
(c)   balances due from new customers;
(d)   debtors exceeding credit limits;
(e)   the matching of cash and invoices;
(f)   correspondence with debtors;
(g)   cash received after date.

Given the seasonal nature of the trade, we will carry out this work on the balances
as at 30 November 1990 (that is the list used for the circularisation) and make
adjustments for any sales to doubtful debtors made in December.

Other cycles
(not reproduced)

4   Advance planning

4.01   We have confirmed with the client that the stocktake will be carried out
on 28 and 29 December with higher value items being covered on 28 December.
An assistant, Kevin Hall, has been requested to attend.

The client will forward his stocktaking instructions to us in early December and
we have agreed to comment on these by 15 December 1990.

4.02   We have confirmed that the debtors aged listing will be ready for us on 5
December 1990 for a debtors' circularisation. We have also reminded the client
to have our standard letter ready for us. The selection will be made using the
client's software enquiry facility.

4.03   We have also confirmed that the creditors' ledger balances and the cumulative purchases by supplier will be ready for us on 7 December 1990. We have
supplied the client with our standard letter and he has agreed to have copies ready
for us. The client has also agreed to retain all suppliers' statements as at 30
November 1990.

4.04   A standard bank letter will be sent by the 15 December.

5   Management letter points

The draft management letter is attached to this memorandum (not reproduced).

Contents noted and approved by manager: ———————————— date———

Contents noted and approved by partner: ———————————— date———

Appendix 8   Points forward to the next audit

As explained in paragraphs **12.43** and **12.44**, the senior should prepare points for the attention of the following year's audit team. The following example, again based on the audit for the year to December 1990 for the *Real Cider Brewery Co Ltd*, shows how these notes may be set out.

The example begins with two accounting decisions taken at the final review stage which affect future audit work. Paragraphs 3 and 4 deal with improvements which we can introduce in next year's audit. The section on creditors, paragraph 5, draws attention to the procedures we need to adopt in the coming months to avoid a particular problem recurring. The final section of the notes is a reminder of planned change in the systems.

In appropriate cases, the permanent audit file must be updated for matters referred to in these notes. In some cases, however, the notes are a reminder that certain parts of the permanent audit file will be out of date by the time of the next audit.

4 March 1991

REAL CIDER BREWERY COMPANY LIMITED
POINTS FORWARD — YEAR ENDING 31 DECEMBER 1990

1   Research and development

At the final meeting with the directors, it was agreed to carry forward the development costs on the Merlin project with a view to their being written off over the first five years of sales. We have examined forecasts and investment appraisals for this project and satisfied ourselves as to the validity of the policy this year. We need to keep the forecasts under review and satisfy ourselves that a more urgent write-off is not required.

2   Allocation of work

An unsatisfactory allocation of work this year led to problems on the audit of fixed assets and stocks. Certain important tests on the valuation of stock had not been carried out by the time of the manager's review; fixed assets had been over-audited in some areas. In future, the audit of stock should be conducted by the senior and the audit of fixed assets should be more carefully planned and supervised by the senior. It should result in a saving of about 6 man hours' work next year.

3   Testing levels

Revenue
Management has decided to introduce a credit check on customers; it will be made before goods are despatched. We will, therefore, be able to reduce our tests in this area provided we check that the new system is operating properly.

Other cycles
(not reproduced)

4   Verification of creditors

Both the client and ourselves had considerable trouble with a major supplier, S Ivel SA, in France whose statements did not correspond with the balance per the client's purchase ledger. They have not responded to our creditors' circularisation or our two telexes although we did manage to speak on the telephone to their sales ledger department. There is a difference of approximately £22,000 which the client maintains represents discounts to be given every quarter once purchases have reached a certain level. The agreement has never been confirmed in writing to the client although Ivel's sales ledger department suggested to us that it might be correct. The client agreed to our request for a board minute detailing these explanations (not reproduced).

Next year, we must contact S Ivel SA and their agent in London at least three months before the year end to request confirmation of balance. We should also confirm with the client in May/June 1991 that this problem has been resolved.

5   Changes in systems

The client intends to computerise the nominal ledger, stock records and purchase ledger during 1991.

We have requested the client to keep us informed of the proposed timetable for the change. The computer audit department will be heavily involved in the changeover and has been invited to comment on the systems at each stage of implementation.

6   Audit time saving

The changes proposed are expected to result in a saving of approximately 20 hours.

Contents noted and approved by manager: _____date _____

Contents noted and approved by partner: _____date _____

Appendix 9 Recording computer systems and assessment of risk

Summary of controls schedule
The summary of controls schedule is a matrix which summarises internal controls, both manual and computer, and weaknesses in the system. The summary of controls schedule is designed to help us assess the risk of error arising in a computer system. For this reason it is normal to complete the summary as part of our audit planning process when we wish to place reliance on internal controls. It may also be useful to do this where we do not rely on internal controls but the system is complex. The schedule helps us assess risk by identifying the likely sources of errors and shortcomings in internal controls. It also helps us identify management letter points.

The summary aims to identify the controls which are in place to ensure:
(a)   all accounting transactions are properly processed; and
(b)   amendments to computer files (for both transaction and standing data) which are unauthorised or inaccurate are detected promptly.

It should also help highlight instances where such controls do not exist.

Completing the summary of controls schedule
Our internal control objectives are shown as column headings. Each significant type of accounting transaction should be identified from the overview flowchart and shown on a separate line. For each type of transaction you should attempt to identify controls which meet the control objectives and complete the appropriate box with a brief description of the control. Where there is no control procedure or it is inadequate or ineffective the reasons should be briefly stated. To aid clarification each box on the matrix grid is marked with:
(a)   a tick to denote a control;
(b)   a cross to denote absence of a control; and
(c)   in addition, a 'P' if the internal control is carried out by the computer.

A tick means there is the equivalent of a 'key' control i.e. one which will prevent material errors in respect of this objective. Where there is a cross in a box the likelihood of error through lack of control must be assessed and audit procedures adjusted if necessary. A tick or a cross should be supported by a brief explanation.

Example 1 (p 284) shows an overview flowchart and *Example 2* (p 285–286) a completed summary of controls for a purchases system. The following should be noted in respect of entries for purchase invoices.

— Completeness of Input

This comprises a computer reconciliation of the number and total value of the invoices input with the totals manually computed prior to entry. These control totals are entered prior to entry of the invoices. As this check is carried out at the input and edit stage and not when the masterfiles are posted it will not ensure that the purchase ledger has been updated, only that all items have been entered.

— Accuracy of Input

The above reconciliation of control totals provides overall assurance that the total value of invoices input is correct but not that the individual analysis (or for example the correct nominal ledger codes) has been correctly entered. The risk of errors in the input of data is reduced by edit and validation checks.

— Validity of Invoices

In the example passwords are used as a means of ensuring that authorised transactions are processed, or approved for payment. A further check on the validity of transactions may be by means of suppliers' statement reconciliations.

— Update of Principal Masterfiles — Purchase Ledger

Control totals have been used to ensure that items have been properly input. To ensure that the accepted items are updated to the purchase ledger the total value and number accepted are reconciled to the movements on the purchase ledger. For example, the total value and number of transactions accepted at the edit stage is agreed to the increase in the outstanding values on the purchase ledger.

— Maintenance of Masterfiles — Purchase Ledger

Reports showing movements on the masterfile are reconciled to the totals reported as accepted for the day as part of the update procedures above. The brought forward totals are reconciled to previous day's closing totals. Any discrepancy would indicate that corruption of the file has occurred or the wrong file has been loaded.

In *Example 2*, service invoices are not formally controlled, although there are suppliers' statement reconciliations and the computer produced cheques are only signed by the chief accountant by reference to supporting documentation.

Using the summary of controls schedule
The summary does not cover controls over reports produced by the computer as a by-product of processing. Sometimes we will rely upon these reports during

the course of our audit. For example, we may rely on the aged debtors listing produced monthly from the sales ledger system. We may use the reverse side of the summary of controls schedule to summarise computer reports of audit significance. We should also record the likelihood of errors in processing due to lack of control or software problems and the consequent effect on the audit procedures. In *Example 2* a number of reports are identified in respect of the purchases system. Only one is included on the reverse side. This is the goods received not invoiced report. It is identified as of audit significance because it is used in calculating the creditors accrual. You should note that the aged creditor listing is not considered significant as it is not relied on during our other procedures.

The completed controls summary should be filed on the permanent file together with the overview flowchart and types, volumes and values information, and updated annually.

EXAMPLE 1

BOUGHT LEDGER

INPUT	EDIT	UPDATE	OUTPUT

ACCOUNTS

- Stores Invoice
- Other Invoices
- Suppliers Details
- Credit Notes/ Transfers
- Amendment to Input

VDU

Supplier Details *

Goods Received not Invoiced *

Bought Ledger *

Edit

Batch Listing D

Suggested Payments D

Items released for Update

Bought Ledger

Supplier Details

Update

Transaction History

To General Ledger

Reports

Review & Amend

* *Reference only, at this stage*

TYPES & VOLUMES

No. of Suppliers 600
No. of Invoices 1000
Average O/S Balance £1.25m

Credit Notes 10 per month
Value £250 average

ROUTINE

- Remittance Lists (W)
- Bought Ledger Print (M)
- Cheques (W)
- Update Analysis (D)
- Cash Requirements (W)

EXCEPTION

- Goods Received, not Invoiced (W)
- Old. outstandings (M)

Example 2

SUMMARY OF CONTROLS

List below:
- — reports of audit significance which summarise, analyse or categorise information held within the computer.

Consider whether the
- — computer programs appear to function correctly. Could material error arise through program error?

- — controls are adequate to ensure proper processing.

COMPUTER REPORT OF AUDIT SIGNIFICANCE	IS MATERIAL ERROR POSSIBLE DUE TO LACK OF CONTROL? OR SOFTWARE FAILURES?	EFFECT ON AUDIT PROCEDURES
Goods received not invoiced.	*Yes*	*No independent check on action of input clerk unless a statement is received. To be noted in analytical review and in deciding levels of test in checking service invoices (if applicable).*

Example 2

SUMMARY OF CONTROLS

Client:

Accounts to:

Transaction and Reference Data

TRANSACTIONS DOCUMENT	COMPLETENESS OF INPUT	ACCURACY OF INPUT	VALIDITY/ AUTHORISATION	UPDATE OF PRINCIPAL MASTERFILES	MAINTENANCE OF MASTERFILES	REPORTS USED IN CHECKING
Purchase Invoice	Computer agreement of manually established control totals. (√)	Total values: as per completeness of input. (√) Correct Accounts: (i) program edit checks for existence (P) (ii) program range checks. (P)	Password controls to restrict entry to authorised staff. (√) (P) Supplier statement reconciliation. (P)	Completeness/Accuracy Reconciliation of number and value of transactions accepted at the input stage to totals reported at the update stage. (√)	Bought Ledger masterfile Reconciliation of opening total values with previously. (√) Reconciliation of opening total values, postings per update stage and reported closing totals. (√)	Goods received not invoiced. (W) Batch/Edit listing. (d) Update report. (D) (√) Aged creditors listing. (M) (√)
Service Invoices	None, unless statements are sent when a reconciliation will be carried out. (X)	None. Input clerk enters these directly as received. (X) Checked by same input clerk. Correct Accounts: As above. (P)	Approved by Dept. Head before input — no assurance amounts are not changed, except cheque signatory receives supporting documentation. (X)	Completeness/Accuracy As per above. (√)	As per above. (√)	As per above. (√)

Index

Accounting policies
changes in
  analytical review, effect on, 4.13
  risk assessment, effect on, 5.15
cycles, and, 2.27

Accounting systems
computerised, 3.29, 14.01 *et seq*
internal controls, 2.38, 2.39, 8.01, 8.02
part of understanding the business, 2.09,
  3.22
record of, 3.26, 3.28, 15.01 *et seq*
review of, 2.12, 3.25, 5.05 *et seq*, App 6

Analytical review
audit evidence, as, 2.37, 7.31
audit plan, 10.09
available information, use of, 4.09
business, ratios specific to the, 16.27
comparisons
  changes in accounting policy, 4.13
  changing price levels, 4.13
  consistency, 4.13
  exceptional items, effect of, 4.13
  extraordinary items, effect of, 4.13
  other companies, with, 4.04, 4.12
  similar businesses in company or
    group, with, 4.04
cost of sales, 16.04
creditors' payment period, 16.17
current ratio, 16.21
debtors' collection period, 16.15
definition, 4.01
expenses, 16.11
explanations, 4.18 *et seq*
gross profit, 16.04
net profit, 16.14
overheads, 16.11
purpose, 2.15, 2.16
quantities, 16.25
ratios specific to the business, 16.27
results, 4.14, 4.22
sales, 16.01
small businesses, 13.09

Analytical review—*cont*
stock turnover, 16.19
substantive tests of details, effect on, 4.23
timing, 2.16, 4.02, 4.07
unexpected results, 4.15
volumes, 16.25
working papers, 4.25

Audit evidence
accountancy work, 7.38
analytical review, 2.37, 7.31
compliance tests, 8.26
computer enquiry packages, 7.41
management representations, 7.35
reliance on internal control, 2.38, 7.27
small businesses, 13.19
sources of, 2.34
substantive tests of detail, 2.35, 7.18 *et seq*
tests in total, 2.36, 7.28 *et seq*

Audit objectives
direction, 2.30, 7.05
link to representations, 2.29, 7.02
sub-objectives, 7.07

Audit opinions
matters covered by, 1.02
qualified, 12.26 *et seq*, 13.24 *et seq*
unqualified, 12.24

Audit planning
approach to audit as a whole, 2.03
approach to each cycle, 2.26
briefing the audit team, 10.21
client expectations, 2.06, 10.05
compliance procedures, 8.23
internal controls, extent of reliance upon,
  8.05
risk, assessment of, 5.05
small businesses, 13.17 *et seq*
taxation work, 10.18
timing, 10.20
understanding the business, 2.10
written plan, 2.43, 10.01, App 5

THE EUROPEAN SECURITY STRATEGY

To François Biscop and Flori Gillis,
my parents

The European Security Strategy
A Global Agenda for Positive Power

SVEN BISCOP
The Royal Institute for International Relations, Belgium

ASHGATE

Published by
Ashgate Publishing Limited
Gower House
Croft Road
Aldershot
Hants GU11 3HR
England

Ashgate Publishing Company
Suite 420
101 Cherry Street
Burlington, VT 05401-4405
USA

Ashgate website: http://www.ashgate.com

British Library Cataloguing in Publication Data
Biscop, Sven
    The European Security Strategy : a global agenda for
    positive power
    1.National security - European Union countries 2.European
    Union countries - Military policy 3.European Union
    countries - Foreign relations 4.European Union countries -
    Defenses
    I.Title
    355'.03354

Library of Congress Cataloging-in-Publication Data
Biscop, Sven.
    The European security strategy : a global agenda for positive power / by Sven
Biscop.
        p.   cm.
    Includes bibliographical references and index.
    ISBN 0-7546-4469-3
    1. National security--Europe. 2. European Union--Military policy. 3. Europe--
Military policy. I. Title.

    UA646B4635 2005
    355'.03304--dc22

                                                                      2005008489

ISBN-13: 978 0 7546 4469 6

Reprinted 2007

Printed and bound in Great Britain by MPG Books Ltd, Bodmin, Cornwall

Contents

Preface

In December 2002, the Security and Global Governance Department of the Royal Institute for International Relations (IRRI-KIIB), the think-tank associated with the Belgian ministry of foreign affairs, initiated a strategic reflection on Europe's security policy, at the request of the ministry. The foreign and security policy of the EU, so it was felt, was lacking strategic clarity, a clear definition of its interests and long-term policy objectives – and 'without strategy, power is a loose cannon and war is mindless' (Betts, 2000, p.5). Under the direction of Professor Rik Coolsaet, the Department's director, and myself, an informal working group was set up, comprising members from the diplomatic, military, intelligence and academic worlds. The aim of our working group was to draft a European strategic concept, in order to stimulate a strategic debate, which at that time, outside of academic circles, was almost nonexistent. Although some academics had already advocated the adoption of a strategic concept, most observers, even those conceding the necessity of a strategic document, held this to be politically unfeasible. Then in early May 2003 at an informal meeting the ministers of foreign affairs of the EU achieved strategic surprise when they tasked the High Representative for the CFSP, Dr. Javier Solana, with the elaboration of a strategic document. Out of the blue the strategic debate that we had hoped to stimulate was all over us. So far for our grand ambitions – which political scientist does not secretly hope to alter the course of history through his writings – but in the wake of the Iraq divide this was marvellous news for the EU indeed.

Henceforth, having rediscovered our modesty, we reoriented ourselves: rather than continuing it as a project on its own, we now explicitly put our work in the framework of Solana's major endeavour, seeing it as a Belgian academic contribution to the broad debate that the EU organized following the presentation of Solana's first draft, *A Secure Europe in a Better World*, to the Thessalonica European Council in June 2003. The result of our project, *A European Security Concept for the 21st Century* (Coolsaet and Biscop, 2004), was formally presented to Javier Solana and the Belgian minister of foreign affairs at the time, Louis Michel, at an IRRI-KIIB conference on 26 November 2003. This conference was organized in collaboration with the three institutes that hosted the seminars that the EU held in the fall of 2003 to discuss the draft Strategy: Aspen Institute Italia (Rome), the EU Institute for Security Studies (Paris) and the Swedish Institute of International Affairs (Stockholm). These three seminars allowed for a thorough debate between EU officials and politicians, diplomats, the military, academics, journalists and NGOs from current and future Member States and from important partner countries of the EU. Following this innovative inclusive method of policy-design, the final *European Security Strategy* was adopted by the Brussels European Council in December 2003.

The Strategy is the first strategic document ever of the EU and therefore a milestone, not only for the CFSP/ESDP, but for EU external action as a whole. The important political choices contained in the Strategy can shape external action in the years to come. Its success is however not guaranteed: the choices made must be translated into specific policies, and those must be effectively and efficiently implemented in order to realise the vision of the EU as a powerful international actor put forward in the Strategy. In all events, the Strategy cannot be ignored, even if those opposed to a strong international role for the EU would prefer to lock it into the dusty drawer of unachievable European ambitions – and present the key to NATO for safekeeping. Choices have been written down and have been rubberstamped by the unanimous heads of State and government in the European Council. Since its adoption, Member States, EU officials and other actors constantly refer to the Strategy to justify their decisions or to strengthen the appeal of their proposals – an initiative based on the Strategy can only be refused with difficulty.

But the Strategy has one drawback: like any set of holy scriptures, it is liable to interpretation. Thus, as Overhaus (2004, p.4) states

> an important indicator for the [Strategy's] prospect for success is not only in the text itself (in terms of its concreteness, binding character and vision of priorities) but also a comparison of how Member States *interpret* the document's content.

How the Strategy is interpreted and then utilized is of major importance for the future of EU external action. And since it is a document of a primarily political, rather than a legally binding nature, there is room for interpretation; the implications of these interpretations for the EU will differ accordingly. The Strategy can be seen as defining the fundamental guidelines for the whole of external action, as containing an ambitious long-term agenda setting forth a global role for the EU and creating the momentum to reshape policies. Or it can be seen as having importance only in a limited timeframe, as a useful way of conciliating Member States after the Iraq divide, a public manifestation of unity confirming some of the EU's policies, but henceforth not very important.

On the basis of IRRI-KIIB's original European Security Concept and ongoing research on different aspects of EU external action, this book aims to offer one such interpretation. IRRI-KIIB is in the business of policy research. Accordingly, this is a normative book: its purpose is to recommend one reading of the Strategy and to think through the implications of that reading for EU external action. The thesis submitted is that the Strategy can be used as the conceptual basis for a comprehensive approach that integrates all dimensions of external action, including the politico-military or 'hard' security field, under the same agenda of 'effective multilateralism' or global governance. This agenda can be operationalized by translating it into, and prioritizing, the core public goods to which every individual on this earth is entitled; promoting everyone's access to these basic public goods can constitute the essence of a distinctive European approach emphasizing long-term stabilization and conflict prevention. Such an approach can then guide the EU in setting policy objectives, choosing instruments and acquiring means and capabilities.

The first two chapters of the book draw the conceptual framework:

- Chapter 1 presents the political and conceptual context of the drafting of the Strategy. The end of the Cold War and the drastic changes in the international security environment that it produced gave rise to several initiatives to re-conceptualize security and elaborate more comprehensive approaches. Although the EU acquired a foreign and security dimension in 1993 and from 1998 onwards it started building a military capability, at first it failed to adopt a single strategic framework to guide policy in these new fields. Only in the wake of the Iraq crisis did it prove possible to translate the broad orientations that could already be deduced from actual policies into the European Security Strategy.
- Following a brief summary of the Strategy, Chapter 2 analyzes its assessment of the international security environment. That analysis and the notion of security implicit in the Strategy constitute the basis for the elaboration of the concept of the comprehensive approach and the global public goods agenda.

The ensuing chapters follow the outline of the Strategy to look into the implications of this approach for EU policies and recommend ways of optimizing their effectiveness:

- At the level of the EU's neighbourhood, relations with the Mediterranean and the wider Middle East are used as a case-study to highlight the challenges presented by the comprehensive European Neighbourhood Policy (Chapter 3).
- At the global level, the central challenge of 'effective multilateralism' is to re-forge a consensus on the collective security system of the UN, which can be based on the recommendations of the High-Level Panel on Threats, Challenges and Change. At the same time, however, the EU needs to address the other, non-politico-military dimensions of global governance (Chapter 4).
- At the intra-European level, the coherence of policies and the enhancement of capabilities must be addressed; the military capabilities especially offer scope for progress through further integration. The implications for EU-NATO relations are obvious, but a broader EU-US partnership, covering all dimensions of global governance, must also be considered (Chapter 5).
- The final Chapter emphasizes the overall importance of recognizing the Strategy as the guiding framework for the whole of EU external action and using it as such. Now that is has a Strategy, the EU can develop a strategic culture.

The book is not as comprehensive as I would have liked it to be – it is in a sense less comprehensive than the Strategy itself. Not all of the important issues are dealt with in detail: the position of Russia in the European and global security architecture; relations with Ukraine and the Caucasus and their place, if any, in the EU; the challenges posed by the need to establish partnerships with China, India and others; the intricacies of the non-proliferation regime; the options to enhance the effectiveness of EU policies in the fields of aid, trade and development; global governance in fields other than the politico-military. On all these accounts, I beg the reader's understanding for the limitations of the author. The dimensions of external action that are covered more elaborately will betray the limits of my expertise. The difficulty of dealing with all of the potential implications of the Strategy for all of the relevant fields can serve as an indication of the daunting task that EU policy-makers are facing. Nevertheless, I hope to have highlighted the main challenges and to have demonstrated how a comprehensive approach to EU external action could be conceptualized, and what it would mean for actual EU policies in a number of fields. Perhaps within that framework others more qualified than myself can fill in the gaps that I have left with regard to the policy fields listed above. I can only hope that my own small contribution will be of some relevance to policy-makers. For if there is one important idea underlying my research, it is voluntarism: the belief that society, *in casu* the global order and the role of the EU in that order, can be changed for the better, and that all of us, through our own work, can and should contribute.

Sven Biscop

Acknowledgements

My first thanks go to the Royal Institute for International Relations for allowing me to sufficiently detach myself from daily business – as far as e-mail and mobile phones permit – in order to be able to spend the time necessary for writing this book. I particularly want to thank Prof. Dr. Rik Coolsaet, director of the institute's Security and Global Governance Department, for his warm support overall, and for his significant contribution to this project through our many talks. Rik kindly volunteered to read large parts of the manuscript and offered his welcome advice – naturally, any remaining mistakes are entirely my own. My colleague in the department, Valérie Arnould, deserves my thanks as well for her large contribution through our almost daily discussions about the subjects covered in this book, for her badly needed help with regard to UN and global governance issues, but also for her perseverance in putting up with me in general, sitting face to face in the institute's modern but rather crowded offices in the heart of Brussels.

A book is not only based on research, documents and academic publications, but is also the product of impressions and insights gained by listening to people at conferences and seminars and, even more importantly, by chatting with fellow academics and officials during the dinners and receptions that usually accompany such events – the 'Brussels scene' is certainly not lacking in this regard. Too many names come to mind to list them all, but I certainly want to express my sincerest gratitude to the members of the institute's informal security working group; without their input of ideas and their informed critiques, this book could never have been written.

List of Abbreviations

ACT	Allied Command Transformation
AU	African Union
BWIs	Bretton Woods Institutions
CCC	Capabilities Commitment Conference
CDM	Capabilities Development Mechanism
C4ISTAR	Command, Control, Communications, Computers, Intelligence, Surveillance, Target Acquisition and Reconnaissance
CFSP	Common Foreign and Security Policy
CSBMs	Confidence and Security-Building Measures
CSCE	Commission on Security and Cooperation in Europe
CSCAP	Council for Security Cooperation in Asia Pacific
DCI	Defence Capabilities Initiative
DPA	Department of Political Affairs
DPKO	Department of Peacekeeping Operations
DRC	Democratic Republic of Congo
ECAP	European Capabilities Action Plan
ECOSOC	Economic and Social Council
EDA	European Defence Agency
EEC	European Economic Community
EGF	European Gendarmerie Force
EMP	Euro-Mediterranean Partnership
ENP	European Neighbourhood Policy
ESDI	European Security and Defence Identity
ESDP	European Security and Defence Policy
EU	European Union
EUMC	European Union Military Committee
EUMS	European Union Military Staff
EUPM	European Union Police Mission
EUROFOR/ EUROMARFOR	European Operational Rapid Force
EYROMESCO	Euro-Mediterranean Study Commission
FYROM	Former Yugoslav Republic of Macedonia
GCC	Gulf Cooperation Council
GMEI	Greater Middle East Initiative
GNP	Gross National Product
GPG	Global Public Goods
HFC	Helsinki Force Catalogue
HG	Headline Goal
HHC	Helsinki Headline Goal Catalogue
HPC	Helsinki Progress Catalogue

HTF	Headline Goal Task Force
IAEA	International Atomic Energy Agency
ICISS	International Commission on Intervention and State Sovereignty
IMF	International Monetary Fund
ISAF	International Security Assistance Force
KFOR	Kosovo Force
MD	Mediterranean Dialogue
MDGs	Millennium Development Goals
MONUC	United Nations Organization Mission in the Democratic Republic of the Congo
NAC	North Atlantic Council
NATO	North Atlantic Treaty Organization
NCW	Network-Centric Warfare
NGOs	Non-Governmental Organizations
NPT	Treaty on the Non-Proliferation of Nuclear Weapons
NRF	NATO Response Force
NSC	New Strategic Concept
NSS	National Security Strategy
NTA	New Transatlantic Agenda
OCCAR	Organisme conjoint de Coopération en matière d'Armements
OCHA	Office for the Coordination of Humanitarian Affairs
ODA	Official Development Aid
OPCW	Organization for the Prohibition of Chemical Weapons
OSCE	Organization for Security and Cooperation in Europe
P5	Permanent Five (in the UN Security Council)
PCC	Prague Capabilities Commitment
R&T	Research and Technology
RMA	Revolution in Military Affairs
SFOR	Stabilization Force
SLG	Group of Senior Level Representatives
TEU	Treaty on European Union
UN	United Nations
UNDP	United Nations Development Programme
UNSCR	United Nations Security Council Resolution
WB	World Bank
WEU	Western European Union
WMD	Weapons of Mass Destruction
WTO	World Trade Organization

Chapter 1

Reinventing Security

In the Oxford English Dictionary definition, *security* is 'the condition of being protected from or not exposed to danger; [...] a feeling of safety or freedom from or absence of danger'. Also described as 'freedom from fear', security thus clearly contains a subjective element, an element of perception. The second part of the definition can also be expressed as 'confidence in the future', which has a more positive ring to it. *Security policy* can then be defined as a policy aiming to keep an object, in this case the values and interests of the EU, safe. Since there are many kinds of danger, security is by nature a very broad concept that comprises several dimensions. Traditionally however, both security and security policy have been associated only with the military dimension, with the use of politico-military instruments to avert military danger.[1] The recognition of the broad nature of security is characteristic of the EU. *Defence policy* is the aspect of security policy that has to do with self-defence against acts of aggression. A *strategy* is a policy-making tool which, on the basis of the values and interests of the EU, outlines the long-term overall policy *objectives* to be achieved and the basic categories of *instruments* to be applied to that end. It serves as a reference framework for day-to-day policy-making in a rapidly evolving and increasingly complex international environment and it guides the definition of the *means* – i.e. the civilian and military capabilities – that need to be developed.

This chapter will explore how, as a consequence of the major change of the security environment, new approaches to security policy have been developed, and how these eventually found their way into a security strategy for the EU.

A New Security Environment

During the Cold War, Europe's security was essentially defined in politico-military terms, as the avoidance of direct *military* danger by a clearly identified foe. This uni-dimensional definition was a product of the bipolar constellation, in which

---

[1] Politico-military instruments comprise, *inter alia*, mechanisms for early warning and peaceful settlement of disputes; confidence and security-building measures (CSBMs), political dialogue and military cooperation; non-proliferation, arms control and disarmament; preventive diplomacy; sanctions regimes; observer, humanitarian, peacekeeping, police and peace enforcement operations (which can be summarised under the general heading of peace support operations and which include a civil dimension); and defence operations.

Europe's security was deemed to hinge on avoiding armed conflict on the European continent by maintaining a nuclear and politico-military balance of power between the US and the Soviet Union. So European security policy was forged under American leadership, mostly within the framework of NATO, and was essentially limited to defence policy. The non-military dimensions of security were regarded as being of much less consequence for Europe's security, as were developments in other parts of the world. There was a tendency to develop security policy without taking other external policy aspects into consideration.

The end of the Cold War produced a drastic change in Europe's security environment. The collapse of the Soviet bloc and of the Soviet Union itself meant the end of a direct and major military threat to Europe's security, i.e. one that could threaten the very survival of the EU. Accordingly, defence policy became less important. The EU Member States had long ceased to be a threat to one another, and through enlargement the deeply integrated European 'security community' was extended to Central and Eastern Europe (Deutsch, 1957). But the end of the Cold War also triggered a wave of inter- and intra-State armed conflicts in the vicinity of the EU. Although they have not threatened the EU directly, they have produced negative spill-over effects, e.g. refugee flows and disruption of trade. At the borders of the enlarged EU, the risk of such conflicts is still very real, while the stabilization of the Balkans is far from complete, as outbreaks of violence in Kosovo showed in 2004. In these conflicts, the civilian population has been targeted more than ever before; they can be described as 'unconventional' or 'small wars' in which the parties do not respect international norms and target society as such (Thiele, 2002, p.68). At the same time, international terrorism poses a much more diffuse and difficult to assess threat, which in the minds of many the issue of the proliferation of weapons of mass destruction (WMD) and their means of delivery is closely intertwined.

Since the EU has recognized that there no longer exists a major direct military threat to its territory, other factors, which can constitute the underlying causes of terrorism or of armed conflict between or within third States, or that can intrinsically affect the values and interests of the EU, have come much more to the fore: organized crime, illegal immigration, social and economic underdevelopment, lack of democratic institutions and respect for human rights, failed States, ineffective multilateral institutions, ecological problems etc. These factors are much less easy to grasp than the previous clearly identifiable threat; they are both more difficult to predict and to manage. Another element of the changing security environment is the growing awareness of the importance of values in international relations, such as democracy and respect for human rights and an effective international legal order. Not only has awareness of other dimensions of security increased, the number of international players – State and non-State, legal and illegal – has grown too. The multidimensional nature of security can no longer be ignored.

The background to this shifting importance of security factors is globalization. The growing dependence on global financial and trade networks has decreased the risk of conflict between the powerful States (NIC, 2005, p.98). Globalization has resulted in interdependence, which has proven to be more than economic: it also has political, cultural and security aspects. As a consequence of globalization, itself a source of tensions between those that benefit from it and those that suffer its negative effects, Europe's interests are inseparably linked to the stability of its worldwide interaction with other players, and vice versa. This interdependency implies that events anywhere in the world can have an immediate impact on Europe – there no longer is a fixed correlation between the importance of developments for European security and their geographical distance from the EU. It further means that the security of one is dependent upon the security of the other, hence the need for multilateral cooperation. As Kay (2004) neatly sums it up,

> under conditions of interdependence, power becomes diffuse – and it works through multiple channels, involves a host of new actors, removes existing hierarchies among issues, and reduces the utility of military force.

In effect, therefore, the security of Europe nowadays is dependent on the stability of the international system as such.

New Approaches to Security

In response to this changing security environment and based on a new assessment of security threats, a number of States and international organizations have sought new ways to deal with security – ways that go beyond the traditional realist, State-centric and defence-oriented, politico-military approach. The use of politico-military instruments can deal effectively with immediate security threats, by ending violence or preventing its eruption, but the underlying causes of instability, conflict and terrorism demand a much broader, long-term and permanent policy of conflict prevention. '9/11' has demonstrated that possession of the greatest military might on earth, including the most advanced technology, cannot by itself guarantee security.

Thus these novel approaches are all much more encompassing than NATO's Strategic Concept adopted by the Heads of State and Government meeting in Washington on 23–24 April 1999. The Alliance does recognize 'the importance of political, economic, social and environmental factors in addition to the indispensable defence dimension'. But because of its very nature, that of a defence organization, NATO can only offer the politico-military part of the answer to the new security environment: collective defence (Article 5), peace support operations ('non-Article 5 missions'), and politico-military dialogue and partnership.

One 'new' approach to security that involves the EU Member States in fact dates back to the beginning of the Helsinki process in 1973: the *comprehensive* view of security taken by the CSCE (Commission on Security and Cooperation in Europe now OSCE), which is reflected in the three baskets of the Helsinki Final Act. The OSCE considers

> the protection and promotion of human rights and fundamental freedoms, along with economic and environmental cooperation [...], to be just as important for the maintenance of peace and stability as politico-military issues.

Security is further seen as indivisible. 'States have a common stake in the security of Europe and should therefore cooperate', to the benefit of all parties, since 'insecurity in one State or region can affect the well-being of all' (OSCE, 2000, pp.1-3). This *cooperative* aspect of the OSCE approach to security amounts to inclusiveness or 'institutionalised consent' (Nolan, 1994; Cohen and Mihalka, 2001): security policy is aimed at reassuring third countries, through cooperation in a wide range of fields, rather than deterring them. In the words of former Australian Foreign Minister Gareth Evans:

> consultation rather than confrontation, reassurance rather than deterrence, transparency rather than secrecy, prevention rather than correction, and interdependence rather than unilateralism (Evans, 1994, p.96).

In practice the OSCE has not emerged as the leading security organization in Europe. It has focussed on a number of specific issues and instruments which have often proved very successful, including confidence and security-building measures, peaceful settlement of disputes, election monitoring and minority rights. Thanks to its pan-European membership, the OSCE also contributes to disseminating the comprehensive and cooperative approach to security. Through their membership of the OSCE, the newly independent countries of the Commonwealth of Independent States e.g. can be familiarized with this approach and its underlying values.

A first limited attempt to draft a distinctive European security strategy was undertaken within the framework of the Western European Union (WEU). In the resulting Common Concept, adopted on 14 November 1995, the WEU states:

> acknowledged that their security is indivisible, that a comprehensive approach should underlie the concept of security and that cooperative mechanisms should be applied in order to promote security and stability in the whole of the continent.

The Common Concept stressed 'Europe's new responsibilities in a strategic environment in which Europe's security is not confined to security in Europe', and described the security environment, highlighting *inter alia* the importance of 'the maintenance of international peace and order and the widest possible observance of generally recognised norms of conduct between States' and of 'democratic institutions, respect for human rights and fundamental freedoms and the rule of law', as well as the need to 'prevent economic imbalances from becoming a threat to our continent'. In terms of how to deal with this new environment however, the document was limited to an assessment of Europe's military capabilities and the identification of partners for cooperation. At that time, a real review of strategy proved to be politically unfeasible because of divisions between the Member States; furthermore the Common Foreign and Security Policy (CFSP), to which WEU provided a military arm, was then still in its infancy. Nevertheless, as the first official European assessment of the changing security environment, it was an important and all too easily forgotten step in the development of the EU as an international actor.

The concept of *human security* is usually thought to have originated in the 1993 and 1994 Human Development Reports (UNDP, 1993 and 1994; Commission on Human Security, 2003). It is also very much present in the report drawn up by UN Secretary-General Koffi Annan in preparation of the September 2000 Millennium Summit (Annan, 2000). Human security takes the individual and his community as point of reference, rather than the State, by addressing both military and non-military threats to his/her security. The security of the State is seen not as an end in itself, but as a means of – and necessary precondition for – providing security for people. Indeed, the State itself can be the source of the insecurity of its citizens. Thus, territorial integrity, traditionally the cornerstone of security policy, is not seen as the overall priority: human life and dignity are the keywords. The UNDP lists seven dimensions of security: economic, food, health, environmental, personal, community and political. This very broad, but therefore also unwieldy definition, with 'vulnerability' as its defining feature, *inter alia* is prominent in Japan; in 1998 then Prime Minister Keizo Obuchi became one of the proponents of human security (Fukushima, 2004).

Another school of thought limits human security to 'vulnerability to physical violence during conflict' (Acharya, 2001). This is the view often found in Canada which under the leadership of former Foreign Minister Lloyd Axworthy became one of the leading promoters of human security. Axworthy (1999a and b) defines human security as 'freedom from pervasive threats to people's rights, safety or lives': that is 'freedom from fear' as opposed to 'freedom from want', the latter corresponding to well-being rather than security. In order to bring the human security concept into practice, Canada has identified five policy priorities – protection of civilians, peace support operations, conflict prevention, governance and accountability, and public safety – which are reflected in a focus on a number of specific issues, including landmines, the International Criminal Court, women and children in armed conflict, small arms proliferation and child soldiers (Nelles, 2002; McCrae and Hubert, 2001). This focus on a number of specific issues has led critics to denounce human security as 'niche diplomacy' (Copeland, 2001). In this Canadian view, the pursuit of human security can involve the use of force. This was also the conclusion of the International Commission on Intervention and State Sovereignty (ICISS), established on the initiative of Canada within the framework of the UN General Assembly to look into the concept of humanitarian intervention. The commission identified as a basic principle that 'where a population is suffering serious harm, as a result of internal war, insurgency, repression or State failure, and the State in question is unwilling or unable to halt or avert it, the principle of non-intervention yields to the international responsibility to protect', including, under strict conditions and if authorized by the Security Council, by military means (ICISS, 2001).

Like comprehensive security, human security highlights the interconnections between different dimensions of security. It seeks to cross the boundaries between humanitarian relief, development assistance, human rights advocacy and conflict resolution (Uvin, 2004). It also underlines the global nature of security challenges, which results in mutual vulnerability. Human security therefore requires comprehensive and cooperative responses. While comprehensive security raises the question 'which threats to our security?' and cooperative security 'which security partners?', human security adds 'whose security?'. Human security is geared to attaining justice and emancipation, not just order and stability. The Council for Security Cooperation in Asia Pacific, a non-governmental grouping of Western and Asian think-tanks, has attempted to merge the two approaches by including the individual level in its formulation of comprehensive security, which is defined as the 'pursuit of sustainable security in all fields (personal, political, economic, social, cultural, military, environmental) in both the domestic and external spheres, essentially through cooperative means', a definition that includes both 'freedom from fear' and 'freedom from want' (CSCAP, 1996).

For its part, the Council of Europe has developed the concept of *democratic security*, building on the assumption that armed conflict between democracies is unlikely, and aiming to protect the individual by guaranteeing the rule of law and respect for human rights. Democratic security thus highlights one specific dimension of security. The Vienna Declaration adopted by the first Council of Europe Summit of Heads of State and Government (9 October 1993) states that

> the end of the division of Europe offers an historic opportunity to consolidate peace and stability on the continent. All our countries are committed to pluralist and parliamentary democracy, the indivisibility and universality of human rights, the rule of law and a common cultural heritage enriched by its diversity. Europe can thus become a vast area of democratic security.

Comprehensive security can be linked to another concept that emerged in the context of the UN at the end of the 1990s: *global public goods* (GPG). Public goods are characterized by non-rivalry in consumption and non-excludability (Ferroni and Mody, 2002, p.6). *Global* public goods provide benefits that are

> quasi universal in terms of countries (covering more than one group of countries), people (accruing to several, preferably all, population groups), and generations (extending to both current and future generations, or at least meeting the needs of current generations without foreclosing development options for future generations) (Kaul, Grunberg and Stern, 1999, pp.2-3).

GPG can be grouped under the following broad headings, the core GPG to which every individual is entitled:

- physical security and stability – 'freedom from fear';
- an enforceable legal order that ensures the equality of all;
- an open and inclusive economic order that provides for the wealth of everyone – 'freedom from want' – and allows all to participate fully in decision-making;
- wellbeing in all of its aspects – access to health, to education, to a clean environment, etc.

GPG are strongly interrelated: ultimately, one cannot be ensured or enjoyed without access to the other. Global stability, and therefore the security of all States, depends on the availability of sufficient access to the core GPG; an excessive gap between haves and have-nots will lead to destabilization. Indeed, it is often only when a threat to the global order is perceived that such deficiencies are taken seriously (Harriss-White, 2002, p.189). Ensuring access to GPG requires effective global governance. An international system that fails to provide the core GPG, as a State should do at the national level, lacks legitimacy. The idea of promoting global governance in order to increase access to GPG is prevalent in the UN's Millennium Development Goals (MDGs): to eradicate extreme poverty and hunger; to achieve universal primary education; to promote gender equality and empower women; to reduce child mortality; to improve maternal health; to combat HIV/AIDS, malaria and other diseases; to ensure environmental sustainability; and to develop a global partnership for development. GPG are usually seen in the context of development, but currently the concept is also being used in more general political terms, as a way of conceptualizing the comprehensive approach to global policy issues, e.g. by Joseph Nye (2002), by the World Economic Forum (2004) and by the US-based Council on Foreign Relations (2004), which sees a world of safety, the rule of law, and the quality of life as the three policy priorities for a renewed transatlantic partnership. The latter is deemed to include the capacity of people to 'feed, clothe, house, and otherwise sustain themselves', as well as 'the obligation of government to provide the conditions – in terms of environment, health, education, and employment, as well as freedom of expression and equality of opportunity – upon which civil society depends'. The definition of the root causes of conflict used by the European Commission in its 'Communication on Conflict Prevention' (2001) is very similar to the notion of GPG, although in the EU GPG are only explicitly mentioned in the context of economic globalization and sustainable development.

This overview of the ongoing re-conceptualization of security highlights the continuity stretching from the origins of the CSCE, one of the first major endeavours to forge a common and autonomous European approach to foreign and security policy, right up to the European Security Strategy. All of these exercises have yielded similar conclusions: only a comprehensive security concept can provide an effective response to the new security environment. Security policy-makers have thus come to try to reflect the inherent multidimensional nature of security in actual policies. Experience also demonstrates however that mainstreaming the comprehensive approach into all of the very diverse policy-fields that then automatically enter the field of vision is far from easy, hence a tendency to focus on specific issues and to try and create integrated policies on a topical basis.

In the US, however, recent developments in strategic thinking have gone in precisely the opposite direction. From merely being reaffirmed when the Bush administration came into office, the traditional 'neo-con' concepts of national sovereignty, national interest and the balance of power became the cornerstones of US policy after '9/11'. In the EU as well, '9/11' brought about a certain renewed emphasis on defence, as reflected in the introduction in the Draft Constitution of a 'solidarity clause' in cases of terrorist attack or natural or man-made disaster (Article I-43), and of an 'obligation of aid and assistance' if a Member State is the victim of armed aggression (Article I-41.7). In the EU, defence issues did not push the comprehensive approach to security off the agenda though – quite the contrary.

Strategic Void

The process leading to the creation of the European Security and Defence Policy (ESDP), the military dimension of the CFSP, was launched in 1998 (Biscop, 1999). The British turnabout that was announced at the informal Pörtschach European Council (24–25 October) and at the Franco-British St-Malo summit (3–4 December), that is London's willingness to build a military capacity in the framework of the EU, was welcomed by all Member States. The need to improve the usability of European armed forces, highlighted by the Member States' difficulties to field 40 to 50 000 troops in Kosovo while having over 1.5 million men and women in uniform, was evident to all. The UK accepted the fact that for the other Member States, for budgetary as well as for political reasons, this would only be feasible through increased European cooperation, a solution implying the creation of EU military bodies: the Military Committee (EUMC) and the Military Staff (EUMS).

Thus there was strong agreement on the need to tackle the military means, but there consensus ended. Member States widely differed on the political/strategic dimension, a debate which goes far beyond ESDP, beyond the CFSP even, as it concerns the whole of EU external action, across all three pillars of the EU. What should be the scope of the EU's foreign and security policy ambitions? What degree of autonomy should the EU have? And what then should be the precise role of the military instrument in EU external action? In the British view, European military capabilities would still primarily be put to use in the framework of NATO, as the main if not exclusive forum for decision-making on security policy. Others certainly preferred the EU to define and implement policies of its own. Even on the assessment of the security environment, Member States differed, with threat perceptions being influenced by individual States' proximity to specific unstable regions (Van Camp and Collins, 2003). The much more unpredictable context renders a common assessment of the security environment upon which to base a strategy very difficult, while in the absence of a single major threat the definition of a strategy is much more determined by political choice rather than by the imperatives of necessity (Murdock, 2004). Because of these deep-running divisions and in order not to lose the momentum, it was decided, as happens so often in European decision-making, to push through with those elements on which an agreement existed, i.e. the means and institutions of ESDP, assuming that once these were in place the strategic debate would inevitably have to follow.

Accordingly, following the December 1999 European Council in Helsinki, where the 'Headline Goal'[2] was defined, the EU started building military – ESDP – and civilian capabilities for crisis management, without possessing an overall

---

[2] 'Member States must be able, by 2003, to deploy within 60 days and sustain for at least 1 year military forces of up to 50 000–60 000 persons capable of the full range of Petersberg tasks'.

strategic framework for its external action. In Article 11, the Treaty on European Union (TEU) does define the objectives of the CFSP,[3] but these are statements of principle rather than policy objectives and hence far too general to provide a framework for daily policy-making. As to the role of the military instrument, the TEU stipulates which types of operations the EU can launch, by including the so-called Petersberg Tasks, as originally defined by the WEU, in Article 17 – humanitarian and rescue tasks, peacekeeping tasks and tasks of combat forces in crisis management, including peacemaking – but it provides no guidelines as to the circumstances under which the use of the military instrument can be considered.[4]

The absence of an explicit strategy need not be a problem if all those involved in policy-making share the same basic views and can thus easily reach a consensus on policies that fit within these general guidelines, even if they are not explicitly written down. But with regard to the external policies of the EU, this was clearly not the case. There was no common strategic vision behind the existing – but incomplete – consensus on the need to develop more effective military capabilities for the EU. Without a strategy, 'belated reactions, decision-making paralysis and coalitions of the willing outside the EU framework are the likely outcome' (Meyer, 2004, p.3). As a consequence, EU external action has lacked direction, determination and consistency. Faced with the initiatives of a dominant global player, the US, that is both very determined and very powerful and that does possess an explicit strategy – the National Security Strategy adopted in September 2002 – the EU has necessarily been restricted to a reactive role. Without having a clear strategy itself, the EU cannot escape the American framework of thought and promote its own policy priorities in terms of both objectives and instruments.

Strategic Indications

That is not to say of course that EU external action has been completely ad hoc. Over the years, a distinctive European approach to security has emerged, which is characterized by the broad, multidimensional or *comprehensive* notion of security, which starts from the interdependence between all dimensions of security – political, socio-economic, ecologic, cultural and military – rather than just focusing

---

[3] 'To safeguard the common values, fundamental interests, independence and integrity of the Union in conformity with the principles of the United Nations Charter; to strengthen the security of the Union in all ways; to preserve peace and strengthen international security, in accordance with the principles of the United Nations Charter, as well as the principles of the Helsinki Final Act and the objectives of the Paris Charter, including those on external borders; to promote international cooperation; to develop and consolidate democracy and the rule of law, and respect for human rights and fundamental freedoms'.

[4] An extended definition of the Petersberg Tasks has been included in the Draft Constitution (Article III-309): 'joint disarmament operations, humanitarian and rescue tasks, military advice and assistance tasks, conflict prevention and peace-keeping tasks, tasks of combat forces undertaken for crisis management, including peace-making and post-conflict stabilisation. All these tasks may contribute to the fight against terrorism, including by supporting third countries in combating terrorism in their territories'.

on the latter; hence the need to set objectives and apply instruments in all of these fields. A further characteristic is a focus on dialogue, cooperation and partnership, i.e. on *cooperative* security or multilateralism. This approach can be deducted from actual EU policies.

In the 2001 Communication on Conflict Prevention the Commission proposed to address the 'root causes of conflict' by promoting 'structural stability', defined as 'sustainable economic development, democracy and respect for human rights, viable political structures and healthy environmental and social conditions, with the capacity to manage change without resort to conflict'. The EU Programme for the Prevention of Violent Conflicts, adopted by the European Council at its meeting in Göteborg on 15–16 June 2001, which is based on the above communication, calls for an integrated policy, surpassing the pillar structure, and defines conflict prevention as a priority for all of the EU's external action. It also lists EU instruments for both long-term structural stabilization and short-term prevention. The EU has now developed instruments such as the Country and Regional Strategy Papers, which outline policy priorities, the Check-List for Root Causes of Conflict and the continually revised Watch List of Priority Countries (countries where there is a serious risk of conflict). But what the EU has been lacking is a conceptual dimension that brings its range of external policies together and that can serve as a framework for the comprehensive and integrated approach that is advocated in the Programme for the Prevention of Violent Conflicts.

A comprehensive approach to security is particularly characteristic of EU policy with respect to its neighbouring States, which it attempts to integrate in an encompassing network of relations: witness the Stability Pact for the Balkans, the Euro-Mediterranean Partnership, and the successful transition of Central and Eastern Europe, probably the most significant European achievement since the start of the European integration project itself. Under the heading European Neighbourhood Policy, this approach has now been adopted as an enhanced framework for relations between the EU and its neighbours (European Commission, 2003a). The aim of the Neighbourhood Policy is to achieve an 'area of shared prosperity and values' by creating close partnerships with the EU's neighbouring States. This should lead to in-depth economic integration, close political and cultural relations and a joint responsibility for conflict prevention. To that end, the EU is to offer very concrete 'benefits', in the fields of market access and investments for example, which should be linked to progress made towards political and economic reforms in the neighbouring States.

When it comes to long-term policies, this comprehensive and cooperative approach to security has emerged as the predominant characteristic of EU external action. Keukeleire (2000 and 2001) calls this 'the structural foreign policy' of the EU. It is less visible than traditional diplomacy or 'high politics', but nonetheless represents a huge and often very successful effort on the part of the EU. A similar picture emerges from Bretherton and Vogler's major study of the EU as a global actor (1999). The EU's profile in these long-term policy areas corresponds to the image of the EU as a 'civilian power', i.e. an actor which seeks to influence the international environment in the long term – which has 'milieu' rather than 'possession goals' (Wolfers, 1962) – which operates mainly through economic, diplomatic and ideological power and via multilateralism, and which is inspired not only by material interests, but also by norms and ideas (Orbie, 2003). A number of implicit strategic assumptions have guided EU policy in this regard; this represents an important *acquis*. Yet these assumptions needed to be substantiated and policy areas needed to be integrated in order to arrive at a framework for maximally consistent, coherent and effective external action.

For when the EU is confronted with acute crises, such as the one in Iraq, these implicit assumptions have proved to be insufficient to arrive at a common policy. More often than not, the EU has failed to achieve consensus on how to respond to such crises, even when the instruments and means to do so were at hand. In the words of former Swedish Prime Minister Carl Bildt (2003): 'Our number one capabilities gap was not in smart bombs, but in smart policies'. As a result, little or no effective action is then taken – hence the need to define a strategy as a framework also for dealing with crisis situations.

'9/11' and its aftermath are a case in point. At first, the EU did react jointly to the terrorist attacks. Its differentiated response, which focuses on the underlying causes of terrorism, actually is another example of the comprehensive approach. The extraordinary European Council meeting of 21 September 2001 called for 'an in-depth political dialogue with those countries and regions of the world in which terrorism comes into being' and 'the integration of all countries into a fair world system of security, prosperity and improved development'. '9/11' was therefore not a turning point for EU external action (nor was the attack in Madrid on 11 March 2004). Rather it served to confirm the view that a policy that focuses exclusively on military instruments cannot achieve long-term stability or ensure national security. If '9/11' influenced CFSP/ESDP, then only in that it accelerated evolutions that had already been put in motion by the it was experiences on the Balkans. The subsequent events, notably Washington's declaration of a 'war on terrorism' and the US-led invasion of Iraq, led to deep divisions within the EU however, between on the one hand those joining the American-led coalition of the willing invading and occupying Iraq – led by the UK, Poland and, initially, Spain – and on the other hand those resisting the use of force without sufficient UN mandate and before the exhaustion of all other options – led by Belgium, France and Germany. Or between 'new' and 'old Europe', as US Defence Secretary Donald Rumsfeld worded it, putting the motto of *divide et impera* to good use. The unwillingness of the latter group to join the invading coalition provoked uncommonly sharp criticism from a US government that could not understand their reluctance; a transatlantic crisis on top of the intra-European one was the result. At an extraordinary meeting on 17 February 2003 the European Council did state that 'force should be used only as a last resort' and emphasized the importance of reinvigorating the Middle East peace process if peace and stability are to be brought to the region. But due to its internal divisions, the EU as such was absent from the scene. It should be noted though that whereas the European governments were highly divided, all polls indicate that a very large majority of public opinion throughout the EU opposed the war.

A clear-cut strategy should be able to avoid such damaging internal divides and ensure the EU's participation in international decision-making. The EU operation in the Democratic Republic of Congo, 'Artemis', even though it was of limited duration (12 June - 1 September 2003) and had limited objectives (the stabilization of the security conditions and the improvement of the humanitarian situation in the city of Bunia), was certainly not of limited risk, and has demonstrated that the EU can act rapidly and decisively if the political will is there. Another, less evident example is provided by the break-up of Yugoslavia in the early 1990s (Crowe, 2004): leaving aside the effectiveness of Europe's policies, one should not overlook the fact that there was a general consensus among the Member States that it was up to the EEC to act and that generally speaking the ECC did develop a common approach that was translated by its high-level representatives on the ground (Lord Carrington, Lord Owen, Carl Bildt).

Thus the taboo on strategic thinking at European level needed to be broken and the strategic concepts of the individual Member States – some more, others less elaborate – aligned. A strategy would not only provide the reference framework that is needed for day-to-day policy-making. It should also determine the instruments and capabilities that are being developed, rather than the other way around. This is especially so with regard to ESDP: the EU's ambitions and the role it sees for the military instrument should guide force planning at the EU level. A Strategy would further bring political benefits (Biscop, 2002a). If consensus can be found on the EU's general approach to security and on what it will and will not do, those Member States that traditionally have been reluctant about the EU's security dimension, out of resistance against a perceived 'militarization' of external action or for fear of undermining the transatlantic alliance, should be persuaded to fully support the efforts to convert the EU into an effective international actor. As stated by Commissioner Pascal Lamy, no State or national parliament would accept to act through the EU if the debate on objectives and principles has not taken place (European Convention, 2002b, p.9). Of course, one can question the degree to which some of the larger Member States, even those that are playing the European card, are really willing to 'Europeanize' their security policies. Will they stop at the technical level of pooling capabilities for efficiency purposes, or will they be willing to accept the full implications, in terms of integration of policy-making and loss of sovereignty, of their demands for a stronger and therefore more unified Europe? In any event, a strategy provides a clear framework for policy-making and thus renders unilateral action more difficult. Such a step might also alleviate the misgivings among the EU's neighbours about a build-up of military capacity which in their view lacks clear objectives, and could thus very well be directed against them. Finally, the adoption of a strategy would increase the openness of CFSP/ESDP and would enable a public debate that is a prerequisite to acquire democratic legitimacy and to gain the vital support of public opinion.

Strategic Momentum

Undoubtedly, '9/11' and Iraq influenced Member States' willingness to consider an exercise in strategic thinking that was impossible when ESDP was created just a few years earlier. The various States may have had differing motivations: defining a distinctive 'European way' for some, so as to distance themselves from a US policy with which they could not agree and to highlight alternatives; aligning European priorities with those of the US for others, to preserve a transatlantic partnership perceived to be threatened in its existence; or a combination of both, reconciling the necessary drafting of an EU agenda with the need for continued transatlantic partnership. Whatever the motivation, the important thing is that this enabled the decisive step to launch a strategic debate in the EU, to translate policy practice into strategy, an endeavour which far exceeds the specific issue of Iraq. In that sense, Iraq can be said ultimately to have been a unifying factor for the EU (Haseler, 2004, p.98).

This endeavour complemented the European Convention which was then in process and the Draft Constitution that it produced, which dealt primarily with institutions and capabilities. Voices in favour of the definition of a new approach to security were raised in the Convention. For example Dr. Wim van Eekelen, former Secretary General of WEU, called for the formulation of a strategic concept which

> would develop the notions of comprehensive security, including conflict prevention, democracy building and economic development and also cooperative security with neighbouring regions, but – in order to be credible – should also contain a military capability underpinning the policies of the Union (European Convention, 2002a, p.4).

The final report of Working Group No. VIII on defence – chaired by European Commissioner Michel Barnier – did state that

> the concept of security is very broad, by nature indivisible, and one that goes beyond the purely military aspects covering not only the security of States but also the security of citizens. On the basis of this broad concept of security, the CFSP and the ESDP which forms part of it promote international security founded on multilateral solutions and respect for international law. Conflict prevention is a key element in the approach followed by the EU in international relations. The ESDP allows the EU military options over and above the civil instruments of crisis prevention and management (European Convention, 2002c, pp.3-4).

The Working Group did not advance such a concept however, as this fell outside of its mandate.

At the informal meeting of the General Affairs and External Relations Council in Greece on 2 and 3 May 2003, Javier Solana was thus – rather unexpectedly – tasked with producing a draft strategic document. At its meeting in Thessaloniki (19-20 June), the European Council welcomed the document submitted by Solana, *A Secure Europe in a Better World*, and charged him with taking the work forward with a view to completing a strategy by its next meeting. The EU then organized three seminars, in Rome (19 September), Paris (6–7 October) and Stockholm (20 October), bringing together officials from the Member States, the future Member States and the European institutions, as well as experts from the academic world, NGOs and the media. This innovative process allowed the High Representative to collect comments and suggestions from a wide variety of actors and observers, a number of which found their way into the final *European Security Strategy*, which was duly adopted by the European Council meeting on 12 December 2003.

Several States and organizations have attempted to implement the comprehensive approach to security and integrate aspects of it in their policies. The EU, as a *sui generis* organization, with a foreign and security policy that has a global scope and covers all dimensions of international relations, now has the opportunity to adopt the comprehensive approach as the foundation of its external action.

Chapter 2

Comprehensive Security

Introduction

At its December 2003 Brussels meeting, the European Council adopted the European Security Strategy and 'warmly congratulated' Javier Solana for the work accomplished. The introduction to the Strategy highlights the fact that 'Europe has never been so prosperous, so secure nor so free' and that 'As a union of 25 states with over 450 million people producing a quarter of the world's Gross National Product (GNP), and with a wide range of instruments at its disposal, the European Union is inevitably a global player', hence 'Europe should be ready to share in the responsibility for global security and in building a better world'. So the Strategy opens with a call to duty, in the interest of global security as well as of our own, for 'Europe still faces security threats and challenges'.

This chapter will first offer a summary of the Strategy, before analyzing the threat assessment included in the Strategy in the light of the new security environment and the development of comprehensive approaches to security. It will then outline how, in the author's view, the Strategy can be seen as an innovative conceptual framework for the whole of EU external action, based on the notion of comprehensive security, and has created the opportunity to structurally integrate all dimensions of external action and thus to implement a distinctive European approach as the potentially most effective response to the current international environment.

The European Security Strategy

The Strategy is organized into three chapters: an analysis of the security environment, the definition of three strategic objectives, and an assessment of the policy implications for the EU.

The Security Environment

Under the heading of 'global challenges', the starting point of the analysis of the security environment is the impact of globalization. On the one hand, globalization has 'brought freedom and prosperity to many people', but 'others have perceived globalization as a cause of frustration and injustice'. Globalization has 'increased European dependence – and so vulnerability – on an interconnected infrastructure, in transport, energy, information and other fields'; as a consequence of globalization, 'the internal and external aspects of security are indissolubly linked'. The Strategy then goes on to specify a number of the worrying features of this globalized world: poverty; disease, especially AIDS; competition for scarce resources, notably water; global warming; migratory movements; and Europe's energy dependence.

In the second part of the analysis of the security environment, which recognizes that 'large-scale aggression against any Member State is now improbable', a jump is then made to the identification of five 'key threats', which are seen as being closely interconnected:

- terrorism, for which 'Europe is both a target and a base'; the Strategy notes that terrorism 'arises out of complex causes', including 'the pressures of modernization, cultural, social and political crises, and the alienation of young people living in foreign societies';
- proliferation of WMD, 'potentially the greatest threat to our security', which in 'the most frightening scenario' could be acquired by terrorists;
- regional conflicts, both worldwide and at the borders of the EU, which 'impact on European interests directly and indirectly' and which 'can lead to extremism, terrorism and state failure';
- state failure, which 'undermines global governance, and adds to regional instability' and which 'can be associated with obvious threats, such as organized crime or terrorism';
- organized crime, an internal threat with 'an important external dimension', such as 'cross-border trafficking in drugs, women, illegal migrants and weapons' as well as gemstones and timber; organized crime 'can have links with terrorism' and is 'often associated with weak or failing states'.

Strategic Objectives

'Addressing the threats' is the first of three strategic objectives outlined in the Strategy, which first lists the initiatives which the EU has already taken in this field:

- the European Arrest Warrant, measures addressing terrorist financing and an agreement on mutual legal assistance with the US;
- the EU's long-standing non-proliferation policies, highlighting its commitment to strong and verifiable multilateral treaty regimes;
- its interventions to help deal with regional conflicts, notably in the Balkans, Afghanistan and the Democratic Republic of Congo.

The Strategy then outlines the approach which the EU will continue to pursue in dealing with the 'key threats', taking into account the nature of these threats and the exigencies of the new globalized security environment. 'In an era of globalization, distant threats may be as much a concern as those that are near at hand', therefore 'the first line of defence will often be abroad'; this statement confirms that the EU cannot be but a global actor. 'The new threats are dynamic' and 'spread if they are neglected', therefore 'conflict prevention and threat prevention cannot start too early'. 'None of the new threats is purely military, nor can any be tackled by purely military means', therefore prevention will require the application of 'a mixture of instruments'. 'The European Union is particularly well equipped to respond to such multi-faceted situations', it is stressed.

'Building security in our neighbourhood' is the second strategic objective. 'Even in an era of globalization, geography is still important', the Strategy points out: 'neighbours who are engaged in violent conflict, weak states where organized crime flourishes, dysfunctional societies or exploding population growth on our borders all pose problems for Europe'. Therefore 'a ring of well-governed countries' must be established, 'with whom we can enjoy close and cooperative relations'. This is to be achieved through partnership and action in the political, economic and cultural spheres as well as in the security field.

This 'ring of friends' or 'neighbourhood' is seen to include:

- the Balkans, where Europe's substantial achievements must be consolidated;
- 'our neighbours in the East', to whom 'the benefits of economic and political cooperation' should be extended;
- the Southern Caucasus;
- the Mediterranean or the Euro-Mediterranean Partnership.

As final strategic objective, the Strategy names the establishment of 'an international order based on effective multilateralism', i.e. 'a stronger international society, well functioning international institutions and a rule-based international order'. The centre of that system is the UN, hence 'equipping it to fulfil its responsibilities and to act effectively, is a European priority'. The institutional architecture further comprises global organizations like the WTO and the international financial institutions on the one hand, and regional organizations such as the OSCE, the Council of Europe, ASEAN, MERCOSUR and the African Union on the other hand. The transatlantic relationship, of which 'NATO is an important expression', is also defined as a core element; it is in the EU's bilateral interest, but also in that of the international community as a whole.

Through this network of regimes and institutions, what amounts to global governance must be pursued, which implies: 'spreading good governance, supporting social and political reform, dealing with corruption and abuse of power, establishing the rule of law and protecting human rights', as well as 'assistance programmes, conditionality and targeted trade measures'. As it is highlighted in the Strategy: 'The best protection of our security is a world of well-governed democratic states'. But the Strategy also emphasizes that for international organizations, regimes and treaties to be effective, the EU must be 'ready to act when their rules are broken'; hence States that 'have placed themselves outside the bounds of international society' are reminded that 'there is a price to be paid, including in their relationship with the European Union'.

Policy Implications

The EU has 'instruments in place that can work effectively', but should 'make a contribution that matches [its] potential'. Therefore under the heading of 'policy implications', in its final chapter the Strategy calls for an EU that is more active, more capable, more coherent and works with others.

'More active' means that the EU should 'develop a strategic culture that fosters early, rapid and when necessary, robust intervention', in order to act 'before countries around us deteriorate, when signs of proliferation are detected, and before humanitarian emergencies arise' – what the Strategy calls 'preventive engagement'. This applies to 'the full spectrum of instruments for crisis management and conflict prevention at our disposal, including political, diplomatic, military and civilian, trade and development activities'.

In order for the EU to become 'more capable', foremost is the need to further 'transform our militaries into more flexible, mobile forces and to enable them to address the new threats'. To that end, the Strategy also calls for 'more resources for defence' and 'more effective use of resources', as 'systematic use of pooled and shared assets would reduce duplications, overheads, and, in the medium-term, increase capabilities'. Other fields mentioned are civilian resources, diplomatic capacity and intelligence sharing.

Under the heading of 'more coherent', the Strategy states that 'the challenge now is to bring together the different instruments and capabilities', for 'diplomatic efforts, development, trade and environmental policies, should follow the same agenda' – an unambiguous call for a comprehensive approach, which should also embrace 'the external activities of the individual Member States'.

Finally, the Strategy states that the EU will be 'working with partners', and this 'both through multilateral cooperation in international organizations and through partnerships with key actors'. The former are listed in the paragraph on 'effective multilateralism'; the latter are deemed to include first of all the US and Russia, and then also Japan, China, Canada and India, 'as well as all those who share our goals and values, and are prepared to act in their support'.

Assessing the Global Security Environment

In the first draft of the Strategy, the emphasis on threats, especially on terrorism and on WMD, was much stronger than in the final version; the first draft was much closer to the National Security Strategy of the US, which focuses very strongly on defence against external threats. More than one European observer thought of the first draft as the EU 'unambiguously re-calibrat[ing] its priorities to match those of the US' (Quille, 2003, pp.1-2; Pailhe, 2004; Gegout, 2005), even though the tone of both documents is decidedly different (Duke, 2004, p.467). Confirming the American threat assessment can be interpreted as a political statement, signalling to Washington, in the aftermath of the transatlantic divide over Iraq, that the EU shares the US' concerns over the threats posed by terrorism and WMD and that the transatlantic partnership is viable yet. That in itself has been a valuable contribution to the healing of transatlantic relations, and has been perceived as such by US observers. But this does not necessarily imply that the EU will adopt the same approach to deal with these threats. The 'strong' first chapter can also be seen as a means of making the much more comprehensive approach to security advocated in the ensuing chapters of the Strategy palatable for the US. One can thus also discern an intra-European compromise reconciling the two camps that emerged during the Iraq crisis: including a firm stand on terrorism and WMD in the threat assessment, in return for an emphasis on comprehensive security in the following chapters.

In the final version of the Strategy, the analysis of the security environment has been elaborated and toned down at the same time:

- more attention is being devoted to the effects of globalization, notably the interdependence of all States' security that results from it, which went almost without mention in the first draft;
- a distinction is no longer being made between 'old' and 'new' terrorism; the first draft seemed to reflect the hypothesis that current, 'new' terrorism is somehow unique, notably as to the scale of its destructiveness and its lack of constraints, but this is being contradicted by scholars pointing out that such waves of terrorism are recurrent throughout recent history (Van de Voorde and Van den Eede, 2004; Rapoport, 2003); if terrorism is not unique, it can be successfully combated, as it has been in the past;
- proliferation of WMD has been re-defined as 'potentially the greatest', rather than 'the single most important' threat, and the statement that 'against small groups having acquired WMD deterrence would fail', has been deleted;
- state failure and organized crime have become separate entries in the list of key threats and regional conflicts have been added to it. Regional conflicts, in the periphery of the EU as well as further away, can threaten Europe's energy supply and the flow of goods and services and provoke refugee flows towards the EU; furthermore, they can undermine the international order as such if acts of aggression, such as the 1990 invasion of Kuwait by Iraq, would remain unpunished (EUISS, 2004, pp.81-2).

These amendments reflect the mood at all three seminars on the draft Strategy that the EU organized in the Fall of 2003, where it was pointed out that the current predominance of terrorism and WMD on the political agenda should not allow policy-makers to forget either 'old' threats, such as regional conflicts, or the need to address the root causes of threats.

Yet it can be argued that even the final version of the Strategy is overemphasizing *military* threats, by exaggerating the importance of both terrorism and WMD specifically, as compared to other threats, and of the need of 'addressing the threats' in general. Placing the threats first among the strategic objectives in the Strategy's next chapter – in the first draft they came last – is further evidence of this, even though this can again be seen as a political message, in order to emphasize once more that the EU shares US concerns.[5] Overemphasizing military threats carries the risk of focusing too much on defence, which is the most obvious, but not necessarily the most effective way of dealing with threats, to the detriment of prevention. Although the links between the five 'key threats' is emphasized, much less is said on the causal relationship between, on the one hand, the 'global challenges', or in other words the 'dark side of globalization', which is the first part of the analysis of the security environment, and, on the other hand, the second part of the analysis, the 'key threats'. In that sense, the threat assessment seems to be lacking coherence.

Terrorism and proliferation of WMD certainly are the most important remaining *direct military* threats to the EU, now that large-scale aggression is no longer a probability. That does not mean that these threats are likely to materialize on a significant scale, however. Most terrorists have an internal political agenda; therefore the most likely target is the domestic regime which they are facing. The bigger threat thus seems to be posed by internal, European terrorists, for example, the ongoing activity of the ETA movement in Spain, or the Corsican separatists in France, or the unexpected letter bomb campaign against the EU institutions by an obscure grouping originating in Bologna at the end of 2003. The same holds true for international terrorism, which as the Strategy states in its most recent manifestation is often linked to extremist Islamism: because of the predominance of domestic agendas, terrorism is not being 'exported' to the EU on any grand scale. Nor does any centralized international terrorist network remain since the effective decapitation of Al-Qaeda by the campaign in Afghanistan – terrorist movements actually have a history of factionalism rather than of cooperation. Although almost anybody can be linked to anybody else, these links for the greater part are just casual contacts and not the manifestation of an organized network. Rather independent groups based in the EU itself or abroad, while often claiming the Al-Qaeda 'trademark' that is certain to attract massive media and political attention, each pursue their own course. Al-Qaeda has thus become an idea rather than an organization, with terrorist groups citing sympathy without having any direct link with it (Coolsaet, 2005; Peña, 2004).

This fragmentation does not mean that the threat has diminished; it is precisely because of it that the threat has become very difficult to assess. On the one hand, attacks against Western targets, like the attacks in Madrid on 11 March 2004, often seem to be linked to specific policies such as a State's involvement in Iraq, so the more balanced policies of the EU, regarding notably the Israeli-Palestinian conflict and the fight against terrorism, might be expected to have a positive impact on the likelihood of further terrorist attacks. On the other hand though, Western targets have been attacked and will probably continue to be, as in the wake of '9/11' and the invasion of Iraq, popular support and media coverage for such acts are easily

---

[5] On the whole, this first strategic objective might appear rather superfluous and repetitive; the actual approach that effectively addresses the threats, or rather global challenges in general, is detailed in the ensuing paragraphs. That in the chapter on the strategic objectives the notion of 'new' threats is still being used, whereas this distinction has been abolished in the chapter on the security environment, seems to be a minor oversight.

forthcoming and thus strengthen the extremists' cause. In that light, provoking retaliation can in fact be the extremists' explicit objective. Countermeasures must therefore be targeted against the specific perpetrators of terrorist acts and must pay attention to the 'hearts and minds' as well, or will be counterproductive. Anti-Western extremism may also be related to frustration and a sense of exclusion from society, a consequence of the xenophobia and racism that are rampant in Europe. For certain individuals, the threshold to revert to violence themselves because of these frustrations has perhaps been lowered as a consequence of the omnipresence of terrorism in the media and in political discourse. The murder of Dutch film-maker and controversial op-ed writer Theo van Gogh by a Dutchman of Moroccan origin in November 2004 can be seen as a sad example. The involvement of irrational actors without a clear structure or agenda has certainly increased rather than decreased the threat, and has rendered it more difficult to combat and predict.

So there undoubtedly is a terrorist threat, but the question is whether quantitatively it is altogether much larger than the threat which so many European countries experienced from domestic and Middle Eastern terrorism in the 1970s and 1980s. Research shows that the shocking events of '9/11' and '11/3' mask a long-term trend: both the number of terrorist attacks and the number of victims have steadily decreased since 1977 (Coolsaet and Van de Voorde, 2004). The murder of Israeli athletes at the 1972 Olympics in Munich, the attacks against US targets in Beirut in 1983 and the explosion of the PanAm flight over Lockerbie in 1988 are just a few examples of large-scale, high-profile terrorist strikes in the past. Should terrorism, and especially the repression of terrorism, therefore be allowed to dominate today's political agenda to the extent that it has – at the risk of ignoring other challenges, which, by the way, often constitute the root causes of terrorism. Besides, an open and democratic society can never be made completely invulnerable to terrorism, except at the expense of abandoning exactly those freedoms that make a democracy. Making the fight against terrorism into a 'war on terrorism' is certainly counterproductive. The murder of van Gogh can again serve as an example: initial 'war-like' reactions by members of the Dutch government only provoked more violence against innocent members of Muslim communities, thus creating the danger of setting in motion a vicious cycle.

Today's terrorists mainly use the same weapons as their predecessors: explosives. In the estimate of the US National Intelligence Council (NIC, 2005, p.95) terrorists will continue to employ primarily conventional weapons. The threat would indeed be increased if a terrorist group were to acquire WMD, but none has done so yet. This fact demonstrates the importance of effective non-proliferation, but should not lead to alarmism. The only parties that do currently possess WMD are therefore States. In their case, the danger is even more limited: no State, apart from the EU's allies, has the means to mount a full-scale offensive and pose any serious threat. Besides, the use of WMD would imply the risk of massive retaliation, by conventional means or otherwise. But the main argument is that in view of the EU's economic might it is hard to imagine which State would not damage its own interests by an act of aggression (Biscop, 2003). All this is not to say that terrorism and WMD can be ignored, but the threat that they pose should be put in the right perspective.

Rather than terrorism, WMD or other military threats, the most important threat emerging from the new security environment is the ever growing gap between haves and have-nots, a gap which can be best expressed in terms of access to the essential global public goods. The 'global challenges' mentioned in the Strategy – poverty, disease etc. – are all symptoms of this gap, which in some form or other often is at the heart of the 'key threats' or, in other words, often reveals their root causes. While this gap and the feelings of exclusion, marginalization and frustration resulting from it certainly do not justify conflict, they do help to explain it, which is a prerequisite for prevention and resolution of conflicts. As High Representative Solana (2004) put it: 'No cause justifies terrorism, but nothing justifies ignoring the causes of terrorism'. In the words of former European Commissioner Chris Patten (2004):

> Of course, there can be no justification for acts of such reckless terrorism and hate. But it would be foolish not to recognize that we can undermine support for extremism by addressing frustration and anger that come with poverty, and particularly with the recognition of relative poverty.

The gap between haves and have-nots is foremost among the challenges of the globalized world, because it is a threat of a systemic nature, i.e. it results from, and impacts on, the functioning of the global order itself. For unless mechanisms of governance are created or rendered more effective so that they can alleviate this situation, at a certain level of inequality, the resulting political upheaval, extremisms of all kinds, economic uncertainty and massive migration flows will become uncontrollable – as Europe and the world already experienced once, in the 1930s (Coolsaet and Biscop, 2004). The gap between haves and have-nots exists both within States and between 'the West' and 'the South'; its consequences can thus not be contained, but will affect 'the West' as well. This is not a new assessment: as early as 1962 then UN Secretary-General U Thant warned that 'an explosion of violence could occur as a result of the sense of injustice felt by those living in poverty and despair in a world of plenty' (Tharoor, 2004, p.87).

Against this background of globalization, specific politico-military challenges do indeed stand out. They include regions of chronic tension and long-standing disputes and conflicts, failed States and civil wars, proliferation of WMD and excessive militarization, and terrorism. These challenges directly threaten people, States and regions. On account of spill-over effects and the challenge that they pose to international stability, they also indirectly affect the EU. They have to be tackled head-on, but as they are symptoms of the 'dark side of globalization', effective global governance, improving access to GPG, must be pursued at the same time as the key to *preventing* such threats. 'Security is the precondition of development', the Strategy states, but this works the other way around as well. As Duffield (2002, p.37) notes: 'the promotion of development has become synonymous with the pursuit of security. At the same time, security has become a prerequisite for sustainable development'. Of course, the strength of the causal relationship between, on the one hand, the gap between haves and have-nots in the broadest sense and, on the other hand, specific politico-military issues differs from case to case. Nonetheless, in the long term no durable settlement of such issues can be achieved unless the stability of the world system itself is assured – the 'enabling environment' must be addressed (von Hippel, 2004). Therefore the feeling of alienation on which recruitment of terrorists draws 'is unlikely to dissipate unless the Muslim world again appears to be more fully integrated into the world economy' (NIC, 2005, p.81). Even in cases where military intervention has proved necessary, addressing the root causes of conflict is vital to post-conflict stabilization, if the EU wants to avoid committing to military presences without end. The outbreak of violence in Kosovo in 2004 has demonstrated that a military presence in itself is insufficient to ensure a return to stable peace.

In its final version the Strategy certainly is much more balanced, mentioning as it does a wide range of global challenges linked to globalization, and presenting a more complete picture of the 'key threats'. It appears though that the inseparable link between the overall challenges of globalization and more specific threats, from which follows the priority need of ensuring the stability of the world system as such, could have been highlighted more in the analysis of the security environment. Recognition of this link is the basis on which a comprehensive security policy can be built. At the same time, one should not overlook the fact that reconciling the threat perceptions of the Member States, all influenced by specific geographic and other circumstances, and representing very different attitudes to security and defence (Pilegaard, 2004), represents an enormous achievement in itself.

Comprehensive Security as an EU Trademark

The Strategy clearly builds on the 'European way' in international relations that can be observed in actual EU policies, especially the EU's encompassing, long-term conflict prevention efforts and partnership arrangements. What the Strategy can do is bring these policies together within a conceptual framework that establishes a link between the various EU external policies, including short-term conflict prevention and crisis management. The latter are the areas where the EU has too often lacked a common approach, as the Iraqi crisis so forcibly demonstrated. This conceptual framework emerging from existing policies can be referred to as *comprehensive security*, which is hereafter analyzed from a normative perspective.

Integration

A comprehensive security strategy starts with the recognition that there are various dimensions of security in the current international environment and that therefore the underlying causes of potential threats to the security of the EU are very diverse in terms of both nature and origin. Kirchner and Sperling (2002) dub this 'the new security agenda'. It is concerned with the ability to protect the social and economic fabric of society, to act as gatekeeper between desirable and undesirable interactions and to foster a stable international economic and political environment. This agenda goes beyond the politico-military dimension, which nonetheless remains a vital element, so according to Kirchner and Sperling 'a broader, holistic definition of the relationship between the "new" and "traditional" conceptualizations of security' is required. Because of the multidimensional nature of security, achieving the overall objective of safeguarding the values and interests of the EU is equally dependent on the specific politico-military dimensions and on the broader, global governance dimensions of external action: on the one hand the continued absence of a direct military threat to the EU itself must be ensured and spill-over effects of politico-military problems, such as conflicts between or within third States, to the EU must be avoided; and on the other hand the stability of the EU's neighbourhood and of the international system as such must be maintained.

In order to achieve these twin objectives, a comprehensive security strategy looks beyond the traditional confines of security policy, i.e. beyond the politico-military dimension: it aims *to integrate a range of external policies*, which together offer a broad set of objectives and instruments that have a worldwide scope and that address the different dimensions of security. This range of policies covers all three pillars of the EU; it includes *inter alia* external trade, development cooperation, humanitarian aid, international environmental policy, international police, justice and intelligence cooperation, immigration policy, foreign policy (multilateral diplomacy and the promotion of the values of the EU) and the politico-military field (including ESDP). The overall objective of this range of policies, which functions as an integrating mechanism, can be summarized as the promotion of every individual's access to the core GPG: physical security and stability, an enforceable legal order and political participation, an open and inclusive economic order, and wellbeing in all of its aspects. By including all of these dimensions, comprehensive security goes beyond 'democratic security', which focuses on just one. 'Traditional' security policy, that is the politico-military dimension, is seen as one aspect of a much broader, integrated framework in which it is on the same level as the other EU external policies, just like all of the GPG are equally important. This integration avoids a 'compartmentalization' of external action.

Within the overall objective of promoting GPG, these external policies all operate according to their own rationale and dynamic. In doing so, they contribute to a permanent or structural policy of prevention and stabilization, and thus to the security of the EU, but the immediate objective is GPG. Thus 'securitization' or 'militarization' of external policies other than security policy in the strict sense is avoided, i.e. specific politico-military concerns and means do not determine overall policy in other fields of external action. Securitization implies the instrumentalization of the non-military fields of external action to avert military dangers and ignores the intrinsic importance of the other GPG – and thus also the inherently multidimensional nature of security itself. It would therefore be detrimental to the legitimacy of EU policies. The GPG agenda on the other hand should provide an answer to the concerns expressed by NGOs and others regarding e.g. the independence of humanitarian aid (Oxfam, 2003; Messner and Faust, 2004).

As it addresses every individual's access to GPG, comprehensive security incorporates the innovation in security thinking brought by human security, taking the individual as point of reference. In the words of Solana (2005): 'The notion of human security – which puts the security of individuals front and centre – is fast gaining ground, and rightly so'. At the same time, by way of the GPG approach, comprehensive security, although it too has a very broad scope, avoids the problems associated with the broad interpretation of human security, i.e. the definition including 'freedom from want'. This view of human security directly includes a wide range of issues in a security discourse and thus entails a greater risk of securitization. If the notion of security is thus extended too far, it becomes meaningless and no longer produces the sense of urgency and importance that the label of 'security' is supposed to generate – if everything is security, nothing is security. A comprehensive security strategy is the exact opposite: by default, issues are dealt with as problems of economic, ecological, political governance etc., in terms of improving the individual's access to the core GPG in all of these fields. Only when issues threaten the access to the core good of physical security, that is when they pose an effective danger of violence and conflict to people, States or regions, or to the international order as such, are they put in the politico-military context and can the use of politico-military instruments be considered.

Prevention

By way of promoting GPG, a comprehensive security strategy gives priority to active *prevention* of conflict and instability as opposed to a reactive and curative approach, which would be much more costly in both human and economic terms. 'An ounce of conflict prevention is worth a pound of humanitarian intervention', as Heinbecker (2000) puts it. Focusing on prevention implies dealing with more issues, at an earlier stage, before they become politico-military problems. In that sense, prevention means assuming more responsibility than an actor following a purely defensive strategy would do. It requires 'meaningful engagement', in the long term, rather than looking for quick fixes (Menon, Nicolaidis and Welsh, 2004). Effective prevention is much more than mere appeasement: it demands a proactive stance, aiming to change circumstances that induce instability and conflict. Duffield (2002, p.42) describes this 'merging of development and security':

> [Development] is no longer concerned with promoting economic growth in the hope that development will follow. Today it is better described as an attempt, preferably through cooperative partnership arrangements, to change whole societies and the behaviour and attitudes of people within them.

In this broad sense, development 'not only leads to the reduction of poverty, more political freedom, and greater affirmation of human rights, but also lays the foundation for more durable peace and security' (Culpeper, 2004). The status quo is not an option, for as it denies access to basic GPG to a large share of the world population, it is inherently instable.

Global public goods are the angle from which prevention can be tackled in the most encompassing and fundamental way. Accordingly, rather than being threat-based, a comprehensive security strategy is a positive approach that aims at achieving positive objectives, GPG, by multilateral means, in the interest not only of the EU, but of all regions and States, and in fact of all human beings. In that sense, working towards GPG can also be said to be a responsibility of the EU. This is what the Commission (2001, p.5) suggests in its Communication on Conflict Prevention:

> Given the importance of the EU on the international scene, its interests and ambitions and the considerable resources it has committed to assistance and cooperation, there is no doubt that the EU should play its part in these efforts.

It lies in their very nature that pursuing GPG serves the mutual interests of both the EU and its partners. As the US-based Council on Foreign Relations (2004, p.6) recommends, indicating at the same time that what holds true for the EU holds true for the US as well: 'Americans and Europeans cannot enjoy [their] privileges in an interconnected world without encouraging their diffusion elsewhere'. Accordingly, 'what for?' rather than 'against whom?' is the question that determines policy. A comprehensive security strategy will thus be able to avoid the classic 'security dilemma' of over-emphasizing threats, leading to unnecessary military build-up and in return provoking distrust and military measures on the part of others (Desportes, 1999). In the terms used by Buzan (1991), comprehensive security amounts to an 'international security strategy', i.e. a strategy addressing the root causes of threats by trying to change 'the systemic conditions that influence the way in which States make each other feel more (or less) secure', as opposed to a 'national security strategy', aimed at reducing one's own vulnerability by taking defensive measures.

The adoption of a comprehensive strategy is thus not a consequence of a lack of military capabilities or of unwillingness to implement military operations, as Kagan (2004) suggests – the combined armed forces of the 25 actually outnumber the armed forces of the US, and EU Member States consistently take part in military operations, including at the high end of the spectrum of violence, in a national, EU, NATO or UN framework. So if necessary, the EU is willing to use force; during the Kosovo crisis, an example which Kagan himself refers to (p.23), the European Allies advised the deployment of ground forces at an early stage, while the US preferred the bombing campaign from high altitude, which carried less risk for the Allied forces. But the EU has made an explicit and principled choice for an approach that aims to minimize the need for military action in the first place, by intervening at an earlier stage with a broader range of instruments (Menon, Nicolaidis and Welsh, 2004). In the words of Cooper (2003, p.159): 'Europe may have chosen to neglect power politics because it is militarily weak; but it is also true that it is militarily weak because it has chosen to abandon power politics'. And of course, as Kagan demonstrates, this choice is partly motivated by Europe's history: the previous decades have demonstrated how a system of intrusive reciprocal openness has been able to forge a durable peace between the very same States whose conflicts previously led to two successive world wars. The 'conscious rejection of the European past, a rejection of the evils of European

Machtpolitik', which Kagan seems almost to deplore, is only logical – and it is equally logical that the EU should now try to export its model. The European integration process thus also has an exemplary function towards other States and regions. The EU interprets the 'lessons of history' differently from the US: whereas the US National Security Strategy emphasizes the end of the Cold War as the confirmation of existing strategies and principles, Duke (2004, p.463) notes that the EU underlines the opportunity 'to offer an alternative to the internecine strife of the first half of the twentieth century'.

Global Scope

Comprehensive security by necessity demands global action: prevention must aim to safeguard and improve access to GPG *worldwide*, for at the level of regions, States and individuals anywhere, insufficient access to GPG provokes tensions and armed conflict and, in case of a major deficiency, can destabilize the international system as such. In a globalized world, the security of one is dependent on that of the other. This global scope does not contradict the specific EU role vis-à-vis its neighbourhood outlined in the Strategy. This is not a question of a hierarchy of priorities: an effective system of governance at the regional level is a component of the overall objective of global governance; because of globalization, stability of the world order as such is equally important as stability in our neighbourhood. Rather the *modus operandi* differs: at the global level the EU chooses to act through the multilateral architecture, in particular through the UN and its associated bodies; in its neighbourhood, where it has more direct leverage, it seeks to assume leadership itself. As without doubt the EU is the most powerful actor in its own neighbourhood, the promotion of peace and stability there can again be seen as a responsibility of the EU.

Traditionally, the EU's interests and, accordingly, scope of action have been seen as a hierarchy of concentric circles. In one of the first pleas for a European strategic concept, Van Staden et al. (2000) distinguish between: 'core or vital interests', i.e. 'bearing on the immediate survival of national societies'; 'essential interests', i.e. 'more remote dangers and indirect threats' such as spill-over of conflicts, refugee flows and the interruption of trade routes; and 'general or subsidiary interests', such as promoting respect for human rights and international law. In a globalized world, such distinctions are not really valid anymore for the EU. The first circle of interests, if equated to territorial defence, can still be clearly distinguished, both geographically, i.e. the territory of the EU and its Member States, and functionally, i.e. assuring the very survival. Since the end of the Cold War, a direct threat to the EU on this scale no longer exists. The ensuing circles overflow into each other: geographically, because the link between the distance of an event and its potential impact on the EU, though often still present, no longer is automatic; and functionally, because in view of the inextricable links between all GPG, in the long-term 'immaterial' issues, such as lack of respect for human rights and the absence of the rule of law, can lead to instabilities and crises that are equally threatening to the EU as more immediate economic or politico-military concerns.

Multilateralism

In order to improve access to GPG, a comprehensive security strategy operates through dialogue, cooperation, partnership and institutionalized, rule-based *multilateralism*. That is exactly what global governance is about: not a world government, but an intricate web of States, regimes, treaties and organizations, i.e. multi-level governance, implicating all levels of authority in a coordinated effort to improve people's access to GPG. The approach that Slaughter (2004, p.18) terms 'global security', i.e. 'an effort at every level – local, national, regional, and global – to protect individuals from violence', applies to all GPG. Although in the spirit of human security the individual is taken as point of reference, the State indeed remains a primary partner, for no effective arrangements can be made with weak and failed States. Well-functioning States are a prerequisite for multilateral institutions to be able to work; accordingly, addressing weak and failing States is one of their responsibilities. Since no power aims for colonization anymore, failed States rapidly become *terra nullius*, a zone of chaos which nobody effectively controls, but which because of globalization will impact on the region and the world (Cooper, 2003). Global governance must further be democratic, i.e. provide for an equitable representation of all States, and participative, i.e. allow for the effective participation of non-State actors (Coolsaet and Arnould, 2004). Like the global scope, the cooperative or multilateral nature of a comprehensive security strategy is an inescapable consequence of globalization. Furthermore, unilateral policies often serve to antagonize potential partners and are harmful for legitimacy. So third States and organizations are regarded as partners for cooperation rather than as mere subjects of EU policies; the aim is to influence rather than to coerce, to use the carrot rather than the stick. The foremost threat which the EU can make is *not* to intervene, i.e. not to offer the benefits of partnership.

But partnership and cooperation cannot be unconditional: benefits granted are linked to progress made in predefined fields, related to the core GPG. In that sense, the EU can be seen as a 'transformative power', which seeks to induce others to reform (Leonard, 2005). The choice for multilateralism thus does not exclude that EU policies can be intrusive, but always on the basis of mutual agreement and in the interest of all parties concerned. Again, comprehensive security is shown to require a proactive stance. A critical dialogue is maintained with partners that do not respect their commitments; if they persist, they will pay the price in their relations with the EU. Coercion, including, as an ultimate instrument, the use of force, is regarded as a last resort in order to prevent or halt violence and conflict. It is not out of the question, but will only be used if all other options have been exhausted and, of course, within the bounds of international law, i.e. with a mandate from the UN Security Council.

There will be cases where the use of force is inevitable, for not all actors that the EU will be confronted with will be amenable to preventive initiatives. This can be expected to happen in what Cooper (2003) in his three-tier description of the world order terms 'the pre-modern world', where weak or failed States do not have the monopoly on the use of force and regimes and/or other actors revert to violence to establish themselves. Very often the continuation of conflict in such States is in the interest of the warring parties, which often include outside actors – they will not always be very responsive to, for example, mediation efforts. But in the 'modern world', 'classical' States too can revert to the use of force when considerations of power and *raison d'état* outweigh respect for international law – and for preventive efforts by third parties. Modern and pre-modern actors' views of the world, and accordingly, policies, can differ distinctively from those of the 'post-modern world' of powers which no longer want to 'fight or conquer', exemplified by the EU. Nye (2002) similarly distinguishes between poor and weak pre-industrial, modernizing and industrial, and post-industrial States. In responding to crises, coercive measures on the part of the multilateral system will sometimes be the only alternative to inaction. An effective military capacity therefore is an indispensable tool in the EU's kit.

For coercive action to be successful a legal mandate from the Security Council is insufficient – legitimacy is a necessary prerequisite. The legitimacy of the EU as an actor that occasionally resorts to the use of force will be strengthened by pursuing a permanent and consistent policy aimed at promoting GPG through multilateral channels. As Nye (2002, p.143) advises the US:

> We gain doubly from such a strategy: from the public goods themselves, and from the way they legitimize our power in the eyes of others.

Partnership can be built on the common aspiration to strengthen GPG, in the mutual interest of all concerned – that is precisely the nature of GPG. In that sense, comprehensive and cooperative security are inextricably linked: the objectives of a comprehensive security strategy can be realized only through cooperation, and cooperation and partnership cannot rely on the politico-military dimension alone, but require a broad base. Any use of force must always be put in the wider context of the prospect of – renewed – partnership and cooperation. This also has implications for the way in which force is used and operations are implemented. In parts of the world where 'the law of the jungle reigns', as Cooper puts it, the EU cannot simply burst in and act along those same laws – neither comprehensive security nor legitimacy can be achieved at gunpoint. The EU's conception of the use of force as an instrument of last resort requires a distinctive doctrine for the implementation of military operations, as was concluded by a Study Group on Europe's Security Capabilities that was established at the initiative of High Representative Solana (Kaldor et al., 2004). Such a doctrine would emphasize the protection of individuals, minimal use of force and 'winning hearts and minds'. The aim must always be to bring the States or regions concerned back within the area of partnership and cooperation.

Paradoxically perhaps, for coercive action to be perceived as legitimate, the EU must intervene sufficiently often. If the EU is perceived to apply too much selectivity in deciding when and where to intervene, and especially if the criteria for intervention are perceived to be based on – economic – self-interest only, this will detract from the EU's legitimacy, even in those cases where intervention is motivated by real humanitarian concerns. Contrasting the world's swift reaction to '9/11' with the hopelessly inadequate reaction to the genocide in Rwanda in 1994, the UN High-Level Panel on Threats, Challenges and Change (2004, p.23) came to this conclusion:

> The credibility of any system of collective security also depends on how well it promotes security for all its members, without regard to the nature of would-be beneficiaries, their location, resources or relationship to great Powers.

Of course, the EU will never be able to intervene in every single crisis; for the time being, effective intervention, militarily or otherwise, in every crisis, by the UN themselves is, regrettably, a utopian perspective. But the EU cannot be seen to ignore any major humanitarian crisis or other threat to international peace and security. This is not to say that the EU should necessarily intervene militarily itself every time the Security Council were so to decide; but the EU should make use of its full range of instruments to bring pressure to bear on those who are at the origin of a crisis, and to put a crisis on the agenda of the Security Council in the first place. The primary objective however remains to avoid the need for coercive action at all, through a structural policy of prevention and stabilization. Indeed, the history of recent military interventions – Iraq, Afghanistan, even Kosovo – teaches modesty: no matter how successful we are in attaining the military objectives of an intervention, there is no guarantee that the political objectives of peace-building will be achieved. Again, Cooper (2003, p.73) can be quoted:

> Nation-building is a long and difficult task: it is by no means certain that any of the recent attempts are going to be successful. Great caution is required for anyone contemplating intervention in the pre-modern chaos. A good rule would be to intervene early before the trouble really begins. But this is not easy either. No state will readily accept that radical interference from outside is needed to prevent its collapse; nor will outsiders want to take on the risks and costs of intervention until it is proved to them that there is no other solution (by which time it is usually too late).

Maintaining the option of having recourse to force as an ultimate instrument need not be contradictory to the picture of the EU as a 'civilian power', contrary to what Smith (2000) claims: the question is *when*, under what circumstances and under which mandate, and not *if* force can be used. This is in line with Maull's (1990) definition of civilian power as including military power 'as a residual instrument'. Without the willingness to apply pressure, sanctions and, if need be, force, EU external action will not acquire the credibility it needs to be effective. The possession of 'hard power' is an 'enabler' for the EU's 'soft power'. This leads Stavridis (2001) to the assertion that 'thanks to the militarising of the Union, the latter might at long last be able to act as a real civilian power in the world'. In that regard, the concepts 'civilian superpower' and 'soft power plus' (Haine, 2004a) have been used. Keukeleire (2002) too concludes that what he terms 'structural foreign policy' can be effective only 'if it goes hand in hand with an effective traditional foreign policy which can be supported by military instruments', or in Haseler's words (2004) if the EU resists the 'great civilian temptation' of relying only on civilian instruments. The deciding factor is that since it has acquired a military capacity, the EU still presents itself, not as a 'traditional' power, playing 'power politics', but as 'a power which is unique because it will be able to use military means as an integrated part of a much broader range of political, economic and diplomatic means' (Larsen, 2002). Or as Cooper (2003, p.85) puts it:

> Power is vital for the defence of peace, but it is a means rather than an end in itself. [...] In pre-modern times war was a way of life; in the modern era it was an instrument of policy; but in the post-modern world war has become something to be avoided if at all possible.

One can conclude, as Gnesotto (2004) does, that 'the great debate of the 1980s over Europe as a civil power or a military power definitely seems to be a thing of the past [...] what the Union intends to become is a *sui generis* power'. Comprehensive security therefore is a term better suited to the EU than civilian power, as it emphasizes the integration of all fields of external action, and avoids the paralysing debate on the validity of the claim to 'civilian power-status' when possessing a military dimension, a debate which is inherent to civilian power literature.[6]

A Power

But civilian or not, a power the EU must be, for in the end, the success of any security strategy depends on *the will to take action*. The EU must be prepared to invest the necessary financial means in effective partnership and cooperation and in developing its own policy instruments, and must also be prepared and able to implement those instruments, including, if need be, the coercive use of military means. In other words, this need for a will to act is tantamount to the need for the EU to behave as a *global power*. In the words of the Laeken Declaration adopted by the European Council in December 2001:

> a power resolutely doing battle against all violence, all terror and all fanaticism [...] a power wanting to change the course of world affairs in such a way as to benefit not just the rich countries but also the poorest. A power seeking to set globalisation within a moral framework, in other words to anchor it in solidarity and sustainable development.

For the EU to become a power, it must have the will and the capacity to weigh on the course of international events and influence the other players on the international stage. This it can only achieve through further progressive integration. Loss of national sovereignty through integration brings increased sovereignty for the EU as a combined international actor (Lübkemeier, 2003). Kagan's assertion (2004, p.1) that 'Europe is turning away from power' and is becoming introvert is only valid if power is solely understood, as Kagan seems to do, as hard or military

---

[6] This division is already apparent in the earliest authors' writings. Whereas the 'founder', Duchêne (1972), used the term 'civilian power' to refer to the EEC, which did not possess a military capacity at all, Maull (1990) applied the concept to Germany and Japan, which do have armed forces.

power. This indeed the EU does not see as a primary instrument of external action – though it does not exclude its use either. The validity of a one-dimensional definition of power is however contradicted by Kagan himself, when he asserts (p.37) the existence of

> a powerful European interest in building a world where military strength and hard power matter less than economic and soft power, an international order where international law and international institutions matter more than the power of individual nations, where unilateral action by powerful nations is forbidden, where all nations regardless of their strength have equal rights and are equally protected by commonly agreed-upon international rules of behaviour.

In these other fields, the existence of which Kagan is forced to recognize, the EU truly is a power, with a global project – a project which is far more attractive than the 'anarchic Hobbesian world' in which military powers thrive which Kagan seems to prefer.

Before the Maastricht Treaty, the question whether Europe should be a power was essentially hypothetical, for the EEC lacked the instruments anyway to play a role in foreign and security policy (Cohen-Tanugi, 2003, p.73). But ever since the EU acquired a foreign and security dimension, the question has been on the table, and has gained in importance because of the evolution of the world, after the end of the Cold War, to a multipolar system. Although the notion of multipolarity is not expressly mentioned, it is certainly underlying the Laeken Declaration, and was in effect often referred to at the time by the Belgian Presidency without provoking any particular reaction (de Schoutheete, 2004, p.56). Only in the wake of the transatlantic divide over Iraq did the notion become controversial, especially in the eyes of Washington. But the fact that not only the EU and the US, but Russia, China and others hold widely differing views – and act accordingly – on how to tackle the challenges of the globalized world, differences which were highlighted in the wake of '9/11' and the US' reaction to it, shows that *de facto* the world is multipolar. The US definitely is the sole remaining superpower in the politico-military dimension of the world order, and it is an explicit objective of its National Security Strategy to dissuade others from surpassing or equalling its military capabilities. But in the economic dimension actors like the EU, China, Japan and the WTO have considerable, and often even more power. In the transnational dimension of the world order too, which concerns post-territorial issues and norms and values, other States and international organizations, as well as NGOs, multinational corporations and the media are equally powerful actors (Nye, 2002). So even though without doubt it is the greatest military power by far, the US on its own cannot deal with all of the world's challenges in these three dimensions:

> The paradox of the present situation is that the United States is an extreme superpower in relation to other powers, but certainly not in relation to the challenges it is confronted with in large areas of the world (Bildt, 2004, p.54).

Nor would the world accept such a US role. As the High-Level Panel states (2004, p.54):

> Since the end of the Cold War, however, the yearning for an international system governed by the rule of law has grown. There is little evident international acceptance of the idea of security being best preserved by a balance of power, or by any single – even benignly motivated – superpower.

For their views and interests to be taken into account, and for effective multilateralism to be possible, the EU and its Member States must consciously and *collectively* muster the will to form one of the poles of this multipolar world. But rather than seeking classic 'strategic multipolarity', based on material power only, the EU can strive to achieve 'normative multipolarity', which takes into account the three dimensions of international relations (Acharya, 2004), and pursue its own distinctive policy: comprehensive security.

A Strategy with Potential

A strategy along the lines suggested above is comprehensive or encompassing in terms of:

- policy objectives, instruments and means: policy fields are integrated under the common agenda of promoting GPG; rather than working only on specific aspects in an ad hoc way, the comprehensive security approach offers a fundamental concept underlying, and thus integrating all fields of EU external action;[7]
- the subjects of policy, which include individuals: on the one hand the security of EU citizens at home and abroad is included in the interests that have to be secured; on the other hand the access of individuals worldwide to GPG is the long-term objective of EU external action – hence a clear link with 'human security', but without ignoring the importance of States and international organizations;
- its worldwide scope, which does not exclude that the EU has a specific responsibility with regard to its neighbourhood;
- its inclusion of third States and organizations in policy-making, through multilateral cooperation and partnership, instead of considering them to be just subjects of EU policy.

As comprehensive security emphasizes the importance of *not* dealing with issues as politico-military problems unless they pose an effective threat to physical security, in order to avoid securitization, and as the comprehensive approach

---

[7] The key elements of comprehensive security are – sometimes in different forms – also included in Ehrhart's (2002) 'cooperative security provider model', but the integrating element is a vital distinction.

focuses on a much broader agenda than military security, 'European Security Strategy' is perhaps not the best title for the document – the Strategy is really much more than that. If it is understood and implemented as proposed above, it will be a *comprehensive strategy for EU external action*, global in scope, and integrating all dimensions of external action.

Comprehensive security in effect translates the principles on which the EU itself is founded – liberty, democracy, respect for human rights and fundamental freedoms, and the rule of law – into the principles underlying EU external action and tries to export these principles to other States. The EU thus combines not only soft/civilian and hard/military power, but also normative power, i.e. the 'ability to shape conceptions of "normal" in international relations' (Manners, 2002). The distinctiveness of this approach lies not in its comprehensive nature as such – every actor in international relations has to solve the problem of how to coordinate the different dimensions of external action. The distinguishing feature is the adoption of GPG as overall integrative agenda as the way of solving the coordination problem. As Everts (2004) notes, the fact that '[...] the EU now explicitly recognizes that it should use its policies on trade, aid and migration in a politically targeted and conditional way' should enable it to fully exploit the potential of its 'soft power'. Ultimately, the GPG approach amounts to exporting what is perhaps Europe's most distinguishing characteristic: the welfare State, the combination of a free market and a strong State, which ensures that the market serves the people rather than the other way around.

The actual European Security Strategy is not equally explicit or precise on all aspects of the comprehensive concept as proposed above. But the general approach chosen by the Strategy is certainly conforming to it:

- 'effective multilateralism' as a global objective and with regard to the EU's neighbourhood in particular, which amounts to global governance in order to provide access to the core GPG;
- putting to use all instruments available to the EU in an integrated way;
- in cooperation with other States, regions and international organizations;
- with the emphasis on prevention of the 'key threats' that are identified;
- and with the ultimate option of having recourse to force if necessary.

The Strategy therefore certainly has the potential to serve as an integrating conceptual framework for EU external action, to be an effective comprehensive strategy for external action.

Chapter 3

A Secure Neighbourhood

The first level at which the Strategy as a framework for a comprehensive approach to EU external action can be put into practice is that of the EU's neighbourhood. 'Building security in our neighbourhood' has in fact been an objective actively pursued by the EU, since the fall of the Berlin Wall as far as the continent of Europe is concerned, and since at least the creation of the Euro-Mediterranean Partnership (EMP) as regards its Southern periphery. It is also the focus of one of the EU's major new projects: the European Neighbourhood Policy (ENP). Focussing on the Mediterranean as an illustrative case-study, this chapter will assess the potential of the ENP as a framework for the implementation of the comprehensive approach, as well as the challenges to be addressed for the ENP to be successful.

The Neighbourhood Policy

'Even in an era of globalization, geography is still important', the Strategy rightly points out. It is indeed the case that, while the security issues arising in the vicinity of the EU are global phenomena that are not specific to this region, their potential effects on the EU can still be greater because of geographic proximity. The EU and its neighbourhood, and certainly its neighbours on the European continent, can be considered a 'security complex' as defined by Buzan (1991): 'a group of States whose primary security concerns link together sufficiently closely that their national securities cannot realistically be considered apart from one another'. It is but logical therefore that in this area the EU assumes responsibility and directly takes the lead in promoting peace and security, for a stable neighbourhood is a necessity for Europe's own security. The actual development of the CFSP and ESDP can be seen in the light of Europe's failure to fulfil exactly this ambition, notably on the Balkans in the early 1990s and, more recently, in Kosovo in 1999. In that sense, the inherent security dimension of the ENP also answers a long-standing call by the US for more burden-sharing, notably with regard to what Washington rightly sees as Europe's backyard: the Balkans. Promoting stability in Europe's neighbourhood can even be seen as a responsibility or a duty, since the EU is the only local actor with the means to do so. Through its force of attraction, the EU has succeeded in stabilizing the European continent; now it has to replicate that success in a wider neighbourhood.

The Strategy offers an ambitious definition of how far this neighbourhood reaches:

- The Balkans: when the conflict in former Yugoslavia first erupted, the EEC proved ill-equipped to deal with such a crisis, even though the Twelve agreed that this should have been 'the hour of Europe'. US intervention was thus a necessity. Since then however the EU has gradually taken over responsibility for the – still far from completed – consolidation of peace in the region. This does not only include the civilian dimension of nation-building, but the peacekeeping role as well: on 2 December 2004 the EU took over the operation in Bosnia-Herzegovina from NATO, under the name of Operation Althea. Even before, the majority of peacekeepers on the Balkans, including in Kosovo, were troops from EU Member States: over 6000 in SFOR (over 50 per cent) and over 16 000 in KFOR (about 70 per cent). The EU has also concluded a military operation in the Former Yugoslav Republic of Macedonia and is running police operations in both Macedonia and Bosnia-Herzegovina. All these initiatives fit into the comprehensive Stabilization and Association Process, while the prospect of eventual EU membership acts as a powerful catalyst. In the meantime, Operation Althea is an important test for the EU's self-professed ability, including in the Strategy, to apply civil and military instruments in an integrated way (Ojanen, 2005).
- 'Our neighbours to the East': here the Strategy refers to Ukraine, Moldova and Belarus, the three remaining countries between the EU and Russia after the accession of Rumania and Bulgaria in 2007. That the explicit reference to these three in the first draft was omitted in the final version of the Strategy can be perhaps be seen as an indication of the fact that to the East the enlarged EU quickly reaches the borders of Russia's 'neighbourhood', and the limits of EU leverage. As the failed attempt of the 2003 Dutch OSCE Presidency to resolve the dispute over the Transnistrian region of Moldova demonstrates, little can be achieved here without the cooperation of Russia – and even less if Moscow actively counteracts EU policy. But the acceptance of the need for a certain degree of *Realpolitik* does not mean that the strategic partnership with Russia that the Strategy calls for cannot include a critical dialogue, including on the most sensitive subjects, such as respect for human rights and fundamental freedoms and the war in Chechnya.
- The Southern Caucasus: that this region, in which since July 2003 the EU is represented by a special envoy, is included in the ENP, goes to show that in effect the EU is not planning to abdicate in favour of a Russian sphere of influence. But the Strategy does not offer any indication of the direction or scope of EU policy towards Georgia, Armenia and Azerbeijan, which however does not stop Georgian President Mikheil Saakashvili from unambiguously stating his European aspirations. Georgia is actively supported by the EU, *inter alia* by the launching, on 16 July 2004, of a rule of law mission in the framework of ESDP, Operation Themis, comprising some ten international civilian experts, and aiming to support the Georgian authorities in addressing urgent challenges in the criminal justice system.
- The Mediterranean: here since 1995 the EU is committed to the comprehensive EMP, now between the 25 and 10 Mediterranean partners:

Algeria, Egypt, Israel, Jordan, Lebanon, Morocco, Syria, Tunisia, Turkey and the Palestinian Authority; Libya has been invited to join on the condition of accepting the *acquis* of the partnership. The EU Strategic Partnership with the Mediterranean and the Middle East, adopted by the June 2004 European Council, widens the scope of Europe's ambitions to the 'Wider Middle East': the members of the Gulf Cooperation Council (GCC), i.e. Bahrain, Kuwait, Oman, Qatar, Saudi Arabia and the United Arab Emirates, plus Yemen, Iran and Iraq. The Strategy does not mention Turkey separately, although this would certainly have pleased Ankara, and would perhaps have better reflected its status as the only remaining Mediterranean candidate for accession after Cyprus and Malta joined the EU; but it is of course one of the Mediterranean partners and thus included in the framework of the EMP.

• Perhaps under the heading of 'building security in our neighbourhood', Sub-Saharan Africa could have been mentioned as well. Not to include it in the Neighbourhood Policy, but as an area where it is the EU's duty, *inter alia* because of historic ties, to play a special role. A more systematic, comprehensive partnership with Sub-Saharan Africa could be envisaged.

The neighbourhood can be seen as the area in which the EU deems it has a specific responsibility for peace and security, and therefore aspires to a directly leading role, as opposed to its general contribution to global stability through the UN as outlined under the objective of 'effective multilateralism'. The Strategy puts down the general principle of building comprehensive and cooperative relations in the political, economic, cultural and security fields with the States concerned, a 'ring of friends', in order to increase security, i.e. an approach that emphasizes a structural, long-term policy of stabilization and prevention. It does not go into detail as to the instruments that the EU can apply to make these relations work, but of course several instruments already exist or are being envisaged.

The potentially most effective instrument is the comprehensive Neighbourhood Policy first proposed by the Commission under the heading of 'Wider Europe'. Somewhat surprisingly, the ENP is not explicitly mentioned in the Strategy, but the title of the second strategic objective has been changed from 'extending the zone of security around Europe' to 'building security in our neighbourhood'. The potential of the ENP, and the challenges that it poses, can be illustrated by the case of the Mediterranean and the 'Wider Middle East' (Biscop, 2004a).

The Mediterranean

The comprehensive approach put forward as a general strategy for EU external action was already underlying the EMP, or Barcelona Process, at the partnership's founding conference in 1995. This is evident from the composition of its three baskets, which cover the whole range of relations between the EU and its Southern neighbours: a political and security partnership, an economic and financial partnership and a partnership in social, cultural and human affairs. The EMP added a politico-military dimension to the traditionally economic focus of Europe's Mediterranean policies, but firmly embedded it in a broad framework of relations. In this framework, there is a strong emphasis on dialogue and co-ownership. The Strategy has thus confirmed the basic orientation of the EMP.

The Mixed Record of the EMP

The ongoing armed conflict between Israelis and Palestinians, which has been clouding the Mediterranean and the 'Wider Middle East' for decades, is of course foremost among the region's security concerns. Although it does not pose a direct security threat to the EU, the conflict has important negative consequences for EU interests: it is an important cause of the stagnation of cooperation in the EMP, in all fields; it serves to radicalize public opinion; and thus creates a breeding ground for extremism. With regard to the Mediterranean, the analysis of the underlying causes of instability, disputes and conflict in terms of access to GPG is particularly revealing. A number of authoritarian regimes lacking legitimacy have to rely on security forces, and the armed forces, to control the opposition and muster popular support. The armed forces are thus primarily an instrument of domestic politics; States have built large military apparatus, absorbing large shares of national revenue and often playing a determining role in politics and society. The lack of legitimacy is a consequence of the inability to provide for the basic public goods to which every human being is entitled and is exacerbated by the repression of political opposition, which from the perspective of the regimes and associated elites is inevitable, for because of their poor performance democratization would undoubtedly lead to their removal from power and thus the loss of the wealth which they acquire by running the State. The result has been a radicalization of the opposition, leading mostly to the growth of Islamist movements, including extreme factions that support the use of violence. The strength of Islamism is closely linked to a dense network of mosques and associated organizations, which often provide certain social services that the State is unable or unwilling to organize. Several regimes haves thus created their own extremists, which primarily have a domestic agenda: overthrowing the current regime.

In the medium to long term, the huge – and widening – gap between haves and have-nots in terms of access to the basic public goods should be considered the primary security concern in the region. Attempting to maintain the status quo is thus not an option, even though at first glance the present situation might appear quite stable, for it contains the root causes of instability.

In order to divert attention away from domestic problems, regimes often revert to fierce nationalist rhetoric, often of an anti-Israeli nature, a theme which strikes a chord with public opinion. At the same time however regimes thus confirm the views of Islamist factions, to whom this theme comes naturally, which also makes it easier for the latter to spread the more general anti-American or anti-Western views that often complement their opposition to the domestic regimes. A number of regimes have thus engaged in a game that they cannot win: going along with anti-Israeli and anti-American/anti-Western views might temporarily soothe public opinion, but in the end serves only to reinforce the legitimacy of the Islamists, as these regimes can never live up to their rhetoric, being as they are dependent on American and European economic – and often military – support. The invasion of Iraq has certainly reinforced the appeal of extremist Islamist factions.

A side-effect of nationalist foreign policies and competition for scarce resources is the very low level of regional integration among the Southern Mediterranean States. Existing regional organizations, such as the League of Arab States, have very limited impact or have been paralyzed by internal differences, such as the Arab Maghreb Union. In the framework of the EMP, the Southern partners therefore do not act as a group and have shown very little enthusiasm for multilateral programmes and activities. This lack of political integration reflects the limited nature of economic relations between the Southern States: intra-Southern trade accounts for just 10% of their trade, while more than half of their trade is with the EU.

From Affirmation to Implementation

The EMP has not fundamentally altered this situation. Simply reaffirming the 'spirit of Barcelona' in the Strategy is therefore insufficient; the partnership is in need of revitalization. Indeed, the Strategy itself states that the Mediterranean:

> generally continues to undergo serious problems of economic stagnation, social unrest and unresolved conflicts. The European Union's interests require a continued engagement with Mediterranean partners, through more effective economic, security and cultural cooperation in the framework of the Barcelona Process.

The ENP offers an opportunity to achieve this objective. The aim of the Neighbourhood Policy is to achieve 'an area of shared prosperity and values' by creating close partnerships with the EU's neighbouring States, bringing them as close to the EU as possible without being a member, which should lead to in-depth economic integration, close political and cultural relations and a joint responsibility for conflict prevention. The aim of the ENP can also be seen as preventing dilution of the EU by putting a brake on enlargement – a neighbour by definition lives in the house next door, as a diplomat worded it. To that end, the EU is to offer very concrete 'benefits', basically a stake in the EU's internal market, to be accompanied by further integration and liberalization to promote the free movement of persons, goods, services and capital – 'the four freedoms'. The Commission proposes *inter alia* the following incentives: extension of the internal market and regulatory structures; preferential trade relations and market opening; perspectives for lawful migration and movement of persons; integration into transport, energy and telecommunications networks and the European research area; new instruments for investment promotion and protection; and support for integration into the global trading system. Through a process of 'positive conditionality', these benefits will be linked to political and economic reform. The Neighbourhood Policy thus has a wide stabilizing and preventive scope. As the Commission (2004) proposes:

The privileged relationship with neighbours will build on mutual commitment to common values principally within the fields of the rule of law, good governance, the respect for human rights, including minority rights, the promotion of good neighbourly relations, and the principles of market economy and sustainable development. Commitments will also be sought to certain essential aspects of the EU's external action, including, in particular, the fight against terrorism and the proliferation of weapons of mass destruction, as well as abidance by international law and efforts to achieve conflict resolution.

The Neighbourhood Policy's ultimate objectives could thus be interpreted as (Coolsaet and Biscop, 2004):

- preventing conflicts in the EU's neighbourhood and acts of aggression against the EU itself;
- settling ongoing disputes and conflicts;
- establishing close economic and political partnerships based on shared values, prosperity and security;
- controlling migration and all forms of illegal trafficking into the EU;
- protecting the security of EU citizens living abroad.

The Neighbourhood Policy does not aim to replace existing frameworks for relations, such as the EMP; rather it wants to supplement and build on them. The idea is to strike a balance between, on the one hand, bilateral Action Plans, so that benefits and benchmarks for progress can be tailored to specific needs and circumstances, in agreement with the individual partner countries, and, on the other hand, multilateral partnerships such as the Barcelona Process, in order to deal with regional issues and to promote regional integration between partners. The latter is the key to mending the institutional unbalance within the EMP, which sees a closely integrated EU of now 25 Member States facing 10 partner States that are only loosely involved in any kind of regional consultation. The Action Plans, to cover the next three to five years, are to address five key areas: political dialogue and reform; trade and measures preparing partners for gradually obtaining a stake in the EU's internal market; justice and home affairs; energy, transport, information society, environment and research and innovation; and social policy and people-to-people contacts (European Commission, 2004).

Among the first batch of Action Plans approved by the EU in December 2004, following exploratory talks with the countries concerned, were those for Israel, the Palestinian Authority, Jordan, Morocco and Tunisia (next to those for Ukraine and Moldova). True to the 'tailor-made principle', these Action Plans reflect the differences in the state of development and the willingness to reform and deepen relations with the EU in the States concerned. In the field of democratization, for example, objectives are decidedly more ambitious, and more concrete, in the Action Plans for Jordan and the Palestinian Authority than in those for Morocco and Tunisia. The Action Plans also have to be approved by the joint bilateral bodies established under the existing bilateral Euro-Mediterranean Association Agreements, which will also be responsible for advancing and monitoring their implementation. The Commission will draw up periodic reports on progress. The next step, if Action Plan priorities are met, could be the conclusion of European Neighbourhood Agreements to replace the current Association Agreements. The Action Plans are not very operational however: they remain very vague on the question of which kinds of reform will be rewarded by which specific additional aid. The degree to which they effectively are 'tailor-made' should not be overstated either: the Action Plans do not allow to distinguish between the main obstacles to reform in the different States concerned (Youngs, 2005, p.6).

Actually, most of the measures that are now being proposed in the framework of Wider Europe are already among the established objectives of the EMP. This holds true for both substance and progress. For example, in the 1995 Barcelona Declaration partners agreed to create 'an area of shared prosperity', to be based on 'the progressive establishment of a free trade area', economic cooperation and 'a substantial increase in the EU's financial assistance to its partners'. The EMP already comprises a mix of multilateral and regional activities on the one hand and Association Agreements and associated programmes that are negotiated bilaterally with the partners on the other hand. The emphasis in the ENP on the bilateral Action Plans should not lead to a dilution of the regional, multilateral dimension (Johansson-Nogués, 2004, p.244). There has certainly never been a lack of ideas to advance the EMP – it is their implementation that has been rather more problematic. The fact that reform has not advanced much further in the Arab States in the EMP than in those outside it, for example, in the Gulf, highlights the Partnership's limitations (Youngs, 2005, p.10).

There is a lack of 'cross-pillar' functioning in the EMP; each basket is run in a more or less autonomous way, without much coordination with the others. The Association Agreements ought to include provisions on political dialogue, human rights, rule of law etc., but in the actual agreements these remain limited to very general stipulations, and even those have never been invoked. The regulations on the MEDA Programme, the financial instrument of EU Mediterranean policy, link economic support to the promotion of human rights, fundamental freedoms and good-neighbourly relations, but here too in actual practice conditionality has been very limited if not non-existent (Lannon, Inglis and Haenebalcke, 2001; Schmid, 2003). The EU's uncritical response to the Tunisian President Bin Ali's 96 per cent election victory in October 2004 can serve as an example (Youngs, 2005, p.3). Not unimportantly, regimes have adopted the discourse of democracy, but tangible results are very limited. As a result, the comprehensive approach, which in theory links all the dimensions of Euro-Mediterranean relations together, has been insufficiently translated into practice. The impression created is that the EU prefers stability over democratization and reform.

On the other hand, for positive conditionality to be effective, a real 'carrot' should be offered by the EU. Currently, it seems as if the Mediterranean partners are suffering all the hardships entailed by the economic reforms necessitated by the projected free trade area, but without, in return, gaining much in terms of effective benefits, or even the near-term prospect of benefits. Undoubtedly, the most sensitive area in this regard is the EU's agricultural policy, the protectionist character of which produces major negative effects for its Southern trade partners –

not to mention for the EU budget. But in the textile sector as well, limits have been imposed; real free trade applies only to oil, gas and industrial products. The level of foreign direct investment from the EU has not significantly increased. It has been argued that the result of these half-hearted policies has actually been a worsening of socio-economic conditions in the partner countries (Tanner, 2004). For this situation to be amended, a substantial effort would be needed on the part of the EU. Today, the predominant feeling in the South seems to be one of resentment, against an EU that imposes difficult reforms but is perceived as not living up to its side of the bargain. It should not be forgotten though that bad management by local authorities, including excessive defence expenditure, and obstacles posed by traditional structures have equally contributed to the worsening of the economic situation, as was forcibly demonstrated by the Arab Human Development Reports. To the extent that local elites manage to control how the resources made available by the EU are applied, these can be made to reinforce the political and economic status quo rather than induce reform (Volpi, 2004, p.149).

With regard to the Mediterranean, the real added value of the Neighbourhood Policy thus is not in the substance of the measures, nor in the working methods proposed. Care should rather be taken to preserve the *acquis* of the EMP, so as not to lose its rich and varied approach to the many dimensions of Euro-Mediterranean relations (Ortega, 2003). What the Neighbourhood Policy does offer is an opportunity to re-launch the EMP, the possibility to have a fresh start.

To fully grasp that opportunity, the EU will have to address a number of major remaining challenges. The Member States will first of all have to muster the necessary political will to invest sufficient means and offer the neighbouring States *real benefits* (Wallace, 2003). Even if membership is not on offer for the remaining Mediterranean partners – except Turkey – other, 'silver' carrots can be devised (Missiroli, 2004). Opening up to agricultural exports for one, or subsidizing major infrastructure projects. Free movement of persons can also be a powerful incentive (Youngs, 2005, p.5). These benefits, or 'new partnership perspectives' as they are called in the Action Plans, ought to be formulated in a sufficiently concrete way in order to be credible. In the longer term, perhaps a 'Marshall Plan' for the Mediterranean could be the next grand project of the EU after enlargement, a major scheme as the only way to substantially and durably improve socio-economic conditions on the Southern shore (Ortega, 2003).

Secondly, allocation of these real benefits should truly be *conditional* on the implementation of the political reforms outlined in the Action Plans if progress is to be achieved within the – per definition non-coercive – partnership approach that characterizes the EU's Mediterranean policy. According to Youngs (2004a), 'The European approach might be likened to a desired "third way" between regime change and undimmed support for autocrats; one focussed on gradual, step-by-step political reform' – but this cannot work without effective conditionality. This requires the definition of clear benchmarks, in order to measure progress, as part of a phased and dynamic process of reform and reward, including a timetable. In a 2003 Communication on human rights and democratization in the Mediterranean, the Commission (2003b) already recommended that national action plans for human rights should include 'a list of specific action points accompanied by measurable benchmarks of performance with clear timelines'. The ENP Action Plans should thus be supplemented by a true roadmap for reform. In the political field, respect for basic human rights and the rule of law must be the minimum condition to be fulfilled, a step which need not directly affect the current regimes' power base, before moving on to gradual but effective democratization. If it does not become more operational, EU policy will not be able to escape the situation described by Youngs (2004a):

> European democracy policy resembles a man trying to learn to swim without letting go of the riverbank: keen to reach the deep, rewarding waters of political transformation but reluctant to let go of the supportive engagement built up with Middle Eastern regimes.

Thirdly, the EU must also address the question of whom it will cooperate with: not only with the regimes in place, but also with reformist actors in civil society? But will the EU cooperate with moderate Islamists? Islamist actors are the backbone of civil society (Volpi, 2004; Fuller, 2004) and can thus hardly be ignored – if in Europe Christian-democracy is an acceptable political current, then certainly 'Muslim-democracy' should be equally acceptable? This requires careful mapping of the political and civil society landscape in all States concerned. The EU must also avoid that its reformist partners have to face negative consequences because of their collaboration, such as imprisonment or other forms of harassment by the regimes in power. An inclusive policy, that is a policy that allows the input of local actors to be taken fully into account, seems to have the largest chance of success. In that regard the EU can build on the Commission's (2003b) idea of organizing regular workshops with civil society at the national level, in order 'to contribute to overall EU knowledge of local conditions'.

Perhaps the basic question is: how far does the EU aim to go? What is the ENP's ultimate objective? If, eventually, full democratization is the aim, are the partnership approach and EU instruments, that is the financial-economic 'carrot', really sufficient to achieve that? For as Youngs (2005, p.5) notes, even the States that are most desirous of economic integration, such as Tunisia, 'show few signs of willing to trade this against improvements in human rights'. And is the EU willing to cope with the potential instability which this implies, and with the Islamist victories that elections might bring? Or will the EU be satisfied with a certain minimum level of respect for human rights, with a *modus vivendi* that is reconcilable with, on the one hand, European consciences and the rhetoric of democratization and, on the other hand, the aims of the current regimes? But is that really an option – would it not be contradictory to the fundamental philosophy of the comprehensive approach to consciously ignore part of the gap in access to the basic GPGs that lies at the root of instability and frustration in the region? A 'traditional' security policy based on containment of threats, which often led to support for authoritarian but seemingly stable regimes, is no longer possible in our globalized world (Kaldor, 2004).

Without a substantial effort the Neighbourhood Policy will suffer the same fate as the 'old' EMP: well-intentioned principles, but very limited implementation. Promises only of the proverbial carrot and mere declarations about democracy will be insufficient, for they have been made too often already. Implementing the Neighbourhood Policy should be nothing less than a top priority. Currently, the EMP constitutes what Attinà (2004) terms a 'regional security partnership': because of the awareness of their security interdependence – the 'security complex' – a number of States that do not necessarily have shared values and institutions have decided, rather than creating opposing alliances, to increase security through cooperation and have gradually agreed to implement international and internal measures to that end. In the long term, if it is successful, the Neighbourhood Policy could, through permanent close interaction and sharing of norms and values, lead to the progressive emergence of a more integrated regional arrangement, to a new 'security community', i.e. 'a trans-national region comprised of sovereign States whose people maintain dependable expectations of peaceful change' (Adler and Barnett, 1998) encompassing the EU – a 'security community' in itself that is expanding through enlargement – and the neighbouring regions or sub-regions.

What of the Politico-Military Dimension?

Even though no direct 'hard' security threats to the EU are emanating from the Mediterranean, the EMP and the Neighbourhood Policy cannot do without a politico-military dimension as a necessary component of a comprehensive approach. The 'hard' security dimension, which is included in the first basket of the EMP, must complement policies in the other fields of external action. On the one hand, politico-military cooperation is an aspect of the long-term stabilization and conflict prevention that the comprehensive approach aims for: exchange of information, exchange of liaison officers, observing exercises, joint manoeuvres and eventually joint operations, arms control, non-proliferation and disarmament all increase mutual trust, both in North-South and South-South relations. Secondly, in the event of crises that may require some sort of military intervention, possibly involving the threat or use of force, established politico-military cooperation provides a much more effective framework for consultation and, preferably, joint action than ad hoc arrangements or unilateral initiatives on the part of the EU or one or more of the Mediterranean partners. As ESDP continues to develop, the EU becomes an ever more capable actor in this field.

Proposals to enhance the security dimension of the EMP are abundant (Biscop, 2003). In its 2000 Common Strategy on the Mediterranean Region the EU already stated its intention 'to make use of the evolving common European policy on security and defence to consider how to strengthen, together with its Med partners, cooperative security in the region'. From the beginning, however, all efforts to add substance to this dimension have failed in the face of the unwillingness of the Mediterranean partners. Consequently, political dialogue has remained at a low level and only a few partnership measures have been implemented: a network of contact points for political and security matters; training seminars for diplomats; the EUROMESCO network of foreign policy institutes; a register of bilateral agreements among the partner countries; exchange of information on partner countries' adherence to international conventions on terrorism, human rights, arms control and disarmament, armed conflict and international law; and a pilot project on natural and man-made disasters. These measures are limited not only in number, but also in scope: they are mainly declaratory and deal with neither military cooperation nor crisis management. Measures regarding arms control, disarmament or non-proliferation are conspicuously absent, even though these are among the region's most important 'hard' security issues.

The Valencia Action Plan adopted by the fifth Euro-Mediterranean Conference (22-23 April 2002), an important attempt to define concrete actions to further the EMP, listed 'effective dialogue on political and security matters, including on the ESDP' among the measures to be taken. Subsequently, on 19 March 2003, the Council endorsed a set of proposals aiming to open up ESDP to the Mediterranean partners. An enhanced dialogue has been created, including meetings between the troika of the Political and Security Committee (PSC) and the Brussels heads of mission of the Mediterranean partners once each Presidency, as well as meetings at expert level; partners can also establish contact with the Secretariat General of the Council and with the Commission. Flexibility has been introduced – partners can themselves decide on the scope and intensity of their participation – and progressiveness. The initial aim is to familiarize partners with ESDP objectives and procedures. In a mid-term perspective partners that are willing can be invited to observe manoeuvres, to appoint liaison officers to the EU Military Staff and to participate in EU training courses. This gradual process should pave the road to participation by Mediterranean partners in actual EU-led crisis management operations, to which the Council can invite them on a case-by-case basis.[8] In spite of this offer on the part of the EU, partner countries initially remained extremely reluctant to engage however and the dialogue at first gained little substance.

Foremost to explain this lack of political will is the Middle East conflict. The eternal conflict between Israel and Palestine is the main stumbling-block for an enhanced security partnership between both shores of the Mediterranean. One cannot expect partners to engage in far-reaching security cooperation when they are divided on the question of an armed conflict that clouds the whole region, and when moreover a number of them criticize EU policy on the issue for being too passive. Furthermore, authoritarian regimes abuse the conflict as a ground of legitimacy. Significant steps towards a resolution of the conflict are a necessary prerequisite for a security partnership to really take off. Proposals for a security partnership that ignore resolution of ongoing conflicts – including the case of the Western Sahara – are not taken seriously. Since EU enlargement on 1 May 2004, the importance of the Middle East conflict for the EMP has become even more pronounced, for with the accession of Cyprus and Malta, and with Turkey having a special status as a candidate member and as a NATO Ally, the partners comprise

---

[8] The situation is different for Turkey: like the other non-EU European members of NATO, it is already involved in a close dialogue on ESDP, it is automatically invited to participate in all EU operations using NATO assets and it can be invited to EU-only operations on a case-by-case basis.

only the Mediterranean Arab countries and Israel (Tanner, 2004, p.140). The Strategy stresses that resolution of the Arab-Israeli conflict is a 'strategic priority', for indeed 'without this, there will be little chance of dealing with other problems'. The Middle East conflict receives additional emphasis in the final version, which as compared to the first draft adds a strong call for a joint effort by the EU, the US, the UN and Russia to implement the 'two state-solution'. Regardless of the position of the US though, as the Commission (2003a) has stated,

> The EU should take a more active role to facilitate settlement of the disputes over Palestine [...] Greater EU involvement in crisis management in response to specific regional threats would be a tangible demonstration of the EU's willingness to assume a greater share of the burden of conflict resolution in the neighbouring countries.

Reaching a 'permanent two-state solution' is listed among the topics for political dialogue and cooperation in the Action Plans with Israel and the Palestinian Authority, but it is doubtful whether this will be translated into operational objectives and benchmarks – until now, the EU has never been willing to utilize the economic instrument to pressurize the parties in the conflict, in spite of its enormous potential, at least if put to use in conjunction with a similar US initiative.

The dissatisfaction with the EU's limited investment in the financial and economic chapter is a second reason. It is often felt that the EU puts undue emphasis on the security aspects of the EMP, to the detriment of the economic basket which the Mediterranean partners consider to be the field for priority action.

Thirdly, there is certain distrust with regard to ESDP itself. With the Gulf War and the intervention in Kosovo in mind, there is a fear of becoming objects of 'Western interventionism'. In the mid-1990s the formation of two multinational military units, EUROFOR and EUROMARFOR, by the EU's Southern Member States was already viewed with considerable suspicion. Indeed, states on the Southern shore of the Mediterranean considered the units to be mainly directed against them. In view of the initial absence of a strategic concept, it was easy to see the development of the ESDP and the creation of a rapid reaction force for the EU in a similar light. It is not difficult to imagine how the debate on 'pre-emption' can fuel this fear of 'interventionism'. Research shows however that more important than actual distrust is a generalized lack of information about ESDP – which can of course easily be abused to create distrust, notably by nationalist and Islamist sectors of society. This lack of information either leads to scepticism regarding the ability of the EU to become an effective international security actor or, quite the opposite, to unrealistically high expectations regarding a potential EU role in the Middle East conflict. There are also positive views of ESDP however, because its development is seen as evidence of multilateralism and as a way to balance the US (de Vasconcelos, 2004; Jünemann, 2003). These positive sentiments must be built upon.

Fourthly, on a more general level, in the partner countries there is limited interest in the Mediterranean as an organizing concept of policy, both among policy-makers and academics. The EMP is mostly seen as a way of addressing bilateral relations with the EU; regional dynamics and South-South regional integration between the Mediterranean partners receive far less attention. From the perspective of the EU, security is an obvious dimension of its Neighbourhood Policy, but for the partner countries, 'Mediterranean security in itself does not seem to have an autonomous *raison d'être*' (Soltan, 2004), hence their lack of enthusiasm for multilateral security cooperation at the regional level. It should also be acknowledged that Mediterranean partners are less familiar with notions such as comprehensive and cooperative security and confidence and security-building measures.

Finally, it must not be ignored that with regard to those partner States that have authoritarian forms of government and where the armed forces play an important part in politics, politico-military cooperation with the EU is a double-edged sword. On the one hand, it could serve to enhance the status of the current regime – which might in some cases run counter to EU objectives in the field of democratization, human rights and the rule of law. On the other hand, cooperation that is conditional upon reform in precisely those fields would undermine the position of these regimes, which explains why they are not very forthcoming. Furthermore, large parts of public opinion are often not in favour of security cooperation with 'the West', which again would have negative consequences for the regimes' internal power base.

Enhancing the Politico-Military Dimension: An Incremental Process

Obviously, in view of the reluctance of the Mediterranean partners, enhancing the politico-military dimension of the EMP cannot be but a very incremental process. In the field of 'hard' security, the EU has a major problem of credibility vis-à-vis its Mediterranean partners, which rules out any grand schemes in the near future. But as this lack of credibility is to a large extent based on a lack of information, which is at the same time an important source of distrust, it is not without potential.

The inclusion of politico-military cooperation in the ENP Action Plans proves as much. Effectively establishing contact points with the ESDP bodies, a deepened dialogue and exploring the possibilities for actual participation in ESDP exercises and operations are mentioned in the Action Plans for Israel, Jordan, Morocco and Tunisia. This seems to indicate that politico-military cooperation is more acceptable if part of a wider, comprehensive framework. Since November 2004, the dialogue on ESDP has been fully integrated in the EMP bodies rather than taking place separately with the heads of mission in Brussels. In the framework of the Action Plans, politico-military cooperation could thus also be promoted through 'positive conditionality'. This increased willingness might also be related to a quest for support in view of the international context, in which terrorism and proliferation – particularly with regard to Iran – continue to be high on the agenda, as well as the fear for the potential spill-over effects of the conflict in Iraq – all of them issues with which the Southern States are most directly confronted.

In fact, the framework of the Action Plans is absolutely necessary, especially in view of the international context, in order to ensure the comprehensive nature of the approach, i.e. to maintain the link between politico-military cooperation, political reform and economic support that is at the core of the Strategy. In the absence of this link, and thus of conditionality, politico-military cooperation might be counterproductive with regard to the objective of promoting democratization, respect for human rights and the rule of law. Security sector reform should actually be among the explicit objectives of the EU, especially in the context of the ongoing fight against terrorism, the label of which is all too easily abused by security agencies and armed forces to silence legitimate opposition. The Commission (2003b) issued a warning in that sense:

> A tension between internal security concerns and the promotion and protection of human rights can result in negative consequences in human rights terms, particularly apparent under the umbrella of the 'war on terror'.

The EU should absolutely avoid a situation where politico-military cooperation strengthens the authoritarian nature of any of the regimes in power or dilutes the focus on conditionality. In that light, it would certainly be counter-productive to put Euro-Mediterranean cooperation too exclusively in the perspective of the fight against terrorism and proliferation, both of which have been high on the agenda of the EMP ever since '9/11'. Rather politico-military cooperation (in the framework of ESDP) and cooperation on justice and home affairs issues should also be subject to the general principle of 'positive conditionality'.

To which extent the Action Plans will succeed in giving substance to the politico-military dimension remains to be seen. The EU could consider accompanying initiatives to enhance the chance of success.

Firstly, the EU could step up its efforts to communicate about the aims and nature of ESDP. The absence of a strategic concept for ESDP was an important cause of suspicion regarding the true intentions of the EU. Now that the Strategy has filled this strategic vacuum, the document should be publicized much more than it is. Even within the EU, the Strategy is little known outside the small circles of policy-makers and experts. The EU could consider an exercise in outreach, not only in the limited framework of the EMP dialogue on ESDP, but also to academia, journalists and NGOs in the partner countries. The EUROMESCO network could play an important role in this regard.

Perhaps in a later stage such a dialogue about the Strategy could lead to a truly joint reflection on the specifics of the Mediterranean region, along the same lines as the Strategy – the challenges posed by the security environment, the objectives, and their policy implications – in order to arrive at a common document at the regional level, next to the bilateral Action Plans, which could put down guidelines for cooperation and serve as a framework for an enhanced security partnership similar to the way the Strategy does – or should – for EU external action. By tackling it from this new angle, the debate on the Euro-Mediterranean Charter for Peace and Stability, which has been moribund ever since the 1999 Stuttgart Ministerial where it was decided to postpone its adoption until 'political circumstances allow', could be given a new impetus, be it not in the short term.

Secondly, the EU need not wait for the dialogue on ESDP to have advanced further to invite partner countries to participate in its operations. The take-over of

SFOR by Operation Althea presents an excellent opportunity for the EU to invite its Mediterranean partners, for a number of them have already taken part in NATO operations in the Balkans. Morocco, which in the first half of 2004 had 350 troops in SFOR and a field battalion in Kosovo (KFOR), participated in Althea from the start. Egypt and Jordan as well have taken part in IFOR, SFOR's predecessor, in the past, while the latter has also participated in KFOR. For these countries at least, taking part in an EU operation using NATO assets, i.e. in a very similar framework, on familiar terrain, ought to be politically feasible. The EU and NATO could very well take a joint initiative to put the proposal to all the States involved in NATO's Mediterranean Dialogue – Algeria, Egypt, Israel, Jordan, Mauritania, Morocco and Tunisia – and to the other Mediterranean partners of the EU. Taking part in an actual EU operation and witnessing ESDP functioning in the field should go a long way to improve the credibility of the EU. Participation would of course be on a voluntary basis, open at all times to the Mediterranean partners that are willing.

As Ministers noted at the Naples Euro-Mediterranean Conference (2-3 December 2003), 'some of the Mediterranean partners already work with the EU in peacekeeping activities (Balkans, Africa) under the UN aegis'. For example, in 2004 Algeria, Egypt, Jordan, Morocco and Tunisia all contributed to MONUC, the UN mission in the Democratic Republic of Congo. On the EU side in that same period Sweden was present with a military contingent of 86, while Belgium, the Czech Republic, Denmark, France, Ireland, Poland, Portugal, Sweden, Spain and the UK contributed observers and/or police. From June to September 2003, the EU at the request of the UN also implemented an operation of its own, 'Artemis', to secure the area around the city of Bunia in the Eastern province of Ituri. Such common participation in a UN operation could be the subject of a fruitful exchange in the framework of the EMP dialogue on ESDP, on lessons learned, best practices etc. It could also lay the foundations for involvement of Mediterranean partners in future EU operations, for example in Africa, particularly operations at the request of the UN. Would an intervention in crises such as that in the Darfur region of Sudan (if the international community could muster the necessary political will) not lend itself to Euro-Mediterranean cooperation? As the EU gradually takes on a more 'expeditionary' role, as can be expected, taking on more responsibility for international peace and security and implementing the Strategy, those Mediterranean partners that are willing could easily be involved.

These very concrete steps would all contribute to increasing confidence between both sides of the Mediterranean and to enhancing the credibility of the EU as an international actor, thus preparing the ground for a deepening and institutionalization of the security dimension of the EMP in the longer term, in which further-reaching steps can then be imagined. These steps should take into account the need for a strong multilateral dimension, as an important South-South confidence-building measure:

- standard procedures for joint crisis management in the event of crises in the EMP area, to allow for joint decision-making and action; taking into account partners' sensitivities, it would seem recommendable to at least provide for automatic consultation whenever the EU considers an intervention in the region; an automatic invitation to participate in any EU operations in the Mediterranean could perhaps follow in an even later stage;

- a Euro-Mediterranean situation centre, to collect and analyze data – provided on a regular basis by partners on both sides of the Mediterranean – on a number of agreed items, and to monitor developments with crisis potential (Calleya, 2002);
- multinational forces including contingents from the Mediterranean partners, e.g. on the basis of EUROFOR and EUROMARFOR;
- joint action on landmines and air/sea search and rescue;
- a wide range of confidence and security-building measures, e.g. prior notification of major manoeuvres, participation in the UN system of standardized reporting of military expenditure, an encyclopaedia of terminology on security.

Finally, and more generally, in the longer term an update of the Common Strategy on the Mediterranean Region can be considered. A new text, concise, along the lines of the Strategy, but also more precise, to be elaborated in much closer consultation with the Mediterranean partners than the current document, could summarize the new approach, based on the Strategy, the Neighbourhood Policy and the joint reflection on security proposed above, and translate this into operational objectives.

Schemes for the Wider – Greater – Broader Middle East

Because of the predominance of the Middle East conflict, without significant steps towards its resolution other schemes for the region have very limited chances of success. The American 'Greater Middle East Initiative' (GMEI) is a case in point. This originally very ambitious scheme to promote democracy in the 'Greater Middle East', which in the American definition includes the Arab States, Israel, Turkey, Afghanistan, Pakistan and Iran, was subsequently watered down in the course of a number of summits taking place in June 2004 (EU-US, Arab League, European Council, NATO), because of the extremely reluctant reactions of the Middle Eastern States concerned. Also at its May 2004 Summit, the Arab League adopted a 'Pledge of Accord and Solidarity', in which leaders called for 'broader participation in public affairs' and for human rights and the strengthening of the role of women 'in line with our faith, values and traditions'. The document can be seen as a local response to the external GMEI, although its value on the ground is questionable.

It is difficult to see how such an initiative on the part of the US could have met with any other reaction, in spite of former Secretary of State Colin Powell's positive picture (2004), in the context of the widely contested American-led occupation of Iraq and of American passivity with regard to, or even outright support for, unilateral actions by the Sharon government that run contrary to the agreed road to peace in the Middle East conflict. It could be said that the Bush administration just lacks the moral authority in the region to propose democratic changes. The GMEI also seems to span too large an area, which comprizes States that are too different for a single unified approach to be workable, and which does not constitute a single 'security complex'. The area of application seems to have been defined by the needs of the US' 'war on terrorism' rather than by any inherent characteristics. These differences imply that even if a stable, democratic Iraq emerges in the short term, a democratic domino-effect in the region is highly unlikely. In the words of former European Commissioner Chris Patten: 'developing democracy is not like making instant coffee' (quoted in Youngs, 2004b, p.5). Furthermore the GMEI has at least been perceived as putting too much emphasis on external intervention, on 'imposing' democracy – as opposed to the partnership approach advocated by the EU – and thus ignoring the internal dynamics that are necessary to achieve any durable change. And popular criticism of current regimes does not necessarily translate into support for external intervention; in the wake of the invasion of Iraq, any American or British involvement in particular is highly sensitive (Niblock, 2003).

These criticisms seem to have been taken into account when on 9 June 2004 the G8 summit finally adopted a much more moderate 'Partnership for Progress and a Common Future with the Region of the Broader Middle East and North Africa'. The G8 document mentions the need to coordinate different initiatives and includes a detailed list of measures envisaging supporting internally driven economic and political reform, but lacks references to budgets and concrete implementation. The focus is on literacy, vocational training, entrepreneurship, business development and microfinance rather than on democratization and references to conditionality are lacking (Youngs, 2004b, p.11). Furthermore, although a new Forum for the Future is to bring together annually the G8 and the States from the region, involvement and commitment from the region actually appears superficial (Gärber, 2004, p.93). The impact of the G8 initiative therefore seems doubtful.

In Search of EU-US Cooperation

All this is not to say of course that promoting reform is not necessary in the States of the region, which is precisely one of the long-standing objectives of the EMP – the EU has not 'discovered' the need for democratization after '9/11' (Perthes, 2004). Youngs (2005, p.1) rightly notes that 'a glance at the Barcelona Declaration encourages the conclusion that much recent debate has been guilty of reinventing this conceptual wheel'. Therefore, US efforts would seem better spent supporting the established EMP and the ENP rather than by launching a separate initiative, with a joint EU-US shift to a higher gear being possible after steps have been taken with regard to the Middle East conflict. The watered-down US proposals are in fact very close to what the EU is already doing – or attempting – in the framework of the EMP/ENP. Looking at the reality behind the rhetoric from Washington and Brussels, one finds that in actual practice the EU and the US fund very similar civil society, governance and education projects, which 'suffices to render unconvincing the notion that the US only does hard power' (Youngs, 2004b, p.7). There certainly is sufficient common ground on which to found close cooperation.

As to the countries outside the EMP, the Strategy states that 'a broader engagement with the Arab world should also be considered'. This can be seen as a reference to the report that Romano Prodi, Javier Solana and Chris Patten submitted to the December 2003 European Council, 'Strengthening EU's Relations with the Arab World', in which they recommend, for the States outside the Barcelona Process, 'to explore proposals for a possible regional strategy for the Wider Middle East, comprising relations with GCC countries, Yemen, Iraq and Iran'. This one sentence in the Strategy thus ambitiously extends the EU's definition of its neighbourhood, but rightly so, for relations with these States are less developed, while at the same time certain security issues affecting the members of the EMP, notably in the Middle East, obviously cannot be tackled without them. Proliferation is the obvious example; the long-standing idea of a WMD-free zone in the Middle East could only be elaborated in such a wider framework. These States would not be included in the Neighbourhood Policy or the EMP, but an additional framework is envisaged which would be closely linked to both existing frameworks. A strategy document to that end was adopted by the June 2004 European Council, the EU Strategic Partnership with the Mediterranean and the Middle East or 'Wider Middle East'. Again, the US could support this initiative and envisage further joint steps in a later stage. Indeed, an effective partnership with the Mediterranean and the Greater/Wider Middle East is more crucial to the EU than to the US, because of geographic proximity, the EU's greater energy dependence and the large Arab population living within the EU. But within the EU itself as well, an exercise in coordination seems absolutely necessary, as it is far from clear yet how exactly the different policy frameworks – EMP, Neighbourhood Policy, Wider Middle East – will relate to each other.

EU-US cooperation is the key, with regard to the Middle East conflict, as each is only accepted as an impartial mediator by one party to the conflict, and with regard to comprehensive partnerships in the Mediterranean and the Gulf regions, as only their combined financial and other efforts will have sufficient impact. The rapid succession of international initiatives with regard to the region certainly calls for thorough coordination. Unfortunately, Brussels and Washington are often divided on the approach to be taken. For example, the former considered the Middle East conflict as the absolute priority to be dealt with before there is the slightest chance of success of dealing with any other matter, while the latter seemed to hope that somehow, the problem will disappear almost by itself if only Iraq can be stabilized and then the process of democratization of the 'Greater Middle East' can be launched. As Ottaway and Carothers (2004) frankly put it: 'The attempt to launch a new initiative without discussing the peace process is a triumph of abstract logic over political reality'. In fact, it can be argued that the US has already missed an enormous opportunity to re-launch the peace process by opting for support for harsh and un-reconciling Israeli policies, under the guise of anti-terrorism, instead of brokering an agreement when, immediately following '9/11', a lull in the violence occurred as everybody was stunned by the horrendous events and their potential impact on the region. Fortunately, the new situation after the death of President Arafat created a new window of opportunity. In any case, the conclusion is that an EU-US forum for permanent consultation and coordination of policies on the Mediterranean and the Greater/Wider/Broader Middle East is more than necessary.

Coordinating with NATO's Mediterranean Dialogue

Since 1994, NATO also has a Mediterranean Dialogue (MD) with seven States: Egypt, Israel, Mauritania, Morocco, Tunisia, Jordan (since 1995) and Algeria (since 2000). At its June 2004 Istanbul summit, NATO decided to enhance the MD, deepening the partnership with current Dialogue countries as well as offering a framework to the States of the GCC through the 'Istanbul Cooperation Initiative'. Although one would expect that Southern States' objections to security cooperation in the context of the EMP would also apply to NATO, they have in fact been less reluctant towards the Alliance, certainly so since the Istanbul summit. The international context of course plays a large role again, but more importantly NATO, which is generally associated with the US, does not suffer the same lack of credibility as ESDP – although in the current context, this perception of American dominance is of course a double-edged sword. NATO has been very successful in the past: without any doubt, the participation of Dialogue countries in NATO operations (IFOR/SFOR and KFOR) is a great success; it is probably the most important achievement of the NATO MD.

The Dialogue suffers from an inherent limitation however. Because of the nature of the Alliance, the NATO MD obviously concerns only the politico-military dimension, which renders the implementation of the comprehensive approach, linking security cooperation to commitments in other fields, very difficult. For example, Algeria, which originally was not invited to join the MD because of its internal crisis, was admitted in 2000, in spite of ongoing violence in which both the government and extremist Islamists were involved; the political opportunity of this move was highly questionable. Clearly, the EMP, which is more comprehensive in terms of both membership and substance, is the framework offering the better prospects for partnership with and reform in the South, which is not to say that the NATO MD is not very valuable as a North-South confidence-building measure (Biscop, 2002b; Malmvig, 2004). It could be argued however that the existence of several frameworks for security dialogue with the Mediterranean alongside each other in itself is one of the causes of Mediterranean States' reluctance to engage in security partnership, as it is not clear to them what is the purpose of all these separate schemes: the EMP, the NATO MD, and the OSCE as well has its 'Mediterranean Partners for Cooperation' – Algeria, Egypt, Israel, Jordan, Morocco and Tunisia.

In view of their similar objectives, and in order to ensure that all actions, including those in the economic and social baskets of the Barcelona Process, are mutually reinforcing, increased coordination of the NATO MD and the EMP certainly is the way ahead. Currently, coordination is limited to informal exchanges of information between NATO and the EU. Perhaps in the longer term, in view of the more comprehensive nature of the EMP, NATO MD activities should be focussed on the EMP agenda, in order to achieve maximuml complementarity. This would also meet at least part of Southern partners' concerns regarding coordination between the different dialogues. EU-NATO cooperation on promoting Mediterranean partners' participation in the EU successor operation to SFOR would be a concrete and extremely useful example. Furthermore, such an arrangement would better reflect the emerging division of labour between NATO and the EU, in which the latter gradually assumes first-level responsibility for security issues in its neighbourhood, as witnessed by the take-over of SFOR. This evolution springs from the long-standing demand, on the part of the US, for more burden-sharing within the Alliance, and the increasing capacity of the EU to respond to that demand, because of the ongoing development of ESDP. Whether the US, apart from welcoming increased military involvement in the Balkans, is also looking forward to an enhanced EU profile in the Mediterranean, and particularly in the Middle East, is a rather different question.

Chapter 4

A Secure World

Under the heading of 'effective multilateralism', the Strategy aims to implement the comprehensive approach at the global level. As in the Neighbourhood Policy, the emphasis is on long-term prevention through the combination of partnership and support in order to promote reforms, but rather than 'leading from the front' itself, as it proposes to do towards its neighbours, the EU will primarily act through the UN and other multilateral institutions and regimes. The central position of the UN is reflected in its place in the text of the Strategy, where it now comes first, contrary to the first draft. 'Effective multilateralism' is perhaps the phrase that best expresses the Strategy's overall approach. It is a global objective, both functionally and geographically, that concerns the world system itself: 'the development of a stronger international society, well functioning international institutions and a rule-based international order'. The other two broad objectives outlined in the Strategy are implied in 'effective multilateralism': 'building security in our neighbourhood' amounts to the application of the same principles at the regional level, while 'addressing the threats' demands a number of immediate politico-military measures, but cannot succeed if not part of a comprehensive root causes approach.

This chapter will primarily assess the contribution that the EU can make to the multilateral system in the field of international peace and security, with particular emphasis on the potential for implementation of the report of the UN's High-Level Panel on Threats, Challenges and Change, while it will also outline the challenges to be tackled with regard to the other dimensions of global governance, that is with regard to the other global public goods.

Power to the System: Reinvigorating Collective Security

The Strategy strongly stresses that for 'international organisations, regimes and treaties to be effective' the EU must be 'ready to act when their rules are broken'. 'Effective multilateralism' thus appears to imply enforceable multilateralism. In the field of international peace and security, that is the politico-military dimension, the multilateral system has indeed been lacking in this respect. As a consequence, the collective security system of the UN has come under attack. Critics of the system feel that its executive body, the Security Council, is insufficiently proactive with regard to what they regard as the 'new' threats of international terrorism and proliferation of WMD and in some instances has failed to deal with such threats altogether. This perceived 'system failure' is often used as a justification for unilateral action, which is presented as being forced upon those States undertaking it by the inability or the unwillingness of the Security Council to act in the face of what they consider to be grave threats. The illegal invasion of Iraq by a US-led coalition of the willing was the sad highlight of this attack on collective security.

Of course, the system is not perfect. First of all, certain crises or developments simply never reach the agenda of the Security Council. These are usually not the issues in which any of the Permanent Five (P5) or any other major actor has a stake, so if in such cases the Security Council is criticized for its inactivity it is mostly by less influential States or by NGOs and civil society actors rather than by the proponents of unilateral action.

Secondly, when issues *are* debated by the Security Council, it sometimes does not act, because the members do not agree on the seriousness of the issue or on the type of action to be taken. In such cases, especially when any of the P5 is in favour of intervention, inaction often produces severe criticism and has led to the bypassing of the UN. This was the case of Kosovo in 1999, when NATO took to the use of force without a UN mandate. Although the NATO operation found wide approval with Western governments, and thus was widely seen as legitimate, though technically certainly not legal, it was widely criticized by other States. As Cooper (2003, p.61) notes, the intervention was perfectly acceptable in the European context, because of the commonality of values that has developed, but outside the continent of Europe, the degree of consensus on universal values quickly drops. Another case of bypassing the UN was that of Iraq in 2003, when the US, faced with the refusal of France to condone military intervention and the intention of Paris to use its veto power, went ahead without UN authorization. The latter case demonstrates that the debate is far from being clear-cut: non-intervention by the Security Council does not necessarily mean that the system does not work – on the contrary, many observers would contend that in the case of Iraq it worked perfectly well. The UN's High-Level Panel on Threats, Challenges and Change illustrated this in its report (2004, p.33):

> Some contend that the Security Council was ineffective because it could not produce Iraqi compliance with its resolutions. Others argue Security Council irrelevance because the Council did not deter the United States and its coalition partners from waging war. Still others suggest that the refusal of the Security Council to bow to United States pressure to legitimate the war is proof of its relevance and indispensability: although the Security Council did not deter war, it provided a clear and principled standard with which to assess the decision to go to war. The flood of Foreign Ministers into the Security Council chambers during the debates, and widespread public attention, suggest that the United States decision to bring the question of force to the Security Council reaffirmed not just the relevance but the centrality of the Charter of the United Nations.

There have been instances of permanent members blocking intervention for fear of creating a precedent that might later be called upon to condemn their behaviour or to warrant intervention in a situation in which they are themselves implicated – the war in Chechnya is a case in point. But a negative response to a proposal for action, even if put forward by one of the P5, can also mean that the other members of the Security Council feel that the issue at hand does not – yet –

warrant action or – first – demands action of a different type. If positive responses only are accepted, than the need to request Security Council authorization becomes meaningless. The so-called 'unreasonable veto', often invoked by the proponents of unilateral action, is thus a very ambiguous concept, as the case of Kosovo illustrates: whereas the proponents of military intervention considered the events in that province sufficiently grave to warrant the use of force, and deplored the Security Council's lack of action in spite of its earlier recognition of the situation as a threat to international peace and security (Dashwood, 2000), the opponents judged the effects of the cure to be worse than the initial problem. It is to be noted that even when States or regional organizations act unilaterally, they often try to legally justify their actions on the basis of Security Council Resolutions and thus formally at least confirm the principles of the collective security system.

Thirdly, when the Security Council does act, the scope of its actions is sometimes felt to be too limited, to be too non-committing. This has often to do with limited willingness on the part of UN Member States to commit sufficient troops and other means.

This illustrates that the Security Council, and indeed the UN as a whole, is nothing without the Member States. If the collective security system is to be restored, it is the Member States that must find a consensus: on the range of issues, or threats, that the Security Council must take in hand, and on the conditions for the use of the range of instruments at the Council's disposal. And it is also up to the Member States to make available the necessary financial, civilian and military means for the Security Council to be able to act effectively. It is to this undertaking that the EU under the heading of 'effective multilateralism' has an important contribution to make.

Debating the Use of Force

The invasion of Iraq in particular spurred an intense debate on the use of force. Under the Charter of the UN (Article 2.4):

> All Members shall refrain in their international relations from the threat or use of force against the territorial integrity or political independence of any state, or in any manner inconsistent with the Purposes of the United Nations.

Legally, use of force, i.e. military intervention against the will of the parties concerned, is therefore possible in two cases only. The first case is use of force authorized by the Security Council. Article 24.1 states the general principle:

> In order to ensure prompt and effective action by the United Nations, its Members confer on the Security Council primary responsibility for the maintenance of international peace and security, and agree that in carrying out its duties under this responsibility the Security Council acts on their behalf.

Chapter VII provides that the Security Council – and it only – can decide what coercive measures to take to maintain or restore international peace and security, including the use of force, as detailed in Article 42:

> Should the Security Council consider that the measures provided for in Article 41 would be inadequate or have proved to be inadequate, it may take such action by air, sea, or land forces as may be necessary to maintain or restore international peace and security. Such action may include demonstrations, blockade, and other operations by air, sea, or land forces of Members of the United Nations.

The second case, which is the only one in which a State, or an organization of States, may use force unilaterally, i.e. without Security Council mandate, is that of self-defence as provided for by Article 51:

> Nothing in the present Charter shall impair the inherent right of individual or collective self-defence if an armed attack occurs against a Member of the United Nations, until the Security Council has taken measures necessary to maintain international peace and security. Measures taken by Members in the exercise of this right of self-defence shall be immediately reported to the Security Council and shall not in any way affect the authority and responsibility of the Security Council under the present Charter to take at any time such action as it deems necessary in order to maintain or restore international peace and security.

Although the wording of Article 51 – 'if an armed attack occurs' – would suggest that use of force in self-defence can only be reactive, it is often accepted that international law allows for a slightly broader interpretation. In this view, Article 51 includes the possibility of 'pre-emptive' action in case of an 'imminent threat', i.e. at a time between the moment when an enemy has decided to attack and the actual launching of that attack, but only if there is an urgent necessity of self-defence against this attack and if there is no alternative to self-defence. These strict conditions go back to those set up by Daniel Webster in the 1837 Caroline Case: 'the necessity of that self-defence is instant, overwhelming and leaving no choice of means, and no moment for deliberation' (Simma, 1994, p.675). International lawyers continue to differ on this issue (Taylor, 2004).

Not all States accept the universal validity of the legal framework of collective security contained in the UN Charter. The US in particular reserves the right to use force without Security Council authorization if necessary and it is often felt that regional organizations, such as NATO, can do the same. The legal justification put forward is often a broadened interpretation of Article 51, or rather of the notion of imminent threat. The presence, in a State considered to be hostile, of terrorist groups, or the possession by such a State, or its intention to acquire, WMD in violation of non-proliferation regimes, is considered sufficient in itself to constitute an imminent threat and thus to legally and legitimately justify use of force in self-defence under Article 51, which therefore does not require Security Council authorization. The 2002 National Security Strategy (NSS) of the US is very explicit in this regard, as it provides for 'anticipatory action to defend ourselves, even if uncertainty remains as to the time and place of the enemy's attack' (p.15).

The covering letter to the NSS by President George W. Bush states: 'And, as a matter of common sense and self-defence, America will act against such emerging threats before they are fully formed'. It is indeed very difficult to prove the imminence of a threat, i.e. the decision to commit an act of aggression. Not often are things as clear-cut as in the schoolbook case: when enemy tanks are rolling, one does not have to wait until they cross the border before launching a counter-strike. But if in order to avoid this difficulty no distinction is made between the possession of a striking capacity and the intention to actually use it, for example with regard to WMD, this would mean that States such as North-Korea and Iran, but also Israel, India and Pakistan constitute imminent threats to any State that might decide to perceive them as potentially hostile. Reinterpreting the Charter thus quickly opens the door to a complete hollowing-out of the collective security system, for if one – Western – State claims a broad right of pre-emptive action, any other State can legitimately do the same. A threat that is not 'fully formed', can hardly be imminent – reinterpretation of pre-emption thus becomes a safe-conduct for plain preventive war, which inherently violates the Charter.

The NSS also states (p.6) that the US 'will not hesitate to act alone, if necessary', i.e. outside the collective security framework of the UN. Another often-used justification for use of force without Security Council authorization is that another grouping of States can confer legitimacy on the use of force in cases where the Council does not act, as long as it is sufficiently broad. For example, Brecher (2003, p.273) submits 'that "legitimacy" is a more fruitful approach than "legality" in the context of an unreformed United Nations'. It is held that an 'international organization of democracies' (Brecher), 'association of democratic nations' (Hoffmann, 2003) or 'coalition of reasonably democratic States' (Buchanan and Keohane, 2004), or also 'the regional organization that is most likely to be affected by the emerging threat' (Feinstein and Slaughter, 2004) can legitimately proceed to use force if the Security Council having been requested to do so does not accord a mandate. Such proposals as well however would fatally undermine the collective security system, for besides being based on the foggy concept of the 'unreasonable veto', they also raise the question of who would decide which States can join such a grouping of democracies, and how legitimate its decisions would be in the eyes of those that can't? And what would stop the latter from forming an alternative grouping that could then claim the same right to use force? Besides, the proposals for a 'democracy caucus' ignore the fact that the fundamental rupture over Iraq occurred between democracies (Dassù, 2004, p.37). As Brunnée and Toope (2004, p.253) rightly note, this idea 'undermines the cosmopolitan aspirations of international law', and 'would only serve to further poison international relations'. Only the universal membership of the UN, represented by the Security Council, can therefore confer legitimacy, and legality, on the use of force. And as Cooper (2003, p.167) notes, legitimacy is ever more important in a world in which early action is required to effectively prevent threats from materializing. In the words of Bildt (2004, p.39):

> If [...] the hard intervention does not fulfil all the criteria under international law, it is obviously deprived of a critical amount of legitimacy, which in turn makes it more

difficult to achieve the third requirement of effectiveness in achieving the aims of the intervention.

The EU view on the collective security system and the use of force can be deducted from the Strategy. As a complement to its long-term structural policy of prevention and stabilization, the EU envisages a two-step approach with regard to politico-military issues that demand short-term prevention and crisis management measures, i.e., in the words of the Strategy, towards States that 'have placed themselves outside the bounds of international society', either because they 'have sought isolation' or because they 'persistently violate international norms'. In the first place, 'the EU should be ready to provide assistance' to help them 'rejoin the international community'. But: 'Those who are unwilling to do so should understand that there is a price to be paid, including in their relationship with the European Union'. At the first instance, this price will be paid in terms of cutting back partnership and cooperation and by imposing economic sanctions, as can be gathered from the use of the notion of conditionality in the Strategy, but when necessary it can also include military intervention, and this at an early stage if needs be. This becomes clear when the chapter on 'effective multilateralism' is read together with the next chapter of the Strategy, on policy implications, and notably the paragraph on an EU that is 'more active in pursuing [its] strategic objectives', an ambition that 'applies to the full spectrum of instruments for crisis management and conflict prevention at our disposal, including political, diplomatic, military and civilian, trade and development activities'. In that context the Strategy stipulates that the EU needs 'to develop a culture that fosters early, rapid and when necessary, robust intervention', for 'we need to be able to act before countries around us deteriorate, when signs of proliferation are detected, and before humanitarian emergencies arise'. Or in other words: 'preventive engagement can avoid more serious problems in the future'. For the thorough assessment of situations that this approach requires, the EU can build on the extensive toolbox for early warning and prevention that the Commission has created.

The emphasis clearly is on the comprehensive approach, on putting to use 'the full spectrum of instruments'. The coercive use of military power therefore certainly is not the priority instrument for short-term prevention and crisis management. Although the Strategy itself does not explicitly say so, the Director of the Policy Unit, Christoph Heusgen (2004, p.7) expressly confirms it: 'Military intervention, however, is only the last resort of EU policy'. This seems to be further confirmed by the fact that – significantly – the notion of 'pre-emptive engagement' in the first draft has been replaced by 'preventive engagement' in the final version. The possibility of unilateral, pre-emptive EU operations thus seems to be ruled out, while 'preventive engagement' obviously is to be understood as conflict prevention. The EU thus also removed the cause of some fierce criticism from a wide range of academics, NGOs, and governments (Schwarz, 2003). That leaves the question of the EU position on the legal mandate required for the use of force, excluding cases of course in which intervention takes place with the consent of the parties, for example in the context of the OSCE, or when the EU is invited, as was the case in Macedonia. On this question the Strategy is not very explicit.

The Strategy states that the EU is 'committed to upholding and developing International Law', an addition – with initial capitals – as compared to the first draft, and says that 'The fundamental framework for international relations is the United Nations Charter. The United Nations Security Council has the primary responsibility for the maintenance of international peace and security'. But it does not expressly say that in principle the EU should seek a UN mandate for coercive military action. The Strategy thus leaves a lot of room for interpretation, and can pragmatically be understood to imply that 'in emergency situations immediate action is not always compatible with a formal application of international public law' (Haine, 2004b, p.110); in other words, the Strategy could be interpreted as allowing a Kosovo scenario. Certainly on this important issue this ambiguity detracts from the Strategy's utility as a framework for policy-making and provides grounds for criticism to those who fear a militarization of the EU, as well as those who feel that the Strategy 'could have been bolder' (Heisbourg, 2004, p.32).

One must of course take into account that the issue is extremely sensitive and was at the heart of the Iraq divide that was rocking the EU at the time of the drafting of the Strategy. But were the conditions for the use of force really the stake at that intra-European debate? It appears in fact that on this issue the Member States have long held the same line: all are willing to use force if necessary, though some have a stronger tradition of intervention than others, often related to a colonial past – for example France in Ivory Coast, the UK in Sierra Leone, Belgium in Central Africa – but none regards the use of force as a first-line instrument and all prefer to do so with a UN mandate. The adoption of the EU Strategy against Proliferation of Weapons of Mass Destruction by the December 2003 European Council, which provides for a very gradual approach, bears witness to this consensus (Spear, 2003). Meyer (2004, p.15) therefore argues that the Iraq crisis demonstrated for the first time that differences between the EU and US approaches are greater than intra-European differences, and 'highlighted and consolidated the intra-European similarities with regard to the norms legitimizing the use of force'. The real issue at stake within the EU thus rather appeared to be the relationship with the US. If in a situation in which the EU would not apply force – yet – the US decides to do so, where do Europe's priorities lie: in upholding its own principles or in supporting its foremost ally?

Another factor to be taken into account is that even if the Strategy itself allows room for interpretation, the need for unanimity in the Council when deciding on military operations serves as a very effective built-in brake on over-hasty military operations: it is difficult to imagine the EU finding consensus on the use of force without unequivocal UN authorization. Nevertheless, it is to be regretted that the principle of Security Council authorization was not expressly included in the Strategy and that the EU renounced from setting an example – and thus from leading by example. Who else would send such a clear message in favour of the collective security system if not the EU?

Seeking Consensus on Collective Security

Inspiration for the formulation of a view on the circumstances justifying the use of force, and the legal mandate required, could have been found in the report of the International Commission on Intervention and State Sovereignty (ICISS, 2001). As mentioned in Chapter 1, the ICISS put forward a very commendable proposal to define common criteria, adapted to today's security environment, for the use of coercive measures, military and other, in order to provide a collective response to States that threaten the security of their own population. The ICISS concluded that if a State is unwilling or unable to stop or prevent serious harm from happening to a population, the principle of non-intervention in the internal affairs of a State must give way to a 'responsibility to protect' on the part of the international community. This implies the possibility, if needs be, of the use of force, that is of humanitarian intervention – although the ICISS preferred not to use that term in order to avoid any militarization of the word 'humanitarian'. The ICISS thus proposed a collective human security system. Unfortunately, partly because of the timing of its release, just months after '9/11', and partly because certain States resisted the concept and blocked its inclusion on the agenda of the UN General Assembly, the report did not receive the attention that it undoubtedly deserves (Fukushima, 2004, pp.34-5).

In the view of the ICISS, the coercive use of military power must be a last resort, to be considered only if all other means have clearly failed or can reasonably be assumed to be ineffective, and subject to an explicit mandate from the Security Council – the 'right authority'. But if these conditions are met, the international community, that is the Member States of the UN, should show no hesitation in taking military action. If, however, the Security Council – whose authorization should in all cases be sought prior to action being taken – proves unable or unwilling to act in a situation where the responsibility to protect is obvious, then the ICISS proposes that the consent of the UN General Assembly can be sought at a meeting in emergency special session under the Uniting for Peace procedure, or that action within its area of jurisdiction by a regional organization under Chapter VIII of the UN Charter can be envisaged, subject to it seeking subsequent authorization from the Security Council. The ICISS thus pragmatically provided for a back door in case of an 'unreasonable veto' in the Security Council, but because of the inherent ambiguity of this concept, severely limited the options.

In the Uniting for Peace Resolution (3 November 1950) the General Assembly resolved that:

> if the Security Council, because of lack of unanimity of the permanent members, fails to exercise its primary responsibility for the maintenance of international peace and security in any case where there appears to be a threat to the peace [...] the General Assembly shall consider the matter immediately with a view to making appropriate recommendations to members for collective measures, including in the case of a breach of the peace or act of aggression the use of armed forces when necessary to maintain or restore international peace and security.

In this first option, the General Assembly can thus only recommend measures, for which a two-third majority is required. By limiting, in the second option, action by a regional organization to its area of jurisdiction, that is the territory of its members or, as was the case of NATO in Kosovo, the periphery of that territory, the ICISS proposes to prevent an organization from claiming a worldwide scope of action. And in all cases a Security Council mandate should first have been sought. The concept of the 'responsibility to protect' can thus not be abused to justify unilateral pre-emptive action under Article 51, without Security Council authorization, as it has been feared it could (Brunnée and Toope, 2004). The case of Kosovo should be seen as the exception that confirms the rule, not as a precedent that can be invoked. It could be argued that the EU, for the same pragmatic reasons, did well in not committing too explicitly to the obligation of Security Council authorization for coercive action. But even though for pragmatic reasons a limited backdoor along the lines proposed by the ICISS can be justified, to allow for exceptional circumstances, the general principle of Security Council authorization should have been included in the Strategy, because of the exemplary function of the EU.

The 'responsibility to protect' applies only to cases of States harming their own population, but the general principles for the use of force that the ICISS advocated can be applied to other threats to international peace and security as well.

A very similar approach has in fact already been developed by the EU with regard to the specific issue of WMD, in the EU Strategy against Proliferation of Weapons of Mass Destruction. This provides for two stages. The first includes strengthening the multilateral non-proliferation treaties and export control regimes, notably with regard to verification, and, in a longer-term perspective, dealing with the underlying causes of proliferation by pursuing political solutions to tensions and disputes and regional arrangements for arms control and disarmament: the 'first line of defence'. The examples of Brazil and South Africa demonstrate that if States feel sufficiently assured by the security guarantees provided by the international system, proliferation can be contained (Guoliang, 2003, p.140). Only when these instruments have failed, can 'coercive measures under Chapter VII of the UN Charter and international law' be envisaged, 'as a last resort'. The Security Council is to play a central part, which implies that its role 'as the final arbiter on the consequences of non-compliance [...] needs to be effectively strengthened'. EU policy with regard to possible nuclear proliferation by Iran can be seen as a successful example of this gradual and comprehensive approach. By engaging with Tehran in a critical dialogue, the UK, France and Germany have been able to exert considerable influence. Although it does not pardon violations of the NPT, Iran's geo-strategic position, notably the possession of nuclear weapons by India, Pakistan and Israel, cannot be ignored when trying to affect its policies. It is too early to judge whether durable results can be achieved, but the approach that has been followed certainly seems more promising than a policy of mere confrontation, which can only be expected to reinforce the position of the hawks within Iran. Given that the Strategy on WMD elaborates upon one aspect of the overall

Security Strategy, it is doubly regrettable that the latter is not more explicit on the use of force itself.

The Security Strategy does expressly recognize though that 'Strengthening the United Nations, equipping it to fulfil its responsibilities and to act effectively, is a European priority'. If the Security Council is indeed to be 'the final arbiter on the consequences of non-compliance', then it must be given the means for effective action – or others will continue to be tempted to act unilaterally in its stead. The same emphasis on the UN can be found in the next chapter of the Strategy, where under the heading 'more active' the EU is said to be 'committed to reinforcing its cooperation with the UN to assist countries emerging from conflicts, and to enhancing its support for the UN in short-term crisis management situations'. Accordingly, the EU has made a significant contribution to the UN's High-Level Panel on Threats, Challenges and Change.

Contributing to the High-Level Panel on Threats, Challenges and Change

At the end of 2003, UN Secretary-General Kofi Annan established the High-Level Panel with the aim of recommending:

> clear and practical measures for ensuring effective collective action, based upon a rigorous analysis of future threats to peace and security, an appraisal of the contribution collective action can make, and a thorough assessment of existing approaches, instruments and mechanisms, including the principal organs of the United Nations (UN, 2003a).

Annan announced his initiative in a brave speech to the September 2003 session of the UN General Assembly, at a moment which he considered to be 'a fork in the road' (Annan, 2003). On the one hand, he heavily criticized States that reserve the right to act unilaterally:

> This logic represents a fundamental challenge to the principles on which, however imperfectly, world peace and stability have rested for the last fifty-eight years. My concern is that, if it were to be adopted, it could set precedents that resulted in a proliferation of the unilateral and lawless use of force, with or without justification.

He added however:

> But it is not enough to denounce unilateralism, unless we also face up squarely to the concerns that make some States feel uniquely vulnerable, since it is those concerns that drive them to take unilateral action. We must show that those concerns can, and will, be addressed effectively through collective action.

'It is a condition of a rule-based international order that law evolves in response to developments such as proliferation, terrorism and global warming', the Strategy says – the High-Level Panel should provide part of the answer. The Panel counted 16 members and was chaired by Anand Panyarachun, former Prime

Minister of Thailand, who submitted the Panel's report to the Secretary-General on 1 December 2004.[9]

In the course of its works, the Panel organized extensive consultations with States, regional organizations, including the EU, academia and NGOs. The EU has made its own contribution to the debate, the Paper for Submission to the High-Level Panel on Threats, Challenges and Change, which was approved by the Council for transferral to the Panel in May 2004. This submission to the Panel is much more explicit on the conditions and the legal mandate for the use of force than the Strategy itself. The EU first reaffirms its commitment to a comprehensive approach, stressing the need for: 'economic, political and legal instruments, as well as military instruments, and close cooperation between states as well as international organizations across a range of sectors'. The paper emphasizes the need for Security Council authorization for use of force:

> In the view of the EU, it should remain for the Security Council, in accordance with its primary responsibility for the maintenance of international peace and security, to decide on the appropriate response to the risks in any situation that is brought to its attention, and to form a judgement on the appropriate course of action in any given situation.

This applies in particular in case of 'actual or threatened failure of state institutions' and in a 'responsibility to protect' scenario, when a State is unable or unwilling to safeguard its own population from harm. The latter scenario is clearly linked to the concept of human security, as it accepts that the security of every individual rather than that of the State is the ultimate objective. The 'responsibility to protect' is thus explicitly included in the EU submission to the High-Level Panel, contrary to the Strategy itself: the first draft of the Strategy spoke of States that 'persistently violate international norms *of domestic governance or of international behaviour* [author's emphasis]', which clearly covers threats posed by States to their own population, but the latter phrase was deleted in the final version. With regard to terrorism and WMD in the hands of non-state actors as well, although recognizing that this is a 'potentially devastating threat', the submission to the High-Level Panel states: 'In this context, the EU is of the view that military action going beyond the lawful exercise of the right of self-defence should be taken on the basis of Security Council decisions'. A gradual and comprehensive process of intervention is outlined:

> Actions that the Security Council might take, in response to an actual or threatened crisis situation, and in the light of political, humanitarian and economic considerations, include, as appropriate, inter alia:

---

[9] The other members were Robert Badinter (France), João Clemente Baena Soares (Brazil), Gro Harlem Brundtland (Norway), David Hannay (UK), Mary Chinery-Hesse (Ghana), Gareth Evans (Australia), Enrique Iglesias (Uruguay), Amre Moussa (Egypt), Satish Nambiar (India), Sadako Ogata (Japan), Yevgeny Primakov (Russia), Qian Qichen (China), Nafis Sadik (Pakistan), Salim Ahmed Salim (Tanzania) and Brent Scowcroft (US).

Calling attention of the authorities of the state in question to the risks in the current situation and to their obligations towards its citizens;

The establishment, with the collaboration of the Secretariat, UN agencies and offices, regional organizations, the BWIs, the donor community and NGOs of an integrated plan for the reinforcement of institutions, the security system, and the promotion of economic and social development;

The mandating of a civilian mission to the country in question, under the leadership of a Special Representative of the Secretary-General, to work closely with the authorities of the state in question, as well as with the UN country team, in the implementation of such an integrated plan;

The imposition, where appropriate, of carefully targeted sanctions, aimed at changing the behaviour of the leadership, without harming the economic and social interests of the general population. Any arms embargo imposed should be strictly monitored and implemented, if necessary through vigorous engagement with the states in which illegally imported arms are manufactured or which they transit;

If warranted by ongoing security conditions and crisis management needs, the mandating of a rapid reaction force and/or a military peacekeeping mission.

The status of this EU submission to the High-Level Panel is perhaps debatable: some regard it more as an academic contribution than as an official EU position. It is explicitly mentioned that Member States can also still submit national contributions. Nevertheless, if read together with the Strategy, this document serves as further confirmation of the fact that for the EU, use of force is an instrument of last resort, to be used only with Security Council authorization. This is the line put forward by the Panel itself in its recommendations, which the EU therefore should wholeheartedly support.

The High-Level Panel's Report

As a first step to the reinvigoration of the collective security system, the Panel stresses the importance of finding a 'new security consensus', i.e. consensus on the range of issues to be dealt with collectively by the Security Council. Such a consensus, which must include *everybody's* primary security concerns, is the basis of the legitimacy of the collective security system, which cannot function if major concerns of specific countries or of a specific nature are felt to be systematically ignored. The Panel identifies six clusters of threats (p.12) which include both the politico-military and other dimensions of international relations:

- economic and social threats, including poverty, infectious diseases and environmental degradation;
- inter-State conflict;
- internal conflict, including civil war, genocide and other large-scale atrocities;
- nuclear, radiological, chemical and biological weapons;

- terrorism;
- transnational organized crime.

The second step is to find consensus on how to deal with these challenges. Following on from its recognition of both military and non-military issues as equally important, the Panel advocates a comprehensive approach – 'comprehensive collective security': the primary objective must be prevention, which begins with development, hence recommendations for States to recommit to the goal of eradicating extreme poverty, to bring official development aid (ODA) to the level of 0.7 per cent of GNP, and to provide greater debt relief to highly-indebted poor countries. Just like the EU in its Security Strategy the Panel has come to the conclusion that all dimensions of international relations are inextricably linked, and that durable results with regard to the politico-military dimension therefore cannot be achieved if the other dimensions, i.e. the other global public goods, are ignored. Prevention especially demands a comprehensive approach. As the Panel itself recognizes, not everybody will agree with defining problems such as poverty and HIV/AIDS in terms of security threats. Although this can be seen as an effort to raise their importance in the eyes of the powers that be, the social and economic issues are different from the other threats identified by the panel in the sense that they do not imply any threat of violence, nor can they be dealt with by politico-military means. Rather, as implied in the Security Strategy, the socio-economic challenges constitute the background to, and the root causes of, the specific politico-military threats. Since according to the terms of reference (UN, 2003) the Panel was to confine itself to the field of peace and security, 'broadly interpreted', its report naturally does not have the same scope and depth when dealing with the non-politico-military aspects. This dimension is covered in detail however by the report of Jeffrey Sachs (2005), also commissioned by the Secretary-General, on the implementation of the MDGs. Presented to the Secretary-General in January 2005, this report should be considered the companion to the work of the High-Level Panel.

With regard to States that violate their international commitments or their obligations towards their own people, politico-military measures can of course be necessary, but a gradual process is recommended, with the use of force as a last resort. With regard to WMD proliferation the primary course of action advised by the Panel focuses on strengthening the treaty regime, particularly in the field of verification, and on reducing the demand for WMD, *inter alia* by including disarmament in negotiations to resolve regional conflicts and by a reaffirmation by the nuclear-weapon States of their commitment not to use nuclear weapons against a non-nuclear-weapon State. With regard to terrorism a strong emphasis is put on addressing the 'causes or facilitators', such as lack of democracy and respect for human rights, occupation and major political grievances, poverty, and State collapse. Just as is the case for the EU individually, the effectiveness of such collective measures will however be enhanced by the possession of a credible capacity for collective coercive action; a credible option to use force serves as a facilitator for the range of non-coercive instruments.

The Panel proposes a set of criteria to judge the need for the use of force (pp.57-8), which are very similar to those proposed by the ICISS (Evans, 2003), thus providing for *ex ante* accountability:

> In considering whether to authorize or endorse the use of military force, the Security Council should always address – whatever other considerations it may take into account – at least the following five basic criteria of legitimacy:
> (a) *Seriousness of threat.* Is the threatened harm to State or human security of a kind, and sufficiently clear and serious, to justify prima facie the use of military force? In the case of internal threats, does it involve genocide and other large-scale killing, ethnic cleansing or serious violations of international humanitarian law, actual or imminently apprehended?
> (b) *Proper purpose.* Is it clear that the primary purpose of the proposed military action is to halt or avert the threat in question, whatever other purposes or motives may be involved?
> (c) *Last resort.* Has every non-military option for meeting the threat in question been explored, with reasonable grounds for believing that other measures will not succeed?
> (d) *Proportional means.* Are the scale, duration and intensity of the proposed military action the minimum necessary to meet the threat in question?
> (e) *Balance of consequences.* Is there a reasonable chance of the military action being successful in meeting the threat in question, with the consequences of action not likely to be worse than the consequences of inaction?

As to the question of the legal mandate for the use of force, the Panel reaffirms the validity of the Charter (p.13):

> In all cases, we believe that the Charter of the United Nations, properly understood and applied, is equal to the task: Article 51 needs neither extension nor restriction of its long-understood scope, and Chapter VII fully empowers the Security Council to deal with every kind of threat that States may confront. The task is not to find alternatives to the Security Council as a source of authority but to make it work better than it has.

The Panel accepts the possibility of unilateral pre-emptive action under Article 51 – apparently ignoring the lack of consensus either way between international law experts – but only within strict limitations (p.54): 'However, a threatened State, according to long established international law, can take military action as long as the threatened attack is *imminent*, no other means would deflect it and the action is proportionate'. The Panel (p.54) even expressly excludes 'the acquisition, with allegedly hostile intent, of nuclear weapons-making capability' from such application of Article 51, so the concept of 'compulsory non-proliferation' as a measure of self-defence that some have advocated is rejected. Analyzing the report, unilateral pre-emptive action thus seems possible only if there is clear proof of a decision to launch an attack by a State or a non-State actor, such as a terrorist group. In the latter case, the criterion of proportionality is particularly relevant: if a terrorist group operates without the consent of the State in which it is based, any action undertaken should be targeted specifically against the implicated individuals and should aim only to pre-empt the planned attack. One can assume that action with a wider scope falls within the scope of Article 51 only if the State concerned actively supports a terrorist group operating from its territory (McMillan, 2004), as was the case of the Taliban regime in Afghanistan, and even in such cases the Panel seems to prefer the Security Council to take the lead. Besides, one should question the effectiveness of military intervention to halt terrorism – most probably an earlier intervention in Afghanistan would not have prevented '9/11', the actual perpetrators of which were based elsewhere. Enhanced cooperation between police and (military and civilian) intelligence services and coordination of legal measures addressing for example, the financing of terrorist groups, which is the EU approach, seem to be the primary instruments to *prevent* terrorism – military intervention is usually a reaction to terrorist attacks. Earlier in the report, the Panel specifically notes (p.47) that non-compliance with anti-terrorism measures is more frequently a matter of a lack of capacity than of insufficient will; hence capacity-building is an important instrument. In order to deal with States willingly refusing to comply, the Panel calls on the Security Council to devise a schedule of pre-determined sanctions.

In any case, *proving* the imminence of an attack will always be very difficult, especially with regard to non-State actors. Since it is difficult to assess by means of objective criteria – as the case of Iraq has demonstrated – the matter is de facto left to the discretion of the individual State concerned (Simma, 1994, p.676) and the risk of abuse therefore great. If the notion of imminence is accepted, it must therefore be interpreted very strictly; if time allows at all, seeking the consent of the Security Council would be highly recommendable.

A related issue which is not specifically addressed by the Panel is the fact that under Article 51 the right to use force in self-defence is of a subsidiary nature: it lasts only until the Security Council has taken the necessary measures to maintain peace and security; this implies that operations would have to be halted when the Security Council seizes the matter. Because of the inaction of the Security Council for a long period of its existence, this restriction has however been almost devoid of practical significance (Simma, 1994, p.677), but in the present circumstances it becomes relevant again. It is unclear how this restriction relates to the situation in Afghanistan, where the initial operation Enduring Freedom, undertaken by a coalition of the willing on the basis of Article 51, as the President of the Security Council recognized, continues to exist alongside the UN-mandated International Security Assistance Force (ISAF). Tensions have arisen because of the different objectives and *modus operandi* of both missions, which at times seem difficult to reconcile – ISAF is primarily a peacekeeping operation, whereas Enduring Freedom concerns combat operations against the remaining terrorist and Taliban elements.

In all other cases than the strict application of Article 51, it is thus up to the Security Council to assume responsibility, that is to decide what measures to take and whether to authorize use of force, including, if necessary, 'preventively and before a latent threat becomes imminent'. So the Panel clearly expects the Security Council to work proactively and resolutely, which is perfectly possible under the present Chapter VII: in recent years the Security Council has already widened the notion of a threat to international peace and security to include such issues as refugees, worsening humanitarian situations (e.g. UNSCR 794 on Somalia in 1992) and terrorism (e.g. UNSCR 748 on Libya in 1992), thus enabling it to act preventively (AIV, 2004b, pp.8-9). Kagan (2004, p.143) rightly notes that 'the real issue may not be prevention itself but who is doing the preventing'. The issues to be dealt with include, in the view of the Panel, the problem of proliferation, with a strong call for strengthened links between the Security Council and the IAEA and the OPCW, in order to inform the Council at an early stage of any serious concerns, allowing it to mandate verification and, if necessary, coercive measures. The Panel (p.57) also explicitly includes the 'responsibility to protect' in the duties of the Security Council, a significant recognition of this human security-related concept:

> We endorse the emerging norm that there is a collective international responsibility to protect, exercisable by the Security Council authorizing military intervention as a last resort, in the event of genocide and other large-scale killing, ethnic cleansing or serious violations of international humanitarian law which sovereign Governments have proved powerless or unwilling to prevent.

The human security approach is further evident in the dedication of a specific chapter of the Panel's report (Chapter XII, pp.62-3) to the importance of taking effective measures to ensure the protection of civilians in armed conflict. The recognition of the 'responsibility to protect' is indeed important, for as Weiss (2004, p.141) notes: 'With Washington's focus elsewhere, the danger is not too much but rather too little humanitarian intervention' – terrorism and WMD often risk pushing human rights and human security off the agenda.

In the same way it has a 'responsibility to protect', the Security Council also has a 'duty to prevent' as Feinstein and Slaughter (2004) submit – but the Security Council only. According to the Panel, the negative consequences of the alternative option, i.e. to broaden the scope for unilateral action, would just be too great:

> in a world full of perceived potential threats, the risk to the global order and to the norm of non-intervention on which it continues to be based is simply too great for the legality of unilateral preventive action, as distinct from collectively endorsed action, to be accepted. Allowing one to act so is to allow all (p.55).

Like the ICISS, the High-Level Panel does provide for a – small – backdoor with regard to use of force by regional organizations. It is indeed a trend that, as the Panel itself recognizes in its report, regional organizations such as the EU act as subcontractors for the UN. As the Panel states (p.71):

> Their efforts need not contradict the United Nations efforts, nor do they absolve the United Nations of its primary responsibilities for peace and security. The key is to organize regional action within the framework of the Charter [...].

This concerns, first of all, the legal mandate: while stressing that 'Security Council authorization should in all cases be sought for regional peace operations', the Panel accepts that 'in some urgent situations that authorization may be sought after such operations have commenced'. The criterion for omitting *a priori* authorization is thus the urgency of the situation rather than, as in the ICISS report, inaction on the part of the Security Council. It is thus less evident that this exception as viewed by the Panel would apply in the case of Kosovo, which inspired the ICISS. Also like the ICISS, the Panel seems to accept operations without prior authorization only within the area of jurisdiction of each regional organization, for the Panel refers to the example of organizations such as NATO (p.71) that 'have undertaken peacekeeping operations beyond their mandated areas' to state that: 'We welcome this so long as these operations are authorized by and accountable to the Security Council'. The Panel thus creates a certain margin for action by regional organizations, principally vis-à-vis their own members, based probably on the fact that these States have subscribed to such organizations, and the commitments they entail, by their own choice, hence the enhanced legitimacy of actions by regional organizations within their area of jurisdiction. Nevertheless, it would be recommendable to interpret this exception very strictly, for its use creates a *fait accompli*: once action has been taken by a regional organization, the Security Council when seized *a posteriori* would have almost no choice but to authorize it or at least to accept its consequences and authorize any follow-up operations. Furthermore, the more emphasis is put on possibilities to act without prior Security Council authorization, the less inclined some will be to seek a mandate from the Council. The fact remains however that there is simply no simple answer to the dilemma posed by inactivity on the part of the Security Council in the face of threats to human life demanding action under the 'responsibility to protect': to bypass the Council and break international law, with the potential consequences for the system which this entails, or to remain passive and allow innocent people to be murdered (Debiel, 2004). Thus one cannot but allow for a certain degree of *Realpolitik*, but because of the need to preserve the collective security system, the *general principle* must be that what applies to States must apply to regional organizations as well: unilateral use of force is limited to the strict application of Article 51.

The members of both the EU and NATO actually seem to prefer the launching of operations on behalf of the UN, rather than contributing troops to UN operations directly under the command of New York. This attitude appears to be motivated *inter alia* by the experience of Rwanda, when communications between the UN Headquarters and the force commander on the ground, and hence decision-making, proved to be slow and cumbersome, which increases the risks for the troops in the field. It is evident however that in all cases the political authority must remain with the Security Council: the body that authorizes an operation and sets its objectives decides when the objectives have been achieved, have to be adjusted or have to be abandoned. In practice however, the exact nature of the relationship between the Security Council and a regional organization implementing an operation on its behalf is often far from clear, hence the importance of the Panel's recommendation (p.71) to formalize cooperation and consultation in an agreement. This could be the objective of the next 'high-level meetings' between the UN Secretary-General and regional organizations, which would thus gain substance. Five such meetings have taken place between 1994 and 2003 to explore ways of strengthening cooperation; the Security Council, in 2003 and 2004, has also held meetings with regional organizations (Graham and Felício, 2004, pp.26-36).

An important related issue that is less explicitly addressed by the Panel is that of the *ex post* accountability of regional organizations as well as States that use force under Article 51, pre-emptively or otherwise, or that implement an operation as subcontractor of the UN. The obligation to report the measures taken to the Security Council is in all cases well-established, but more specific use could be made of these reports to evaluate whether the action was effective, proportionate and undertaken in a way consistent with the principles of the UN. In this context the relevance is evident of the conviction, expressed by the Solana-inspired Study Group on Europe's Security Capabilities (Kaldor et al., 2004), that military operations aiming to achieve comprehensive and human security-related objectives require a distinctive doctrine. In the case of pre-emptive action, the Security Council could also assess the validity of the claim of the existence of an imminent threat. The idea has been raised to link certain consequences to the result of such evaluation, e.g. the obligation to compensate those who suffered harm as a result of the action or to provide financial support for the restoration of infrastructure (Buchanan and Keohane, 2004). This would seem particularly relevant with regard to those that have undertaken pre-emptive action and could perhaps function as a useful brake on such use of Article 51.

A New Consensus?

In conclusion, the Panel does not recommend a major overhaul of the system. The significance of the High-Level Panel report is that it can serve as a basis to forge a political consensus again between the principal world actors – in the first place among the P5 – about the validity, interpretation and implementation of the collective security system such as it is. Such a consensus is essential: it is indeed a condition of the international order that law must evolve in response to developments, as the Security Strategy says, but it must remain an international *order*, not an anarchy in which every State acts unilaterally at his own discretion.

The first part of this consensus concerns the range of threats to collective security to be addressed by the system, i.e. by the Security Council. If such a consensus can be found, the inclusion of terrorism and WMD proliferation in the six clusters identified by the Panel should be welcomed in Washington as proof that its current main concerns are shared by the whole world, and that accordingly the will is there to deal with them resolutely. On the other hand, the inclusion of non-military, economic and social threats among the priorities on the agenda of the Security Council, and the incorporation of human security, should be welcomed by the major actors of the developing world, and by the EU, since the recognition of their importance equal to the politico-military dimension is the basis of the comprehensive approach. If agreement can be found on the threats, then consensus on how to deal with them is the next step. Again, Washington should be pleased by the recognition of the possibility of pre-emptive action under Article 51, including against terrorists, be it within strict limitations, and by the recommendation to deal with security threats, including proliferation, collectively but resolutely and preventively. The emphasis on collective action and on a gradual process of intervention should be welcomed by most others. The Panel has in fact adopted the approach to the use of force advocated by the ICISS, based notably on the five criteria, but has widened its scope of application to include not only the 'responsibility to protect', but other politico-military threats as well.

The Panel's report thus contains the elements of a suitable compromise. On the one hand, the call for a policy of capacity-building in order to empower third States in the framework of the fight against terrorism could be the basis for increased concrete cooperation between the EU and the US. Existing cooperation between police, intelligence and judicial services could be supplemented by a stepped-up joint effort to set up similar cooperation with other States and to help them increase their capacity to deal with terrorism. The EU's Mediterranean partners could very well be the priority target States. This could be done in the framework of wider coordination of policies towards such States, for example with regard to setting objectives for political and economic reform and defining incentives; joint initiatives could be imagined to rebuild failing and failed States and devise support programmes. Strengthening and reforming States is an instrument that serves effective governance with regard to all global public goods, from the fight against terrorism to democracy promotion (Slaughter, 2004). The financial contribution of the EU as well as its expertise would be greatly welcomed by the US; the ongoing development of deployable civilian capabilities by the EU is geared to just such undertakings. Such civilian cooperation extends to Afghanistan, where major efforts are undertaken but much remains to be done, and, once the security situation has stabilized, to Iraq. Furthermore, acceptance by the EU of the possibility of pre-emptive action against imminent terrorist attack would be an important gesture vis-à-vis the US. On the other hand, the US could subscribe to the collective approach to deal with, in the first place, proliferation issues, and support *inter alia* a strengthening of the treaty regimes, as well as EU policy towards Iran – Washington does not have a viable alternative anyway, for as long as it is tied up in Iraq, military intervention is not an option.

In the end, everything boils down to the political will of the members of the Security Council and of the UN in general to assume the huge – and exclusive – responsibilities that the Charter accords to the Council and to make the system work. The efficacy of the collective security system depends on the will of the Member States sitting in the Security Council to effectively address crises and developments relating to the six clusters of threats, preventively and using *all* the instruments at hand, and on the will of all to contribute the necessary means for the Security Council's decisions to be implemented and, if necessary, enforced. Only then will the UN be able to enhance its authority with regard to both those who would risk acts of aggression against others or against their own population and those who would risk unilateral action outside the UN system, either alone or in the framework of a coalition of the willing.

A political framework based on the High-Level Panel report – notably on the five criteria to judge the use of force – would not be a panacea: political will would have to be found on a case-by-case basis; action will still be more easily forthcoming when what are perceived as 'key states' are involved (Mair, 2005, p.92); difficult decisions would still have to be faced when the use of the 'carrot' does not yield results; members of the Security Council would have to stop taking decisions on the course of action in function of limited national interests and fears of precedents; no overall solution for the promotion of democracy and the inevitability of dealing with authoritarian regimes presents itself; the resources available do not weigh up to the number of crises, failing States and human rights violations requiring some sort of action by the international community. But it would be a start. If the Panel's recommendations were implemented, the chance would at least be greater that *more* security concerns would come to the attention of the Security Council, at an *earlier* stage – and the earlier action is taken, the bigger the chances of success and the smaller the need for coercive measures. Such a political framework could also be referred to by NGOs and civil society to put pressure on members of the Security Council to act when faced with situations covered by it. It would make it more difficult not to act in the face of public opinion. In the words of Panel member Gareth Evans (2004, p.77):

> I am a firm believer that good process produces, if not always optimal, at least better outcomes. If the process demands that criteria have to be systematically discussed, it is much more difficult to duck, weave, fudge, dissimulate and simply ignore critical issues: colleagues will ask harder questions, and even the press will sometimes start asking the right questions. At the end of the day strong arguments will look stronger and weak arguments weaker, and these appearances do matter.

Implementing this part of the Panel's recommendations does not require an amendment of the Charter. A consensus could however be expressed in a 'solemn declaration', a document of constitutional significance, such as the Millennium Declaration, in which the Member States of the UN would express their commitment to collective security (Ortega, 2004).

The EU Contribution to Collective Security

As one of the Panel's members, Lord David Hannay (2005), noted, 'the fit between the Panel's proposals and EU objectives is astonishingly close', a fact which, as he emphasizes, has consequences:

> But this presents the EU with a fundamental challenge: can its foreign policy move beyond warm words and fine-sounding communiqués to action; and can it deploy its influence to convince less enthusiastic members to move forward?

With two of the P5 among its Member States, the EU is one of the primary addressees of the High-Level Panel report, although the EU as such is of course not a member of the UN. Secretary-General Annan himself presented the report to the December 2004 European Council, which welcomed the work of the Panel, 'in particular the comprehensive approach to collective security', and clearly stated that 'The follow-up to the European Security Strategy [...] should aim at supporting the efforts of the UN Secretary-General'. Earlier, on 8 December, an EU Presidency Statement to the UN General Assembly had expressed strong support for the Secretary-General, commending him 'for his leadership and vision to establish the High-Level Panel'. As External Relations Commissioner Benita Ferrero-Waldner (2004) stated just after the report's release, the Panel's 'holistic approach echoes the EU's own commitment to a comprehensive conception of security'. It is only logical therefore that the EU should wholeheartedly support the implementation of the Panel's recommendations, which are so much in line with the EU's Security Strategy.

Perhaps the two European permanent members of the Security Council, France and the UK, who belonged to opposite 'camps' on the Iraq crisis, could *together* play an important role in promoting consensus. Together, and jointly with High Representative Solana, they could reach out to the other permanent members: to Washington, echoing London's efforts, before the invasion of Iraq, to steer the US towards a solution in a multilateral framework; to Moscow, which along with Paris opposed the invasion; and to Beijing, perhaps the most difficult of all to convince of the merits of the Panel's work. But one should not forget that for many Southern governments as well the Panel's recommendations, especially the notion of the 'responsibility to protect', are highly controversial (Berdal, 2004, p.95). The EU could include the Panel's report among the topics for multi- and bilateral political dialogue in its regional partnerships and with its partner countries, emphasizing that the 'responsibility to protect' is but one element in a comprehensive approach, be it one that for reasons of principle and humanitarian concerns is highly important. As Annan (2004) said to the European Council: 'As we move ahead, full European engagement will be essential. [...] the world now looks to you to support a global multilateral framework'.

The EU also has a practical contribution to make to the UN: as a global actor and with two of the P5 in its ranks, it must assume its part of the responsibility for the maintenance of international peace and security. The enlarged EU is in any case an essential part of the UN; the EU-25 account for 38 per cent of the UN's general budget. Based on the similarity of both organizations' approaches, which was of course evident long before the publication of the European Security Strategy and the High-Level Panel report, a close partnership has been established. In the field of peace and security, the major step was the adoption, by the June 2001 Göteborg European Council, of a declaration on EU-UN Cooperation in Conflict Prevention and Crisis Management, which named three priority areas for the strengthening of cooperation: conflict prevention, the civilian and military aspects of crisis management, and particular regional issues (the Balkans, the Middle East, the Great Lakes Region, the Horn of Africa and West Africa). In the field of conflict prevention and early warning, both the EU and the UN have created extensive instruments, such as indicators of conflict potential, for the worldwide monitoring of developments, the efficacy of which can only increase by combining the assembled information. On 24 September 2003 both organizations signed a joint declaration on cooperation in crisis management, with the aim of increasing coordination and compatibility of mission planning units, training, communication (between situation centres as well as desk-to-desk dialogue and exchange of liaison officers) and best practices. A Steering Committee at working level was established in February 2004. Regular meetings now take place between staff from both organizations, involving, on the side of the EU, the Policy Unit, the

EU Military Staff, the Council Secretariat and the Commission, and, on the side of the UN, DPA, DPKO, OCHA and the UN Situation Centre (Manca, 2004). A specific Council Working Group, CONUN, covers EU-UN relations.

The EU-25 contribute about 40 per cent of the UN's peacekeeping budget, making the EU the largest contributor by far (European Union, 2004), but their contribution in terms of manpower is rather smaller. In November 2004 the EU-25 provided 4,836 military observers, civilian police and troops for UN operations or only about 7.5 per cent out of a total of about 64,000 (UN, 2004). In recent years, the absolute numbers of EU troop contributions have not varied that much, but the overall number of UN operations and of troops engaged has risen enormously – for example in November 1998 only about 15,000 troops were deployed on UN operations – so the relative weight of the EU contribution has greatly diminished. This is a distorted image however, since these figures only take into account operations under direct UN command. EU Member States further contribute in much more substantial numbers to operations mandated by the UN but undertaken by the EU and NATO: about 7,000 in Bosnia-Herzegovina (EU operation Althea), over 16,000 in Kosovo (about 70 per cent of NATO's KFOR) and about 4,000 in Afghanistan (over 60 per cent of NATO-led ISAF). If these operations are counted as well, the EU Member States are on average deploying some 32,000 men in support of the UN, which represents about half of the average total deployment of European forces at any one time in 2003–2004.

The first ESDP military operation which the EU implemented completely autonomously, that is without the use of NATO assets, was in fact an operation requested by the Security Council, which in Resolution 1484 (30 May 2003) authorized the deployment of an 'interim emergency multinational force' in Bunia in the Democratic Republic of the Congo, where armed militias threatened the security of the local population and humanitarian aid workers, in order to allow the UN time to reinforce the military presence of MONUC, the UN mission, in the region. The EU operation, baptized Artemis, was one of limited scope, in time (12 June – 1 September 2003), in scale (about 2,000 deployed, including 400 at the support base at Entebbe airport in Uganda) as well as geographically (securing the town of Bunia in the Eastern province of Ituri), but it certainly was a high-risk operation, in an extremely volatile environment, undertaken at very short notice at a great distance from the EU. Its successful implementation served to boost Europe's confidence in the abilities of ESDP. France acted as framework nation for this operation, providing the operational headquarters in Paris, the operation commander, Major General Bruno Neveux, and the force commander on the ground, Brigadier General Jean-Paul Thonier, as well as the bulk of the troops, with 17 States in all participating. Artemis can be seen as an expression of the EU's commitment to the UN, as well as of its – developing – special interest in helping to maintain peace and security in Africa, which seems to be much lower on the agenda of NATO or the US, at least as far as contributing to peace support operations goes. The operation also highlighted the need to detail the relations between the Security Council and the EU when acting on behalf of the former (Tardy, 2004, pp.63-4). On a practical level, the EU and France at first appeared reticent to communicate all information regarding the deployment. At the political level, the EU apparently did not accept any subordination of the Political and Security Committee to the Security Council, though it did of course report to the Security Council on the implementation of the mandate as stipulated in Resolution 1484.

Operation Artemis subsequently served as a model for the so-called battlegroup concept. Acting on the original proposal by France, Germany and the UK, the EU has decided to create battlegroups, each some 1,500 strong (one combat battalion plus supporting units), which must be able to deploy no later than ten days after an EU decision to launch an operation and be sustainable for 120 days until the termination of the operation or relief by another, larger and longer-term force. By 2007 the EU aims to be able to undertake two concurrent battlegroup-sized operations. Member States' commitments made in November 2004 are to eventually create 13 national and multinational battlegroups. The EU has stated its intention to deploy the battlegroups primarily at the request of the UN, either for small-scale stand-alone operations, or as the initial entry force pending the deployment of a longer-term UN operation (or an operation by another regional organization, such as the African Union), or as an interim force between two such operations – the so-called bridging model. As the UN's force generation process tends to be rather cumbersome, this would represent a very welcome addition to the UN's capabilities. The High-Level Panel expressly welcomed the EU initiative and recommended that 'Others with advanced military capabilities should be encouraged to develop similar capacities at up to brigade level and to place them at the disposal of the United Nations' (p.59).

However, a military contribution equal to its economic and political weight – and its share in the UN's peacekeeping budget – would demand a greater effort from the EU than the implementation of the battlegroup concept, important though this may be. The offer to undertake interim operations for the UN is extremely useful, but one would expect an effective commitment to, for example, peace in the DRC also to be translated into long-term participation in peacekeeping, *in casu* MONUC. Interim work is fine, but it does not bring the same status and recognition as a permanent contract. Even when taking into account the participation of Member States' forces in 'subcontracted' operations, the current contribution of about 32,000 by the EU-25 does not seem proportionate to their combined capacity or to the position of the EU in the UN system, especially when considering that its members have two permanent seats in the Security Council. In comparison, in November 2004 the *seven* largest contributors of military forces and civilian police together also provided over 32,000 personnel for ongoing UN operations: Bangladesh, Pakistan, Nigeria, India, Ethiopia, Ghana and Nepal (the first two accounting for 8,212 and 7,503 respectively) – countries that do not exactly have the same wealth or sophisticated military capabilities as the EU. It must also be noted that the UN-mandated EU and NATO operations are either taking place on the European continent, or, as regards Afghanistan, as a follow-up to an initial operation of self-defence. The EU thus seems to assume only a limited part of the UN's responsibility for the maintenance of *worldwide* peace and security, apart from its financial contribution to the peacekeeping budget. Mainly financing other States' troops falls short however of the burden-sharing that can be expected from one of the most powerful global actors. Likewise, highly commendable efforts to empower other regional organizations to undertake peace support operations, such as the African Union through the African Peace Facility, do not absolve the EU from its own responsibility, certainly not while the AU's capacity is still far from fully-fledged (Gowan, 2004b). It would in effect detract from the universality of the UN if people could only count on the security which their own regional organization could provide (Goulding, 2002). An increased EU contribution of military and police forces is of paramount importance if the UN is to fulfil its collective security role, for currently, in view of the number of crises, 'there remains a glaring gap between the demand and the supply of capable peacekeeping forces that the international community can mobilize' (O'Hanlon and Singer, 2004, p.79).

It has to be recognized that currently the EU is constrained by the limited deployability of a large share of the Member States' armed forces. The High-Level Panel says as much (p.59): 'The developed States have particular responsibilities here, and should do more to transform their existing force capacities into suitable contingents for peace operations'. It is recommendable therefore that in the framework of 'effective multilateralism' the EU would include a future larger-scale contribution to UN-led or UN-mandated peace support operations around the world in the objectives of the capability-building process in ESDP. While it is sometimes feared in New York that fewer EU troops will be available for UN operations (Tardy, 2004, p.74), the further development of ESDP should actually enable the EU to contribute more:

- Assigning forces to UN-led operations remains a national decision, on a case-by-case basis, and several Member States have bilateral stand-by arrangements with the UN Department of Peacekeeping Operations (DPKO) in which they commit to maintain specific capabilities on stand-by in order to be able to react rapidly to requests from the UN Secretary-General if they so wish. This does not mean though that the Member States cannot jointly undertake to increase their contribution, agree a quantitative objective and take that into account when planning capability needs and defining requirements in the framework of ESDP. In its June 2004 declaration on EU-UN Cooperation in Military Crisis Management Operations the European Council launched the idea of a 'clearing house process' as a complementary role for the EU in this regard, with the aim of providing a framework for Member States to exchange information and coordinate their national contributions to UN operations.
- Similarly, a quantitative objective could be set, looking beyond the battlegroups and including both military and civilian capabilities, with regard to EU operations at the request of the UN, defining how many operations of which type – including peacekeeping – and at which scale the EU would be willing to undertake. These could be short and long-term EU-led operations, such as Artemis and Althea, under EU-command and under the political control of the Council and the Political and Security Committee and only indirectly of the Security Council. Perhaps specific components or modules

within the structure of a broader UN mission could also be envisaged, with an EU force commander in the field, but under the operational command of UN Headquarters in New York and under the direct political control of the Security Council. In both cases the relations between the various bodies involved in both organizations need further clarification. A specific type of high-intensity operation in which the UN is interested, but with regard to which the EU appears rather reluctant, is that of an 'over the horizon reserve' or 'extraction force', that is a EU reserve force that would be on stand-by if rapid response were required in support of a UN operation, for example in support of, or to evacuate, peacekeeping forces in case of an escalation of violence.

The EU also has civilian capabilities to contribute to deployment as part of integrated civil-military operations or for exclusively civilian missions. This is particularly relevant in the light of the Panel's recommendation (pp.83-5) to establish a Peacebuilding Commission, and a Peacebuilding Support Office, to fill a gap in the institutional architecture of the UN and create a body that can identify States in risk of collapse and coordinate international assistance to frail States and States in post-conflict situations. The ongoing development of the EU's civilian capabilities means that the EU could make an eminent contribution to such peacebuilding missions.

Security Council Reform

An issue that is closely related to the reinvigoration of the collective security system is that of Security Council reform. The legitimacy of UN decisions and actions in the field of international peace and security is inherently linked to the composition of its main decision-making body. The High-Level Panel has therefore taken up the long-standing demand for reform, hoping however that the debate over this high-profile issue would not overshadow the other important recommendations in its report.

As the Panel notes (p.66), the P5 in return for their veto power were expected to shoulder an extra burden in promoting global security, but in practice 'The financial and military contributions to the United Nations of some of the five permanent members are modest compared to their special status'. Obviously, the Security Council's decisions cannot be implemented by the members of the Council alone, but require contributions from all Member States, but 'the paucity of representation from the broad membership diminishes support for Security Council decisions'. The P5's veto power and the under-representation of certain continents thus combine to affect the legitimacy of Security Council decisions and the willingness of the Member States to help to implement them. The Panel therefore recommends enlarging the Security Council in order to involve more Member States in decision-making, especially those that contribute most to the UN. Two alternative models are put forward, both bringing the number of seats to 24, by creating either six additional permanent seats – without veto – and three additional two-year seats, or eight new four-year seats and one additional two-year seat. The Panel further recommends that when electing the additional permanent or new four-year members the General Assembly should give preference to the largest contributors to the UN. As to the veto power, while noting its 'anachronistic character that is unsuitable for the institution in an increasingly democratic age', the Panel pragmatically admits that is sees 'no practical way' of changing this (p.68), stressing however that reform should not lead to expansion of the veto.

Whether these recommendations will be acted upon is highly doubtful. Although many States are objective allies in demanding Security Council reform, they are competitors as soon as the question arises of which States are to sit on an enlarged Council, especially in schemes that provide for additional permanent members. The EU as well is highly divided on this issue, with some Member States supporting Germany's claim to a permanent seat and others opposing it. These differences are reflected in the EU's submission to the High-Level Panel, which simply says that 'The EU regrets that efforts to achieve a comprehensive reform of the Security Council have not so far proved successful'. The EU then reconfirms the commitment contained in the UN's Millennium Declaration, wherein Member States resolve 'to intensify our efforts to achieve a comprehensive reform of the Security Council in all its aspects' – but without actually putting forward any concrete proposal. At the same time, although technically France and the UK under Article 19 of the TEU should 'in the execution of their functions, ensure the defence of the positions and the interests of the Union, without prejudice to their responsibilities under the provisions of the United Nations Charter', in practice they all too often still pull the national card.

In the long term, a single permanent seat for the EU would be the logical consequence of the evolution of the CFSP towards ever deeper integration. This seat could be taken up by the EU Presidency, or better still, by the (representative of) the EU Foreign Minister provided for in the draft Constitutional Treaty. Of course, a single EU seat would require a truly common foreign policy, but this works both ways: having but one representative on the Security Council would oblige the EU to speak with a single voice or be absent from the debate altogether. Such an evolution would also be in line with the growing trend for the Security Council to rely on regional organizations as agents for the implementation of its decisions. Schemes have been elaborated for the composition of an enlarged Security Council based on regional organizations, which would each be represented in rotation by one of their Member States (Graham and Felício, 2005; Tavares, 2004). Presently, integration has not sufficiently advanced in all regions of the world for such a scenario to be feasible, but regional integration certainly is on the rise, as evidenced by the example of the African Union.

Even without enlargement, the representation of the Security Council could be enhanced by amending the arrangement of Member States in five regional groups in the General Assembly, which form the basis for the election of the ten non-permanent members of the Security Council: five are elected from the combined groups of African and Asian States, two from the group of Latin American and Caribbean States, two from the group of Western European and other States, and one from the group of Eastern European States. Clearly, this arrangement no longer corresponds to the current world order – the EU now spans two different regional groups – and it results in an over-representation of the Western world. Without amending the Charter, the Member States could also informally agree on a number of guidelines for the election, for example the contribution made to the UN budget and to UN peacekeeping (Holmes, 2004; Ortega, 2004).

Security Council reform will most probably remain difficult for some time to come and therefore care should be taken not to allow this issue to paralyze the debate on reforming and reinvigorating other aspects of the UN system. At the same time however one should not lose sight of Security Council reform as an ultimate objective.

Improving Global Governance

The High-Level Panel and the Sachs reports together constitute one single agenda, which in its entirety concerns all members of the UN. It is indeed the founding philosophy of the Charter itself that security and economic development are indivisible (Arnould, 2005b, p.3). For 'effective multilateralism' to be implemented, and in order to address the root causes of 'hard' security threats, enhancing the efficacy of global political, social, economic and environmental governance, at all levels, is as important as reinvigorating the global collective security system. Strong international institutions are required to manage globalization and ensure that it benefits all. This goes beyond even the social and economic threats identified by the Panel; all global public goods have to be covered. This need for global governance is also recognized in the redefinition of the overall objectives of EU external action in the Draft Constitution (Article III-292), which when compared with the present Article 11 of the TEU puts a stronger emphasis on 'an international system based on stronger multilateral cooperation and good global governance' – the latter notion a rather peculiar combination of two quite distinct concepts – and which adds a number of very ambitious objectives:

(d) foster the sustainable economic, social and environmental development of developing countries, with the primary aim of eradicating poverty;
(e) encourage the integration of all countries into the world economy, including through the progressive abolition of restrictions on international trade;
(f) help develop international measures to preserve and improve the quality of the environment and the sustainable management of global natural resources, in order to ensure sustainable development;
(g) assist populations, countries and regions confronting natural or man-made disasters.

The Strategy does not go into detail as to how effective global governance in these other fields is to be primarily pursued, i.e. how the institutional architecture can be improved and which are the priority policy fields in which action must be taken. With regard to the institutional dimension of EU-UN cooperation the Commission (2003c) has already elaborated extensive proposals. Perhaps at least a general direction could have been indicated in the Strategy. Now the need for global governance overall is rather obscured by the emphasis in the document on the politico-military dimension; the Strategy thus lends itself to criticism for lack of balance between the different dimensions or global public goods.

An important potential field of action is the reform of the UN's Economic and Social Council (ECOSOC) (Arnould, 2005a). The EU could step up its efforts to promote its reform so as to enable it to play a central role in crisis management in case of financial crisis, economic stagnation or famine, when a large number of different actors have to be brought together. Next to its traditional role of coordinating different spheres of economic and social development, ECOSOC would thus function as a sort of 'socio-economic security council', be it without the same binding powers. This would imply strengthening the links between ECOSOC and the Security Council, the World Bank, the International Monetary Fund and the World Trade Organization. ECOSOC's role as a portal for relations between the UN and the NGO and business communities should also be strengthened. The recent past demonstrates that the EU can act as a 'front-runner' in developing multilateral instruments:

> Where the EU has lent its active and undivided support to the adoption and effective implementation of key multilateral legal instruments – such as the Kyoto Protocol or the International Criminal Court – its voice has often been decisive in ensuring the 'critical mass' to facilitate their entry into force (European Commission, 2003c, p.5).

Next to reforming the global multilateral institutions, the EU must also reform itself. It is all too easily forgotten that although the EU is often seen as a proponent of multilateralism (González, 2004, p.67), in the South the EU's image often is that of an aggressive economic actor, quite the opposite of the 'benign' way in which the EU perceives itself as an international actor. Correcting that image requires an earnest effort on the part of the EU to take into account the South's access to global public goods. The Millennium Development Goals agreed upon by the UN provide an obvious beacon, which could serve to enhance coherence between the different international organizations (Culpeper, 2005, p.15). Integrating the targets and criteria agreed in the UN in its own bilateral and multilateral relations should be an integral part of the EU's comprehensive approach (European Commission, 2003c). As the biggest donor, the EU's part in the achievement of the MDGs is crucial. Through its development policy the EU is heavily committed to the MDGs, but more fundamental changes in EU policy, notably with regard to trade, will be needed in order to create an economic order that is truly inclusive and to effectively combat poverty. This will require substantial efforts on the part of the EU, such as debt relief, opening up its agricultural market – equally important at the global and the neighbourhood level – and to stop dumping subsidized agricultural products on the world market. By thus gaining the confidence of the developing countries, the EU could also win their support for its efforts in the WTO to reconcile global trade with its environmental and health policy objectives (Lagendijk and Wiersma, 2004, pp.111-14). The advantages to be gained work both ways, for promoting citizens' access to global public goods in the South implies raising their standard of living and setting minimal norms for wages and social security – and thus ultimately closing the wealth gap that is so destructive to the EU's model of the welfare state.

A very promising option would be the introduction at the European level of the so-called Spahn Tax. This is a variant of the Tobin Tax, the original proposal to impose a tax of 0.1 to 0.5 per cent on all speculative currency transactions. Since it is almost impossible to distinguish speculation from regular transactions however, the Tobin Tax would have to apply to all transactions and would thus have a paralyzing effect on the financial markets. The Spahn-variant proposes a more practicable, two-step approach: a general tax of 0.02 per cent, sufficiently low not to disturb the markets, would be imposed on all currency transactions; but if a currency would move outside certain pre-determined borders, a heavy tax of 80 per cent would apply in order to stop speculation and avoid financial crises and the disastrous socio-economic consequences that they entail. The tax would thus bring a double benefit: the general tax would generate an estimated 50 billion euro, which can be put to use for development, while the prohibitive 80 per cent tax would have a stabilizing effect on the financial markets. In 2004 Belgium adopted a law introducing the Spahn Tax conditional upon its adoption by all members of the Euro-zone. In the wake of the tsunami disaster in South-East Asia on 26 December 2004, Belgian Minister of Development Cooperation Armand De Decker repeated the appeal to his colleagues to earnestly consider the introduction of the tax in order to create a structural source of funds for reconstruction and development.

In these various fields of global governance as well, the EU is enhancing concrete cooperation with the UN. On 28 June 2004 the Commission and the United Nations Development Programme (UNDP) announced a strategic partnership focussing on governance, conflict prevention and post-conflict reconstruction, with particular attention for countries that emerge from conflict. While previous cooperation had been on an ad hoc basis, more systematic and targeted collaboration should now be possible. This partnership is to be the first in a series of partnerships with UN and associated agencies. On 19 July 2004 already it was followed by a partnership with the International Labour Organization in the field of poverty reduction and improvement of labour conditions in developing countries.

'Effective multilateralism' if effectively implemented would thus shape all dimensions of EU external action, not in function of 'hard' security concerns, but in function of the overall objective of improving every individual's access to the basic global public goods.

Chapter 5

Securing the Capabilities

The final part of the Strategy deals with the 'policy implications for Europe' of the strategic choices outlined in the previous chapters. This comprises the instruments and means which the EU needs to develop in order to implement the comprehensive approach, but also the decision-making process in the EU and the EU's partnerships. In the words of the Strategy: an EU that is more active, more capable and more coherent, and that works with partners. The first objective refers to 'a strategic culture that fosters early, rapid, and when necessary, robust intervention'. As put forward in Chapter 4, this commitment to effective preventive engagement is an integral part of the attempt to re-forge a global consensus on the reinvigoration of the collective security system of the UN. This chapter will focus on the need for coherence between the different dimensions of external action, on the opportunities for enhancing the EU's military and civilian capabilities, and on the future of the EU's most important partnership, that with the US.

Building Coherence

EU external action comprises a broad range of policy fields, from aid and trade to ESDP, in each of which the EU has a wide array of instruments at its disposal – the EU is an international actor well-equipped to deal with the complex international environment, as the Strategy itself stresses repeatedly. Objectives in different policy fields can be contradictory, however, and instruments are not always applied in a coherent and consistent manner. The dilemma between stability and democratization that the EU faces in its Mediterranean neighbourhood is a case in point: political support for the regimes in power and unconditional economic cooperation are often contradictory to objectives in the field of democracy and human rights. The protectionist agricultural policy and development policy provide another example of potentially clashing objectives, with damaging consequences for the EU's image in the South. The potential for conflict is equally evident between support for third States in the fight against terrorism and the promotion of human rights and the rule of law, although the EU very carefully attempts to avoid any abuse of the label of anti-terrorism by its partners. Very rightly therefore the Strategy states that 'the challenge now is to bring together the different instruments and capabilities'. A not to be misunderstood call for a comprehensive approach is included: 'Diplomatic efforts, development, trade and environmental policies, should follow the same agenda'. The promotion of global public goods can provide this integrative agenda.

Since coordination and integration of all dimensions of external action are at the heart of the comprehensive approach, coherence, although it may perhaps seem to be a vague and theoretical notion, is crucial to its effective implementation. By way of the integrative GPG agenda, coherence should be achieved at the level of policy objectives, instruments and means, across the three pillars. The comprehensive approach should ensure that this would not entail any securitization of the non-politico-military aspects of external action. Rather the CFSP/ESDP would be shaped by the overall objective of promoting GPG. As the Neighbourhood Policy demonstrates, this implies recognizing the links between the different GPG: to fully enjoy them, one has to have access to them all, so policies focussing on just one dimension cannot achieve durable results, hence the need to make military and economic cooperation conditional on respect for human rights. Because of the scale of the EU and the diversity of the policy fields and of the European and national actors involved, increasing coherence is far from an easy task.

One way of enhancing coherence would be to institutionalize it, that is to build in coordination and integration in the organization of the decision-making process, from the early stages of policy-design to the implementation of the decisions adopted. In that regard, the Draft Constitution (Articles I-28 and III-296) already includes far-reaching proposals, particularly the creation of a Union Minister of Foreign Affairs, who would combine the current positions of Commissioner for External Relations Benita Ferrero-Waldner and High Representative for the CFSP Javier Solana (Grevi, Manca and Quille, 2005). He/she will thus head the relevant departments of the Commission administration, dealing with the Community aspects of external action, such as development, trade, humanitarian aid and environmental cooperation, as well as of the Council administration, dealing with CFSP and ESDP. The Minister will also take part in political decision-making in both fields. As Vice-President of the Commission, he/she will be responsible for ensuring the consistency of all aspects of external action within the remit of the Commission and will thus have to work closely with the Commissioners responsible for specific aspects of external action. At the same time the Minister will not only represent the EU and its CFSP/ESDP and carry out Council decisions, which is the function of the current High Representative, but he/she will also have right of initiative, and will thus be able to propose policies, and more importantly still, will chair the Council when it deals with foreign affairs. Because of his/her 'double-hatted' position, the Minister will have the possibility of truly coordinating and integrating all dimensions of external action; as chair of the Foreign Affairs Council, he/she will moreover have the opportunity to act as an effective engine of external action in general.

Although different decision-making procedures will remain in vigour for Community and CFSP matters, this scheme constitutes a significant break-through of the pillar system, which currently greatly hinders effective coordination of policies. And although decisions on most CFSP issues will still require unanimity in the Council, the important responsibilities of the EU Minister of Foreign Affairs also imply a certain move away from an exclusively intergovernmental approach. Perhaps the way the Strategy was drafted, with a strong central role for Solana and the Policy Unit, but with the involvement of national diplomats, EU officials, academics and NGOs, can serve to illustrate the huge potential of a powerful EU Minister of Foreign Affairs. Member States allowed Solana to play a very proactive role (Grevi, 2004, p.3); without the direction of Solana and his staff, the classic negotiation process between the Member States would certainly have resulted in a much vaguer document.

The Draft Constitution (Article III-296.3) further provides that the Minister of Foreign Affairs will be assisted by a European External Action Service, which 'shall comprise officials from relevant departments of the General Secretariat of the Council and of the Commission as well as staff seconded from national diplomatic services of the Member States' (Maurer and Reichel, 2004). The different dimensions of external action could thus be integrated at the administrative level as well. This External Action Service could be limited to a small coordinating body that comprises just a few officials from all of the relevant departments, but ideally, in order to gain maximal coordination, its creation would entail a complete merger of all relevant Council and Commission departments, so as to establish a single unified administration dealing with all dimensions of external action. In the same line, the Commission representations abroad could then be reformed into EU representations that cover all of these dimensions. Including national diplomats in the External Action Service, as is the case in NATO's administration as well, would enhance the possibilities for effective coordination with Member States' national policies, for as the Strategy states coherence should also embrace the external activities of the individual Member States. Such detachment of national diplomats would at the same time strengthen Member States' sense of ownership of EU external action; one can hope that this would further stimulate the gradual Europeanization of foreign policy.

With regard to national diplomatic representations abroad, the Draft Constitution (Article III-306) merely provides that they 'shall step up coordination by exchanging information and carrying out joint assessments'. The Strategy includes a call for a 'stronger diplomatic capability', notably 'a system that combines the resources of Member States with those of EU institutions', but the reference to the desirability of pooling national diplomats in the first draft has been omitted, as the debate in the Convention and the IGC on the Constitution did not yield any result on this matter. Perhaps the detachment of national diplomats to the Commission/EU representations as well could forebode greater integration in this field too.

In its final version the Strategy adds that 'Better coordination between external action and Justice and Home Affairs policies is crucial in the fight both against terrorism and organized crime'. In the EU approach to both problems, international police and legal cooperation, within the EU and with third partners, plays a major role in prevention and repression. Since in the current security environment, the distinction between internal and external security has become blurred, these dimensions too must be coordinated with external action. Referring to the examples of the Balkans and West Africa – and the Great Lakes Region perhaps illustrates this even better – the final version of the Strategy also emphasizes that 'coherent policies are also needed regionally, especially in dealing with conflict', because 'problems are rarely solved on a single country basis, or without regional support'. This demonstrates the importance of working with partners and of the EU objective to support regional integration efforts in other parts of the world.

Building a Military Capacity

The military capabilities acquired through ESDP are the most recent addition to the EU's toolbox. As discussed in Chapter 1, since the inclusion of the Petersberg Tasks in the Amsterdam Treaty, it has been clear which *types* of military operations the EU can undertake. The Petersberg Tasks in effect mean everything but collective defence, which remains the prerogative of NATO, but including 'non-Article 5' operations at the high end of the spectrum of violence. The Strategy now also defines in support of which *objectives* military operations can be undertaken: building security in our neighbourhood and 'effective multilateralism' at the global level. The EU thus appears to show a clear resolve to contribute militarily to international peace and security, including if necessary through high-intensity operations. The EU's resolve has been demonstrated by the intention to create rapidly deployable 'battlegroups' to be projected mainly at the request of the UN and by the first EU military operations: Concordia in the FYROM and Artemis in the DRC. Implementing 'effective multilateralism' thus entails an important expeditionary military capacity as the ultimate instrument in the EU's toolbox (Biscop, 2004b).

EU-US: Mind the Gap

Quite regardless of recent developments in ESDP, a number of observers, on both sides of the Atlantic, still see the EU as incapable of autonomous military action, as increasingly incapable even of operating alongside the US, as a consequence, in their view, of not keeping up with technological developments and spending too little on defence. Putting aside the issue of the political will to use the military instrument, they feel that, based on the comparison with the US, the EU would have difficulties to act without the US or NATO, for lack of capabilities. To quote Kagan (2003, p.53):

> The effort to build a European force has so far been an embarrassment to Europeans. Today, the European Union is no closer to fielding an independent force, even a small one, than it was three years ago.

This opinion, currently shared by all too many European observers, contrasts sharply with the confidence in Europe's capacity to act militarily that was prevalent in the early 1990s, long before the creation of ESDP, before the entry into force of the Maastricht Treaty even. The civil war in Croatia is a case in point. To stop the fighting between Croats and Serbs and prevent escalation to Bosnia-Herzegovina, on 6 August 1991 the Twelve requested the Western European Union (WEU) to assess options for the deployment of a European interposition force.

Driven in particular by the French Chief of Staff, Admiral Jacques Lanxade, and his Belgian colleague, General José Charlier, four scenarios were elaborated, including one for a 30,000-strong force. All of these provided for autonomous European operations, without having recourse to US or NATO assets, since at the time Washington was not willing to intervene in what it considered to be a European problem. In October 1991 however the UK, the Netherlands and Portugal vetoed WEU involvement on the ground that military operations should remain the exclusive competence of NATO; British reluctance was also motivated by experiences in Cyprus and Northern Ireland and the fear that military intervention would lead to a difficult-to-manage guerrilla war. But from the point of view of military capabilities, Europe's ability to act apparently was never in doubt (Coolsaet, 2001, pp.529-30).

However, when Washington did intervene in former Yugoslavia, this was seen by many as proof of Europe's weakness as compared to the US and NATO. More recently, the Kosovo air campaign, which demonstrated the difficulty of European air forces to interoperate with their technologically more advanced US counterpart, seemed to confirm that judgement. The EU is of course not the military superpower that the US is, but the seemingly clear-cut comparison with the US hides a number of ambiguities. First of all, EU military capabilities should also be compared with those of other States, for they are the ones that EU forces will possibly be confronted with – the EU will not be fighting the US. Secondly, EU Member States have but a single set of forces, which can be deployed in a national, coalition of the willing, EU, NATO, OSCE or UN framework. The often lauded effectiveness of NATO thus depends on the quality and availability of European forces as well; conversely, a critique of European capabilities inherently is a critique of NATO. Evidently, it is quite impossible that the same forces are effective only when operating in a NATO framework and powerless when deployed under the EU flag. This further implies that two issues must be distinguished: the quantity and quality of EU Member States' forces per se, and the availability of assets and mechanisms such as command & control allowing them to be put to use in an EU context. Finally, the question must be asked whether the EU, in the light of its view on the use of force, needs the same types and size of capabilities as the US. A more objective look at European forces is thus required in order to assess the current military capacity of the EU as well as its future capability needs.

European Forces: The State of the Realm

The combined armed forces of the 25 EU Member States total over 1.8 million. From these, the Headline Goal (HG) agreed at the Helsinki European Council (December 1999) aims to make available to the EU the necessary capabilities, including the necessary command & control, intelligence, logistics and air and naval assets, to enable the deployment of 60,000 troops within 60 days and sustainable for a year. Given the need to rotate forces the HG would require a pool of some 180,000, allowing for forces on stand-by and standing down equal to the force deployed. As defined in the Capabilities Development Mechanism (CDM), follow-up of the HG is ensured by a working group of experts, the Headline Goal Task Force (HTF), with the support of the EU Military Staff (EUMS). First the Helsinki Headline Goal Catalogue (HHC) was drawn up, listing the capabilities required to achieve the HG; a call for voluntary contributions was then made; following the first Capabilities Commitment Conference (CCC; November 2000), the results of this call were listed in the Helsinki Force Catalogue (HFC). These amounted to about 100,000 troops, 400 combat aircraft and 100 naval vessels. Both the HHC and the HFC are regularly updated, taking into account additional requirements and adding new contributions (Lindstrom, 2004; WEU Assembly, 2003). At the May 2003 CCC, contributions from the ten new Member States and the six non-EU European members of NATO were added. This process led to the identification of a number of substantial qualitative shortfalls, listed in detail in the Capability Improvement Chart. The Audit of Assets and Capabilities for European Crisis Management Operations, conducted by the WEU in 1999, had already arrived at similar conclusions.

Following the second CCC (styled Capabilities Improvement Conference; November 2001) a European Capability Action Plan (ECAP) was therefore adopted, setting up 19 panels of national experts, with at least one lead-nation each, to propose solutions to remedy this original list of 42 shortfalls (Schmitt, 2004). Progress was not as rapid as expected however: out of a total of now 62 identified shortfalls, the May 2004 Capability Improvement Chart showed only seven to have been solved and four where the situation has improved; 23 of the remaining are considered 'significant in the assessment of capability'. These concern attack and transport helicopters, air-to-air refuelling, precision-guided munitions, deployable force headquarters, (high-tech) intelligence collection and strategic air- and sealift. The main problem seems to be the voluntary, bottom-up nature of the process, especially with regard to those shortfalls that require long-term investment in the development of new capabilities, for example satellite observation or strategic lift. ECAP remains an essentially intergovernmental process, with limited leadership and coordination, and with insufficient incentives for Member States to take action. At the 2003 CCC a second phase of ECAP was therefore launched. On the basis of the Helsinki Progress Catalogue (HPC), an analysis of the updated 2003 HHC and HFC, the ECAP panels were transformed into 15 project groups,[10] each with a lead-nation, which were to focus on the implementation of concrete projects, giving due attention to options such as leasing, multinational cooperation and specialization. The same drawbacks still applied however, and at the November 2004 CCC it was made clear that without additional measures the scope for further progress of the project groups was limited.

---

[10] Air-to-air refuelling; combat search and rescue; headquarters; nuclear, biological and chemical protection; special operations forces; theatre ballistic missile defence; unmanned aerial vehicles; strategic airlift; space-based assets; interoperability issues and working procedures for evacuation and humanitarian operations; intelligence, surveillance, target acquisition and reconnaissance; strategic sealift; collective medical protection; attack helicopters; support helicopters.

Quantitatively, an important pool of forces is thus available to the EU in the HFC, be it not sufficient to ensure rotation in the case of a full corps-sized deployment of 60,000, but that is a rather unlikely scenario. Qualitatively, a number of important shortfalls remain, notably in the fields of secure and deployable command, control and communications, intelligence, and strategic transport. Quality also relates to the 'usability' of forces. Out of the combined Member States' armed forces, about 10% or 170 to 180,000 have been estimated to be usable for deployment as combatants (Lindley-French and Algieri, 2004, p.27; EUISS, 2004, p.100). Given the need for rotation, about a third of these could be deployed at any one time; this number could therefore be increased for operations of short duration. For observer and peacekeeping missions of low intensity, the percentage of usable forces is probably larger. Nevertheless, the objective must be that all deployable combat forces should be able to deal with operations across the whole spectrum of violence, because every operation implies the risk of escalation; it is not recommendable therefore to divide the armed forces into distinct peace enforcement and peacekeeping branches. To this all too limited definition of usability, one should add the numerous supporting forces needed to sustain the combatants (e.g. logistics); in most armed forces, the ratio of combatants to personnel in combat support and combat service support is actually one in three (Mileham, 2001, p.622). Nonetheless, this does leave over 420,000 conscripts of very limited usability in 17 Member States, plus a very important number of forces that are still geared to 'traditional' territorial defence and therefore less usable for deployment abroad. A minimum capacity for territorial defence should always be maintained though, to provide for potential long-term developments, a view which is certainly shared by the new Member States, which still perceive a certain risk implied by their proximity to the former USSR. Finally, it should not be forgotten that deployments imply a severe budgetary impact that is often difficult to sustain for Member States with limited defence budgets and a high percentage of personnel costs. It has been estimated that the UK's participation in the invasion of Iraq will cost the equivalent of its defence budget for two years, which could severely limit the possibilities for large-scale commitments in the near future (Pilegaard, 2004, p.23).

How then to assess the EU's expeditionary capacity? Three dimensions have to be addressed: the number of troops that the EU can deploy, the types of operations that it is able undertake and the efficiency of the budgets that are spent to enable these deployments.

With regard to the numbers, the remaining shortfalls have not stopped EU Member States from almost permanently deploying a number of troops equal to the HG in a number of concurrent operations. In the framework of NATO, in 2003-2004, Member States have been contributing over 6,000 troops to SFOR in Bosnia-Herzegovina (over 50% of total SFOR strength), over 16,000 to KFOR in Kosovo (about 70%) and over 4,000 to ISAF in Afghanistan (over 60%). The EU presence in Bosnia-Herzegovina has increased to over 7,000 since operation Althea took over from SFOR. Also in 2004, after the withdrawal of Spanish forces in July, 12 EU Member States had a total of some 19,000 troops in Iraq. If UN operations around the globe, previous EU operations Concordia and Artemis, and occasional national operations (e.g. British and French operations in Sierra Leone and Ivory Coast) are taken into account, EU Member States are permanently sustaining at least 50 to 60,000 troops in operations abroad, not including troops in permanent foreign bases such as those held by the British and French armed forces (Giegerich and Wallace, 2004). This figure corresponds perfectly to the HG; it also amounts to about one third of the most conservative estimate of the number of usable forces, that is the number of troops in that estimate which the EU actually *can* deploy, taking into account the need for rotation. In the current state of capabilities, EU Member States could thus not deploy substantially more troops, certainly not for operations nearer the high end of the spectrum of violence; perhaps for low-intensity operations some additional deployments would be possible.

Not all of the existing capabilities of all Member States needed to sustain the current average level of deployment have been included in the HFC, but one can safely assume that they would be made available if Member States, in whatever framework, agreed on an operation. The HFC itself is no more than that anyway: a catalogue of forces that can be made available for EU operations by national decision on a case-by-case basis. Otherwise, these forces remain under national command and do not train together on a systematic basis. Effectiveness and interoperability, i.e. the ability of armed forces to work together, could thus still be increased. An exception to some extent are the multinational units in which a number of Member States have organized part of their forces and that have been declared as such to the HFC. Though the 'catalogue' system is applied as well, most of these have a permanent staff element and regularly hold combined exercises. The most integrated is the 60,000-strong Eurocorps, in which Belgium, France, Germany, Luxemburg and Spain participate, the headquarters of which (970 strong, comprising a multinational support battalion) has been certified by NATO as a Rapid Deployable Corps HQ; it has been deployed in Kosovo and provided the core of the HQ of ISAF VI in Kabul. In many of these multinational units the permanent elements are rather limited though.

With regard to the types of operations, in May 2003 the Council's assessment in its Declaration on EU Military Capabilities was that:

> the EU now has operational capability across the full range of Petersberg Tasks, limited and constrained by recognized shortfalls. These limitations and/or constraints are on deployment time and high risk may arise at the upper end of the spectrum of scale and intensity, in particular when conducting concurrent operations.

This assessment can be broken down to the level of the various Petersberg Tasks, and taking into account the combined armed forces of the Member States:

- The EU certainly has the capabilities to undertake low and medium intensity operations, including of large scale and long duration, such as military advice and assistance tasks, conflict prevention and peacekeeping tasks. A greater portion of Member States' forces is 'usable' for such operations, although it must be taken into account that the risk of escalation of violence is always present. The most important shortfall in this regard is strategic transport, so the further the distance, the more difficult is the ability to move forces to the theatre of operations, and sustainability, that is the ability to logistically support deployed forces, especially for large-scale operations.

- The EU is also capable of undertaking substantial non-combatant humanitarian operations and rescue and evacuation tasks; the latter can be, or evolve into, high-intensity operations, usually of short duration; the same shortfall applies.

- With regard to tasks of combat forces undertaken for crisis management, the EU can mount combat operations, certainly of small and medium scale, but this is where the shortfalls have the greatest impact. The number of usable forces is smaller, so the needs of rotation come to bear more rapidly; insufficient strategic transport increases reaction time and renders sustainability more difficult; shortfalls in command & control, intelligence and precision-guided munitions increase the risk of casualties and collateral damage. In other words, if needs be the EU can undertake significant combat operations, but implementation will be less quick and less 'clean' than comparable US operations – although how 'clean' these really are, is perhaps a matter for debate itself.

Finally, the efficiency of the EU's military capacity must also be assessed: how does the output in terms of capabilities relate to Member States' combined defence budgets? At 180 billion euro, the EU-25 has the world's second-largest defence budget, equivalent to the next six put together: China, Russia, Japan, Saudi Arabia, India and South Korea (Howorth, 2004a) – this clearly demonstrates that even today the EU effectively is a military power of global magnitude. But the comparison with the US' 330 billion euro budget for 2002, for a total of 1.4 million troops, including at least 400,000 deployable ground troops and the availability of high-technology equipment, also demonstrates that the EU-25 budget should generate much more usable capabilities than it does. US capabilities should not be idealized either – for example it is often forgotten that the US has to have recourse to civilian strategic lift to replenish its military capabilities (Schweiss, 2003, pp.223-4) – but in comparison the EU clearly suffers from huge inefficiencies. The causes are evident: on the one hand, EU Member States still maintain large numbers of conscripts and forces for territorial defence of limited usability; on the other hand, limited multinational cooperation implies negative effects of scale. This is a consequence of separately procuring equipment – the simultaneous development of three European combat aircraft, Rafale, Eurofighter and Gripen, is a case in point – of useless duplication of overhead facilities – headquarters, planning, training, logistics, bases etc. – and of maintaining a wide range of often very small capabilities in all of the individual Member States. The financial consequence is that limited means remain for defence procurement and defence-related R&T, in other words for enhancing the usability, and for operations. The defence budgets of the EU-25 are simply spent unwisely.

Enhancing Capabilities: An Ongoing Effort

Important decisions have been taken regarding the process of enhancing EU military capabilities. The June 2004 European Council endorsed the new Headline Goal 2010. This will involve the continued updating of the HHC and HFC, on the basis of focused military scenarios, in order to finalize a more detailed Requirements Catalogue by 2005. No additional quantitative objectives have been set; the focus is instead on qualitative issues: interoperability, deployability and sustainability. To that end benchmarks in these fields will be developed, on the basis of which all forces declared to the HFC will then be categorized in terms of effectiveness in relation to the range of possible tasks, thus introducing peer-pressure. Forces will be tested making use of the opportunities offered by national and multinational exercises so, apart from HQ exercises, apparently no EU-organized real 'mud on the boots' manoeuvres are being considered – the UK has always resisted this in favour of NATO manoeuvres. Common concepts and procedures are to complement the existing collection of doctrines. Building on the ECAP project groups, the HG 2010 also includes a number of more specific objectives, addressing the identified shortfalls: the implementation of 'strategic lift joint coordination' by 2005, with a view of achieving all the necessary capabilities and full efficiency by 2010; a space policy by 2006; the availability of an aircraft carrier and associated air wing by 2008; an information-sharing policy by 2010; compatibility and network linkage of all terrestrial and space based communications assets by 2010; harmonization of future military requirements and procurement calendars by 2010.

Another specific aspect of the HG 2010 concerns rapid response. Although it is often styled the 'rapid reaction force', the original HG provides for a reaction time of up to 60 days. Only part of the force in the HFC can be deployed sufficiently quickly to provide real rapid response, that is within a few days, which might be necessary in case of rescue operations or humanitarian crises. It was therefore decided to further develop the rapid response dimension of the HG, which is now reflected in the HG 2010. On the one hand the EU is to further develop decision-making procedures so as to allow the decision to launch an operation to be taken within five days of the approval by the Council of the Crisis Management Concept, the selection of a military option in response to a crisis. Secondly, the EU has adopted the British-French-German proposal to create 'battlegroups', to be used mainly at the request of the UN, each about 1500 strong (one battalion plus supporting units), which can be deployed within 10 days of the decision to launch an operation and are sustainable for 120 days. By 2007, seven to nine battlegroups, either national or multinational, would be made available, adding 10,500 to 13,500 rapidly deployable combat troops for high-intensity operations to the HFC. The EU then wants to be able to deploy two battlegroups at any one time; a rotation scheme will be implemented between the battlegroups so that two are always on stand-by.

At the November 2004 CCC Member States committed to eventually create 13 battlegroups. The first four to be available will be national battlegroups, comprising France, Italy, Spain and the UK. Benchmarks will have to be developed to allow for 'certification' of declared battlegroups; national forces assigned to battlegroups will thus rotate through training and certification, stand-by and standing-down. For the multinational battlegroups to be able to operate swiftly and smoothly, which is especially required for the type of rapid response operations that is being envisaged, manoeuvres would be highly recommendable. In this regard, the battlegroups could serve to break the British veto on manoeuvres in an EU context. The question remains though whether the battlegroups will simply be existing rapid response forces that had not been declared to the HFC before, as is likely to be the case with national battlegroups, or whether Member States by pooling resources in multinational battlegroups can deliver additional 'usable' forces and/or enhance the usability of existing forces. One must note that the battlegroup concept, which has been modelled on Artemis, does not provide an answer to all scenarios demanding rapid response; perhaps the possibility to deploy several battlegroups together in a brigade-formation should also be explored to allow for larger-scale operations if necessary (van den Doel, 2004, pp.35-7).

In delivering the HG 2010, an important part is to be played by the European Defence Agency (EDA), established by Council Joint Action of 12 July 2004. The role of the EDA is to be one of promotion and coordination: identifying further capability needs (HHC); evaluating Member States' contributions against agreed benchmarks (HFC); coordinating the implementation of ECAP; promoting the harmonization of Member States' military requirements; proposing multinational cooperative equipment projects to meet these; and managing specific projects through OCCAR (Organisme conjoint de coopération en matière d'armements, created in 1996 to manage cooperative equipment projects, uniting France, Germany, Italy and the UK) or other arrangements. The EDA is further to promote defence-related R&T and the restructuring of the European defence industry. What is envisaged is not a large administration, but a small body that coordinates all existing mechanisms for cooperation in procurement and that attempts to stimulate Member States into action by means of peer-pressure. This implies a *real* evaluation of Member States' contributions to the HFC, which until now have never been the subject of a thorough assessment, which can lead to doubts as to the effective availability and quality of promised contributions. A great innovation entailed by the EDA is that it does not just focus on the possibilities for cooperative projects based on Member States' current procurement needs, but that it aims to exert influence far more upstream in the decision-making process: the definition of long-term military requirements and the orientation of R&T. The additional guidance provided by the EDA should promote the achievement of concrete results by the ECAP project groups.

Given that a number of specific objectives have been set and taking into account the additional impetus to be provided by the EDA, one can reasonably expect that by 2010 substantial progress can be achieved in resolving a number of the remaining shortfalls with regard to the HG, be it that the voluntary character of the process has been preserved. Some scepticism seems in order though as to major shortfalls requiring substantial investment and therefore best addressed through multinational cooperation, e.g. strategic air- and sealift and space-based communications assets. It is to be hoped that peer-pressure applied by the EDA will be sufficient to convince Member States to relinquish procurement policies based primarily on national considerations (i.e. national military requirements and the preservation of national defence industries) in favour of harmonization of requirements and a policy driven by the needs of the EU as a whole. In that regard, a promising option would be the creation of a limited procurement budget at the EU level, which the EDA could manage as a function of the implementation of ECAP, thus circumventing the national dimension. As to the forces declared to the HFC, the implementation of the battlegroup concept and further incremental additions in function of the ongoing updating of the HHC would probably deliver the numbers required to achieve the full HG of a sustained 60,000-strong deployment by forces *within* the HFC.

Beyond the Headline Goal?

The whole process of enhancing European capabilities is geared to the HG, which however concerns only part of the combined Member States' armed forces – no vision as yet exists on the future of the remaining 1.5 million. Of course, Member States are conscious of the need to pursue the transformation of their armed forces from territorial defence to expeditionary operations and are taking important steps. This is evident from the Strategy itself, in which under the heading of 'more capable' foremost is the need to further 'transform our militaries into more flexible, mobile forces and to enable them to address the new threats'.

At the same time it is equally evident that the financial means available for transformation are limited, and that for budgetary and efficiency reasons, most Member States are unable to continue to provide the whole range of capabilities in their army, navy and air force, and cannot maintain certain capabilities unless in cooperation with others. This certainly holds true for the new Member States, a number of which have only just begun transformation. This is related to the problem of defence inflation (Alexander and Garden, 2001): as in most European countries the annual cost of defence capabilities rises faster than yearly inflation, capabilities decline even if defence budgets are kept level in real terms – and in many countries, budgets are still decreasing. In any event, clinging to the 'full toolbox' is useless, as the range of necessarily small-scale (and thus inefficient) capabilities would not allow smaller – and medium-sized – States to implement autonomous operations, so they are dependent on other states anyway – although not all States concerned have yet come to realize this. Pilegaard (2004, p.28) summarizes the situation well:

> In some ways, the typical European nation state is arguably locked in an inefficient local optimum: the defence posture is inadequate to mount a credible national defence, but still sufficiently important to quell critical questioning of the rationale of 'mini-mass armies' organized on a national scale.

Because of the efficiency and budgetary imperatives, further substantial transformation of national capabilities by necessity will have to imply a certain degree of specialization and multinational cooperation.

Multinational cooperation is possible in many ways, at different levels of integration:

- coordinating supporting capabilities in multinational frameworks, such as the European Air Transport Coordination Cell in Eindhoven (Netherlands) which coordinates the air transport of the participating Member States to ensure optimal use of all flights, or pooling such capabilities in single multinational units;
- creating integrated multinational combat units such as the multinational battlegroups, but including larger scale formations in army, navy and air force;
- pooling can also mean creating collective capabilities, that are no longer owned by the participating Member States but by the EU as such, along the lines of the NATO-owned AWACS; this is probably the way forward to acquire capital-intensive assets such as space observation.

Specialization (De Neve, 2003) implies that certain capabilities are no longer maintained by a Member State or are maintained only through participation in a multinational cooperative framework. A certain degree of specialization has always existed, since many Member States have never possessed all types of capabilities; submarines or aircraft carriers are an obvious example. But in recent years, specialization and cooperation are simultaneously on the rise. For example, Belgium at the same time as reducing its number of mechanized brigades from three to two has decided to replace all tracked vehicles, including its entire stock of Leopard tanks, by more easily deployable wheeled armoured vehicles (which entails a loss of firepower). Another example of far-reaching cooperation is the integration of the Belgian and Dutch navies under a single operational command. There is also a consciousness of the need to downsize forces in favour of usability and to deal with conscription; Italy has already decided to abolish conscription and the debate is ongoing in some other countries.

The problem with all these national, bilateral and multilateral initiatives is that decisions are being made without reference to any European framework – for the simple reason that apart from the HG, none exists. Decisions are thus based on national considerations only, on national capability needs or often even simply on the need to save money, without reference to the usefulness for the EU as a whole of the capabilities that are either cut or strengthened. The risk is that without coordination, in the end Member States' combined capabilities will represent an incoherent whole, with surpluses of one capability and shortages of another, that does not answer to the needs of the EU. What is required therefore is top-down planning and coordination at the EU level, starting neither from the limitations of the current HG nor from the comparison with the US, but from the objectives of the EU as expressed in the Strategy. Current levels of deployment demonstrate that the EU is capable of a number of concurrent operations, but the Strategy has yet to be translated into more detailed quantifiable military ambitions – now it just says that the EU 'should be able to sustain several operations simultaneously', without going into detail. Only with regard to the battlegroups has it been decided, at the November 2004 CCC, that in 2007 the EU should be able to undertake 'two concurrent single battlegroup-size rapid response operations' and to launch them 'nearly simultaneously'.

A political decision is needed: how many concurrent operations, at which scale, of which type and at which level of intensity, does the EU want to be able to implement, in view of its commitments towards its neighbourhood and 'effective multilateralism'? On that basis, a comprehensive catalogue of capability needs for the EU as a whole could be drawn up that looks beyond the HG and that could serve as a framework for the further transformation of Member States' combined armed forces. This would effectively amount to a 'strategic defence review' at the EU level (Quille, 2004a). For most Member States, who *are* willing to continue transformation, such a framework is indispensable, for without it multinational cooperation and specialization, the only way forward because of budgetary and efficiency constraints, are difficult if not impossible. Within such an EU framework it could be decided which capabilities would be contributed by which Member States, allowing the largest Member States to maintain a wide range of national capabilities, but enabling the others to focus their contribution and to deliver it in cooperation with others by making specialization and pooling possible. The capability needs of the EU would thus be integrated in national force planning from the onset, rather than being inputted at the end of the process, when most decisions have already been taken on the basis of national considerations. Only on the basis of the definition of capability needs at the EU level, would true harmonization of the requirements of capabilities be possible, as well as maximal coordination of procurement, either by jointly ordering equipment 'off-the-shelf' or through cooperative production projects. And since NATO does not offer such far-reaching integration, the EU is the only option to implement such a scheme.

In defining its overall capability needs, the EU must take into account the need to continue its presence on the Balkans and the possibility of future deployments further East, the possibility of operations in its Mediterranean periphery, as well as the need to increase its troop contribution to international peace and security in the framework of the UN. Given also the view on the use of force as a last resort only that is implicit in the Strategy, and the emphasis on the integrated use of civil and military means, such a comprehensive planning exercise would presumably arrive at capability needs above the HG, but far below the level of current US capabilities and of a different composition. Further downsizing of European armed forces is thus implicit in this scenario. The EU need not strive for a military capacity equal to that of the US, but must carefully plan its capability needs according to the Strategy, abandoning the all too simple logic of ever more troops and equipment and daring to downsize overcapacities in certain areas (Groupe d'officiers du CHEM, 2003). That the EU already succeeds in sustaining ongoing operations on the scale envisaged by the HG, demonstrates that the HG corresponds well to the capabilities currently available, but it does not mean that in order to fully implement the Security Strategy, more capabilities are not needed.

Network-Centric Warfare?

This planning exercise should also address the outstanding question of how far the EU should go along with 'network-centric warfare' (NCW) as entailed by the current 'revolution in military affairs' (RMA) which the US is in the process of implementing. This issue is directly linked to the problem of interoperability between European and American forces. NCW amounts to information superiority, based on advanced command, control, communications, computers, intelligence, surveillance, target acquisition and reconnaissance (C4ISTAR), enabling geographically dispersed units at all levels of command to be all connected to a single network, which results in 'increased combat power irrespective of weather conditions, increased speed of command, a higher tempo of operations, increased survivability and a degree of self-synchronisation' (EUISS, 2004, p.107). A number of limitations of the NCW concept should be recognized (Cohen, 2004; Desportes, 2004; Stone, 2004). First of all, NCW primarily applies to high-intensity operations against other organized forces, so is not applicable to all Petersberg Tasks. As stated earlier, all combat forces must be able to operate across the whole spectrum of violence, which implies that designing specific peacekeeping forces is unwise, but it is equally true that forces that are exclusively designed for 'war-fighting' can find themselves deficient in other operations (Nardulli and McNaugher, 2002, p.104). This is why in the US one side of the debate argues that transformation should be reoriented to take more account of lower intensity operations (Tangredi, 2002, p.8). Furthermore, technological innovation is not an end in itself, but is useful only in so far as it is integrated in doctrine and enhances the effectiveness of forces. Finally, for the EU achieving full NCW-interoperability with the US would demand a huge investment.

As apparently already indicated in the HG 2010, the EU had therefore better aim for the possibility of enabling ad hoc network linkages between European forces engaged in types of operations that demand so, and for a more limited degree of 'cooperability' with the US to provide for combined EU-US operations. This means focusing on specific NCW assets, as a number of Member States are already doing, on the basis of European experience and doctrines for different types of operations, rather than setting up a single encompassing US-like network at the EU level (Lindley-French and Algieri, 2004, p.43; De Neve and Mathieu, 2004). The third option, to simply rely on ad hoc access to the US network, would entail a degree of dependency that ignores the specific needs of the EU, or in the words of Boyer (2004, p.87): 'Such a situation would be reminiscent of the status of colonial forces serving in British and French armies during the colonial period'. NCW is not the only determinant of interoperability: doctrine, readiness, sustainability and equipment are important as well, and all of these are the subject of ongoing work in the context of ESDP. Nor should it be forgotten that the US transformation toward NCW is far from complete: full operational capability is envisaged in the 2008-2015 timeframe, i.e. the period when major European investment schemes should also generate substantial enhancement of EU capabilities (Barry, 2002).

Permanent Structured Cooperation

Apart from the vague reference in the HG 2010 that 'between 2006 and 2010 [...] a longer term vision beyond 2010 will be formulated with the objective of identifying trends in future capability developments and requirements', there is no indication that all Member States would be willing to subscribe to comprehensive planning and coordination at the EU level in the near future. Nor can the EDA, the prime focus of which remains the HG, be expected to generate such a far-reaching innovation in the short term, in spite of its potentially substantial impact on Member States' commitments. It is recommendable therefore to offer those Member States that are willing to go further with cooperation and specialization a framework to do so. The answer could be 'permanent structured cooperation', one of the innovations brought by the Draft Constitution (Howorth, 2004b).

Articles I-41.6 and III-312 provide that Member States willing to fulfil higher capability criteria can establish permanent structured cooperation; their commitments to one another will be set out in a protocol annexed to the Constitution. As up till then defence had been excluded from the possibility of 'enhanced cooperation', this was one of the major breakthroughs engineered by the Convention. The first objective of structured cooperation is to 'proceed more intensely to develop [...] defence capacities', which entails:

• achieving a still to be determined level of investments in defence equipment, which amounts to the introduction of a financial convergence criterion;
• working on the ECAP shortfalls, including through multinational approaches, and participating, where appropriate, in joint projects in the framework of the EDA;
• enhancing the availability of forces by setting common objectives regarding the commitment of forces to operations;
• bringing their forces 'into line with each other as far as possible' by harmonization of requirements, pooling and, where appropriate, specialization.

Participating Member States' contributions shall be assessed by the EDA. The second objective however, to deliver a national or part of a multination battlegroup by 2007, has come to dominate the agenda, seemingly to the detriment of the other useful applications of the mechanism. If used only to set up the battlegroups, structured cooperation brings little added value and is hardly necessary. Of course, the battlegroups are a necessary addition to the HFC, but they constitute just one specific (rapid response) capability. When a form of enhanced cooperation or 'defence Euro-zone' was originally proposed in the Convention, what was envisaged was 'participation in multinational forces with integrated command and control capabilities' (European Convention, 2002c). During the preparation of the Belgian-French-German-Luxembourg defence summit or 'chocolate summit' in Brussels on 29 April 2003, proposals were raised as well to progressively integrate existing multinational units. This summit intended to look into the possibilities for creating a 'core group' or 'avant-garde' to accelerate the development of ESDP, and eventually strongly supported structured cooperation.

Such a scenario is still possible. In the framework of structured cooperation, Member States that are willing could look for partners with similar needs and identify the possibilities for cooperation and specialization. They could then start creating a number of integrated multinational capabilities, including both combat and support units, in army, navy and air force, going beyond the battlegroup scale, into which they can integrate a much larger share of their national armed forces; the existing multinational units could be the core. The primary focus should be on deployable force packages, with modules that can fit together according to the needs of the operation at hand. Greater permanency in such arrangements, for example standing multinational staffs, joint manoeuvres and pooled capabilities, would greatly enhance interoperability. Though short of maximum coordination at the level of the EU-25, more coherence would be ensured than when Member States continue cooperation and specialization at a purely national and ad hoc basis; the involvement of the EDA and the EUMS can ensure that the exercise is geared to the capability requirements of the EU.

The Belgian air force can illustrate the usefulness of such a platform to identify partners for cooperation. Belgium currently operates a relatively large number of combat aircraft (two wings of F16), of relatively old age; in view of the country's limited defence budget it is easily predictable that replacing them when eventually necessary will be extremely difficult. Two options then present themselves: either abolish the combat element in the air force altogether and lose the country's expertise in that field, or look for partners of a similar scale, such as. the Czech Republic or Hungary, to set up one multinational unit, with joint headquarters and training, and thus a heavily reduced overhead, in which each participates with a more limited number of aircraft and can thus remain an actor in that field at his own level of possibilities. In fact aircraft capabilities offer the most promising prospects for pooling in the short term, because air procedures are already harmonized to a very large extent and because many States operate the same equipment, while the high cost of aircraft acts as a powerful stimulus for multinational cooperation (Alexander and Garden, 2001, p.522). In the field of strategic lift, an ideal opportunity for integration presents itself: the acquisition of 170 A400M, the new transport aircraft, by 5 Member States – Belgium (with Luxembourg financing one of the eight aircraft ordered), France, Germany, Spain and the UK. Supporting services are the least sensitive in this regard, but there are opportunities in combat units and in the army and navy as well, as the example of Belgo-Dutch naval integration demonstrates.

To be effective, multinational cooperation and specialization pose a number of conditions. For the sake of solidarity within the EU, it would not be acceptable for a Member State to assume a free-rider's position and specialize in non-combatant forces only. Member States could focus on just one or two major capabilities or types of forces, but in order to create a sense of ownership it would be better if through multinational cooperation and pooling they would participate in a somewhat wider range of capabilities. Specific capabilities should not be limited to just one Member State or multinational arrangement; it is recommendable to always have more than one set of resources available. Nevertheless, cooperation and specialization do entail a loss of national military autonomy and require a large degree of trust, but that is nothing new for the large majority of Member States. An official Dutch inquiry shows that a number of Member States would be willing to seriously consider specialization; hesitation seems to be a matter of a lack of framework and the classic question of 'who jumps first?' (IBO, 2003). But as Haine (2004b, p.111) says: if the answer to the question whether European countries are allies forever is yes, there should be no problem.

Spending Wisely

The combined armed forces of the EU Member States already present a powerful military capacity, second only to that of their foremost Ally, the US. The ongoing HG process will ensure that the most usable forces will be made available to the EU and will address the remaining major capability shortfalls, particularly in the fields of command and control, intelligence and strategic lift. Better spending of existing defence budgets should generate far *more* usable capabilities though, which would enable the EU to fully implement the Strategy. This would require further transformation of national armed forces, moving to professional armies and replacing territorial defence as the major guiding principle for capabilities planning; and a major advance in the harmonization of military requirements to enable fully coordinated procurement. For smaller Member States, effective transformation is only possible in cooperation with others. In the absence of comprehensive top-down planning of capabilities at the level of the EU-25, permanent structured cooperation could enable a quantum leap forward by offering a framework for multinational cooperation and specialization to those Member States that are willing.

The accession of 10 new Member States, with armed forces that for the greater part are only in the earliest stages of transformation, presents an additional challenge, but at the same time it might lower the threshold for moving to deepened military integration. Obviously, in view of their huge needs in so many fields, the new Member States are not in a position to implement a 'big bang' and transform the whole of their militaries at once. Consequently, they have opted for multinational cooperation – the Baltic States provide a good example of far-reaching integration – and for concentration on specific capabilities that are most usable in the current international context, which entails *de facto* specialization – the Czech Republic has focussed its efforts on NBC protection units. This opens prospects for other Member States that are looking for opportunities for cooperation, although the severe budgetary difficulties of many new Member States might serve as an obstacle. Setting up multinational capabilities involving both older and new Member States could be one of the ways of preventing the emergence of a durable divide along the 'old' and 'new' line within the EU.

The size of European defence budgets thus is not the problem; if better spent, existing budgets should be sufficient to build all the capabilities required for the EU's ambitions as expressed in the Strategy. Frans Osinga of the Clingendael Institute in The Hague estimates that at the EU level filling the major capability gaps would cost about €42 billion; if spread over a ten year period, this requires shifting resources within the existing defence budgets to allow for a ten per cent increase of the means for procurement (De Wijk, 2004, p.140). Calls for increased defence spending are therefore senseless, besides being politically unfeasible in a context demanding huge efforts on the part of Member States to maintain the welfare state. Shifting resources from social programmes to defence, as Kagan (2004) calls for, is not only unnecessary, but contrary to the fundamental idea of the comprehensive approach. The Strategy does call for 'more resources for defence', but also, in its final version, for 'more effective use of resources'. The latter addition reflects the budgetary and political unfeasibility of increasing defence spending in the majority of the Member States, a fact which was voiced at the last of the three EU seminars on the Strategy. Hence the need to make better use of current budgets; as the first draft already said, 'systematic use of pooled and shared assets would reduce duplications, overheads, and, in the medium-term, increase capabilities'. The problem, though, is that the measures needed to enhance the efficiency of existing budgets, that is downsizing capabilities of limited usability and investing in others, would at first instance entail additional costs, before positive effects of scale would be generated – or, 'nothing ventured, nothing gained' (AIV, 2004a, p.9). Therefore, either transformation is spread over a significant number of years, or perhaps a number of Member States could consider introducing a one-time special budget during a few years in order to achieve some substantial progress in a shorter term.

Locking European capabilities into each other makes sense only if crowned by a consensus at the political level on the role of the EU as an international actor and the part to be played therein by the military instrument. Imperfect though perhaps it may be, the Strategy provides such a framework, which can serve as the basis for a precise assessment of the capability needs of the EU. Then the EU must also muster the political will to make use of the tool it has acquired. What counts is not so much the size of the armed forces, but the willingness and ability to use them (Bertram, 2003). The decision not to intervene directly in the humanitarian crisis in Darfur and the limited participation of EU Member States in MONUC, the UN operation in the DRC, shows that this is not always the case. But EU operations on the Balkans and Artemis, as well as the commitment of European forces in other frameworks, demonstrate that the EU can make a significant contribution.

Coherence between Civilian and Military Capabilities and Doctrines

The EU's long-term stabilization and conflict prevention policies, notably through the different partnerships that it has established with third States and regions, its early warning mechanisms and its diplomatic tools, are complemented by deployable civilian capabilities. A Committee for Civilian Aspects of Crisis Management has been established under the Council. At the June 2000 European Council in Feira, civilian Headline Goals were set in four fields, along the lines of the Helsinki HG, to establish a catalogue of capabilities available to the EU:

• police: 5,000 police officers, 1,400 of whom to be deployable within 30 days;

- rule of law: 300 prosecutors, judges and prison officers;
- civil administration: a pool of experts, deployable at short notice;
- civil protection: two or three assessment and/or coordination teams, deployable within three to seven hours, and intervention teams of up to 2,000 for deployment at short notice.

The first civilian CCC in November 2002 concluded that these goals had been met and even exceeded through Member States' voluntary contributions. The latest civilian CCC, in November 2004, confirmed the availability of 5,761 personnel in the field of police, 631 for rule of law, 562 for civilian administration and 4,988 for civil protection, as well as 505 for an additional monitoring capability, and 391 experts in the added fields of human rights, political affairs, gender and security sector reform, which should enhance the EU's capacity to deploy targeted multidimensional missions. Another additional capability is the European Gendarmerie Force (EGF), a pool of paramilitary police forces established by France, Italy, the Netherlands, Portugal and Spain for deployment abroad in order to guarantee public order in more demanding circumstances, tasks for which they are more specifically trained than the military. All of these capabilities can be deployed for capacity-building in frail and failed States, monitoring missions, crisis management, and post-conflict reconstruction. The aim is to deploy multidimensional, integrated packages, the size and composition of which can vary according to needs. The EU has already launched four civilian operations: the rule of law mission in Georgia (Operation Themis); and three police missions, in Macedonia (Proxima), in Bosnia-Herzegovina (EUPM) and in Kinshasa, in the DRC (EUPOL). As is the case for the military capabilities, certain gaps have to be addressed: the same shortfalls in the field of strategic transport apply, as well as in the field of planning capacity. The 2004 CCC stressed the importance of urgently establishing sufficient operational planning and support capabilities to allow the EU to conduct several civilian crisis management operations simultaneously. Analogous to the European Defence Agency, a European Peacebuilding Agency could be imagined, to provide guidelines for capacity-building, harmonize training – currently an important shortfall – and assess the availability and expertise of capabilities declared by the Member States (EPLO, 2004; ICG, 2005, p.31). Future capability planning could take into account the desirability of enhancing the EU's contribution to UN peacebuilding efforts, in view of the High-Level Panel's recommendation to increase the UN's effectiveness in this field through the creation of a Peacebuilding Commission.

The EU is the only international organization, next to the UN, that covers all dimensions of international relations (Rummel, 2003, p.8). The Strategy stresses that the EU 'could add particular value by developing operations involving both military and civilian capabilities' and calls for 'a greater capacity to bring all necessary civilian resources to bear in crisis and post crisis situations'. The same emphasis on the combination of military and civilian instruments as a distinctive feature of the EU approach can also be found in the December 2003 European Council decision to add a 'cell with civil-military components' to the EU Military

Staff, which is to function as a core that can be rapidly expanded into an operations centre for EU operations without the use of NATO assets when no national HQ of one of the Member States is being used, and particularly when a joint civil and military response is required – which nowadays applies to most if not all operations. Military operations must not only be determined by the wider political goals to be achieved, at the operational level as well they must ideally integrate a civilian component from the outset, to be able to launch the state-building efforts that must accompany any military intervention as soon as possible. The scale of the civilian involvement will of course vary according to the type of operation: in high-intensity operations, it will be limited at first, to be gradually strengthened as the security situation is stabilized.

The EU must therefore not only increase its deployable civilian capabilities *per se*, but should also continue work on the integration of civilian and military capabilities. In order to achieve maximal coordination and effectiveness, the civilian and military components should not only be integrated at the level of the operational headquarters, that is in the new Civil-Military Cell and in the future European External Action Service, but deployable civilian components could also be integrated with the military capabilities, as suggested by the Kaldor Study Group (Kaldor et al., 2004). Civilian experts could notably be attached to the different deployable force headquarters available to the EU, and to the battlegroups; the civilian dimension could also be included in the exercises organized by the EU. Since for civilian personnel it is more difficult to take leave from their positions at short notice for deployment abroad, unlike the military, who prepare for just that, the Kaldor Group suggests that the EU could subsidize small cadres that are on stand-by and receive special training, but that otherwise serve in their domestic capacity. Perhaps in a later stage, a full-time core of EU personnel could be created, to serve during the initial entry phase of operations and as leading officials. The Draft Constitution (Article III-321.5) also provides for a voluntary capability, the European Voluntary Humanitarian Aid Corps, which would consist of school-leavers and students; the European Parliament has proposed the creation of a Civil Peace Corps of mid- or post-career voluntary professionals with useful skills. Both elements could in one form or another be combined into a single capability, for example as a Human Security Volunteer Service, as proposed by the Kaldor Group.

As mentioned in Chapter 2, the EU's view of the military instrument as an integral part of a comprehensive approach putting to use the whole range of EU instruments in the framework of the overall agenda of GPG, and its view of the use of force as an instrument of last resort, requires a distinctive doctrine for the implementation of military operations. Doctrine must reflect not only strategy, but also the norms and values of the society from which it emanates (Münkler, 2004, p.22). The Kaldor Group puts forward substantial elements of such a doctrine (Glasius and Kaldor, 2005), based on the notion of human security, which can also be found in the existing doctrines of several Member States, in which the emphasis, including for high-intensity operations, is on the protection of civilians; on the need to minimize the use of force, killing, injury, and material destruction, in order to avoid creating opposition; on neutral policing; and on the determination to work well with the local population, on the overall objective of winning hearts and minds. This approach is the opposite of the *zéro mort*-attitude that prioritizes force protection and the avoidance of casualties among the deployed forces at the cost of 'collateral damage', including human lives, for the local population; the high-altitude bombing campaign over Kosovo in 1999 exemplifies this approach. In the words of the Kaldor Group (Kaldor et al., 2004, p.20):

> In human security operations, the lives of those deployed cannot be privileged. The aim should be to protect people and minimize all casualties. This is more akin to the traditional approach of the police, who risk their lives to save others, even though they are prepared to kill *in extremis*, as human security forces should be.

Though this formulation is perhaps too far-fetched, it is clear that a balance must be sought between the evident requirements of force protection and the need to protect civilians. The overall experience of the British forces in Iraq demonstrates that such an approach, a different style, does make a difference on the ground, even in a very difficult environment. Indeed the British armed forces in particular have acquired considerable expertise in this respect (Spear, 2004). At present, no European body of doctrine exists (Bono, 2004). The creation of the battlegroups could be seen as an opportunity to devise a common doctrine for the types of operations that all of the battlegroups, national and multinational, will have to implement, on the basis of existing doctrine and experience in the individual Member States. In this regard too, the battlegroups could thus stimulate integration in a field hitherto not directly addressed by ESDP. Common doctrines would serve as an important stimulus for harmonization of capability requirements and would strengthen the Europeanization of Member States' armed forces in general (Reiter and Frank, 2004, p.5).

Re-Building the Transatlantic Partnership

Even though its own capabilities are ever increasing, the EU expressly aims to cooperate with other partners in pursuing its objectives; this is one of the core elements of the comprehensive approach. Foremost among the EU's partners is the US; as the Strategy rightly notes the transatlantic relationship, of which NATO is the most concrete expression, is 'irreplaceable'. Close EU-NATO relations have been established, including since 2001 two annual joint meetings at the level of the foreign ministers, at least three joint meetings per semester at ambassadorial level between the Political and Security Committee and the North Atlantic Council, and two joint meetings per semester between the Military Committees of both organizations, as well as regular meetings between subordinate committees and staff-to-staff contacts. The Security Strategy was discussed at a joint ambassadorial meeting in the fall of 2003 and amendments suggested by NATO were incorporated in the final version, notably a reference to the importance of EU-NATO permanent arrangements for the enhancement of the EU's operational capabilities and as a framework for the strategic partnership in crisis management between both organizations (De Witte, 2004, p.5). Both organizations have also concluded an agreement on the security of information, which has made possible a more substantial exchange of data. The 'Berlin Plus' arrangements provide for guaranteed EU access to NATO planning, the availability of NATO command structures for EU operations, as well as the availability of other NATO assets.

The transatlantic relationship, and NATO in particular, has suffered greatly however as a consequence of the Iraq crisis. 2003 especially was a mixed year for the Atlantic Alliance. On the one hand, it was a year of crisis. In February 2003 it took the Allies several weeks to agree on defensive measures to assist Turkey, as Belgium, France and Germany insisted that the other US requests for NATO action that were joined to the proposed decision be discarded, since they took these to start from the assumption that military action against Iraq was inevitable, while the 'three rebels' as they got to be known still thought a peaceful solution possible at that time. The US requests which they resisted included making available air bases to the US, protection of passageways for US Navy vessels in the Eastern Mediterranean by Allied ships, replacing US troops on the Balkans and in Afghanistan and considering a NATO post-conflict mission in Iraq (Pailhe, 2003). Their action caused a deep rift within the Alliance, and within the EU, which was itself deeply divided on the issue of military intervention. EU-US relations suffered accordingly. The US Senate even adopted a resolution recommending the President to look into the possibility of establishing a procedure to suspend the NATO membership of Allies which 'no longer comply with the NATO principles of democracy, individual liberty, and the rule of law' (Michel, 2003, p.4).

On the other hand, NATO for the first time took on a mission evidently outside the Euro-Atlantic area when on 11 August 2003 it assumed strategic command, control and coordination of ISAF in order to provide continuity to the operation, which was being hampered by lead nations rotating every six months. From June onwards NATO also provided low-profile support to the Polish participation in the stabilization force in Iraq, in the fields of force generation, communication, logistics and movements, and following the June 2004 Istanbul summit a NATO training mission was deployed to Iraq. These conflicting developments indicate that the future course of the Alliance is far from being evident. The Strategy however only highlights the importance of transatlantic relations, within NATO as well as with the US more generally – it does not offer any guidelines as to how these relations can be rebuilt and strengthened.

The End of the Out-of-Area Debate

When NATO was founded, a geographic limit was imposed on its actions by keeping the number of Member States limited and by limiting the applicability of the collective defence commitment to Europe – including, until their independence, France's Algerian *départements* – and North America, in order to focus Allies' efforts on what was considered to be the primary security threat emanating from the Soviet Union. Over the years, 'out-of-area operations', as they are commonly known, have regularly been on the agenda of the Alliance however. Allies, at first the Europeans during the period of decolonization, and later the Americans as they started to feel the effects of over-extension, solicited direct or indirect support for their global involvements. Or Allies were concerned because fellow Allies' actions were deemed to be diverting attention away from the main 'front' or were seen as an infringement upon what they considered a *domaine réservé* of their own, for example a former colony. The dominating presence of a common enemy ensured that during the whole period of the Cold War the main thrust of NATO policy was always preserved (Stuart and Tow, 1990).

This 'out-of-area debate' became really prominent when, following the end of the Cold War and the demise of the Soviet Union, the Alliance started looking for a new role, a quest which directly raised the questions of 'what' and 'where':

> The original notion of the Alliance's purpose – 'to keep the Soviets out, the Germans down and the Americans in' – is quaintly anachronistic. With the Soviets not simply 'out' but vanished entirely, the Germans buried deeply and irreversibly inside the European Union, and the Americans not only 'in' but seemingly everywhere, a new understanding of what the Alliance is all about is obviously needed if, as Atlanticists on both sides of the ocean desire, the Alliance is to endure (Rhodes, 2004, p.123).

In 1991 the Alliance's Strategic Concept was modified, be it rather modestly; the revision probably came too soon for a real departure from Cold War strategic thinking to be possible (NATO, 1991). The second revision, at the 1999 Washington Summit where the New Strategic Concept (NSC) was adopted, was much more thorough. NATO resolutely chose to reorient itself and added to its mission the task 'to engage actively in crisis management, including crisis response operations' – clearly an extension of Article 5 on collective defence and thus a silent amendment of the North Atlantic Treaty (NATO, 1999).

The NSC already hinted that geographic limitations on these non-Article 5 missions would not be as strict as for the traditional collective defence role, as it referred to 'uncertainty and instability in and around the Euro-Atlantic area and the possibility of regional crises at the periphery of the Alliance' that might demand action. Just like collective defence can require action against the territory of the aggressor, it may be necessary to operate outside the North Atlantic area in order to maintain the stability of that region. There is of course a much larger grey area, which did give rise to debate. As a consequence of Allied divisions on the subject, and notably of French reticence, NATO did not play any operational role in the 1991 Gulf War. At the time of the crisis in Albania in 1997 the US itself passed the clear message that NATO would not be the world's policeman and that neither the US nor the Alliance would intervene in a conflict in which, in Washington's judgement, no American interests were at stake – which can just as well be interpreted as meaning that according to the US worldwide NATO action must be possible when American interests effectively are in jeopardy. The debate on NATO's intervention in Kosovo in 1999 rather concerned the legal basis of the operation, because of the absence of an explicit Security Council mandate. As with other NATO operations on the Balkans, the Alliance's geographic authority was not a matter of debate, since operations took place on the European continent.

At the November 2002 Prague Summit the Alliance ended this ambiguity, as it approved the creation of the NATO Response Force (NRF), a high-readiness and fully integrated land, air and sea capability of eventually 21,000, able to deploy in five days and sustain itself for 30 days, for both crisis response and collective defence or Article 5 operations. The NRF is to have a global reach; as the Prague Summit Declaration stated it must be 'ready to move quickly to wherever needed, as decided by the Council' (NATO, 2002). Allowing for global NATO involvement, this formulation, agreed upon by all Allies, thus apparently made an end to the 'out-of-area debate'.

In the current security environment, where there no longer is one major direct military threat, too strict a geographic limitation does indeed seem obsolete (Gärtner, 2003). In a globalized world, events anywhere can affect the security of the Euro-Atlantic area; an effective security policy thus demands a global scope of action. In Washington and Prague, and on the ground in Kabul, all Allies have come to accept the additional tasks of conflict prevention and crisis management *and* the wider scope of action – and have implicitly amended the North Atlantic Treaty in the process. After Prague, a new era thus seemed to beckon for a 'global NATO'. The Alliance's involvement in Afghanistan since August 2003 could be seen to prove that the Alliance is now confidently taking on its new tasks.

Strategic Differences between Allies

But if the out-of-area debate has come to a close, another, much more fundamental divide has arisen between the Allies: the February 2003 crisis over Iraq has highlighted the existence of fundamentally different approaches to security on both sides of the Atlantic; these differences effectively amount to *different strategies*.

Throughout the US National Security Strategy (NSS) adopted in September 2002, direct threats and defence against them are the dominant theme. All fields of policy are seen as a function of the fight against proliferation of WMD and 'rogue states' and particularly of the 'war' against terrorism, a struggle that 'will be fought on many fronts against a particularly elusive enemy over a long period of time'. This struggle is considered to be the overall strategic priority. In order to deal with these threats, the NSS relies heavily on the use of the military instrument, including pre-emptively and even, as the wording of the NSS makes clear, preventively. It was the explicit inclusion of the doctrine of pre-emption that led to a high-profile debate about the NSS, whereas usually its predecessor documents, which have to be submitted to the US Congress regularly, have attracted little attention. In Hunter's estimate (2004a, p.36) rather than really functioning as a guiding document, such a strategy 'usually serves more to "tick a block" in meeting a congressional requirement'; he therefore also doubts whether the NSS was as 'painstakingly and widely-discussed and debated' within the administration as external observers would perhaps assume.

The NSS also breathes unilateralism: even though 'allies and friends' are mentioned throughout the text, it is always clear that these are assumed to accept US leadership and that the US 'will be prepared to act apart when our interests and unique responsibilities require'. The EU is left almost without mentioning: it is primarily seen as 'our partner in opening world trade' and even though the US 'welcome our European allies' efforts to forge a greater foreign policy and defence identity within the EU', the basic concern is 'to ensure that these developments work with NATO'. The NSS does mention other dimensions of security and corresponding policy instruments, such as trade and aid and democratization. But these too are primarily put in the context of the 'war on terrorism' and are instrumentalized to that end. Besides, actual US policies have evidently focussed on the use of the military instrument; Iraq is the obvious example. Other dimensions of security than the military, although they are present, have thus been eclipsed by the predominantly military discourse and policies of the Bush administration.

The emphasis on unilateralism and on the military dimension, as well as the often rather blunt style used by members of the Bush administration, has served to antagonize many governments and other actors around the world. As Joffe (2001) notes, the US has always been seen as an important provider of global public goods, but: 'To the extent that the United States turns unilateralism into a habit or cuts its contribution to the production of public goods, others will feel the string of American power more strongly'. Another major factor that contributes to distrust towards the US is that American policies have come to be perceived as unpredictable and as no longer aiming for the stability of the international system; not only the invasion of Iraq has contributed to this perception, but also the repeated allegations since then that military intervention in such a wide range of countries as Iran, Yemen, Syria and North Korea might be considered as well. To word it in Nye's terms (2002), the NSS has cost the US a lot in terms of soft power.

At the same time, the EU has adopted a comprehensive strategy, which even after the threat assessment was amended in the final version shares an emphasis on similar key threats, but which advocates a much more positive approach to deal with these threats. The same threats may have been identified, but the intensity of the threat perception is certainly different (Skiba, 2004, p.11); unlike the US, the EU does not consider itself to be engaged in a new war (Berenskoetter, 2004). As a diplomat summarized the differences: according to the American document, the world is dangerous; according to the European document, the world is complex.

The growing awareness in the EU of its distinctive identity in international relations and the increasing will to make a proper mark on the course of events, as evidenced by the Security Strategy, is a major new structural factor in transatlantic relations. This self-awareness is reinforced by and itself reinforces the building of an EU military capability able to operate autonomously if needed. It is a consequence of the observation that European and American interests do not always coincide and that, even when overall objectives are generally very similar, there are different conceptions of the way to achieve them. In the post-Cold War era this is a logical evolution, which undoubtedly was accelerated by different reactions to the events of '9/11' on both sides of the Atlantic. Existing conceptions of foreign and security policy in 'neo-con' circles, which had always focussed on the national interest, were suddenly hugely reinforced and were allowed to determine US policy. But whereas the US – understandably perhaps, as an instinctive reaction – launched a 'war on terrorism', the European Council, meeting in extraordinary session on 21 September 2001, called for 'an in-depth political dialogue with those countries and regions of the world in which terrorism comes into being' and 'the integration of all countries into a fair world system of security, prosperity and improved development' – a most explicit call to address the root causes of the problem. The EU position on the Iraq crisis further illustrated the Union's preference for non-coercive instruments to be exhausted before reverting to the use of force. At an extraordinary meeting on 17 February 2003 the European Council stated that 'force should be used only as a last resort' and emphasized the importance of reinvigorating the Middle East peace process if peace and stability are to be brought to the region. France, Germany and Belgium went furthest in letting this view determine their diplomacy on the Iraq issue, which led to the February 2003 crisis in the Alliance.

The Union's affirmation as an international actor is of course an ongoing process. Member States still differ as to how far the ambitions of the EU should reach, and much will depend on whether the EU will be able to muster the will to act. But the course has certainly been set towards Europe as a power – a new structural factor in transatlantic relations. The important fact for the future of NATO is that power is conceived very differently in the NSS and in the Security Strategy. At the same time, now that the two main pillars of NATO, the EU and the US, have defined their security strategies, a more equitable partnership can be built, within NATO and between the EU and the US more generally, starting from both partners' policy priorities. The European Council Declaration on Transatlantic Relations, adopted on 12 December 2003, refers to the common threat assessment – although the final version of the EU Strategy focuses much less exclusively on the 'new' threats of terrorism and WMD than the NSS – and calls for a common agenda and 'a permanent dialogue as strategic partners'. For such a renewed partnership to be possible, a number of issues must be addressed.

Of Forces and Headquarters

First of all, at the level of the military capabilities full complementarity must be ensured between NATO and ESDP. As states have but a single set of forces, NATO when assessing the capabilities of the European Allies obviously identified a range of 58 shortfalls very similar to those identified by the EU. At the April 1999 Washington Summit, before the adoption of the HG, NATO launched the Defence Capabilities Initiative (DCI), providing a roadmap aimed to guide Allies' national efforts towards five priorities: mobility and deployability, sustainability, effective engagement, survivability and interoperable communications. Guaranteeing interoperability between European and American forces was a major concern. Just as in the first phase of the ECAP, initial progress was very limited for lack of coordination and of incentives for states to change their policies. Like the transition from ECAP panels to project groups in 2003, and setting similar priorities, at the December 2002 Prague Summit NATO therefore adopted the more focussed Prague Capabilities Commitment (PCC), targeting more specific capabilities.[11] Because of the single set of forces principle, and because apart from collective defence NATO and the EU have taken up exactly the same 'non-Article 5' or Petersberg Tasks, NATO and EU processes are in this regard perfectly complementary; in order to ensure coordination, an EU-NATO Capability Group has been set up. Double work is avoided by relying where possible on existing data from NATO's Defence Planning Process; to that end experts from both organizations can meet in a configuration known as HTF Plus. It has been suggested however to further increase coordination by reviewing the annual Defence Planning Questionnaire that is sent to NATO Allies, in order to incorporate to a larger extent the specific needs of the EU. Obviously, if in the longer term the EU would be able to introduce a scheme for comprehensive top-down planning, the relations with NATO force planning should be reassessed more thoroughly.

Another part of the Prague decisions on transformation was the creation of the NRF, which is to reach its full operational capacity of 21,000 in 2006. Like the EU, NATO too aims to increase its capacity for rapid response. The NRF will consist of national forces that are assigned to it for a fixed period of time and which, like the battlegroups, rotate through three phases: training to achieve 'certification' as a high-readiness force, stand-by (for six months) and standing-down. As consecutive national forces rotate through the NRF, the certification process serves as a very important mechanism to enhance the usability of forces, notably with regard to high-intensity, rapid response operations, just as the battlegroups; criteria for participation could thus be coordinated. A large number of Member States do not have sufficient rapid response forces to contribute both to a battlegroup and to the NRF in the stand-by phase at the same time. The rotation schemes of the battlegroups (3,000 on stand-by) and the NRF (21,000 on stand-by) can be coordinated however so that national forces can alternate between both. National forces that constitute battlegroups could also as such take part in the NRF rotation.

Nevertheless, in the current state of European capabilities both schemes could interfere, if the forces on stand-by in the framework of the NRF could during those six months not be called upon for operations in any other framework. If a crisis would occur in which NATO would decide not to intervene and the EU subsequently would, but would then not be able to call on the European forces in the NRF, the EU would be deprived of a relatively large portion of its most deployable capabilities. This is especially relevant for larger-scale operations and in the light of the EU's ambition to implement operations at the request of the UN. The 21,000 troops on stand-by in the NRF, which equals about one third of the average number of forces constantly deployed by the EU-25 in different frameworks, would thus be deadlocked. This issue is all the more important

---

[11] Chemical, biological, radiological, and nuclear defence; intelligence, surveillance, and target acquisition; air-to-ground surveillance; command, control and communications; combat effectiveness, including precision guided munitions and suppression of enemy air defences; strategic air and sea lift; air-to-air refuelling; and deployable combat support and combat service support units.

because of the more fundamental strategic divide that has arisen: in view of the huge differences on the rules for the use of force between the Allies, and in view of different geo-strategic interests (see for example the willingness to join in peace support operations in Africa), it is difficult to imagine a scenario in which unanimity could be found on the need to deploy the NRF, except perhaps for low intensity operations which do not require an NRF-type force in the first place. Although its utility with regard to force transformation is undeniable, the operational value of the NRF seems questionable. It would be recommendable therefore to provide for double-hatting and allow the use of European forces in the NRF for EU-operations. The EU forces engaged in the NRF would thus at the same time be available to NATO and the EU.

At the strategic level, EU-NATO relations are forever clouded by the issue of autonomy – this too is a consequence of the complete overlap between the EU's Petersberg Tasks and NATO's non-Article 5 operations. Although it was envisaged from the beginning that 'where NATO as a whole is not engaged', the EU can act, with the use of NATO assets or without, actual initiatives to provide the EU with the necessary capabilities for the latter scenario have always caused friction. Among the EU Member States, the UK especially has always been very fearful of ESDP duplicating or undermining NATO. Even though in 1998 London, together with Paris, was instrumental in launching ESDP, its motivation was to enhance the performance of European military capabilities, which the British acknowledged for the other Member States was only possible through European cooperation, both for budgetary and political reasons. When it came to the political decision-making however, London was much more reluctant, preferring enhanced European military capabilities to be used in a NATO framework rather than by an autonomous EU, although inevitably – as the British soon found out – ESDP evolved in the latter direction.

Thus the proposal of the April 2003 'chocolate summit' to set up 'a collective capability for planning and conducting operations for the European Union' in the Brussels suburb of Tervuren met with fierce criticism, especially in the UK and the US. Secretary of State Colin Powell had it known that Europe needs more means, not more headquarters. The critics' main thrust was that such a capacity would be a useless duplication of NATO's operational headquarters, SHAPE. Only after a hot-tempered debate, which saw vociferous opposition from the UK – which presented a counter-proposal to set up a more distinctive European cell within SHAPE – and intense pressure from the fiercely opposed US administration, was a compromise finally reached. This agreement was formally adopted by the December 2003 European Council, the same summit where the Heads of State and Government proved unable to agree on the Draft Constitution. Ironically, the most controversial ESDP-related item was thus the only one to be decided upon in 2003. After so much discussion, it passed very easily even – *'l'affaire est passée comme une lettre à la poste'*, as a French diplomat worded it. The compromise provides for a three-tier structure:

• An EU cell at SHAPE provides for the scenario in which the EU conducts an operation having recourse to NATO assets under the 'Berlin Plus' framework.

This would ensure that such an operation would have a more distinct European character and it would facilitate the exercise of political control and strategic direction by the Political and Security Committee – both were sometimes sensed to be inadequate during the Concordia operation in Macedonia, which was implemented under the 'Berlin Plus' framework. In spite of the 'Berlin Plus' agreement, the availability of NATO's command structure can never be an absolute certainty however; relying on it as sole option would make EU military action dependent on the goodwill of individual Allies who could easily frustrate EU use of NATO assets (EUISS, 2004, p.109).

• Therefore the EU can also undertake fully autonomous operations, in cases when NATO is unwilling or unable to intervene or lend its help. This scenario is far from unimaginable: on the one hand, NATO and the US have no interest in peace support operations in Africa for example, as the EU did in the case of 'Artemis'; on the other hand, the operational planning capacity in SHAPE, which is not exactly unlimited either, might very well be unavailable because of other NATO involvements, as in Afghanistan. An EU capacity is thus indispensable if the Union is to be able to use the military instrument available to it at all times. The first option then is to make use of a national operational HQ provided by a Member State, which is then to be 'multinationalized' by adding on personnel from the other Member States.

• When no national HQ is identified, and especially when a joint civil and military response is required (which seems to cover the majority of, if not all, operations), the new Civil-Military Cell and Operations Centre in the EUMS, which will integrate planning of the civil and military dimension of interventions, can be used. The EUMS does strategic planning, that is managing the force catalogue in function of a typology of possible operations, but originally had not been equipped for planning and conducting actual operations. The Civil-Military Cell is not a fully-fledged standing HQ as in the original 'Tervuren-proposal', but a core that can be rapidly built on as required; it is to be capable of conducting operations on the scale of Artemis.

One can expect that the EU Cell and Operations Centre will expand, acquiring more standing elements and the capacity to manage larger-scale operations. In the eyes of the participants in the 'chocolate summit', it is certainly only the beginning of what will grow into a larger autonomous European planning capacity. Currently five national operational HQs have been declared available, though usually only the French and British are considered capable of conducting large-scale operations; the question is whether these will always be available as the EU takes on more operations, as envisaged by the battlegroup concept, and including long-term commitments, as on the Balkans. Expanding the EU body would be preferable to a proliferation of national HQs, which is the true duplication problem. Furthermore, multinationalization of national HQs is not always easy. A European HQ would offer all Member States, including those incapable of setting up a national structure, the chance to participate, promoting the harmonization of doctrine, a sense of joint ownership and the emergence of a European *esprit de corps*. It would also offer the possibility to build on the EU's experience with combined civil-military operations and create a body of expertise and mechanisms and procedures that are not readily available elsewhere (Zilmer-Johns, 2004, p.64); a European HQ could thus embody the distinctive approach of the EU. Perhaps ultimately such a European HQ could be merged with existing NATO assets into a jointly owned 'EU-NATO Operational Planning and Command Centre' that would replace SHAPE (Lindley-French and Algieri, 2004, pp.40-2). The eternal duplication debate would thus be overcome, but the condition would of course be that the decision-making autonomy of the EU would be preserved and access to the capability guaranteed.

The Security Architecture up for Revision

However, rebuilding the transatlantic partnership will take more than reconciling the capability-planning and HQ arrangements of NATO and the EU – more than 'Berlin Plus' can settle (von Platen, 2003, p.10). Without political transformation, the defence transformation sponsored by NATO is unlikely to succeed (Binnendijk and Kugler, 2004). A much more fundamental rethinking of the Alliance is in order.

NATO still has a role to play. First and foremost, the Alliance is based on a community of values. 'Shared values and common interests form the basis of our partnership with the US and Canada', reads the December 2003 European Council Declaration on Transatlantic Relations. This fact outweighs the strategic differences between the EU and the Bush administration. Besides, another administration might change elements of the US strategy again; and the differences for the greater part concern instruments, and not the overall objectives of foreign policy. The principles enshrined in the EU Treaty – liberty, democracy, respect for human rights and fundamental freedoms, the rule of law – are common to all Allies. It is logical therefore that the sense of community that is thus created – and which has been strengthened through mutual contributions to one another's security in the course of history – continues to be translated into a collective defence commitment, as a long-term insurance against threats to the very survival of any of these like-minded States, even when no such threat is imaginable in the near future. Europe and North America can indeed be said to constitute a 'security community' (Pouliot and Lachmann, 2004). It is because of the communality of values that even though not all EU Member States line up behind the US on every occasion, Europe still remains the US' most solid ally (Cohen-Tanugi, 2003, p.54); the motivations of other States who join ad hoc coalitions of the willing are often more of a tactical or opportunistic nature and therefore less steadfast. Secondly, NATO has proved its efficacy as an operational organization for non-Article V missions; it is therefore the obvious – and most efficient, for permanence – framework to use when all Allies agree on the need to intervene militarily. Thirdly, through its defence planning, the NRF, Allied Command Transformation (ACT) etc., NATO is an instrument for the permanent enhancement of military capabilities in terms of usability and interoperability.

But even though the EU and NATO can be made to be complementary from the *military* point of view, with regard to operations and capabilities, a redefinition of the transatlantic partnership is in order, to take into account the Union's *political* ambitions as an international actor as expressed in the Security Strategy – a structural factor – and the fact that these do represent a different approach from that of the current NSS – a conjunctural factor. The implications for the Alliance go well beyond the specific case of Iraq. That NATO can act out-of-area for non-Article 5 missions is agreed, in view of the mandate of the NRF and the actual deployment, under the NATO flag, in Afghanistan. But is the operation in Afghanistan really foreboding a global role for NATO or will it remain the exception, motivated perhaps by some of the Allies' desire to make amends after their refusal to support the military intervention in Iraq? Will NATO only act out-of-area when there is a direct link to collective defence and the security of one of the Allies, as was the case with the Taliban regime in Afghanistan, which was linked to the perpetrators of '9/11'? Or will it also take on other operations, for example, at the request of the UN?

In the past, the US has often sought political and indirect military support from its Allies, but actual military operations have usually been implemented by American forces alone or by ad hoc coalitions of the willing. The initial operations against the Taliban are a case in point. Even though the Alliance for the first time in its history invoked Article 5, US Secretary of Defence Donald Rumsfeld declined any direct military support, which illustrated US reluctance to submit its forces to the authority of NATO, or 'warfare by committee', as for the Kosovo campaign – as one senior Pentagon official explained, 'If anyone thinks that the US is ever going to use the North Atlantic Council to run another major military campaign, they must be smoking pot' (quoted in Grant, 2004, p.67). Rumsfeld's rejection, under the motto 'the mission defines the coalition', badly damaged the cohesion of the Alliance. With the creation of the NRF at the end of 2002, which is to consist mainly of European forces, the US did demand a major military contribution from its Allies, to a force with a global mandate. But the March 2003 intervention in Iraq was also undertaken by a coalition of the willing, which was expanded afterwards for the stabilization force. Again the US requested political support for the intervention, notably in the Security Council, and, in February 2003, only indirect military support from NATO, which led to the well-known rift in the Alliance.

Then in mid-August 2003 the Alliance took over command of ISAF in Afghanistan. And at the end of August, in the light of the American inability to pacify Iraq, so dramatically highlighted by the terror attack on the UN headquarters in Baghdad, and because of the difficulty of further increasing its already enormous troop presence, the US started to consider a UN-mandated operation, under an American force commander, in order to overcome the objections of non-participating states against joining in. This change in US thinking became even more pronounced when at NATO's Ministerial Meeting in Brussels on 4 December 2003 Colin Powell urged the Alliance to examine how it might do more to support peace and stability in Iraq than the low-level support to the 23-nation division then led by Poland in central Iraq – the first appeal to NATO since the invasion. The US apparently came to realize that the self-declared 'war on terror' implies such a huge commitment that support of 'Allies and friends' is indispensable. Shunning NATO, like the 'neo-cons' had done, tempted perhaps by the even further-going prospect of eventually freeing budgets and troops by downscaling US involvement in the Alliance altogether, was no longer an option. Some, like Haseler (2004, p.165), even argue that in the present circumstances the US needs the EU and NATO more than the other way around, as indispensable allies and support bases for its global politico-military designs, whereas the EU, not having military ambitions of a similar magnitude, has much less to demand.

Accordingly, 2004 saw the establishment of the NATO training mission in Iraq and continued American attempts to convince other Allies of sending troops, both for the training mission and for the occupation forces. It has been argued however that training Iraqi forces outside of Iraq, as a number of Allies are doing, is actually much more efficient than doing it in the country, because this requires huge measures to assure the security of instructors and recruits alike. Taking part in the occupation is not feasible for those Allies that opposed the invasion in the first place: as demonstrated above, the current potential of EU Member States to deploy additional capabilities for high-intensity operations is limited, so their involvement would have little impact on the ground anyway, but the costs would be enormous, in terms of credibility in the eyes of their own public opinion, and in terms of political leverage towards the countries of the region. If all EU Member States or the EU as such were militarily involved in Iraq, no alternative voice would be available.

So whereas the Allies had been willing to accept NATO involvement in operations against the Taliban in Afghanistan in the context of Article 5, and did agree to direct involvement in UN-mandated ISAF, the February 2003 crisis which saw Belgium, France and Germany objecting to even the indirect use of NATO means, and thus of their forces, for a strategy vis-à-vis Iraq with which they disagreed, had in the meantime made it crystal-clear that all Allies will not condone the implication of NATO in just any case. From the comprehensive security point of view, the use of force can be an ultimate instrument only and requires a sufficient legal base – which was present in the case of Afghanistan, but not in that of Iraq. In other words, the US cannot expect the Alliance to step in simply whenever Washington feels it appropriate. As a number of Allies will not see NATO instrumentalized in function of US foreign policy, involvement of the Alliance, and of the newly-created NRF, is far from automatic.

If the Alliance is to survive, and it has an *acquis* well worth preserving, then a rethinking of relations within NATO is in order. A more flexible attitude towards non-Article 5 missions is needed, acknowledging the fact that Allies will not always agree on such operations. Nor can they be expected to just on the ground of transatlantic solidarity, because of the inherently political nature of missions that do not concern the territorial integrity of an Ally itself. Furthermore, what holds true for the NRF in particular also goes for NATO operations in general: in view of the current strategic differences between Allies, there do not seem to be many scenarios in which unanimity could be found in the North Atlantic Council. Even Nick Witney, Chief Executive of the EDA, has suggested that 'in the short to medium term, it was perhaps easier to envisage new ESDP operations than new NATO missions' (European Union Presidency, 2004, p.27). Therefore scenarios other than involvement of NATO as such are required, in order to avoid recrimination between Allies every time one of them proposes an operation that not all of the others consent to. The growing international actorness of the EU, and its military capabilities in particular, have to be taken into account. Without fundamental rethinking, the Alliance plainly risks lapsing into disuse and to stop functioning as an operational organization. Differences and disputes between Allies are manageable as long as they are addressed within the framework of genuinely shared strategic objectives, but in the absence of such a framework they have the potential to become debilitating (Council on Foreign Relations, 2004, p.8).

A Two-Pillar NATO

The concept that might bring a solution is that of a two-pillar Alliance, in which there is a more equitable balance between, in particular, the US and the EU.

A two-pillar NATO would not necessarily imply setting up a formal European caucus within the Alliance. Rather it would automatically follow from the further enhancement of collective foreign and security policy-making in the EU that within NATO, EU Member States will share viewpoints on issues that they have previously debated and decided upon in the framework of the EU. In a certain sense a two-pillar constellation is *de facto* already coming into existence, as since the creation of ESDP ever closer formal relations are being established between the EU as such and NATO. This is certainly felt by the non-EU European members of NATO, which perceive an 'ESDP-ization' of the Alliance (Knutsen, 2002; Missiroli, 2002), and probably even more so by Canada – one Canadian diplomat once described NATO as 'US-dominated euro-centrism'.

Given the development of ESDP, in a two-pillar NATO the EU and the US – plus Canada – each could assume first-level responsibility in the case of events in their respective neighbourhoods which they judge require a – coercive or non-coercive – military response, as far as non-Article 5 situations go. Each pillar could either act autonomously or making use of NATO assets according to pre-arranged mechanisms, such as Berlin Plus. The US would thus also have to agree a 'Washington Plus' with the Alliance. With regard to the respective neighbourhoods, the second tier NATO level would then only be activated and operations only implemented under the NATO flag: either if the means of one pillar prove insufficient to quell the crisis, a development which in a worst-case scenario might evolve into an Article 5-situation; or if the EU and the US politically agree to both become involved from the beginning, because they both feel important interests are at stake. The two-pillar scheme must not be limited to the respective neighbourhoods. Although the EU certainly has a specific responsibility for security in its own neighbourhood, it is at the same time a global actor – a division of labour in which the EU would only deal with its neighbourhood and the US with the global challenges (Tertrais, 2002, pp.21-2) is not feasible. Therefore, both the EU and the US could also initiate non-Article 5 operations in support of their global policies or at the request of the UN or a regional organization such as the OSCE, again either with or without the use of NATO assets according to pre-arranged mechanisms. Only if they both agree to become involved could such operations be implemented under the NATO flag, regardless of their geographical scope.

For all non-Article 5 missions, the respective pillars rather than NATO as such would thus be the 'default level'. The pillar initiating an operation would have an obligation to consult with the other Allies; if they choose to join in, the initiative can become a NATO operation. Otherwise, the initiating pillar can implement it under its own (EU or US) flag, with or without the use of NATO assets; it can then choose, if it wants to, to invite other Allies to participate in its operation. Article 4, which contains the obligation for Allies to consult, thus acquires a pivotal role (von Plate, 2003, p.21). As far as the EU is concerned, the existing mechanisms for participation of non-EU members of NATO in EU operations could remain valid, that is they will be automatically invited to participate in operations making use of NATO assets; for EU-only operations it belongs to the discretionary authority of the Council to invite them or not. In both cases the States concerned will take part in the daily running of the operation on an equal footing with the EU Member States, but political control and strategic direction will remain with the Council and the Political and Security Committee.

Rather than attributing a formal 'right of first refusal' to NATO, which if interpreted strictly means that the EU can only act when NATO formally adopts a decision not to, it would thus be a matter of consultation between the Allies whether an operation would be run by one or other of the pillars or by NATO as such. An unconditional right of first refusal just is too rigid a mechanism, which does not answer well to all contingencies, nor is it possible to lay down so rigorous a set of procedures as to preclude different interpretations of what each organization is permitted to do (Brenner, 2002, p.75). Operation 'Artemis', an EU operation without the use of NATO assets, proves as much. The decision to launch the operation (5 June 2003), the project of which apparently was the object of fierce US criticism at NATO's Madrid summit two days before, was taken following a request by UN Secretary General Kofi Annan. In such cases, the spirit of the Alliance calls for transparency, and the EU did offer other Allies the possibility to participate, but making such operations conditional on formal NATO assent would inordinately detract from the autonomy of both the EU and the UN. As the US was not interested in contributing to peace support operations in Central Africa in the first place – and in fact voted in favour of the mandating resolution in the Security Council – this was certainly the case with 'Artemis'. NATO does not exercise a right of first refusal with regard to national operations undertaken by the Allies, and should not do so vis-à-vis the EU either.

A two-pillar constellation would imply a pragmatic attitude, choosing according to the situation at hand the framework that is most suitable, NATO or one of the pillars, or, for rapid response operations, the battlegroups or the NRF. Other ideas that have been raised, for example to do away with the consensus rule, as was suggested in some American circles following the February 2003 crisis (Michel, 2003), would reduce NATO to a mere toolbox for utterly ad hoc coalition-making and would ultimately lead to the irrelevance of the Alliance, just as leaving things as they are would do. The advantage of the two-pillar structure would be that non-participation in a non-Article 5 operation initiated by the other pillar, perhaps because of political objections such as in the case of the invasion of Iraq, would no longer need to give rise to accusations of breaching transatlantic solidarity, while the NATO emblem could only be used for operations that all Allies consent to. At the same time, mere ad hoc coalition-making would be avoided thanks to the delineation of first- and second-level responsibility for non-Article 5 missions. The Alliance as a community of values expressed in a collective defence commitment would be preserved, while building in the necessary flexibility to prevent divergences between Allies on issues of 'day-to-day policy' from endangering the organization as such.

As a pragmatic solution, the two-pillar concept could perhaps constitute the middle ground between staunch 'atlanticists' and fervent 'europeanists', since neither organization would receive overall preference over the other. The option of a division of labour along the lines of 'soft' and 'hard' security which is often put forward, for example by Moravcsik (2003), or which is implicitly present in many critiques of the EU's ambitions, would be unworkable in practice. The EU as well as the US needs to be able to implement the whole range of instruments in order to effectively respond to multi-dimensional contingencies. Besides, there always is a risk of operations at the low end of the scale of violence evolving into effective conflict as the situation on the ground changes; the initiating pillar must then have the means to respond. And an EU 'hard security' capacity is needed to be able to act in cases when NATO/US assets are unavailable. Without a 'hard' capacity, the EU would have to count on the willingness of the US to solve all of its problems, which it cannot, and should not, do. Such a situation would easily lead to resentment on the US side as well, who would have to face much greater risks and assume a much larger share of the burden than the EU; it would thus prove politically divisive, also because Europeans and Americans would less frequently share common tasks and experiences (Council on Foreign Relations, 2004, p.12). A 'hard' capacity is also essential for the credibility of the EU. The Petersberg Tasks should not be interpreted as concerning only 'soft' operations, as is so often done by those opposed to an autonomous EU role. The Petersberg Tasks in fact imply all types of operations short of collective defence, which is indeed clear from their extended formulation in the Draft Constitution. The rejection of a soft-hard division of labour has implications for the US as well: while the US possesses the most effective war-fighting capacity in the world, important capability deficiencies will have to be addressed with regard to lower-intensity missions and the civilian dimension of operations.

A two-pillar constellation would meet the long-standing US demands for more burden-sharing within the Alliance and for a greater effort with regard to defence and crisis management on the part of the European Allies. These demands were put in very explicit terms after the Kosovo operation, but they date back to the early days of the post-Cold War period, if not of the Alliance itself. It should not be forgotten that the US only intervened in the civil wars ravaging the territory of former Yugoslavia after all European attempts at conflict resolution had failed.

Likewise, when Albania collapsed into anarchy in 1997, the US made it quite clear that it was not considering an intervention in what it regarded as a European problem in which no important American interests were directly at stake. If the EU were formally to take on primary responsibility for crises in its neighbourhood and would continue to build the necessary military capabilities to that end, then US assets would become available for other global contingencies. Although part of them may be redeployed, this would not imply a complete withdrawal of US troops in Europe, if only because of the need for European bases for the projection of force. Making Europe more capable thus certainly will not be at the expense of NATO as some observers fear (Cimbalo, 2004).

But, there is an inextricable link between burden-sharing and power sharing (Hulsman, 2000). In its December 2000 strategic document, Strengthening Transatlantic Security – A US Strategy for the 21st Century, the Clinton administration recognized that 'development of a foreign and security policy for the EU is a natural, even an inevitable, part of the development of broader European integration', and expressly stated that: 'real cooperation requires a two-way street'. The US cannot expect a greater defence effort on the part of the EU Member States without allowing them a greater say in the running of the Alliance, and vice versa. In the end, increasing the performance of Europe's military capabilities will unavoidably change the political constellation, especially in view of the EU's enhanced role as an international actor. A two-pillar Alliance would at the same time value European capabilities and provide for the flexibility that would allow for the EU to play its proper part on the international scene. Introducing the two-pillar notion could be the subject of a revision of the Alliance's Strategic Concept, which at the same time could be amended so as to do away with the vague references to NATO's out-of-area role in favour of an unambiguous statement of Alliance missions.

A Vital Transformation

Pleas for a more equitable Alliance are not new. Back in 1962, President John F. Kennedy made a well-known reference to the importance of the European pillar. The reactivation of the Western European Union (WEU) starting in the 1980s was a first attempt to build a 'European Security and Defence Identity' (ESDI) within the Alliance, which the Maastricht Treaty also designated as the military arm of the EU. Crises are not a new thing for the Alliance either; France's withdrawal from the integrated military structure in 1966 and the massive protests following the 'double-track decision' of 1979 are just two of the most prominent examples.

What is new however, is on the one hand the end of the bi-polar world order and with it of the cohesive force that the perceived Soviet menace generated, and on the other hand the emergence of an ever more self-conscious and ambitious EU that wants to pursue its own agenda in international relations – and that is equipping itself with the necessary capabilities to that end. The transfer of WEU's newly established operational role to the EU following the inclusion of the Petersberg Tasks in the 1997 Amsterdam Treaty and the launching of ESDP signalled the definite end of the taboo on security and defence as subjects of European integration. It is for the first time therefore that a real possibility exists to create an equitable transatlantic partnership in NATO. This window of opportunity has not gone unnoticed. Belgian Prime Minister Guy Verhofstadt, among others, has repeatedly called for a strong European pillar within NATO, while Finnish general Gustav Hägglund when Chairman of the EU Military Committee held a remarkable plea for a thorough reorganization of the security architecture. The 'chocolate summit' was put in this perspective too: 'In NATO, we do not have too much America, we have too little Europe, and that is what we want to change', German Chancellor Gerhard Schröder declared after the summit.

Restructuring the Alliance would not only allow for a global role for NATO and for more burden-sharing, to the benefit of the US, and provide more scope for the EU policy agenda. Restructuring appears to be vital to the future of the Alliance. Tensions between the US administration and the EU demonstrate that a fundamental reappraisal of the Alliance is in order, taking into account the changes in the international environment and in relations between Allies, if NATO is to remain a useful and performing organization. The future of NATO is of course related to the broader picture of the global security architecture. If the EU and the US, and their strategic partners, can find a new consensus on how to deal collectively with global security issues, as discussed in Chapter 4, it will be easier for them to find agreement on joint actions for which NATO can be put to use. The agreement on NATO involvement in Afghanistan has gone some way to restore transatlantic relations after the rift over Iraq, even though it remains a source of constant friction between Allies. This renewed goodwill can be put to use to rethink the Alliance.

Collective Defence

Next to permanent structured cooperation, two other breakthroughs in the field of ESDP resulted from the Convention and were introduced in the Draft Constitution, both related to collective defence; just like structured cooperation, both were strongly supported by the participants in the 'chocolate summit'. Although the issue is absent from the Strategy, it is nevertheless being addressed.

Firstly, the 'solidarity clause' (Articles I-43 and III-329) will allow for the use of all instruments, including ESDP, to prevent terrorism and to assist Member States, at their request, in case of terrorist strikes or natural or man-made disasters on their territory; currently, ESDP instruments can only be used outside of the EU. As its title makes clear, this is an important expression of solidarity between the Member States. But its importance is more than symbolic: concrete measures in the field of ESDP are already envisaged, *inter alia* for the protection of infrastructure and major events – such as the role NATO played in the security of the 2004 Olympic Games in Athens – as well as for consequence management. The primary role in the prevention and repression of terrorism remains with the criminal justice, police and intelligence services. It is indeed important to note that for the EU the military instrument plays only a secondary, complementary role with regard to internal security, hence European reluctance towards the American concept of 'homeland security', often perceived as entailing the militarization of this policy field. In the European context, civil protection is a much more viable concept. This is naturally related to the different threat perception on both sides of the Atlantic: since Europeans do not feel the same intense threat, and certainly do not consider themselves to be at war, they reject an internal security policy that would inordinately limit civil liberties and accord a major role to the military. In the 'solidarity clause' the emphasis is less on the defence of territory than on the safeguarding of the functions of a democratic State and on the protection of citizens (Ekengren, 2005); in the field of internal security as well, the EU approach appears to be inspired by human security.

Secondly, the Draft Constitution includes a more explicit reference to collective defence, in this context dubbed 'mutual defence'. Article I-41.7 stipulates that, 'If a Member State is the victim of armed aggression on its territory, the other Member States shall have towards it an obligation of aid and assistance by all means in their power, in accordance with Article 51 of the United Nations Charter'. Just like Article V of the WEU Treaty, on which it is clearly based, this collective defence commitment is worded more strongly than NATO's Article 5, which obliges each Ally to assist the aggressed party 'by taking forthwith [...] such action as it deems necessary'. Previously, Member States had been unable to agree on the inclusion of Article V of the WEU Treaty in the TEU, so this is a major symbolic step in the evolution of the EU towards a fully-fledged political community. Symbolically it will remain however, at least for the time being, for just as WEU upon its creation in 1954 had delegated the implementation of Article V to NATO, the Draft Constitution states that:

> Commitments and cooperation in this area shall be consistent with commitments under NATO, which, for those States which are members of it, remains the foundation of their collective defence and the forum for its implementation.

The actual planning and organization of collective defence by the EU is thus not foreseen and will remain the prerogative of NATO. In fact, under the Draft Constitution NATO is implicated further in the defence of Europe than perhaps some had preferred or understood. In a hypothetical scenario of an EU Member State which is not a member of NATO being attacked, the other EU Member States will have an obligation of assistance, *through* NATO for those that are members of it – NATO will thus be drawn into the defence of a non-member. Of course, no such threat exists in the foreseeable future and, more importantly, an act of aggression against any Member State of the EU equals an act of aggression against the EU as a whole and thus *de facto* constitutes an attack on the Alliance as well. Nevertheless, the legal construction in the Constitution seems to increase the probability of what in the past the US has always wanted to avoid: automatic implication in a European conflict.

In a reformed, two-pillar NATO, solidarity in the event of an effective Article 5 situation would naturally still be complete and unquestionable. Article 5 should be interpreted strictly though, so as not to detract from the value of this ultimate security commitment. NATO would thus remain the foundation of collective defence and the ultimate guarantee for the security of all Allies. The prospect of effective EU action in this field still remains though, for the Draft Constitution resumes the stipulation in Article 17 of the Treaty on European Union that ESDP 'shall include the progressive framing of a common Union defence policy. This will lead to a common defence, when the European Council, acting unanimously, so decides'. In the current security environment, this is hardly a priority for the EU however.

In order to take into account the concerns of the 'neutral' EU Member States, Article I-41.7 also stipulates that the obligation of aid and assistance 'shall not prejudice the specific character of the security and defence policy of certain Member States', the standard phrase used in the successive Treaties to indicate that these States shall not be obliged to give up their 'neutral' status. During the Cold War, a neutral or unaligned status was a viable third way between the two superpowers and their associated alliances, but one has to question the validity of neutrality in the current world order. EU Membership and the reciprocal intrusiveness which it implies certainly make for a strong and ever closer union and a powerful sense of solidarity; by third parties, the EU is already often perceived as a single actor – perhaps exaggerating the degree of harmonization and unification. Member States' economic, political and other interests have become inextricably intertwined. *De facto* an act of aggression against any EU Member State therefore constitutes an attack on the Union as a whole. Ideally therefore all Member States should subscribe to the principle of 'mutual defence'.

A Broader EU-US Partnership

The US often functions as 'the other' and thus helps to stimulate the emergence of an ever stronger European identity (Cohen-Tanugi, 2003). The existence of effectively different strategic approaches means that the EU and the US will continue to have differences of opinion as to how to deal with the problems – current and future ones – of this world. Yet, these differences need not be irreconcilable. By focussing on Iraq, it is easily forgotten that on other issues, e.g. North Korea, policies are remarkably similar. Nor should the European Strategy be interpreted as being directed against the US. On the contrary, the EU and the US should aim to reinforce the transatlantic partnership in all fields of external policy, not just in NATO, in order to put their combined means to use in the most efficient and effective way. The Strategy words it clearly: 'Acting together, the European Union and the United States can be a formidable force for good in the world'. But the Strategy immediately adds that the aim should be 'an effective and balanced partnership'. An equitable partnership is indeed required, one which both partners enter into on the basis of their own priorities and their own distinctive approaches to security, then to jointly define common interests and policies. As long as the EU had not defined its own agenda, a balanced partnership was impossible; the intra-European strategic debate is inextricably linked to the debate on the autonomy of EU policy-making vis-à-vis the US (WEU, 2003a). So the adoption of the Security Strategy has been a necessary first step towards an enhanced transatlantic partnership.

The transatlantic partnership is more than NATO, as the Strategy itself points out; NATO concerns just the politico-military dimension of what should be a much broader EU-US partnership. Its military structures are an instrument of choice in cases when both pillars of the Alliance decide to act together, but are of no use to deal with the fundamental gap in terms of access to the basic public goods that is underlying more immediate politico-military concerns. In other words, the Alliance is a very useful tool, but with a limited field of application – it is therefore ill-adapted to address the comprehensive range of problems that at least the EU has identified in the current globalized security environment. This also means that NATO is not the most suitable forum to discuss EU-US cooperation in all of these other areas. Because of this fundamental reason, NATO *de facto* no longer is the structuring factor in transatlantic relations, nor can it remain the primary political forum. At the same time, the strategic divide that has arisen between the Allies in the wake of Iraq means that in the politico-military sphere of action, in which it does remain one of the primary actors, its effectiveness is hampered as well – unless, as suggested, a rethinking is possible that takes into account the new state of Euro-American relations. Next to their military cooperation in the framework of NATO, the EU and the US therefore also need to consult directly, and build cooperation, on a broad range of issues – and not only their military assets, but all of their other capabilities as well must be brought into the equation (von Plate, 2003, p.12; Hunter, 2004b).

Since the 1990 Transatlantic Declaration, annual EU-US Summits bring together the President of the US, the President of the European Commission, the Head of State or Government of the EU Member State holding the EU Presidency and the High Representative. Relations were enhanced following the adoption of the New Transatlantic Agenda (NTA) in December 1995, which focuses on four topics: promoting peace and stability, democracy and development around the world; responding to global challenges; contributing to the expansion of world trade and closer economic relations; and building bridges across the Atlantic. The annual Summits are now prepared by a Group of Senior Level Representatives (SLG), composed of senior officials from the European Commission, the EU Presidency and the US State Department, which meets four to six times a year and prepares a report to the Summit leaders on achievements and new priorities. It is supported in its work by an NTA Task Force, which follows closely the day-to-day implementation of the NTA, prepares the SLG meetings, and recommends areas for SLG input. These high-level summits lack focus however and, although 'endless shopping lists of key priorities' have been produced (Heisbourg, 2004, p.38), they have not served to effectively coordinate policies. Actual cooperation therefore is still very much ad hoc and, in general, rather limited. Concrete cooperation has been established, a number of difficult debates notwithstanding, in the fight against terrorism and non-proliferation, notably between police, intelligence and judicial services; on these specific issues, an intense dialogue is in place, not least at the request of the US. But the general approaches to terrorism and proliferation are not being coordinated, nor are policies in all the other areas of mutual concern, in spite of the fact that in many areas, regional as well as thematic, it is easy to see how increased coordination of policies and effective joint action would greatly increase the leverage of Brussels and Washington vis-à-vis third States and enhance the chances of success.

As shown in Chapter 3, the Middle East peace process in particular and political reform in the Arab world in general are obvious examples of issues on which a lack of transatlantic cooperation has slowed down if not paralyzed progress. The peace process can only advance if the EU and the US work together, for their respective leverage is limited to one of the parties to the conflict. Promoting democratization in the Arab world would greatly benefit from a harmonization of objectives, benchmarks and benefits allocated between Brussels and Washington, making it impossible for a number of regimes to continue to play off one against the other. Other regional issues of evident mutual interest are the relationship with Russia and its role as a global partner in the Security Council, the future place of Ukraine in the European system, and the future of the Caucasus, a region where the US is very active, but which gains more and more importance on the agenda of the EU as well. In this regard, not only a rethinking of NATO, but a thorough reconsideration of the role and structures of the OSCE as well is in order. While the OSCE certainly has a wealth of experience in the field of CSBMs and performs some very useful tasks, for example with regard to the protection of the rights of minorities, its role is also more and more being encroached upon by the EU. As a forum uniting the EU, the US and Russia, the OSCE obviously has a great potential value, but perhaps thought should be given to a refocusing of the organization, so as to allow it to concentrate on the fields where its added value is evident and to terminate its actions in areas that are nowadays more effectively covered by other actors. The need for EU-US consultation is evident. With regard to the global level as well, a harmonization of views between the EU and the US is at the core of the attempt to forge a consensus again on the collective security system of the UN. As demonstrated in Chapter 4, a 'grand bargain' could be possible on the basis of the recommendations of the High-Level Panel.

Coordination on such a broad range of topics requires much more elaborate mechanisms for consultation than currently exist. While the annual EU-US Summit could remain the forum where the broad orientations are defined and priority issues are debated, this could be complemented by more regular high-level but informal consultation, as well as ad hoc meetings, between the future EU Foreign Minister and the US Secretary of State, along the lines of the informal 'Gymnich' meetings in the EU. Almost daily direct consultation between the relevant desks of the Council and the Commission and the State Department and the Pentagon, at senior official and expert level, would be needed in order to implement concrete cooperation and to operate jointly within the framework defined by the summits. The New Transatlantic Agenda's tenth anniversary would be the ideal occasion to renew the EU-US partnership and adopt a new declaration, which would provide for more extensive consultation and concrete cooperation. As the example of the EU-UN partnership shows, no heavy legal basis is required – it would probably be counterproductive. The possibility of concluding a transatlantic treaty, as Guérot (2005) suggests, could perhaps in a much later stage be considered as the symbolic expression of EU-US cooperation. For a renewed transatlantic partnership to be possible, both sides of the Atlantic would have to muster the political will to recognize each other as equal partners and to talk on that basis. The US specifically would have to accept the EU as the primary interlocutor rather than attempting to steer EU policies by way of bilateral contacts with individual Member States. And perhaps such recognition on the part of the US would stimulate Member States to commit more earnestly to the CFSP. Of course, consensus will not be found in all cases and joint action will certainly not always be possible. But more extensive consultation would at least ensure that the reasons behind the respective policies would be known, and would diminish the chance that different policies would again lead to emotional debates and mutual recriminations.

Strategic Partners and Multilateralism

Because of historic ties and the similarity in basic values, the US remains the EU's primary strategic partner. Whenever Brussels and Washington can agree on a common position and act together within the relevant multilateral institutions, they certainly can make an enormous contribution to global governance, in all policy fields, including the reform of the multilateral architecture itself. But the Strategy rightly calls for the development of other 'strategic partnerships' as well, first of all with Russia, and also with Japan, China, Canada and India – in the first draft, Russia was set on an equal par with the latter four, but in the final version it receives additional emphasis. The partnership with Russia, a permanent member of the Security Council, must indeed extend beyond the European continent and address global issues. The same obviously holds true for China, with whom, a number of obvious difficulties notwithstanding, relations are gradually increasing. In October 2003 China adopted its first policy document on the EU, which calls *inter alia* for increased cooperation to strengthen the UN. Relations with Japan and India are following the same trend: mutual recognition as important global actors and widening of the political dialogue to issues of global governance. Gradually, opportunities for concrete cooperation can now be identified.

It could be argued, as Thiele (2002, p.70) does, that 'Europe holds the key to a cooperative world order in its own hands', or at least partly, in the sense that by assuming itself a larger share of the burden of global governance in its different dimensions, it can then with more authority call on other powers to do likewise. A strong EU-US partnership is only a first step; together they could probably solicit other powers' commitment to global governance much more effectively. In the view of the US National Intelligence Council (NIC, 2005, p.116) therefore 'the transatlantic partnership would be a key factor in Washington's ability to remain the central pivot in international politics'. Calleo (2004, p.32) rightly notes that:

> The real transatlantic issue, therefore, is whether Europe and America can accommodate each other sufficiently so that Europe can continue its integration to a point where the West can come into a harmonious balance. Europe and America will then be able to play together a creative role in shaping the world's future. Otherwise, the West seems likely to grow increasingly preoccupied and disabled by its own internal conflicts.

With Canada, a NATO Ally, long-standing cooperation has been established in many fields, including ESDP; Canadian forces regularly participate in EU operations. European and Canadian approaches are remarkably similar, both advocating a comprehensive view of security, the strengthening of the multilateralism system, and taking into account the human security perspective. This similarity is evidenced by the frequency with which the EU and Canada vote together in international fora. In March 2004 a new EU-Canada Partnership Agenda was adopted, which reconfirmed the commitment to 'effective multilateralism' and established a Coordination Group to ensure the implementation of decisions taken at the political level.

Overcoming the dark side of globalization, closing the gap between haves and have-nots in all aspects, requires the cooperation of all States. Great powers have the greatest responsibility for projecting stability in the world. By further developing its own instruments and capabilities, and working together with strategic partners, the EU can enhance the effectiveness of its contribution.

Chapter 6

Securing Implementation

The adoption of the Strategy by the December 2003 European Council was a major step for EU external action, a step which before the Iraq crisis seemed unimaginable. The challenge now is to put this breakthrough to value and to effectively implement the Strategy's comprehensive approach, or as the European Council worded it, 'to draw all the consequences of those strategic orientations and to mainstream them into all relevant European policies'. The Strategy has clearly been based on trends in existing EU policies and practices – now it has to be translated back into practice again.

In the Strategy, the EU for the first time has a document with the potential to serve as an overall policy framework guiding and thereby integrating the whole of external action, across the pillars. The Strategy should function as a tool for policy-makers, as a set of guidelines for day-to-day policy-making in all of these fields; this applies to setting objectives as well as choosing the instruments to apply and acquiring the necessary means and capabilities. At the same time, the ambitious agenda set forth in the Strategy serves as an affirmation of the EU as a global actor. By the mere adoption of the Strategy, the EU has emphasized its ambition to make a proper mark on the course of global events. Therefore, effectively implementing the Strategy is essential to the credibility of the EU. In that sense, the Strategy also is a measure of performance and the objectives of the Strategy must guide the evaluation of policies as well.

Strategic Choices and Specific Policies

The mission statement of the EU as an international actor can be found in the Treaty. Article III-292.2 of the Draft Constitution contains the revised list of the eight primary missions of the whole of EU external action, which indicates which type of actor the EU aspires to be. The Strategy is more than that, but it is not an operational document either: it is not a plan of action that details individual measures, sets a timeframe or creates a specific capability. Nor was that to be expected, since this is not the objective of such a high-level exercise in strategic thinking. The Strategy lays down the long-term overall objectives of EU external action, the primary instruments and the overall way of achieving these objectives, as well as broad guidelines for the development of means and capabilities. These constitute a set of political choices. The overall choice is that of the comprehensive approach, that is promoting access to the basic public goods as the way to long-term stabilization and conflict prevention. This choice is the most important; it determines all dimensions of external action. This is the approach that the EU will implement in its neighbourhood, which geographically is defined very ambitiously. Here, the EU seeks the leading role itself; resolving the Arab-Israeli conflict is a strategic priority. At the global level, a clear choice is voiced for reinforcing the multilateral system, of which the UN is the core. A strong commitment to actively pursue these objectives, in cooperation with strategic partners, and to enhance capabilities and coherence accordingly completes the picture. All of these choices in all of their aspects have to be elaborated upon and translated into specific policies, sub-strategies – such as those on terrorism and WMD – and action plans, across the pillars, with regard to States, regions and global issues, as well as with regard to the development by the EU itself of the instruments and capabilities that the implementation of the Strategy requires.

The difficulty is that whereas the Strategy words a clear choice for the general approach of comprehensive security, it remains rather vague and prone to interpretation on a number of particular issues, and does not always offer a clear choice with regard to more specific objectives or the instruments to apply. In that sense, not all parts of the Strategy lend themselves as easily to translation into practice. In some instances significant political choices have yet to be made and a number of difficult debates might still lie ahead. In the meantime, on the issues concerned, the EU still lacks a clear and unambiguous framework for day-to-day policy-making, which can render the elaboration of specific policies more difficult.

The Strategy does not offer much guidance with regard to dimensions other than the politico-military ones of global governance or 'effective multilateralism'. Global governance is at the core of the comprehensive approach, and the Strategy does mention a whole range of issues or public goods that are seen as determining 'the quality of international society', such as good governance, social and political reform and respect for the rule of law and human rights. But the Strategy does not prioritize between policy fields or name more specific objectives and instruments, nor does it contain any guidelines as to how the international institutional architecture in general and the UN in particular are to be improved. Similarly, under the heading of 'more capable' the Strategy does not mention capabilities in the fields of *inter alia* aid and trade. The EU certainly is one of the most active and most powerful players in the vast and diverse fields of international trade, development, humanitarian aid, environmental policy etc., most of which fall within the Community competence – all the more reason to make clear strategic choices. Member States are still very much divided on such issues as the reform and future composition of the Security Council, particularly on the desirability of the additional permanent seat desired *inter alia* by Berlin. With regard to international trade and development as well, Member States, according to the political party in power, have different views on how best to organize relations to the benefit of all involved, and on the efforts and sacrifices which the EU itself should be willing to make to that end. Nevertheless, an evident beacon such as the MDGs could have been integrated. It would have been understandably difficult and perhaps unfeasible to include all of these issues at once in the debate on the Strategy, but they cannot remain unaddressed. As it is, although the overall choice for a comprehensive approach is clear, there is an imbalance in the Strategy between the politico-military and the other dimensions of global governance, which risks undermining the credibility of the EU's assertion to pursue a distinctive course in international relations, and which provides a ground for criticism by those in fear of securitization and militarization of EU external action.

Even concerning the politico-military dimension of 'effective multilateralism', the Strategy is much less explicit than it could have been. Implicitly, the Strategy opts for the use of force as a last resort only, and always with a UN Security Council mandate, but the text leaves rather too much room for interpretation. If the Strategy is read together with other documents, such as the EU submission to the UN High-Level Panel, this implicit meaning is confirmed, and policy practice also indicates that this is the view held by the majority of, if not all, the Member States. Nevertheless, on this issue an unambiguous expression of principle is urgently needed, because of the exemplary function of the EU vis-à-vis other States and regions – who will yet support the collective security system of the UN if not the EU? In this regard, the EU has missed an important opportunity, which can however be repaired through its strong support for the efforts to re-forge a consensus on the collective security system on the basis of the Panel's recommendations.

Another question on which the Strategy is not very outspoken is that of transatlantic relations. NATO is mentioned of course, as an important 'strategic partnership' for the EU, specifically with regard to crisis management and enhancing the EU's military capabilities, but no indication is given as to how relations within NATO could evolve in view of the shifting role of the Alliance and its growing global involvement, the creation of the NRF and the affirmation of the EU's own ambitions as an international actor. That 'an effective and balanced partnership' with the US is wanted might indicate that some sort of re-balancing is sought. Partnership with the US includes far more than NATO, as the Strategy says, but no details are given with regard to other policy fields. The EU's degree of military and, by implication, political autonomy vis-à-vis NATO remains a subject of debate between the Member States, as is the nature of the partnership with the US. This dividing line between 'atlanticists' and 'europeanists' is not to be found in all policy fields covered by the EU; on issues such as agriculture, Member States align in completely different ways. It is not even to be found in all fields of external action: for instance, on trade the EU effectively speaks with one voice most of the time. Yet without a consensus on this fundamental issue, the resoluteness and effectiveness of EU external action, especially in the field of CFSP/ESDP and when reacting to crises, will always be in doubt. The internal EU divide on Iraq, which was really caused by the lack of consensus on EU-US relations, has shown as much. If a number of Member States continue to wait for Washington's guidelines before deciding how to act, the EU can never be a true strategic actor. In the field of external action, the future of the transatlantic partnership therefore is the single most important debate, which determines the future of the EU as an international actor – the question that was already on the table when ESDP was created in 1998-1999 thus still requires an answer. This is not to say that the further strengthening of the EU's position as an international actor is aimed against the US. It is not a matter of 'us versus the US'. On the contrary, a comprehensive partnership is called for – but a partnership between equals, for which the self-assertion of the EU is a precondition.

Fewer details are provided of what strategic partnership with Russia, Japan, China, Canada and India might entail. Relations with Russia and China especially, both permanent members of the Security Council, will grow in importance as the EU enhances its profile as an international actor. Because of the many difficulties that both relationships entail, as in the field of promotion of respect for human rights, they are far from uncontroversial and thus demand stronger strategic guidance than is now offered by the Strategy.

An organization that is hardly covered by the Strategy is the OSCE, which is mentioned just once as a regional organization of 'particular significance' to the EU, on a par with the Council of Europe. EU-OSCE relations are certainly very close, but at the same time raise a number of significant questions. As a consequence of ever-growing EU activity, particularly with regard to its neighbourhood, the geographic as well as functional overlap between the two organizations is increasing. The naming of an EU Special Representative for the Southern Caucasus, which is now also mentioned in the Strategy as an area of special interest for the EU, is a case in point. A clearer division of labour, with each organization focussing on the areas in which it can offer the greatest added value, would enhance the efficiency and efficacy of both the EU and the OSCE. The internal functioning of the OSCE offers scope for rethinking. The OSCE is the least visible of all security organizations in Europe, but even though it is perhaps not something that ought to have been included in the Strategy, as a pan-European forum that brings together the EU, the US and Russia, its future role and potential certainly deserve more attention than they currently receive.

The Strategy does not address the issue of nuclear capabilities; France and the UK, the two nuclear weapons states within the EU, are simply not considering Europeanizing their nuclear strategies in any way. In the absence of a direct military threat to the EU, and in view of the limited applicability of deterrence to the remaining politico-military issues that the EU is facing, this can hardly be considered a priority for the EU. The position of the nuclear weapons is of importance however for the non-proliferation policy of the EU: the lack of effective measures in the direction of nuclear disarmament, as demanded by Article VI of the NPT, is an often-used argument by other States seeking to justify the acquisition of a nuclear weapons capacity.

Finally, little guidance is offered with regard to Sub-Saharan Africa, although the Strategy's general approach is evidently applicable to the African continent. A very ambitious comprehensive approach is in fact outlined in the Common Position on conflict prevention, management and resolution in Africa adopted on 26 January 2004, which puts a strong emphasis on empowering African States and regional organizations to deal with crisis and conflict themselves. The EU has repeatedly demonstrated its willingness to contribute to peace and stability in Africa, *inter alia* through its support for the African Union and by staging Operation Artemis (Gowan, 2004a). If this represents a long-term, strategic option, it could have been high lighted in the Strategy, especially since after the UN and its associated organizations, the EU seems to be the international actor that is the most inclined to a strong involvement in Africa in the fields of development and peace support operations.

Institutionalizing Strategic Culture

The December 2003 European Council immediately defined four priority areas of action with regard to the implementation of the Strategy: 'effective multilateralism' with the UN at its core, the fight against terrorism, a strategy towards the region of the Middle East, and a comprehensive policy towards Bosnia-Herzegovina; the European Council also adopted a sub-strategy on WMD. The crucial challenge is however to establish the Strategy, in spite of its imperfections, as *the* reference framework for external action, effectively guiding *all* of the EU's external policies. In the first place therefore, it must be recognized as such by all relevant actors in the EU bodies and the Member States.

Reference to the Strategy should come intuitively to all policy-makers involved in the design, implementation and evaluation of EU external action. A strategic culture should be developed, first of all in the sense that policy-makers should at all times refer back to the fundamental choices contained in the Strategy and make their decisions accordingly. Greater consistency and coherence of EU policies will follow automatically. This applies to the individual Member States as well, and their representatives in the different EU bodies, who continue to be the key decision-makers in large fields of external action. Ideally, the Member States would act through the EU when dealing with issues covered by the Strategy, instead of acting under the national flag as often they still do, especially when specific actions are thought to have a big chance of success and would thus enhance national prestige. Recommendable though the objectives and results of national initiatives often may be, in the end they detract from the image of the EU as a coherent international actor and carry with them the risk of inconsistency and lack of coordination. Of course, individual Member States have specific interests and expertise with regard to certain regions; informal groups of Member States with shared interests can offer an important input to EU policy-making. But the EU remains the most effective platform to translate interests and expertise into policies that matter: the influence of individual Member States, even of large countries, is limited, but acting together, as the EU, they can have a major impact. And Crowe (2004, p.32) emphasizes that 'it is the EU which alone can provide the glue to keep them together, and combine the resources [...] to give muscle to European efforts'.

Reference to the Strategy could also be formally included in the mechanisms and procedures for all aspects of external action. Institutionally, the strengthening of coherence as put forward in Chapter 5 would also serve to reinforce the focus on the Strategy; the EU Minister of Foreign Affairs and the unified External Action Service proposed in the Draft Constitution offer the best prospects for effectively integrating all fields of external action, with the Strategy as conceptual basis. The effective implementation of the Strategy is thus linked to the institutional reform of the EU that the Constitution should provide. The role of the Minister of Foreign Affairs especially would be crucial: through his/her role as chair of the Foreign

Affairs Council and as Commissioner for external action, he/she could ensure that the agenda put forward by the Strategy effectively guides policy. As exemplified by the drafting of the Strategy itself, a policy-making process with due involvement from the Member States but starting from and coordinated by the Foreign Minister, could result in a less divisive process of negotiation and thus in more substantive decisions being taken; bargaining could give way to joint problem-solving (Grevi, 2004). The Foreign Minister could also serve as the focal point for rapid decision-making when events demand short-term preventive measures or crisis management. In the words of Rynning (2003): 'Coercive power demands executive authority to make decisions and command resources'. In this sense too should the EU develop a strategic culture, as called for in the Strategy itself. Policy-makers should not look for politico-military or 'robust' answers to problems by default – it is a mistake to think that strategy concerns only military means (Haglund, 2004, p.482) – but should be disposed to act resolutely and preventively, using all the instruments at their disposal including, if necessary, but certainly not exclusively, coercive means, in order to address problems effectively at an early stage, before they escalate into difficult-to-manage crises.

The evaluation of policy in the light of the Strategy could be institutionalized as well, reorienting existing mechanisms like the annual report on the CFSP and the annual Council debate on the effectiveness of external action. As the Strategy sets objectives and defines approaches for the whole of external action, it can also be used as a tool for the assessment of policies in all fields concerned. In each of the areas covered by the Strategy, such an assessment could list EU documents currently in force and the actions undertaken since the previous assessment, and could then evaluate the effectiveness and efficiency of EU policy in all of these fields, that is the measure in which objectives have been achieved and the relation between the achieved objectives and the means spent to that end. The evaluation would thus highlight the areas in which the EU is most active, as well as those aspects of the Strategy demanding further elaboration into operational policies. Such a comprehensive assessment would also be an ideal occasion to judge the degree of coherence of policies in the different fields of external action and would quickly expose any contradictory actions. A regular evaluation of the Strategy would thus be an important stock-taking exercise, and create the momentum to review policies in the light of the assessment of their effectiveness and efficiency, the orientations of the Strategy, and changes in the international environment. Such a comprehensive evaluation cannot be organized annually – that would be too cumbersome and would carry the risk that evaluations would quickly become formal exercises without much content, while a true assessment of the substance of policies is required.

Grevi (2004) proposes a bi-annual process of evaluation, starting with a report on the implementation of the Strategy drafted by an inter-institutional task force under the authority of the High Representative, a task which could later be assumed by the External Action Service. This report would be debated by the European Parliament as well as by the national parliaments, who would forward their recommendations to the European Council, which according to Grevi should devote at least half a session to the evaluation of the Strategy, in order to be able to really take the matter in hand and provide political guidance at the highest level. Grevi emphasizes the importance of involving the national parliaments: a national debate on external action would raise public awareness and could also positively influence the political will of Member States to enhance integration in this field. Furthermore, there now is a lack of democratic scrutiny of CFSP/ESDP issues in particular, as the European Parliament has limited powers in this field, while the national parliaments lack the capacity and the willingness to effectively address it. An effective communication strategy would be a necessary complement to such a process trying to involve national parliaments and public opinion.

Another way of institutionalizing strategic culture would have been to include a reference to the Strategy in Article III-292 of the Draft Constitution, which lists the missions of EU external action. The final paragraph of this Article could have been amended so as to stipulate that the Strategy that is adopted by the European Council shall define how these objectives are to be pursued throughout the different dimensions of EU external action, thus formalizing the obligation to link all external action-related decisions to the Strategy. Currently, the Strategy basically is a political document, a European Council declaration; contrary to what its name might suggest, it does not have the legal status of a Common Strategy, the more specific and rather more binding CFSP-instrument that the European Council can adopt. Including a binding reference to the Security Strategy in the Constitution would thus have significantly enhanced its status.

The different ways of institutionalizing the reference to the Strategy in policy-making processes would not of course provide any guarantees as to the implementation of the Strategy. In the end, the political will of the Member States is the decisive factor. But without doubt it would increase the chance of the Strategy really becoming the driver of external action.

A Global Agenda for Positive Power

The adoption of the Strategy is a major achievement in itself. Until the Iraq crisis, defining a joint agenda for external action for all Member States was considered by many observers to be a necessary, but also a highly unlikely step, given the different views existing within the EU. By convincing the Member States of the necessity of defining a strategy, the Iraq crisis has at least achieved one very positive short-term result.

But the Strategy is much more than a formal reconciliation after the divides over Iraq. Building on existing partnerships and policies, the Strategy contains an ambitious agenda for an EU that assumes the responsibilities of a true global actor. In order to implement this agenda, the Strategy outlines a distinctive European approach, based on the concept of comprehensive security. Aiming to integrate the full range of the EU's policies, instruments and capabilities under the overall positive objective of effective governance at both the global and the regional level, that is promoting every individual's access to the basic public goods, the Strategy renders explicit a comprehensive approach that was already apparent throughout actual EU policies and partnerships. Like all human achievements, the Strategy is not perfect; not on all issues is it sufficiently clear; not all the necessary choices have already been made. But as a tool for policy-makers, the Strategy has enormous potential. This potential cannot be wasted. A strategic culture must be developed; at all times policy-makers must decide and act with the objectives and the approach of the Strategy in mind. This will increase the coherence of EU external action, harmonizing the agendas of all policy fields; it will increase efficiency, putting the available means to better use; and ultimately it will increase effectiveness, achieving the objectives that the EU has set.

It is crucial for the success of the Strategy to recognize that it does not just concern security policy in the narrow sense, that is the politico-military dimension, but that because of its distinctive and ambitious comprehensive approach it directly covers *all* dimensions of EU external action. In that sense, it really is more than a Security Strategy. The Strategy can, and should, be a global agenda for positive power – global, because it has a worldwide scope and covers all aspects of external action, and positive, because it claims effective power to achieve positive objectives.

Bibliography

Acharya, A. (2001), 'Human Security: East versus West', *International Journal*, Vol. 56(3), pp. 442-60.

Acharya, A. (2004), 'Regional Security Arrangements in a Multipolar World: The EU's Contribution', in M. Ortega (ed), *Global Views on the European Union*, Chaillot Paper No. 72, EU Institute for Security Studies, Paris, pp. 93-102.

Adler, E. and Barnett, M. (1998) (eds), *Security Communities*, Cambridge University Press, Cambridge.

AIV (2004a), *Military Cooperation in Europe. Possibilities and Limitations*, Advice No. 31, Advisory Council on International Affairs, The Hague.

AIV (2004b), *Preëmptief Optreden*, Advies No. 36, Advisory Council on International Affairs, The Hague.

Alexander, M. and Garden, T. (2001), 'The Arithmetic of Defence Policy', *International Affairs*, Vol. 77(3), pp. 509-29.

Annan, K. (2000), *We the Peoples. The Role of the United Nations in the 21st Century*, UN, New York.

Annan, K. (2003), *Secretary-General's Address to the General Assembly*, UN, New York.

Annan, K. (2004), *Statement to the European Council*, Press Release SG/SM/9653, UN, New York.

Arnould, V. (2005a), 'De Economische en Sociale Raad', in Vereniging voor de Verenigde Naties (ed), *60 Jaar Verenigde Naties: Terugblik en Vooruitblik*, Acco, Leuven.

Arnould, V. (2005b), *Security in the 21st Century: EU and UN Approaches*, Paper presented at the Japan-EU Think-Tank Roundtable on Next Steps in Global Governance, 13-15 January, Tokyo.

Attinà, F. (2004), 'European Neighbourhood Policy and the Building of Security Around Europe', in F. Attinà and R. Rossi (eds), *European Neighbourhood Policy: Political, Economic and Social Issues*, University of Catania, Catania, pp. 16-24.

Axworthy, L. (1999a), 'NATO's New Security Vocation', *NATO Review*, Vol. 47(4), pp. 8-11.

Axworthy, L. (1999b), 'La Sécurité Humaine: La Sécurité des Individus dans un Monde en Mutation', *Politique étrangère*, Vol. 64(2), pp. 333-42.

Barry, C.L. (2002), 'Coordinating with NATO', in H. Binnendijk (ed), *Transforming America's Military*, National Defense University Press, Washington DC, pp. 231-258.

Berdal, M. (2004), 'The UN after Iraq', *Survival*, Vol. 46(3), pp. 83-102.

Berenskoetter, F. (2004), *Mapping the Mond Gap: A Comparison of US and EU Security Strategies*, Fornet Working Paper No. 3, Fornet, London.

Bereuther, D. (2004), 'NATO and the EU Security Strategy', *Oxford Journal on Good Governance*, Vol. 1(1), pp. 23-7.

Bertram, C. (2003), 'Europe's Best Interest: Staying Close to Number One', *Internationale Politik und Gesellschaft*, No. 1, pp. 61-70.

Betts, R.K. (2000), 'Is Strategy an Illusion?', *International Security*, Vol. 25(2), pp. 5-50.

Bildt, C. (2003), *We Have Crossed the Rubicon – But Where Are we Heading Next? Reflections on the European Security Strategy versus the US National Security Strategy*, lecture at the Centre for European Reform, London, 17 November 2003.

Bildt, C. (2004), 'Peace and War in the World after Westphalia: Some Reflections on the Challenges of a Changing International Order', in A.-M. Slaughter (ed), *The New Challenges to International, National and Human Security Policy*, Triangle Paper No. 58, Trilateral Commission, Washington-Paris-Tokyo, pp. 29-58.

Binnendijk, H. and Kugler, R.L. (2004), 'The Next Phase of Transformation: A New Dual-Track Strategy for NATO', in D.S. Hamilton (ed), *Transatlantic Transformations: Equipping NATO for the 21st Century*, Johns Hopkins University, Washington DC, pp. 37-74.

Biscop, S. (1999), 'The UK's Change of Course: A New Chance for the ESDI', *European Foreign Affairs Review*, Vol. 4(2), pp. 253-68.

Biscop, S. (2002a), 'In Search of a Strategic Concept for the ESDP', *European Foreign Affairs Review*, Vol. 7(4), pp. 473-90.

Biscop, S. (2002b), 'Network or Labyrinth? The Challenge of Coordinating Western Security Dialogues with the Mediterranean', *Mediterranean Politics*, Vol. 7(1), pp.92-112.

Biscop, S. (2003), *Euro-Mediterranean Security: A Search for Partnership*, Ashgate, Aldershot.

Biscop, S. (2004a), 'The European Security Strategy and the Neighbourhood Policy: A New Starting Point for a Euro-Mediterranean Security Partnership?', in F. Attinà and R. Rossi (eds), *European Neighbourhood Policy: Political, Economic and Social Issues*, University of Catania, Catania, pp. 25-36.

Biscop, S. (2004b), 'Able and Willing? Assessing the EU's Capacity for Military Action', *European Foreign Affairs Review*, Vol. 9(4), pp. 509-27.

Biscop, S. (2004c), *The European Security Strategy – Implementing a Distinctive Approach to Security*, Sécurité et Stratégie No. 82, Royal Defence College, Brussels.

Biscop, S. (2004d), 'La Stratégie Européenne de Sécurité: Un Agenda Ambitieux', *Défense Nationale*, Vol. 60(5), pp. 55-66.

Biscop, S. and Arnould, V. (2004), 'Global Public Goods: An Integrative Agenda for EU External Action', in E.B. Eide (ed), *Effective Multilateralism: Europe, Regional Security and a Revitalised UN*, Global Europe Report No. 1, The Foreign Policy Centre, London, pp. 22-32.

Biscop, S. and Coolsaet, R. (2003a), *The World is the Stage – A Global Security Strategy for the European Union*, Policy Paper No. 8, Notre Europe, Paris.

Biscop, S. and Coolsaet, R. (2003b), 'Une Stratégie de l'UE pour la Sécurité: Définir la Voie Européenne', *Défense Nationale*, Vol. 59(10), pp. 125-33.

Bono, G. (2004), 'The EU's Military Doctrine: An Assessment', *International Peacekeeping*, Vol. 11(3), pp. 439-56.

Boyer, Y. (2004), 'The Consequences of US and NATO Transformation for the European Union: A European View', in D.S. Hamilton (ed), *Transatlantic Transformations: Equipping NATO for the 21st Century*, Centre for Transatlantic Relations, Washington DC, pp. 75-90.

Brecher, I. (2003), 'In Defence of Preventive War. A Canadian's Perspective', *International Journal*, Vol. 58(3), pp. 253-80.

Brenner, M.J. (2002), *Europe's New Security Vocation*, McNair Paper No. 66, National Defense University, Washington DC.

Bretherton, C. and Vogler, J. (1999), *The European Union as a Global Actor*, Routledge, London.

Brunnée, J. and Toope, S.J. (2004), 'Canada and the Use of Force. Reclaiming Human Security', *International Journal*, Vol. 59(2), pp. 247-60.

Buchanan, A. and Keohane, R.O. (2004), 'The Preventive Use of Force: A Cosmopolitan Institutional Proposal', *Ethics & International Affairs*, Vol. 18(1), pp. 1-22.

Bunn, E. (2003), *Pre-emptive Action: When, How and to What Effect?*, Strategic Forum No. 200, Institute for National Strategic Studies, National Defense University, Washington DC.

Buzan, B. (1991), *People, States and Fear. An Agenda for International Security Studies in the Post-Cold War Era*, 2nd Edition, Harvester Wheatsheaf, Hemel Hempstead.

Calleo, D.P. (2004), 'The Broken West', *Survival*, Vol. 46(3), pp. 29-38.

Calleya, S. (2002), 'Conflict Prevention in the Mediterranean: A Regional Approach', in B. Huldt, M. Engman and E. Davidson (eds), *Euro-Mediterranean Security and the Barcelona Process. Strategic Yearbook 2003*, Swedish National Defence College, Stockholm, pp. 41-59.

Cameron, F. (2004), 'The EU's Security Strategy', *Internationale Politik*, No. 1, pp. 16-24.

Cimbalo, J.L. (2004), 'Saving NATO from Europe', *Foreign Affairs*, Vol. 83(6), pp. 111-120.

Cohen, E.A. (2004), 'Change and Transformation in Military Affairs', *The Journal of Strategic Studies*, Vol. 27(3), pp. 395-407.

Cohen, R. and Mihalka, M. (2001), *Cooperative Security: New Horizons for International Order*, Marshall Center Paper No. 3, The Marshall Center, Garmisch-Partenkirchen.

Cohen-Tanugi, L. (2003), *An Alliance at Risk. The United States and Europe since September 11*, Johns Hopkins University Press, Baltimore-London.

Commission on Human Security (2003), *Human Security Now*, UN, New York.

Coolsaet, R. (2001), *België en zijn buitenlandse politiek 1830-2000*, Van Halewyck, Leuven, pp. 529-30.

Coolsaet, R. (2005), *Al-Qaeda: The Myth. The Root Causes of Contemporary International Terrorism and How to Tackle Them*, Academia Press, Ghent.

Coolsaet, R. and Arnould, V. (2004), *Global Governance: The Next Frontier*, Egmont Paper No. 2, Royal Institute for International Relations, Brussels.

Coolsaet, R. and Biscop, S. (2004), *A European Security Concept for the 21st Century*, Egmont Paper No. 1, Royal Institute for International Relations, Brussels.

Coolsaet, R. and Van de Voorde, T. (2004), *International Terrorism. A Longitudinal Statistical Analysis*, Research Note, University of Ghent, Ghent.

Cooper, R. (2000), *The Postmodern State and the World Order*, Demos, London.

Cooper, R. (2003), *The Breaking of Nations. Order and Chaos in the Twenty-First Century*, Atlantic Books, London.

Copeland, D. (2001), 'The Axworthy Years: Canadian Foreign Policy in the Era of Diminished Capacity', in F.O. Hampson, N. Hillmer and M.A. Molot (eds), *The Axworthy Legacy*, Canada Among Nations 2001, Oxford University Press Canada, Don Mills, pp. 152-72.

Cornish, P. and Edwards, G. (2001), 'Beyond the EU/NATO Dichotomy: The Beginnings of a European Strategic Culture', *International Affairs*, Vol. 77(3), pp. 587-603.

Council on Foreign Relations (2004), *Renewing the Atlantic Partnership. Report of an Independent Task Force*, Council on Foreign Relations, New York.

Crowe, B. (2004), 'A Common European Foreign Policy after Iraq?', in M. Holland (ed), *Common Foreign and Security Policy. The First Ten Years*, 2nd edition, Continuum, London – New York, pp. 28-43.

CSCAP (1996), *The Concepts of Comprehensive and Cooperative Security*, Memorandum No. 3, Council for Security Cooperation in Asia Pacific, Singapore.

Culpeper, R. (2005), *Human Security, Equitable and Sustainable Development: Foundations for Canada's International Policy*, NSI Paper on the International Policy Review, The North-South Institute, Ottawa.

Dashwood, H.S. (2000), 'Canada's Participation in the NATO-Led Intervention in Kosovo', in M.A. Molat and F.O. Hampson (eds), *Vanishing Borders*, Canada Among Nations 2000, Oxford University Press Canada, Don Mills, pp. 275-302.

Dassù, M. (2004), 'UNdone', *Aspenia*, No. 25-26, pp. 34-37.

Debiel, T. (2004), 'Souveränität verpflichtet: Spielregeln für den neuen Interventionismus', *Internationale Politik Und Gesellschaft*, No. 3, pp. 61-81.

De Neve, A. (2003), *La Spécialisation des Tâches: Une Révolution pour l'Europe? Approches Théoriques*, Sécurité et Stratégie No. 79, Royal Defence College, Brussels.

De Neve, A. and Mathieu, R. (2004), *La Défense Européenne et la RMA: Convergences Possibles ou Disparités Inéluctables*, Sécurité et Stratégie No. 84, Royal Defence College, Brussels.

de Schoutheete, P. (2004), *La Cohérence par la Défense. Une autre Lecture de la PESD*, Chaillot Paper No. 71, EU Institute for Security Studies, Paris.

Desportes, V. (1999), 'Pour la pensée stratégique', *Défense nationale*, Vol. 55(8-9), pp. 109-21.

Desportes, V. (2004), 'Quelle doctrine pour quelles forces ?', *Défense Nationale*, Vol. 60(7), pp. 104-116.

Deutsch, K.W. (1957), *Political Community and the North Atlantic Area. International Organization in the Light of Historical Experience*, Princeton University Press, Princeton.

de Vasconcelos, A. (2004), *Launching the Euro-Mediterranean Security and Defence Dialogue*, EUROMESCO Brief, Instituto de Estudos Estratégicos e Internacionais, Lisbon.

de Wijk, R. (2004), 'The Implications for Force Transformation: The Small Country Perspective', in D.S. Hamilton (ed), *Transatlantic Transformations: Equipping NATO for the 21st Century*, Centre for Transatlantic Relations, Washington DC, pp. 115-46.

De Witte, P. (2004), *The Need for Strengthened EU-US Relations?*, Paper presented at a Workshop on the EU's Role in International Security Management, Lund University.

Duchêne, F. (1972), 'Europe's Role in World Peace', in R. Mayne (ed), *Europe Tomorrow*, Fontana, London.

Duffield, M. (2002), *Global Governance and the New Wars*, Zed Books, London.

Duke, S. (2004), 'The European Security Strategy in a Comparative Framework: Does it Make for Secure Alliances in a Better World?', *European Foreign Affairs Review*, Vol. 9(4), pp. 459-81.

Ehrhart, H.G. (2002), *What Model for CFSP?*, Chaillot Paper No. 55, EU Institute for Security Studies, Paris.

Ekengren, M. (2005), 'From a European Security Community to a Secure European Community', *CFSP Forum*, Vol. 3(1), pp. 5-7.

EPLO (2004), *Resolution for a European Peacebuilding Agency*, European Peacebuilding Liaison Office, Brussels.

EUISS (2004), *European Defence. A Proposal for a White Paper*, EU Institute for Security Studies, Paris.

European Commission (2001), *Conflict Prevention*, COM (2001) 211 final.

European Commission (2003a), *Wider Europe – Neighbourhood: a New Framework for Relations with our Eastern and Southern Neighbours*, COM (2003) 104 final.

European Commission (2003b), *Reinvigorating EU Actions on Human Rights and Democratisation with Mediterranean Partners*, COM (2003) 294 final.

European Commission (2003c), *The European Union and the United Nations: The Choice of Multilateralism*, COM (2003) 526 final.

European Commission (2004), *European Neighbourhood Policy – Strategy Paper*.

European Convention (2002a), Working Group VIII on Defence, Working Document 2, 19 September.

European Convention (2002b), Working Group VII on External Action, Working Document 10, 15 October.

European Convention (2002c), Final Report of Working Group VIII – Defence, WG VIII 22, 16 December.

European Union (2004), *The Enlarged European Union at the United Nations: Making Multilateralism Matter*, Agreed by the Troika and Member States in New York, EU, Luxembourg.

European Union Presidency (2004), *Conference on International Military Cooperation. Improving Capabilities: A Shared Responsibility*, Wassenaar, 11–12 October 2004, Conference Report, The Netherlands Ministry of Defence, The Hague.

Evans, G. (1994), 'Cooperative Security and Intra-State Conflict', *Foreign Policy*, Vol. 25(3).

Evans, G. (2003), *Waging War and Making Peace*, Annual Hawke Lecture, University of South Australia.

Evans, G. (2004), 'When is it Right to Fight?', *Survival*, Vol. 46(3), pp. 59-82.

Everts, S. (2004), 'Two Cheers for the EU's New Security Strategy: Soft Power and Hard Power', *Oxford Journal on Good Governance*, Vol. 1(1), pp. 39-42.

Feinstein, L. and Slaughter, A.-M. (2004), 'A Duty to Prevent', *Foreign Affairs*, Vol. 83(1), pp. 136-50.

Ferrero-Waldner, B. (2004), *The Future of the UN: Results of the Kofi Annan High-Level Panel on Threats, Challenges, and Change*, Speech at the conference organized by the European Policy Centre and the Konrad Adenauer Stiftung, Brussels, 8 December.

Ferroni, M. and Mody, A. (2002), 'Global Incentives for International Public Goods: Introduction and Overview', in Ferroni, M. and Mody, A. (eds), *International Public Goods: Incentives, Measurement and Financing*, Kluwer Law – World Bank, Washington DC.

Freedman, L. (2003), 'Prevention, not Pre-emption', *The Washington Quarterly*, Vol. 26(2), pp. 105-14.

Fuller, G.E. (2004), *Islamists in the Arab World: The Dance Around Democracy*, Carnegie Paper No. 49, Carnegie Endowment for International Peace, Washington DC.

Fukushima, A. (2004), *Human Security: Comparing Japanese and Canadian Governmental Thinking and Practice*, Canadian Consortium for Human Security Visiting Fellow Paper, Liu Institute for Global Issues, Vancouver.

Gärber, A. (2004), 'Transatlantische Initiativen für den Mittleren Osten und Nordafrika – Eine unvollständige Agenda', *Internationale Politik Und Gesellschaft*, No. 4, pp. 87-110.

Gärtner, H. (2003), 'European Security: The End of Territorial Defence', *The Brown Journal of World Affairs*, Vol. 9(2), pp. 135-47.

Gegout, C. (2005), 'Europe Has a Strategy, but Is the EU a Strategic Actor?', *CFSP Forum*, Vol. 3(1), pp. 8-11.

Giegerich, B. and Wallace, W. (2004), 'Not Such a Soft Power: The External Deployment of European Forces', *Survival*, Vol. 46(2), pp. 163-82.

Glasius, M. and Kaldor, M. (2005), 'Individuals First: A Human Security Strategy for the European Union', *Internationale Politik und Gesellschaft*, No. 1, pp. 62-82.

Gnesotto, N. (2004), 'European Strategy as a Model', EU Institute for Security Studies, *Newsletter*, No. 9, pp. 1-4.

González, F.E. (2004), 'Mexico's Future International Orientation: The European Union as a Model and Influence', in M. Ortega (ed), *Global Views on the European Union*, Chaillot Paper No. 72, EU Institute for Security Studies, Paris, pp. 55-69.

Goulding, M. (2002), *Peacemonger*, John Murray, London.

Gowan, R. (2004a), 'Can the EU create Africa's NATO?', in E.B. Eide (ed), *Effective Multilateralism: Europe, Regional Security and a Revitalised UN*, Global Europe Report No. 1, The Foreign Policy Centre, London, pp. 38-44.

Gowan, R. (2004b), 'The EU, Regional Organizations and Security: Strategic Partners or Convenient Alibis?', in S. Biscop (ed), *Audit of European Strategy*, Egmont Paper No. 3, Royal Institute for International Relations, Brussels, pp. 8-17.

Graham, K. (2004), *Towards Effective Multilateralism. The EU and the UN: Partners in Crisis Management*, Working Paper No. 13, European Policy Centre, Brussels.

Graham, K. and Felício, T. (2004), *Regional Security and Global Governance. A Study of Interaction Between Regional Agencies and the UN Security Council with a Proposal for a Regional-Global Security Mechanism*, Discussion Paper, United Nations University / Comparative Regional Integration Studies, Bruges.

Graham, K. and Felício, T. (2005), *Regional Security and Global Governance: A Proposal for a 'Regional-Global Security Mechanism' in Light of the UN High-Level Panel's Report*, Egmont Paper No. 4, Royal Institute for International Relations, Brussels.

Grant, C. (2004), 'Conclusion: The Significance of European Defence', in S. Everts et al. (eds), *A European Way of War*, Centre for European Reform, London, pp. 55-71.

Grevi, G. (2004), *European Security: No Strategy without Politics*, Idea No. 4, Ideas Factory, European Policy Centre, Brussels.

Grevi, G., Manca, D. and Quille, G. (2005), *A Foreign Minister for the EU – Past, Present and Future*, Fornet Working Paper No. 7, Fornet, London.

Groupe d'officiers du CHEM (2003), 'Un Concept de Sécurité et de Défense, pour la France, pour l'Europe?', *Défense Nationale*, Vol. 59(8-9), pp. 113-24.

Guérot, U. (2005), *Towards a Renewed Transatlantic Community*, Idea No. 6, Ideas Factory, European Policy Centre, Brussels.

Guoliang, G. (2003), 'Redefine Cooperative Security, not Pre-emption', *The Washington Quarterly*, Vol. 26(2), pp. 135-45.

Haglund, D.G. (2004), 'What Good is Strategic Culture? A Modest Defence of an Immodest Concept', *International Journal*, Vol. 59(3), pp. 479-502.

Haine, J.-Y., (2004a), 'The EU's Soft Power. Not Hard Enough?', *Georgetown Journal of International Affairs*, Vol. 5(1), pp. 69-77.

Haine, J.-Y., (2004b), 'Idealism and Power: The New EU Security Strategy', *Current History*, Vol. 103(671), pp. 107-12.

Hannay, D. (2005), 'Making Multilateralism Work', *CER Bulletin*, Issue 40.

Harriss-White, B. (2002), *Globalisation and Insecurity. Political, Economic and Physical Challenges*, Palgrave, New York.

Haseler, S. (2004), *Super-State. The New Europe and its Challenge to America*, I.B. Tauris, London – New York.

Heinbecker, P. (2000), 'Human Security: The Hard Edge', *Canadian Military Journal*, Vol. 1(1), pp. 11-16

Heintze, H.-J. (2004), 'Das Völkerrecht wird unterschätzt: Internationale Antworten auf den internationalen Terrorismus', *Internationale Politik Und Gesellschaft*, No. 3, pp. 38-60.

Heisbourg, F. (2004), 'The "European Security Strategy" is not a Security Strategy', in S. Everts et al. (eds), *A European Way of War*, Centre for European Reform, London, pp. 27-39.

Heusgen, C. (2004), 'Implementing the European Security Strategy', in S. Biscop (ed), *Audit of European Strategy*, Egmont Paper No. 3, Brussels, Royal Institute for International Relations, pp. 5-7.

High-Level Panel (2004), *A More Secure World: Our Shared Responsibility*, Report of the Secretary-General's High-Level Panel on Threats, Challenges and Change, UN, New York.

Hoffmann, S. (2003), 'America Goes Backward', *New York Review of Books*, Vol. 50(10).

Holmes, K.R. (2004), 'A Democracy Caucus', *Aspenia*, No. 25-26, pp. 49-56.

Howorth, J. (2004a) *Able and Willing? Does Europe Have the Means to Stage a Military Operation if it wants to*, in Royal Defence College – Royal Institute for International Relations, Proceedings 16 March 2004, Royal Defence College, Brussels, pp. 17-33.

Howorth, J. (2004b), 'The European Draft Constitutional Treaty and the Future of the European Defence Initiative: A Question of Flexibility', *European Foreign Affairs Review*, Vol. 9(4), pp. 483-508.

Hulsman, J.C. (2000), *A Grand Bargain with Europe: Preserving NATO for the 21st Century*, Backgrounder No. 1360, The Heritage Foundation, Washington DC.

Hunter, R.E. (2004a), 'The US and the European Union: Bridging the Strategic Gap?', *The International Spectator*, Vol. 34(1), pp. 35-50.

Hunter, R.E. (2004b), 'A Forward-Looking Partnership. NATO and the Future of Alliances', *Foreign Affairs*, Vol. 83(5), pp. 14-18.

IBO (2003), *Taakspecialisatie: het schiet niet echt op*, Interdepartementaal Beleidsonderzoek, The Hague.

ICG (2005), *EU Crisis Response Capability Revisited*, Europe Report No. 160, International Crisis Group, Brussels.

ICISS (2001), *The Responsibility to Protect*, International Development Research Centre, Ottawa.

Joffe, J. (2001), 'Who's Afraid of Mr. Big? Global Relations with the United States', *The National Interest*, No. 64.

Johansson-Nogués, E. (2004), 'A "Ring of Friends"? The Implications of the European Neighbourhood Policy for the Mediterranean', *Mediterranean Politics*, Vol. 9(2), pp. 240-7.

Jünemann, A. (2003), 'Repercussions of the Emerging European Security and Defence Policy on the Civil Character of the Euro-Mediterranean Partnership', *Mediterranean Politics*, Vol. 8(2-3), pp. 37-53.

Kagan, R. (2004), *Paradise & Power. America and Europe in the New World Order*, Atlantic Books, London.

Kaldor, M. et al. (2004), *A Human Security Doctrine for Europe*, The Barcelona Report of the Study Group on Europe's Security Capabilities, presented to EU High Representative for Common Foreign and Security Policy Javier Solana.

Kaul, I., Grunberg, I. and Stern, M.A. (1999), *Global Public Goods. International Cooperation in the 21st Century*, Oxford University Press – UNDP, Oxford.

Kay, S. (2004), 'Globalization, Power and Security', *Security Dialogue*, Vol. 35(1), pp. 9-25.

Keukeleire, S. (2000), *The European Union as a Diplomatic Actor*, Diplomatic Studies Programme Discussion Paper No. 7.

Keukeleire, S. (2001), 'Au-dela de la PESC. La Politique étrangère structurelle de l'Union européenne', in *Annuaire français de Relations internationales*, Bruylant, Brussels, pp. 536-551.

Keukeleire, S. (2002), *Reconceptualising (European) Foreign Policy: Structural Foreign Policy*, Paper presented at the ECPR First Pan-European Conference on European Union Politics, Bordeaux, 26-28 September 2002.

Kirchner, E. and Sperling, J. (2002), 'The New Security Threats in Europe: Theory and Evidence', *European Foreign Affairs Review*, Vol. 7(4), pp. 423-52.

Knutsen, B.O. (2002), *ESDP and the non-EU NATO Members*, FFI Rapport No. 01212, Norwegian Defence Research Establishment, Kjeller.

Lagendijk, J. and Wiersma, J.M. (2004), *Na Mars komt Venus. Een Europees Antwoord op Bush*, Balans, Amsterdam.

Lannon, E., Inglis, K. and Haenebalcke, T. (2001), 'The Many Faces of EU Conditionality in Pan-Euro-Mediterranean Relations', in M. Marescau and E. Lannon (eds), *The EU's Enlargement and Mediterranean Strategies. A Comparative Analysis*, Palgrave, New York, pp. 97-138.

Larsen, H. (2002), 'The EU: A Global Military Actor?', *Cooperation and Conflict*, Vol. 37(3), pp. 283-302.

Leonard, M. (2005), 'Europe's Transformative Power', *CER Bulletin*, Issue 40.

Leonard, M. and Gowan, R. (2004), *Global Europe: Implementing the European Security Strategy*, The Foreign Policy Centre, London.

Lindley-French, J. and Algieri, F. (2004), *A European Defence Strategy*, Bertelsmann Foundation, Gütersloh.

Lindstrom, G. (2004), *The Headline Goal*, Fact Sheet, EU Institute for Security Studies, Paris.

Lübkemeier, E. (2003), 'Abenteuer Europa. Aus der EU kann und sollte ein weltpolitischer Akteur werden', *Internationale Politik*, Vol. 58(12), pp. 45-50.

Mair, S. (2004), 'Intervention und "State Failure": Sind schwache Staaten noch zu retten?', *Internationale Politik Und Gesellschaft*, No. 3, pp. 82-98.

Malmvig, H. (2004), *From Diplomatic Talking Shop to Powerful Partnership? NATO's Mediterranean Dialogue and the Democratisation of the Middle East*, DIIS Brief, Danish Institute for International Studies, Copenhagen.

Manca, D. (2004), 'Follow-up to the European Security Strategy: Effective Multilateralism', *European Security Review*, No. 23, pp. 3-5.

Manners, I. (2002), 'Normative Power Europe: A Contradiction in Terms?', *Journal of Common Market Studies*, Vol. 40(2), pp. 235-58.

Maull, H. (1990), 'Germany and Japan: The New Civilian Powers', *Foreign Affairs*, Vol. 69(5), pp. 92-3.

Maurer, A. and Reichel, S. (2004), *Der Europäische Auswärtige Dienst. Elemente eines Drei-Phasen-Plans*, SWP-Aktuell No. 53, Stiftung Wissenschaft und Politik, Berlin.

McCrae, R. and Hubert, D. (eds), *Human Security and the New Diplomacy. Protecting People, Promoting Peace*, McGill-Queen's University Press, Montreal – Kingston.

McMillan, J. (2004), *Apocalyptic Terrorism: The Case for Preventive Action*, Strategic Forum No. 212, National Defense University, Washington DC.

Menon, A., Nicolaidis, K. and Welsh, J. (2004), 'In Defence of Europe. A Response to Kagan', *Journal of European Affairs*, Vol. 2(3), pp. 5-14.

Messner, D. and Faust, J. (2004), *Development Policy – A Core Element of European Security Policy*, Briefing Paper No. 3, German Development Institute, Bonn.

Meyer, C.O. (2004), *Theorising European Strategic Culture. Between Convergence and the Persistence of National Diversity*, Working Document No. 204, Centre for European Policy Studies, Brussels.

Michel, L.G. (2003), *NATO Decision-Making: Au Revoir to the Consensus Rule?*, Strategic Forum No. 202, National Defense University, Washington DC.

Mileham, P. (2001), 'But will they fight and will they die?', *International Affairs*, Vol. 77(3), pp. 621-9.

Missiroli, A. (2002), 'EU-NATO Cooperation in Crisis Management: No Turkish Delight for the ESDP', *Security Dialogue*, Vol. 33(1), pp. 9-26.

Missiroli, A. (2004), 'The EU and its Changing Neighbourhood. Stabilization, Integration and Partnership', in R. Dannreuther (ed), *European Foreign and Security Policy. Towards a Neighbourhood Strategy*, Routledge, London, pp. 12-26.

Moravcsik, A. (2003), 'Striking a New Transatlantic Bargain', *Foreign Affairs*, Vol. 82(4), pp. 74-89.

Münkler, H. (2004), 'Angriff als beste Verteidigung? Sicherheitsdoktrinen in der asymmetrischen Konstellation', *Internationale Politik Und Gesellschaft*, No. 3, pp. 22-37.

Murdock, C.A. (2004), *Improving the Practice of National Security Strategy. A New Approach for the Post-Cold War World*, Center for Strategic and International Studies, Washington DC.

Nardulli, B.R. and McNaugher, T.L. (2002), 'The Army: Toward the Objective Force', in H. Binnendijk (ed), *Transforming America's Military*, National Defense University, Washington DC, pp. 101-28.

NATO (1991), *The Alliance's Strategic Concept Approved by the Heads of State and Government Participating in the Meeting of the North Atlantic Council*, Rome, 8 November 1991.

NATO (1999), *The Alliance's Strategic Concept Approved by the Heads of State and Government Participating in the Meeting of the North Atlantic Council*, Washington DC, 23-24 April 1999.

NATO (2002), *Prague Summit Declaration Issued by the Heads of State and Government Participating in the Meeting of the North Atlantic Council*, Prague, 21 November 2002.

Nelles, W. (2002), 'Canada's Human Security Agenda in Kosovo and Beyond', *International Journal*, Vol. 57(3), pp. 459-79.

Niblock, T. (2003), 'Reform and Reconstruction in the Middle East: Room for EU-US Cooperation?', *The International Spectator*, Vol. 38(4), pp. 47-58.

NIC (2005), *Mapping the Global Future*, Report of the 2020 Project, National Intelligence Council, Washington DC.

Nolan, J.E. (1994), 'The Concept of Cooperative Security', in J.E. Nolan (ed), *Global Engagement, Cooperation and Security in the 21st Century*, The Brookings Institution, Washington.

Nye, J.S. (2002), *The Paradox of American Power: Why the World's Only Superpower Can't Go it Alone*, Oxford University Press, Oxford.

Ogura, K. (2004), 'Coping with Threats to Human Security', in A.-M. Slaughter (ed), *The New Challenges to International, National and Human Security Policy*, Triangle Paper No. 58, Trilateral Commission, Washington-Paris-Tokyo, pp. 59-66.

O'Hanlon, M. and Singer, P.W. (2004), 'The Humanitarian Transformation: Expanding Global Intervention Capacity', *Survival*, Vol. 46(1), pp. 77-100.

Ojanen, H. (2005), 'Operation Althea: Healing, Testing, or Testing the Healing?, *CFSP Forum*, Vol. 3(1), pp. 11-13.

Orbie, J. (2003), *Conceptualising the Role of the EU in the World: Civilian Power Europe?*, paper presented at the EUSA 8th International Biennial Conference, Nashville, 27–29 March 2003.

Ortega, M. (2003), 'A New EU Policy on the Mediterranean?', in J. Batt et al. (eds), *Partners and Neighbours: A CFSP for a Wider Europe*, Chaillot Paper No. 64, EU Institute for Security Studies, Paris, 2003, pp. 86-101.

Ortega, M. (2004), 'The EU and the UN: Strengthening Global Security', in E.B. Eide (ed), *Effective Multilateralism: Europe, Regional Security and a Revitalised UN*, Global Europe Report No. 1, The Foreign Policy Centre, London, pp. 11-21.

OSCE (2000), *OSCE Handbook*, OSCE, Vienna.

Ottaway, M. and Carothers, T. (2004), *The Greater Middle East Initiative: Off to a False Start*, Policy Brief No. 29, Carnegie Endowment for International Peace, Washington DC.

Overhaus, M. (2004), 'The European Security Strategy – Paper Tiger or Catalyst for Joint Action?', *German Foreign Policy in Dialogue*, Vol. 5(13), pp. 3-6.

Oxfam (2003), *Letter to European Union Foreign Ministers regarding EU Security Strategy*, 26 November.

Pailhe, C. (2003), *L'Engagement de l'OTAN en Irak: La Fracture Transatlantique*, Note d'Analyse, Groupe de Recherche et d'Information sur la Paix et la Sécurité (GRIP), Brussels.

Pailhe, C. (2004), *Un Concept Stratégique Utile mais Dangereux*, Note d'Analyse, Groupe de Recherche et d'Information sur la Paix et la Sécurité (GRIP), Brussels.

Pally, M. (2004), 'Mach's besser, Europa!', *Internationale Politik*, Vol. 59(9), pp. 73-86.

Patten, C. (2004), 'A Security Strategy for Europe', *Oxford Journal on Good Governance*, Vol. 1(1), pp. 13-16.

Peña, C.V. (2004), 'Strategy for the War on Terrorism', *Cato Policy Report*, Vol. 26(4), pp. 1-17.

Perthes, V. (2004), *America's Greater Middle East and Europe. Key Issues for the Transatlantic Dialogue*, SWP Comments No. 3, Stiftung Wissenschaft und Politik, Berlin.

Pilegaard, J. (2004), 'The European Security and Defence Policy and the Development of a Security Strategy for Europe', in J. Pilegaard (ed), *The Politics of European Security*, Danish Institute for International Studies, Copenhagen, pp. 11-38.

Pouliot, V. and Lachmann, N. (2004), 'Les Communautés de Sécurité, Vecteurs d'Ordre Régional et International', *La Revue Internationale et Stratégique*, No. 54, pp. 131-140.

Powell, C. (2004), 'A Strategy of Partnerships', *Foreign Affairs*, Vol. 83(1), pp. 22-34.

Quille, G. (2003), 'Making Multilateralism Matter: The EU Security Strategy', *European Security Review*, No. 18, pp. 1-2.

Quille, G. (2004a), 'Turning the Rhetoric of European Defence Cooperation into Reality', in NDA (ed), *Fresh Perspectives on European Security*, New Defence Agenda, 2004, Brussels, pp. 27-31.

Quille, G. (2004b), 'The European Security Strategy: A Framework for EU Security Interests?', *International Peacekeeping*, Vol. 11(3), pp. 422-38.

Rapoport, D.C. (2003), 'The Four Waves of Rebel Terror and September 11', in C.W. Kegley Jr. (ed), *The New Global Terrorism. Characteristics, Causes, Controls*, Prentice Hall, Upper Saddle River (NJ), pp. 36-52.

Reiter, E. and Frank, J. (2004), *The European Security Strategy – Austrian Perspective*, Bundesministerium für Landesverteidigung, Vienna.

Rhodes, E. (2004), 'The Good, the Bad, and the Righteous: Understanding the Bush Vision of a New NATO Partnership', *Millennium*, Vol. 33(1), pp. 123-43.

Rühl, L. (2004), *Conditions for a European Intervention Strategy in Application of the ESDP and US/NATO Crisis Management*, Discussion Paper No. 138, Zentrum für Europäische Integrationsforschung, Bonn.

Rummel, R. (2003), *Konfliktprävention: Etikett oder Markenzeichen europäischer Interventionspolitik?*, SWP-Studie No. 45, Stiftung Wissenschaft und Politik, Berlin.

Rynning, S. (2003), 'The European Union: Towards a Strategic Culture ?', *Security Dialogue*, Vol. 34(4), pp. 479-496.

Sachs, J. (2005), *Investing in Development: A Practical Plan to achieve the Millennium Development Goals*, UN, New York.

Salmon, T.C. and Shepherd, A.J.K. (2003), *Toward a European Army. A Military Power in the Making?*, Lynne-Rienner, Boulder-London.

Schmid, D. (2003), *Interlinkages within the Euro-Mediterranean Partnership. Linking Economic, Institutional and Political Reform: Conditionality within the Euro-Mediterranean Partnership*, EUROMESCO Paper No. 27, Instituto de Estudos Estratégicos e Internacionais, Lisbon.

Schmitt, B. (2004), *European Capabilities Action Plan (ECAP)*, Fact Sheet, EU Institute for Security Studies, Paris.

Schwarz, K.-D. (2003), *Die erste Sicherheitsstrategie der EU. Ein Kommentar zum Solana-Entwurf*, SWP-Aktuell No. 47, Stiftung Wissenschaft und Politik, Berlin.

Schweiss, C.M. (2003), 'Sharing Hegemony. The Future of Transatlantic Security', *Cooperation and Conflict*, Vol. 38(3), pp. 211-34.

Simma, B. (1994), *The Charter of the United Nations. A Commentary*, Oxford University Press, Oxford.

Skiba, A. (2004), *Die Nationale Sicherheitsstrategie der USA und die Europäische Sicherheitsstrategie im Vergleich*, Sonderband No. 3, Wissenschaft & Sicherheit, Bonn.

Slaughter, A.-M. (2004), 'Old Rules, New Threats: Terrorism, Proliferation and Anti-Americanism', in A.-M. Slaughter (ed), *The New Challenges to International, National and Human Security Policy*, Triangle Paper No. 58, Trilateral Commission, Washington-Paris-Tokyo, pp. 11-28.

Smith, K.E. (2000), 'The End of Civilian Power EU: A Welcome Demise or a Cause for Concern?', *The International Spectator*, Vol. 35(2), pp. 11-28.

Solana, J. (2004), 'Three ways for Europe to Prevail against the Terrorists', *Financial Times*, 25 March.

Solana, J. (2005), *Shaping an Effective EU Foreign Policy*, Speech for the Konrad Adenauer Stiftung, 24 January, Brussels.

Soltan, G. (2004), *Southern Mediterranean Perceptions and Proposals for Mediterranean Security*, EUROMESCO Brief, Instituto de Estudos Estratégicos e Internacionais, Lisbon.

Spear, J. (2003), 'The Emergence of a European "Strategic Personality"', *Arms Control Today*, No. 11.

Spear, J. (2004), 'Is there a Distinctive European Approach to Stability and Reconstruction Operations?', *ACES Cases*, No. 3, pp. 1-29.

Stavridis, S. (2001), '"Militarising" the EU: The Concept of Civilian Power Revisited', *The International Spectator*, Vol. 41(4), pp. 43-50.

Stone, J. (2004), 'Politics, Technology and the Revolution in Military Affairs', *The Journal of Strategic Studies*, Vol. 27(3), pp. 408-27.

Stuart, D. and Tow, W. (1990), *The Limits of Alliance. NATO Out-of-Area Problems since 1949*, The Johns Hopkins University Press, Baltimore.

Tangredi, S.J. (2002), 'Assessing New Missions', in H. Binnendijk (ed), *Transforming America's Military*, National Defense University, Washington DC, pp. 3-30.

Tanner, F. (2004), 'North Africa. Partnership, Exceptionalism and Neglect', in R. Dannreuther (ed), *European Foreign and Security Policy. Towards a Neighbourhood Strategy*, Routledge, London, pp. 135-50.

Tardy, T. (2004), *L'Union Européenne et l'ONU dans la Gestion de Crise: Opportunités et Limites d'une Relation Déséquilibrée*, Recherches & Documents No. 32, Fondation pour la Recherche Stratégique, Paris.

Tavares, R. (2004), 'Contribution of Macro-Regions to the Construction of Peace: A Framework for Analysis', *Journal of International Relations and Development*, Vol. (7)1, pp. 24-47.

Taylor, T. (2004), 'The End of Imminence?', *The Washington Quarterly*, Vol. 27(4), pp. 57-72.

Tertrais, B. (2002), 'ESDP and Global Security Challenges: Will There Be a Division of Labor Between Europe and the United States?', in E. Brimmer (ed), *The EU's Search for a Strategic Role. ESDP and its Implications for Transatlantic Relations*, Center for Transatlantic Relations, Washington DC, pp. 117-33.

Tharoor, S. (2004), 'Globalization and the Human Imagination', *World Policy Journal*, Vol. 21(2), pp. 85-91.

Thiele, R. (2002), 'Projecting European Power: A European View', in E. Brimmer (ed), *The EU's Search for a Strategic Role. ESDP and its Implications for Transatlantic Relations*, Center for Transatlantic Relations, Washington DC, pp. 67-84.

UN (2003a), *Secretary-General names High-Level Panel to Study Global Security Threats, and Recommend Necessary Changes*, Press Release SG/A/857, 4 November.

UN (2003b), *The High-Level Panel. Terms of Reference*, UN, New York.

UN (2004), *Monthly Summary of Contributions (Military Observers, Civilian Police and Troops) as of 30 November 2004*, UN, New York.

UNDP (1993), *Human Development Report 1993*, UN, New York.

UNDP (1994), *Human Development Report 1994*, UN, New York.

US (2002), *The National Security Strategy of the United States of America*, White House, Washington DC.

Uvin, P. (2004), 'A Field of Overlap and Interactions', *Security Dialogue*, Vol. 35(3), Special Section: What is 'Human Security'?, pp. 352-3.

Van Camp, S. and Collins, D. (2003), *Les Etats Membres de l'UE et la PESD, Eléments de Convergence et de Divergence*, Sécurité et Stratégie No. 78, Institut Royal Supérieur de Défense, Brussels.

Van de Voorde, T. and Van den Eede, M. (2004), 'Internationaal Terrorisme als een Fenomeen van Transities', in C. Devos (ed), *Schijn of Scharnier? Politieke Trendbreuken in de Jaren Negentig*, Academia Press, Ghent, pp. 377-413.

van den Doel, T. (2004), *De militaire ambities van de Europese Unie: retoriek of werkelijkheid?*, Clingendael Institute, The Hague.

Van Staden, A. (2004), 'Effectief Multilateralisme: Van Retoriek naar Daadkracht', *Internationale Spectator*, Vol. 58(7-8), pp. 343-9.

Van Staden, A., Homan, K., Kreemers, B., Pijpers, A. and de Wijk, R. (2000), *Towards a European Strategic Concept*, Netherlands Institute of International Relations 'Clingendael', The Hague.

Volpi, F. (2004), 'Regional Community Building and the Transformation of International Relations: The Case of the Euro-Mediterranean Partnership', *Mediterranean Politics*, Vol. 9(2), pp. 145-64.

von Hippel, K. (2004), *Dealing with the Roots of Terror – A Progress Report Three Years On*, Fundación para las Relaciones Internacionales y el Diálogo Exterior (FRIDE), Madrid.

von Platen, B. (2003), *Die Zukunft des transatlantischen Verhältnisses: Mehr als die NATO*, SWP-Studie No. 17, Stiftung Wissenschaft und Politik, Berlin.

Waheguru Pal Singh, S. (2004), 'Regionalisation of Peace Operations', in E.B. Eide (ed), *Effective Multilateralism: Europe, Regional Security and a Revitalised UN*, Global Europe Report No. 1, The Foreign Policy Centre, London, pp. 32-37.

Wallace, W. (2003), *Looking after the Neighbourhood: Responsibilities for the EU-25*, Policy Paper No. 4, Notre Europe, Paris.

Weiss, T.G. (2004), 'The Sunset of Humanitarian Intervention? The Responsibility to Protect in a Unipolar Era', *Security Dialogue*, Vol. 35(2), pp. 135-53.

WEU Assembly (2003a), *A European Strategic Concept – Defence Aspects*, Document A/1841, Western European Union, Paris.

WEU Assembly (2003b), *European Defence: Pooling and Strengthening National and European Capabilities*, Document A/1842, Western European Union, Paris.

Wolfers, A. (1962), *Discord and Collaboration: Essays on International Politics*, The Johns Hopkins Press, Baltimore.

World Economic Forum (2004), *Global Governance Initiative*, Annual Report 2004, WEF, Geneva.

Youngs, R. (2004a), *Europe's Uncertain Pursuit of Middle East Reform*, Carnegie Paper No. 45, Carnegie Endowment for International Peace, Washington DC.

Youngs, R. (2004b), *Transatlantic Cooperation on Middle East Reform: A European Misjudgment?*, Civility – The Foreign Policy Centre, London.

Youngs, R. (2005), *Ten Years of the Barcelona Process: A Model for Supporting Arab Reform?*, Working Paper No. 2, FRIDE, Madrid.

Zilmer-Johns, L. (2004), 'The Convention, the IGC and the Great Powers: The ESDP and New Security Threats', in J. Pilegaard (ed), *The Politics of European Security*, Danish Institute for International Studies, Copenhagen, pp. 55-81.

Index